HUMAN ADJUSTMENT

Student Study Guide

JANET A. SIMONS
The University of Iowa

SETH KALICHMAN · JOHN W. SANTROCK
Medical College of Wisconsin   University of Texas–Dallas

Prepared by Janet A. Simons and Seth Kalichman

WCB Brown & Benchmark
PUBLISHERS

Madison, Wisconsin · Dubuque, Iowa

Contents

Preface

This study guide is designed to help you master the material in the text *Human Adjustment* by Janet A. Simons, Seth Kalichman, and John W. Santrock. Used along with your textbook, this guide will help you learn, review, retrieve, and evaluate course material.

The study guide opens with a brief guide to better studying. Use these ideas along with the textbook's Preface. Together, you will learn several tips that will improve your studying habits both in this course and in your other college courses. The goal is to help you use your available studying time more effectively. Your school library has additional material on how to study, improve memory, and do better on tests, and you are encouraged to find and use these additional resources. Some colleges also have short courses or handouts to refresh your study habits and improve your testing skills.

Following this section is an important section on how to get maximum benefits from this particular study guide. Each chapter has eight sections that are designed to help you learn. Reading the part called "Using This Study Guide" will help you use all eight available sections well.

Good luck in your psychology of adjustment course. Your efforts in taking notes in class, reading the textbook, using this study guide, and other study skills should help you do well in this course as well as improve your knowledge of topics that affect your daily living. We hope that you find the materials in this study guide useful in being successful in your course.

Janet A. Simons, Ph.D.
University of Iowa, School of Social Work
Central Iowa Psychological Services

Seth Kalichman, Ph.D.
Medical College of Wisconsin

How to Study Efficiently

Psychologists have studied learning, attention, memory, thinking, and attitudes for years. Some of the research findings are useful in learning how to study more effectively. Even though psychologists and educators know much about how one should study, few students are instructed in the best learning and remembering tips. If you have never learned about the best studying techniques you probably waste time and effort in your studying and are not remembering anywhere near your potential. Please take time to try some of the suggestions that follow. By incorporating some of these ideas, you should be able to learn more in less time.

Managing Your Study Time

A Studying Schedule

Are you the typical student who always ends up cramming the night before the test? Typing up your report just hours before its final deadline? One of the hardest tasks to accomplish is to manage your time in ways that will help you to be a successful student. It is useful to plot out a typical week's schedule so that you can see how your time is spent. Mark in your hours in which you will be in class (class attendance is significantly related to grade performance), and also mark in necessary time for sleep, meal preparation and eating, household and family responsibilities, exercise and leisure activities, employment hours, commuting time, and other built-in activities.

Now, is there any time left for studying? Ideally, you should have more studying time than classroom time (a common guideline is 2 hours of studying per hour of class). Figure out which hours are good ones for you to study, and pencil them in. Are there other activities that need to be switched, reduced, or eliminated for awhile so that you can do your best as a student? Try to figure a practical and manageable schedule.

You needn't find two- or three-hour studying blocks. Some students do their very best by studying in frequent half-hour blocks rather than in a few massive studying blocks in which they get bored and frustrated. You need to experiment with whether you do better in marathon studying or mini-studying blocks, and then do it! Utilize your best time for studying—if you are a morning person, do some of your studying then. If you are a night owl, then burn the midnight oil with your books.

Establishing Priorities

If you are taking a full load of courses, and especially is you have family and work responsibilities, you will probably not be able to finish every project and reading assignment and learn all that you should in your courses. Instructors assign heavy assignments and there is an infinite amount that you could learn about and think about in every college course; therefore, it is important that you establish priorities in your studying. Too many students fail to analyze what aspects of each course are most important to spend time on. For example, if a term paper makes up 40 percent of one grade and a book report makes up 5 percent, it is crucially important to do an excellent term paper. It is also good to do an outstanding book report, but the payoff is not as large as it is for the term paper. If your time is limited, put the most effort into the term paper. Ideally, of course, you will put sufficient effort and talent into both projects.

For each course, examine the high payoffs (HIPOS) and low payoffs (LOPOS) of the course. Make a list of each at the beginning of the course. For almost every course, a HIPO is class attendance (in one research study 85 percent of A and B students almost always attended class while 48 percent of those earning a C or lower were often absent). Other generalized HIPOS include note-taking, using required textbooks, completion of assignments and projects, and good preparation for exams. Each week, examine your list for crucial HIPOS (or HIPO I activities) and important, but less urgent HIPOS (or HIPO II activities). At the beginning of the course, starting a project due at midterm is a HIPO II, but in just a couple of weeks this activity should be moved to a HIPO I.

LOPOS should be divided into necessary items that must be regularly accomplished (LOPO III), but quickly attended to (e.g., clarifying hastily written notes, clearing off your study space, rereading parts of the course syllabus) and other activities that are a complete waste of activity (LOPO IV). A common LOPO IV activity is using precious study time to restudy information that you already know well. As you study, spend your time learning new, difficult material, or material that you have confused with other information. It is a comfortable but unnecessary waste of time to study known information. Give familiar material just a "once over" review prior to the exam.

Banishing Procrastination

Are you putting off studying, reading a certain textbook, or getting started on the term paper? Do you spend your time calling yourself lazy and stupid? Are there projects that you aren't starting because you fear that you cannot do them well? Or do you delay tasks because you aren't quite certain what is expected of you?

Do you know that the number one cause of procrastination is perfectionism? You may want to do such a good job on a task that it becomes forbidding to get started. You must break through that perfect roadblock and just get started. Remind yourself that nobody is perfect, and that you just need to begin and make revisions toward a better project as you get into it. It is helpful to break down a big test or project into more manageable, less threatening components. Today you are not doing the term paper—today your project is to find six sources of information in the library, a very manageable task. Today you are not studying for a six-chapter task—you are learning the information of just one chapter.

Managing Your Study Space

Almost as important as when to study is where to study. If you are going to do some of your studying on campus, explore the campus for the best studying location. Are there study areas in the library? Are there areas that are relatively quiet where you can read while sipping coffee or cola? If you are capable of studying outdoors, are there locations that are practical for learning outside? If you plan to do some small group studying, are there appropriate lounge, cafeteria, or classroom areas where this can be accomplished? Make some decisions, and try to keep some regularity in your time for studying on campus. A regular habit makes it easier for your brain to "expect to study now."

In your living space, explore whichever areas are best for encouraging serious studying. You may do best formalizing your studying at a desk or study table. You may prefer and do better in a soft chair that you come to associate only with studying. Some individuals can study in bed, but for many this is an inappropriate answer because they tend to fall asleep while studying. Some students do well studying at a kitchen table, but here environmental cues may lead to an increase in eating!

If possible, choose a study area in which studying will be the only major activity done in that place. In that way, you will develop environmental cues that will help you become a more efficient student. Also provide yourself with the best level (for you) of lighting, sound, and temperature.

Studying Strategies

Analyzing Your Learning Style

Know yourself! Explore your own learning style. It has already been suggested that you need to know your time tolerance for studying—can you study in marathon sessions, or do you do better at many mini-sessions? If you find that you can only concentrate on your material for five minutes, begin there. Study for five minutes, listen to a song on the radio, and then study for another five minutes. Gradually build up your studying attention span—five minutes now, eight minutes tomorrow, and twelve minutes the day after that. As you become an efficient student and learn to put fun and variety into your studying, you will be able to build your studying time to a half hour, hour, or a couple of hours.

Know yourself in the studying environment—formal or informal, barren or interesting. Are you distracted by your visual environment? If so, darken the room and use a study lamp that focuses on your studying material. Are you distracted by sounds? If so, turn off the radio and use the music as a reward after studying so many minutes. Is studying most efficient early in the day or late in the day? Do you study better with snacks and beverages, or without these edibles around?

Do you do better studying by yourself in isolation? By studying by yourself in an area where others are also studying? Would you benefit by doing some of your studying with others in your class? If you form a small study group, it may be very useful to first study by yourselves, and then as a group quiz each other, analyze ideas offered in the course, and help each other retain the more difficult parts of the course material. If you are well prepared, you may find yourself instructing other students on some of the course concepts, and in explaining the material to others you will firmly place the information into your own long-term memory.

SQ5R—Survey, Question, Read, Recite, wRite, Relate, and Review

Many studying systems are available for increasing your efficiency in studying. Here is one system proposed by my colleagues (Don Irwin and Bev Drinnin) that I think is helpful because it emphasizes active recitation. It is an expansion of the SQ3R technique developed by Francis Robinson in the 1940s.

Although many students study be reading and rereading their text and notes, this rather passive system really does not promote the most efficient studying. The more actively you study, and the more senses you engage in your studying, the more you will learn in less time. Isn't that a worthy goal—study better while studying less? Try this system during this semester, and I think you will like the results. The following section explains how this study guide incorporates this system.

Don't begin to study for this or other courses by picking up your book and reading straight through the assigned chapters. This exercise will fill your study time but will not leave you with much useful learning. Instead, start with taking a **survey** of what you are about to read. Just as you consult a map before taking a trip, begin your journey through a textbook by checking out the route. You can do this by using headings to note the major topics, glancing at photos and charts to scan the major attractions along the way, and briefly looking at the list of key terms and other special features in your textbook. If there is a chapter summary in the book, it is often more useful to read this summary before you actually read the text. At this point, you have developed a sense of the important facts and ideas within the chapter.

As you return to the beginning of the chapter and get ready to read, instead of just reading, ask **questions.** Take a heading and turn it into a question (the question to this section would have been "What is SQ5R?"), or use a sentence in a paragraph to propose a question (e.g., "Why ask questions?"). You can also formulate questions about figures and boxed materials. By more actively processing the information in this way, you will spend less time reading the chapter.

As you formulate a question, it is time for the third step, which is to **read.** However, you should not read every word. Instead, actively search for the answer to your formulated question. This technique gets you to focus on the important material in the text—material that is likely to show up in tests and material that you will want to know long after you are done with the course.

This strategy is designed to make you an active learner, and so part of the strategy is to **recite.** When you locate an answer to your question, recite it to yourself. Recitation helps you to practice retrieval—the task that you will need to employ during tests. Try to visualize your answer whenever possible—visual memories are easier to retrieve than auditory memories. Refer back to the text as needed to develop your answer. Put these answers into your own words rather than trying to memorize passages from the book.

It is also useful to **write** information—a task that engages more senses and actively involves you in the material you are learning. Write down a key term and try to write out the briefest definition possible. Or draw a doodle of an example of the key term. As you read the text, jot down ideas in the margin. It is recommended that you do limited underlining in your textbook (if you underline a lot, it loses its usefulness of cutting down on rereading time); a common mistake is underlining passages that you already understand, while ignoring complex ideas. It may be more useful to make a check mark in the margin for an important point, a + sign for important definitions, and a ? if you need to review some information again in order to understand it.

An important step in studying is to **relate** the material to information that you already know. Forming associations helps you to retain and understand the information. This type of integration of the material is superior to rote memorization. Relating material can involve finding examples of the concepts in your own life. (This may be difficult to do with a calculus course, but is fairly easy with a child development course.) Apply ideas to common experiences. Visualize the examples provided by the authors of the text. Imagine using some of the information in the future.

Relating can also involve using memory techniques. It has already been mentioned that vivid visual images are easier to retrieve than auditory images. Try to build pictures of things you wish to learn. Another memory technique is the acronym technique—using the initial letters of the items to be remembered to form a "word" that eases recovery. For example, PIES can help you remember that Sigmund Freud's concept of personality is that Personality = Id + Ego + Superego. In the acrostic technique, a sentence rather than a word is used. For example, the order of Piaget's cognitive stages can be aided by the sentence "Some policemen can frown," which helps one to recall that the order is Sensorimotor, Preoperational, Concrete operations, and Formal operations. Likewise, to learn Freud's five psychosexual stages in order (oral, anal, phallic, latent, genital) remember that "Ollie and Patricia like giraffes." The crazier and more imaged the phrase, the more helpful.

Review is the final step of the SQ5R technique. It involves using reciting, writing, and relating until the material is mastered. Remember to make the review as active as possible. Say aloud the answers to possible questions, study with friends and take turns quizzing each other, write out possible answers to likely questions, and so forth.

Use the SQ5R technique to improve your note-taking, too. Listen actively to the lecture and class discussion and formulate questions about what is being said—then write brief answers to these postulated questions as your class notes. This technique is superior to trying to copy all of the instructor's words. After all, the typical instructor will speak at least 125 words per minute, and the average student writes about 25 words per minute. Be brief and write down the essential and the important. Later, you can add related ideas and text material to your notes. Also, take brief notes during films and videotapes—the lecturer is including them in the course to provide information, not to entertain the class.

Using This Study Guide

Each chapter in this study guide has eight sections to help you learn the text material. Read this section to provide you with information on how to utilize these sections to learn the chapter's material.

1. **Chapter Outline.** Each chapter begins with a detailed outline of the main points of the text chapter. Before you read the text, scan this summary outline so that you can preview the topics that you will read about. You might benefit from turning the major points into questions and searching for the answers to your questions while you read. What this does is make you a more active learner, who will be able to retain more material than if you just passively read from page to page. Answering questions is a good retrieval practice for taking tests. The detailed nature of the outline allows you to use it when you are studying but don't have your textbook with you.

2. **Learning Objectives.** This list provides guidelines for mastery of chapter material. You will know much text material when you know and can understand the goals of the learning objectives. If you are tested with essay questions, these learning objectives can provide clues to possible test questions.

3. **Guided Review.** The guided review consists of fill-in-the-blank items that help you do thorough reading of the chapter. It is the most detailed studying task in this chapter, and should help you to be more challenged and active to reread your chapter if you need to hunt down answers. The guided review will help you become familiar with detailed information so that you can better recognize appropriate answers to multiple-choice questions. Answers are provided nearby so that you can immediately provide feedback about your efforts.

4. **Key Terms.** The key terms for the chapter are listed next. Space is provided for you to write in a brief definition in your own words. It is important that you avoid learning definitions exactly from the textbook. Not only would this be a difficult and arduous task, but is more important for you to understand a term than to have rote memory of a precise definition. Make it a challenge to capture the essence of a definition in just a few words. It might be possible to draw an answer rather than writing it out, and you are encouraged to think of vivid visual examples of the definitions. This section of the study guide allows practice with the studying aspects or reciting, writing, relating, and review. It may also encourage you to come up with mnemonic aids for some of the key terms. When you know a term very well, mark an X by the term and stop studying it—spend the rest of your studying time on key terms that are still confusing and difficult rather than rehearsing that which you already know. This section of the study guide is useful for preparing for both multiple-choice tests and essay tests.

5. **Study Aids.** In this section, two to four mnemonic aids are provided to help you learn the material in the chapter. You should try to develop mnemonic aids on your own.

6. **Understanding Concepts.** The questions in this section help you think about the various concepts in the chapter. This is a very useful section for studying for essay tests.

7. **Applying Concepts.** This section requires additional critical thinking or personal applications of the chapter's material. Relating the material to your own life will help you have control over the material in the chapter. This section is especially useful in studying for essay tests.

8. **Chapter Practice Tests.** Each chapter provides you with two fifteen-item multiple-choice tests. Each of the two tests provides a sampling of the entire chapter material. Questions vary from easy to quite hard and there are factual, applied, and conceptual questions included. If your instructor uses multiple-choice items in exams, these practice tests will help you prepare for that format. However, your instructor will use different items than are in the study guide—do not waste your time trying to memorize these specific items. Instead, use them to notice which concepts you do not yet understand, to be a better analyzer of test item wording, and to diagnose how well prepared you are for your next exam. You may benefit from checking specific items for possible variations. For example, if the question asks, "Which of the following is *least* likely to be true?," try figuring out the correct answer if you change the wording to "Which of the following is the *most* likely to be true?" The answers are provided in the study guide, along with the learning objective and text page number.

Chapter Outline

I.   What Is Adjustment?
   A. Coping in Today's World
      1. Today people are exposed to more information than were earlier generations.
      2. Americans must learn to cope with the United States' diminishing role as the industrial giant.
      3. Another change is that the work force is more diverse with more ethnic minorities and more women in the workplace.
      4. Understanding the nature of adjustment helps to reduce conflict while coping with challenges in better ways.
      5. Psychology provides useful knowledge about people's personality, behaviors, thinking, and coping; therefore, psychology can help improve the quality of our lives.
   B. Defining Psychology
      1. Psychological findings include some surprising ones along with those that fit our "common sense" ideas.
      2. Psychology is defined as the scientific study of behavior and mental processes in contexts.
      3. As a science, psychology uses systematic methods to observe, describe, explain, and predict behavior and mental processes.
      4. While some psychologists conduct scientific research, others are more involved in applied psychology, such as clinical and counseling psychologists.
      5. Psychiatrists are physicians who specialize in abnormal behavior and psychotherapy, while counseling and clinical psychologists receive doctoral degrees in graduate schools and have internships in mental health facilities.
      6. Contexts refer to the historical, economic, social, and cultural factors that influence mental processes and behavior, and all human behavior occurs in a cultural context.
   C. Defining Adjustment
      1. Adjustment is the psychological process of adapting to, coping with, and managing the problems, challenges, and demands of everyday life.
      2. Adjustment is important to all areas of human lives.
II. Psychology and Pseudopsychology
   A. Defining Pseudopsychology
      1. Pseudopsychologies are nonscientific systems that only superficially resemble psychology.
      2. Unlike psychology, the descriptions, explanations, and predictions of the pseudopsychologies cannot be directly tested, or when tested turn out to be unfounded.
      3. Astrology is a pseudopsychology that uses the position of the stars and planets at a person's birth to understand the person's personality and behavior.
      4. Graphology is a pseudopsychology based on handwriting analysis.

B. Pseudopsychology Movements
   1. The New Age Movement involves a distrust of science while engaging in a search for hidden "spiritual dimensions" using aspects such as crystal power, channeling, past lives regressions, and astrology.
   2. A pseudopsychology human potential movement popular in the 1970s was Werner Erhard's EST; although EST claimed to increase self-esteem and life satisfaction, it has no scientific value.
   3. Scientology, a pseudopsychology developed by Hubbard, supposedly attacks engrams, or automatic behavior programming.
C. Problems with Pseudopsychologies
   1. Pseudopsychologies tend to promise too much through supposedly wondrous powers and supernatural forces.
   2. They can divert people from coping with their lives in a rational and realistic way.
   3. For distressed persons with serious problems, following the advice of mystics or scientologists can delay appropriate problem solving.
III. Sociocultural Issues in Adjustment
A. A Sociocultural Approach
   1. A sociocultural approach emphasizes the roles of culture, ethnicity, and gender in understanding adjustment and behavior.
   2. Culture refers to the behavior patterns, beliefs, and other products of a particular group of people including values, work patterns, music, dress, diet, and ceremonies.
   3. Ethnicity is based on cultural heritage, national characteristics, race, religion, and language, and involves descent from common ancestors.
   4. Ethnic identity occurs when ethnicity is important in defining our self-identity.
   5. Sex is a biological dimension of being female or male, while gender is a sociocultural definition of female or male.
B. Sociocultural Issues
   1. People can make wrong assumptions and behavioral errors because of underestimating or overestimating the strength of another person's ethnic identity.
   2. Another common error is basing someone's ethnicity on physical features believed to be typical of an ethnic group.
   3. Few aspects of existence are more central to identity and to social relationships than are sex and gender, and as our gender-related attitudes and behavior are changing, people must cope with the results of these changes.
   4. Within the discipline of psychology, feminist psychologists note that much of psychology has traditionally had a "male dominant theme."
   5. Another important change in psychology is its increasing concern with a sociocultural approach that explores and validates our diverse cultural backgrounds.
   6. One special concern is the prejudice and discrimination faced by many cultural and ethnic groups.
   7. Women have lesser roles in politics, lower-paying jobs with fewer career opportunities, fewer educational opportunities, more likely to be victims of domestic violence, and experience higher incidence of depression.

IV. The Science Base of Psychology and Adjustment
  A. Theory and the Scientific Method
    1. A theory is a coherent set of ideas that help to explain observations and aid in making predictions.
    2. A theory's hypotheses can be tested by the scientific method.
    3. The scientific method has the following steps: identify and analyze problems, take observations, draw conclusions, and revise theories.
    4. When data is collected, statistical procedures are used to understand their meanings.
  B. Collecting Information about Adjustment—Measures
    1. Systematic and controlled observation is used in scientific studies.
    2. Laboratory studies allow the most controlled observation while naturalistic observation allows real-world observations but less control.
    3. Surveys and questionnaires can be the most efficient way to get information, but even well-designed questions are subject to inaccurate answers and socially desirable answers.
    4. Random samples are used to achieve subjects that best represent the population being studied.
    5. A case study looks in-depth at a single individual and is especially valuable in studying unique individuals and situations.
    6. Standardized tests allow an individual's scores to be compared to norm groups and provide information about individual differences.
  C. Strategies for Setting Up Research Studies on the Psychology of Adjustment
    1. The correlational strategy describes the strength of relations between two or more events or characteristics.
    2. Correlations are useful in making predictions, but they do not indicate cause and effect.
    3. The experimental strategy allows causal statements because its features allow control and manipulation of the variables.
    4. In the experimental group, the independent variable (or manipulated variable) is given but the control group receives no independent variable. The dependent variable is measured for both groups.
  D. Reducing Sexism in Research
    1. Both sexes need to be studied in order to draw proper conclusions about topics rather than basing selection of one sex on assumptions and stereotypes.
    2. Gender differences should not be inaccurately magnified.
    3. Titles and summaries of research articles should reflect the actual research participants rather than a broader group.
  E. Ethics in Research on the Psychology of Adjustment
    1. All colleges and universities have review boards that evaluate the ethical nature of research conducted at their institutions.
    2. Psychologists follow the research ethics guidelines of the American Psychological Association (APA).
    3. APA guidelines include informed consent and the subject's right to withdraw from the study at any time.
  F. Being a Wise Consumer of Psychological Knowledge
    1. The media often reports on psychological research and clinical findings from journals, professional meetings, and psychologists.

2. The media often focuses on sensational and dramatic psychological findings, or make errors in interpreting studies.
3. Self-help books are often useful, but some are written by persons who have no specialized training.
4. Nomothetic research is conducted at the level of the group while idiographic needs refer to what is important for the individual, a distinction that is often missing from media reports.
5. A common error is overgeneralization based on a small sample or a clinical sample.
6. Multiple studies provide better knowledge about issues and problems than does a single study.
7. Causal conclusions from correlational studies cannot be made.
8. It is important to consider the source of psychological information and evaluate its credibility.

Learning Objectives

After reading and studying this chapter, students should be able to:

1. Define what psychology is and what psychologists do.
2. Define adjustment.
3. Distinguish psychology from pseudopsychology.
4. Know what sociocultural issues play a central role in psychology.
5. Identify the role of theory in science.
6. Identify and discuss the various aspects of the scientific method.
7. Know how psychologists go about studying human adjustment.
8. Understand the basic principles behind setting up scientific studies.
9. Know about sexist bias in research and how scientists try to control it.
10. Identify the key ethical concerns in research.
11. Understand how to be a good consumer of psychological research.
12. Distinguish between nomothetic research and idiographic needs.
13. Understand the principle of generalization and how it is related to the size of a study.
14. Understand the limitations of any one scientific study.
15. Know what a causal relationship is in a scientific study and how the credibility of research can be evaluated.

Guided Review

After you have read the chapter one time, search through the chapter to find the appropriate words to complete these statements. Material is covered in the same order as the chapter.

1. Psychology is the _____ study of behavior and _____ processes in contexts.
2. Because they can be directly observed, talking, smiling, and combing one's hair are examples of _____, while private experiences such as thoughts, feelings, and motives make up _____ _____, which cannot be observed directly.

3. As a science, psychology uses systematic methods to achieve the four goals of psychology, which are to observe, _____, explain, and _____ behavior and mental processes.

4. The most widely practiced specialization in psychology is _____ and _____ psychology, which involves evaluating and treating people with psychologically related problems.

5. _____ are trained in graduate schools and internships in mental health facilities while _____ are trained in medical schools, but both specialize in abnormal psychology and improving the lives of people with mental health problems. One major difference is that only the _____ can prescribe drugs for mental health problems.

6. All human behavior occurs in a _____ _____, which includes historical, economic, social, and cultural factors that influence mental processes and behavior.

7. _____ is the psychological process of adapting to, coping with, and managing the problems, challenges, and demands of everyday life.

8. A nonscientific system that only superficially resembles psychology is called a _____. Examples include _____, which studies the influence of the stars and planets in one's life and _____, which involves handwriting analysis. Both are difficult to scientifically test, but when tested, astrology and graphology are _____.

9. The _____ _____ movement utilizes several pseudopsychologies in a nonscientific exploration of hidden spiritual dimensions. Other pseudopsychology movements include Erhard's _____ and Hubbard's _____, which seeks to clear oneself of _____, or automatic behavior patterns.

10. A _____ _____ to adjustment emphasizes that culture, ethnicity, and _____ are essential to understanding adjustment and behavior.

11. _____ refers to the behavior patterns, beliefs, and other products of a particular group of people, whether it is a large and diverse group such as the United States or as small and unified as an African hunter-gatherer tribe.

12. _____ involves descent from common ancestors, usually in a specific part of the world, and includes a cultural heritage, nationality characteristics, race, religion, and language. For an African-American, the culture is the _____ _____ and the ethnicity is _____.

13. _____ (All, Some) people have culture; _____ (all, some) people have ethnicity; _____ (all, some) people have ethnic identity.

14. Psychologists use the term _____ to refer to the female and male biological dimension and the term _____ to refer to the sociocultural definition of female and male. As such, _____ changes more with time and culture than does_____.

15. Because psychologists now address sociocultural issues, psychology has moved from being a study of _____-_____ _____ to being meaningful and relevant for culturally diverse people.

16. Worldwide, as of 1990, _____ made up less than 10 percent of national legislatures and about 5 percent of ministerial level positions; only 10 countries had national laws that supported maternity leave and guaranteed jobs.

17. Science is defined by _____ (how, what) it investigates, and scientists can be characterized as _____ (skeptical, trusting).

18. A _____ is a coherent set of ideas that help explain observations and aid in making predictions. Its _____ are assumptions that can be tested to determine their accuracy.

19. The _____ _____ involves identifying and analyzing the problem, taking observations, drawing conclusions, and revising _____.

20. The step of making observations involves collecting _____ which is then analyzed using _____ procedures to understand their meaning. These analyses are used by psychologists to draw _____ and to _____ theories.

21. Scientific research involves _____ observations in situations where factors that are not the focus of inquiry are _____, often in a _____ setting.

22. Non-controlled, but more realistic observations are called _____ _____.

23. _____, which can occur face-to-face or over the telephone, vary in how _____ they are. Highly structured interviews that involve reading and writing are called _____.

24. In a _____ sample, every member of a _____ has an equal chance of being selected.

25. Some subjects respond in socially acceptable rather than truthful ways; this tendency is referred to as _____ _____.

26. A _____ _____ involves an in-depth look at a single individual and is especially used by _____ psychologists. They provide information about unique and dramatic situations, but caution must be taken in _____ from this information and involve researcher judgments of unknown _____.

27. _____ tests allow psychologists to compare one person's scores with others.

28. The _____ strategy looks at relations between two or more events or characteristics, with the _____ of the relationship determining the effectiveness of one's _____.

29. To deal with cause-and-effect, psychologists rely on the _____ strategy. In this strategy, the _____ is the event being manipulated and _____ is the behavior that changes because of the manipulation.

30. In an experimental study, the _____ group has a manipulated experience while the _____ group receives no manipulated factor. Subjects are assigned to the two groups using _____ _____.

31. The _____ variable is the manipulated factor in an experiment while the _____ variable is the factor measured in an experiment. Therefore, only the experimental group receives the _____ variable.

32. In Florence Denmark's comments about nonsexist research, she suggests that one problem with data analysis has been an overemphasis on gender _____ (differences, similarities).

33. In order to conduct ethical research, colleges have ethics research committees that review proposed research; in addition, psychologists follow guidelines established by the _____ _____ _____.

34. The _____ often covers psychological research and clinical studies but sometimes focuses on _____ findings. Likewise, _____-_____ books can be excellent or written by persons with little professional background.

35. _____ _____ is conducted at the level of the group, while _____ _____ refer to what is important for the individual.

36. As a consumer of psychological information, avoid: (1) _____ from a small sample or a clinical example; (2) viewing a single study rather than a set of studies as a definitive answer; (3) making _____ conclusions from correlational studies; and always evaluate the credibility of the source of the psychological information.

37. The small, everyday life events to which you must adjust are called _____.

38. Guidelines for selecting self-help books include: (1) not judging a book by its cover, (2) look for _____ recommendations, (3) examine the quality of the evidence reported in the book, (4) select books that recognize that problems are _____ and involve multiple factors and alternative solutions, (5) choose books that focus on a particular problem over a generally approach, (6) don't be fooled by _____, or self-improvement jargon, and (7) check out the author's educational credentials and the author's attitude toward psychological findings.

Guided Review Answers

1. scientific, mental; 2. behaviors, mental processes; 3. describe, predict; 4. counseling, clinical; 5. Psychologists, psychiatrists, psychiatrists; 6. cultural context; 7. Adjustment; 8. pseudopsychology, astrology, graphology, unfounded; 9. New Age, EST, scientology, engram; 10. sociocultural approach, gender; 11. Culture; 12. Ethnicity, United States, Africa; 13. All, all, some; 14. sex, gender, gender, sex; 15. European-American males; 16. women; 17. how, skeptical; 18. theory, hypotheses; 19. scientific method, theories; 20. data, statistical, conclusions, revise; 21. systematic, controlled, laboratory; 22. naturalistic observations; 23. Interviews, structured, questionnaires; 24. random, population; 25. social desirability; 26. case study, clinical/counseling, generalizing, reliability; 27. Standardized; 28. correlational, strength, prediction; 29. experimental, cause, effect; 30. experimental, control, random assignment; 31. independent, dependent, independent; 32. differences; 33. American Psychological Association; 34. media, unexpected, self-help; 35. Nomothetic research, idiographic needs; 36. overgeneralizing, causal; 37. hassles; 38. realistic, complex, psychobabble.

Key Terms

For each term, briefly define the term in your own words and provide an example or situation (especially one you can visualize) that will help you retain the meaning of the concept. Key terms are presented in the order they are presented in the chapter.

1. psychology (p. 7)

2. behavior (p. 7)

3. mental processes (p. 7)

4. science (p. 7)

5. clinical and counseling psychology (p. 8)

6. psychiatry (p. 8)

7. contexts (p. 8)

8. adjustment (p. 8)

9. pseudopsychology (p. 9)

10. astrology (p. 9)

11. graphology (p. 9)

12. New Age Movement (p. 9)

13. EST (p. 10)

14. scientology (p. 10)

15. sociocultural approach (p. 11)

38. hassles (p. 23)

39. psychobabble (p. 36)

Study Aids

Students who do well on tests develop mnemonic aids to help them remember important terms and concepts. A few are suggested here, and you are encouraged to develop your own additional aids.

PSEUDO. *Pseudo* is an important prefix to understand. It means "false." Therefore, when it is paired with another word or word root, it means that it is an inaccurate, opposite, or false version. For example, you may have used the word *pseudonym,* which means "false name," such as an author's pen name. Used in this chapter with *pseudopsychology,* the rough translation is "false psychology." Since psychology is a science, you know that a pseudopsychology is not a science.

CORRELATIONS. It is best to memorize a phrase such as Correlation does not equal causation, to help emphasize in your memory that the correlational strategy cannot be used for the explanation goal of psychology.

INDEPENDENT VARIABLE (IV) AND DEPENDENT (DV) VARIABLES. These two terms are often confused, so you might want to develop a couple of strategies to help you remember how to distinguish these terms. One way is to think of an IV delivering medicine to a patient (in the experimental group), *causing* a change in the condition. This change (or *effect*) is the dependent variable. Another helpful strategy is to come up with an example of IV and DV in your own life. Such as "If I study 10 hours for this test (IV), it will cause me to have a good grade (DV)" or "If I stay up all night (IV), I yawn during my morning psychology class (DV)."

NOMOTHETIC RESEARCH AND IDIOGRAPHIC NEEDS. You are probably not familiar with the words *nomothetic* and *idiographic,* so use the initial letters to key in their definition. Since nomothetic and numbers both start with N, nomothetic research is conducted at the level of the group, and since idiographic and individual both start with I, idiographic needs refer to what is important for the individual.

Understanding Concepts

Answer these questions to develop your understanding of the important ideas in this chapter.

1. Discuss how a psychology of adjustment course can help a person cope with life's challenges.

2. Some psychologists have believed that psychology should study only behavior, and not behavior and mental processes. What are the advantages and disadvantages of including mental processes in the science of psychology?

3. What's the difference between a counseling and clinical psychologist and a psychiatrist?

4. Compare and contrast psychology and pseudopsychology.

5. Show that you understand the chapter's position that everyone has ethnicity, but not everyone has ethnic identity.

6. How do psychologists define the terms *sex* and *gender?* Do you agree that it is important to have two separate terms? Why, or why not?

7. Compare and contrast a laboratory experiment with a naturalistic observation study. What are the advantages and disadvantages of each setting?

8. If another student said, "Since only experiments can show cause and effect, it is the only research strategy that should ever be used," how might you respond so that you defend the use of other methods such as case studies, surveys, and correlations?

9. How do you distinguish between nomothetic research and idiographic needs? Why is the distinction important?

10. Summarize the major points involved in being a wise consumer of psychological knowledge.

11. Summarize the guidelines for choosing self-help books.

Applying Concepts

Answer these questions to develop your ability to apply this chapter's material to your life and the world. Your own responses may differ from other students' in the class, and it is helpful to share your ideas with the other students.

1. The chapter begins with a contrast in the lives of Charles Joseph Whitman and Alice Walker. Then the Preview asks, "What leads one person, so full of promise, to cope poorly with life's problems while another turns poverty and trauma into a rich harvest of adjustment?" Briefly describe two other well-known individuals whose lives seem to defy their childhood beginnings. Then briefly speculate on the causes of individual differences—is biology or environment more important, for example?

2. The chapter mentions that one issue of the *New York Times* contains more information than a person in the Middle Ages acquired during a lifetime. Discuss the advantages and disadvantages of the amount of information available to us.

3. A college student confides in you that she is feeling quite depressed. Advise her on what to expect if she makes an appointment with a counseling and clinical psychologist or with a psychiatrist.

4. Think about the important contexts in your life. Which ones have had the most impact on you? How would you define your culture, ethnicity, and ethnic identity? Given that you are a person of a particular ethnicity, cultural background, gender, and sexual orientation, can you ever get beyond your personally biased perspectives to see another's?

5. Why do you think that pseudopsychologies such as astrology and crystal power are so popular today when scientific reasoning is so highly valued? Do you see the New Age Movement and other pseudopsychology movements as frivolous, useful, or dangerous? Why?

6. The Sociocultural Worlds 1.1 mentions that women are twice as likely as men to be diagnosed as depressed. Do you think that this is the result of sex or gender?

7. Take Self-Assessment 1.1, the Crown & Marlowe Social Desirability Scale and score and evaluate your results. Summarize your evaluation here. Are you the kind of person who says basically what you feel and believe, or do you often say what will be approved of by others? Did knowing ahead of time what the scale measured affect your answers? How?

8. Discuss the ways in which psychologists are trying to reduce sexism in research. Why do you think that psychology has traditionally been dominated by a European-American male perspective?

9. Review this week's newspapers and assess how often psychology makes the news. Do the results of psychological studies seem to be adequately reported? Did you find any shortcomings, such as overgeneralizing from small samples or using correlational findings to talk about cause and effect?

10. How well do you handle life's "hassles"? What are the most common hassles that you face as a college student?

11. Go to a library or a book store and look at the variety of self-help books that are available. What are the most popular topics? Could you locate many of the books suggested in table 1.1? Locate a couple of books that you would like to read, and explain your choices.

Chapter Practice Tests

Answer these multiple-choice test questions to help you assess your understanding of the chapter's material. Evaluate your answers to determine which sections you need to further review.

Practice Test A

1. Factors that involve history and culture that influence behavior and mental processes refer to
   a. controls.
   b. context.
   c. confounds.
   d. co-factors.
   p. 7

2. Adjustment involves
   a. coping only under certain conditions.
   b. both coping with catastrophe and everyday stressors.
   c. coping only with catastrophe.
   d. none of the above.
   p. 8

3. Which of the following is a pseudopsychology?
   a. graphology
   b. scientology
   c. EST
   d. all of these
   p. 9-10

4. A person's sense of membership to a group that shares her language, race, religion, and values is referred to as her
   a. culture.
   b. psychological core.
   c. ethnic identity.
   d. self-identity.
   p. 11

5. Science is characterized by
    a. the content area studied.
    b. a theory.
    c. the methods used to study a problem.
    d. the training of scientists.
    p. 12
6. A psychologist who wishes to conduct a naturalistic observation study of children's relationship to each other in school settings would possibly
    a. develop a survey for teachers and children to complete.
    b. have teachers and students come to a laboratory and observe their interactions.
    c. go to a classroom for an extended period of time.
    d. interview children about their feelings for teachers.
    p. 16
7. A study that questions criminals about their crimes will likely face problems with
    a. relating findings to the real world.
    b. not being able to ask such questions in a questionnaire.
    c. social desirability.
    d. finding a standardized test for this problem area.
    p. 17
8. Hannah conducted a study where she found that people placed in rooms with more intense light became more irritable as compared to people placed in rooms that were lit dimmer. What is the most likely type of research strategy that was used?
    a. case study
    b. a correlation
    c. an experiment
    d. observational study
    p. 19

9. A researcher selects women and men from a liberal arts class and conducts a study concerning sex differences in engineering aptitude. Which of the following is a potential bias of the study?
    a. assumptions underlying the measures used
    b. assumptions underlying the sample
    c. assumptions underlying the theory
    d. All of these are potential biases.
    p. 21
10. Whenever a person participates in a psychological study they should expect to receive
    a. standardized tests.
    b. informed consent.
    c. routine counseling.
    d. payment in cash for participation.
    p. 21
11. A study published in a psychological journal was discussed in a local newspaper. Which of the following is most likely to be true?
    a. Adequate space was available to discuss the findings.
    b. The information was presented in its true scientific form.
    c. The findings underwent professional review processes.
    d. Only the sensational aspects of the study were highlighted.
    p. 21
12. When research is conducted at the level of groups rather than individuals, the research is referred to as
    a. experimental.
    b. nomothetic.
    c. idiographic.
    d. correlational.
    p. 22
13. A study with a small sample is most likely to
    a. rely on correlations.
    b. have a diversity of subjects.
    c. be idiographic and not nomothetic.
    d. not generalize to other people.
    p. 22

14. The university conducted a large study with over 10,000 men that showed that testicular self-examination helped detect more than 80% of cancerous tumors. Which of the following is a best conclusion from the study?
    a. Self-examination is all that is necessary to detect testicular cancer.
    b. Men who regularly conduct self-examination do not need to see a doctor unless they feel a lump.
    c. The study is likely invalid because it was not conducted by a government agency.
    d. More research than just one study is needed to draw a conclusion.
    p. 22
15. Men who have committed sexual assaults against women report drinking more alcohol than non-assaultive men. Which of the following is a reasonable conclusion?
    a. Drinking causes men to assault women.
    b. The tendency to be assaultive causes men to drink.
    c. Society promotes drinking which in turn promotes assaulting women.
    d. It can be concluded that drinking and being assaultive are related.
    p. 22

Practice Test B

1. In which way is psychology different from psychiatry?
    a. Psychology concerns treating persons with problems; psychiatry does not.
    b. Psychiatry is an area of medicine; psychology is not.
    c. Psychiatry is distinguished as a subspecialty of psychology.
    d. Psychologists specialize in psychotherapy; psychiatrists do not.
    p. 7

2. Which of the following is true of adjustment as defined by the text?
    a. Adjustment only involves everyday coping.
    b. Adjustment involves both coping with catastrophe and everyday stressors.
    c. Adjustment is only involved in coping with catastrophe.
    d. Coping is only one aspect of adjustment.
    p. 9
3. Which of the following is a pseudopsychology?
    a. Zen Buddhism
    b. scientology
    c. counseling psychology
    d. psychiatry
    p. 10
4. Behavior patterns and beliefs of people in a particular group that are passed on from generation to generation are referred to as
    a. ethnicity.
    b. gender.
    c. culture.
    d. sociodemography.
    p. 11
5. Theories in science
    a. rely on correlations.
    b. explain observations.
    c. eliminate the scientific method.
    d. formulate the opinions of scientists.
    p. 14
6. Which of the following is a role of the scientific method?
    a. to provide information only in support of theories
    b. to identify and analyze problems
    c. to determine truths about human nature
    d. to test ideas studied by philosophers
    p. 14

7. Laboratory research is limited by which of the following?
   a. the lack of control over outside influences
   b. the lack of resemblance to the real world
   c. the overemphasis on precision
   d. difficulty in making observations in that setting
   p. 15

8. An advantage of questionnaires is
   a. they allow for more open and detailed responding.
   b. they can be easily administered to large numbers of people.
   c. they are inexpensive.
   d. they are not scientific.
   p. 16

9. A researcher examines the SAT scores of men and women over the past several years and concludes that men are better at math than women. Which of the following is a potential bias in this research?
   a. assumptions underlying the measures used
   b. assumptions underlying the sample
   c. assumptions underlying the theory
   d. All of these are potential biases.
   p. 21

10. When potential research participants comes to a study, the first thing they should expect is
    a. to be counseled.
    b. to be evaluated by a psychologist.
    c. to be fully informed about the study.
    d. to be provided with a brief overview of scientific methods.
    p. 21

11. Which of the following influences how the media presents research findings?
    a. availability of experts
    b. the general knowledge of the public about science
    c. a tendency to focus on scientific advances
    d. All of these are influences.
    p. 21

12. When research is conducted at the level of groups rather than individuals, the research is likely to overlook
    a. the natural environment.
    b. the needs of individuals.
    c. the nomothetic aspects of study.
    d. the differences between groups.
    p. 22

13. Studies with small numbers of subjects
    a. should be interpreted with caution.
    b. provide the same results as larger studies.
    c. generalize to other people like the subjects.
    d. are better because they are cheaper.
    p. 22

14. Which of the following is necessary to have in order to conclusively answer a research question?
    a. multiple studies with common results
    b. an experimental study
    c. a study with a large sample size
    d. a correlational study
    p. 22

15. A correlation between two factors allows the researcher to conclude that
    a. one factor is causing the other.
    b. some third factor is causing them both.
    c. neither factor is causing the other.
    d. None of the above can be concluded.
    p. 22

Key for Practice Test A

1. Answer b; Contextual influences, such as culture and historical period impact behavior through subtle but powerful means; page 7; Learning Objective 1
2. Answer b; Coping is a broad concept that involves adjustment to a multitude of life events and conditions; page 8; Learning Objective 2
3. Answer d; Pseudopsychologies have features that parallel the interests of psychology but are nonscientific; page 9-10; Learning Objective 3
4. Answer c; Ethnic identity encompasses all features of persons that correspond to their heritage; page 11; Learning Objective 4
5. Answer c; Science studies many of the same questions that other disciplines do, but science is defined by the methods used to answer the questions; page 12; Learning Objective 5
6. Answer c; Naturalistic observation involves the unobtrusive study of organisms in their natural environment, such as when a biologist camps out in a jungle to study gorillas; page 16; Learning Objective 6
7. Answer c; Social desirability occurs when persons try to present themselves in a positive light, overshadowing the reality of their behavior or attitudes; page 17; Learning Objective 7
8. Answer c; Experiments manipulate something to show cause and effect. Here, the light of the room was manipulated and compared; page 19; Learning Objective 8
9. Answer d; The study is obviously biased to find sex differences because it does not control for numerous factors related to engineering aptitude; page 21; Learning Objective 9
10. Answer b; All research must provide a person with an expectation of what will occur, and the costs, benefits, and risks of participating; page 21; Learning Objective 10
11. Answer d; News coverage of science tends to focus only on the most sensational aspects because news is driven by public interest; page 21; Learning Objective 11
12. Answer b; Nomothetic research is concerned with groups of people rather than any given individual; page 22; Learning Objective 12
13. Answer d; Study results become more generalizable when samples sizes get large; page 22; Learning Objective 13
14. Answer d; Regardless of the size of a study and its results, one study cannot be taken to be conclusive; page 22; Learning Objective 14
15. Answer d; This finding concerns a correlation between two things and cannot allow for a causal conclusion; page 22; Learning Objective 15

Key for Practice Test B

1. Answer b; Psychiatrists obtain a medical degree and can prescribe drugs. Psychologists complete a Ph.D. program and are expert in researching behavior and mental processes; page 7; Learning Objective 1
2. Answer b; Adjustment is a part of common and uncommon life events and challenges; page 9; Learning Objective 2
3. Answer b; Pseudopsychologies are unscientific and involve aspects related to the usual domains of psychology, but are not to be confused with areas within psychology, related disciplines, or religions; page 10; Learning Objective 3
4. Answer c; Culture is passed on to generations within groups; page 11; Learning Objective 4
5. Answer b; Scientific theories are constructed to explain phenomena; page 14; Learning Objective 5

6. Answer b; The scientific method systematically and objectively evaluates problems; page 14; Learning Objective 6
7. Answer b; Laboratory research may not represent how things operate in natural settings; page 15; Learning Objective 7
8. Answer b; Questionnaire research typically involves a large number of respondents because they are easy to administer; page 16; Learning Objective 8
9. Answer d; Sex difference research tends to be biased on multiple levels; page 21; Learning Objective 9
10. Answer c; Informed consent should be the first part of a research experience; page 21; Learning Objective 10
11. Answer b; The media cannot present the details of research because the public would find the information of limited use; page 21; Learning Objective 11
12. Answer b; Group, or nomothetic research gathers information across individuals to find generalities; page 22; Learning Objective 12
13. Answer a; Studies with small numbers of subjects may not generalize to larger groups; page 22; Learning Objective 13
14. Answer a; No single study can provide conclusive answers. It requires several studies conducted by several different researchers; page 22; Learning Objective 14
15. Answer d; Correlations do not allow for causal conclusions or a direction of the relationship to be inferred; page 22; Learning Objective 15

Chapter **2**   **Personality**

Chapter Outline

I.   What Is Personality?
   A. Defining Personality
      1. Personality involves enduring, distinctive thoughts, emotions, and behaviors.
      2. Personality is the characteristic way an individual adapts to the world.
      3. Personality deals with individual differences.
   B. Personality Theories
      1. Theories describe why individuals respond to the same situation in different ways.
      2. Theories differ in their emphasis on biology versus life experiences.
      3. Theories differ in their emphasis on how we think about ourselves and on how we behave toward others.
      4. No one theory can account for all aspects of personality.
II. Psychoanalytic Perspectives
   A. Freud's Theory
      1. Freud, a neurologist and psychiatrist during the early part of the twentieth century, developed his theoretical ideas from his work with his patients.
      2. Freud emphasized the importance of unconscious motivations on our everyday life; he believed that most of our personality exists below the level of awareness.
      3. The three personality structures are the id, ego, and superego.
      4. The id consists of instincts, is totally unconscious, and works according to the pleasure principle, which means the id's goal is immediate gratification.
      5. The ego, operating from the reality principle, deals with the demands of reality and tries to achieve pleasure within the norms of society.
      6. The superego is the moral branch of personality and views being good as the self's primary goal.
      7. Defense mechanisms are unconscious methods by which the ego distorts reality to protect itself from anxiety.
      8. The most powerful and pervasive defense mechanism is repression, in which unacceptable id impulses are pushed from awareness into the unconscious mind.
      9. Other defense mechanisms include rationalization, displacement, sublimation, projection, reaction formation, and regression.
      10. Freud stated that personality develops during five psychosexual stages in which varying erogenous zones are the strongest focus for pleasure-giving qualities; overgratification or undergratification of these erogenous zones results in fixations that are expressed in one's adult personality.
      11. The most important psychosexual stages are the first three: the oral stage (one's first eighteen months), the anal stage (from one-and-a-half to three years), and the phallic stage (from three to six years).

12. During the phallic stage, boys experience the Oedipus complex, which involves a process of falling in love with their mothers and then blocking this love and identifying with the strength of the father's gender role; girls undergo a more complex and less satisfactorily resolved Electra complex which ends with girls identifying with the weakness of the mother's gender role.

13. From six years until puberty, individuals are in the latency stage during which sexual interest is repressed and social and intellectual skills are developed.

14. The final stage is the adult genital stage in which there is sexual reawakening and the development of mature love.

B. Psychoanalytic Criticism
1. Freud is criticized for overemphasizing the role of sexuality.
2. Freud underplayed the role of later childhood and adolescence in shaping adult personality.
3. Freud did not give enough credit to the ego and conscious thought processes.
4. Sociocultural factors are much more important than Freud believed, and Freud overemphasized the biological basis of personality.

C. Horney's Sociocultural Approach
1. Horney downplayed Freud's biological emphasis in favor of a sociocultural approach including assessing gender differences.
2. Horney believed that the need for security was the prime motive in human existence.
3. Three strategies for coping with anxiety are moving toward people (i.e., seeking love and support), moving away from people (i.e., becoming more independent), and moving against people (i.e., becoming competitive and domineering), with secure individuals using all three ways in moderation and balance.
4. Nancy Chodorow adds that more women than men define themselves in terms of their relationships with some men using more denial in their relationships.

D. Jung's Depth Psychology
1. Jung divided the unconscious into two parts. One, the personal unconscious, is similar to Freud's unconscious.
2. The other part, the collective unconscious, is an impersonal, deep layer of the unconscious mind shared by all human beings.
3. The content of the collective unconscious is in the form of archetypes, and include anima (woman) and animus (man).
4. The archetypal self has two aspects—the persona, or socialized, civilized self, and the shadow, which is the darker self—which both need to be acknowledged by the individual.
5. Jung believed the personality growth continued throughout one's life, with the early primary task to grow in areas that come easily and the task of the second half of life to become more balanced.

E. Adler's Individual Psychology
1. Adler's theory emphasizes the uniqueness of each individual and the role of social factors on shaping personality.
2. The concept of striving for superiority emphasizes the human motivation to adapt, improve, and master the environment.
3. Feelings of inferiority that come from interacting with more powerful others and through sibling rivalry usually leads to striving for improvement.

4. Compensation is the individual's attempt to overcome imagined or real inferiorities or weaknesses by developing one's ability; while overcompensation is denying one's weakness and making an exaggerated effort to conceal the weakness.

5. The striving for superiority can be hindered by an inferiority complex (being overwhelmed by extreme feelings of inadequacy) or a superiority complex (using exaggerated self-importance to mask actual feelings of inferiority).

F. Evaluation of the Psychoanalytic Perspectives

1. All psychoanalytic theories view personality as determined by both current experiences and by earlier experiences.

2. They postulate that we mentally transform environmental experiences and form subjective, personal realities.

3. They speculate that the mind is not all conscious, and unconscious motives lie behind behaviors.

4. This perspective emphasizes conflict and anxiety and the fact that adjustment is a complex, difficult task.

5. Psychoanalytic theories are difficult to translate into testable hypotheses and much of the supporting data comes from therapists' subjective evaluations.

III. The Behavioral and Social Learning Perspectives

A. Classical Conditioning and Pavlov's Views

1. The behaviorist traditions emphasize that personality is no more than observable behavior.

2. Pavlov's classical conditioning occurs when a neutral stimulus (the conditioned stimulus) acquires the ability to produce a response originally produced by another stimulus (the unconditioned stimulus).

3. Classical conditioning plays a role in automatic, emergency reactions, in some stress and illness situations, in the conditioning of emotional responses, and in the formation of fetishes.

B. Operant Conditioning and B. F. Skinner's Views

1. Skinner's operant conditioning occurs when behavioral consequences change the probability of a behavior's occurrence.

2. Reinforcement increases the probability that a behavior will occur, and punishment decreases the probability of the behavior.

3. Positive reinforcement is receiving a pleasant stimulus after a behavior and negative reinforcement is the removal of (or avoidance of) an unpleasant stimulus after a behavior.

C. Social Learning Theory and Bandura's Views

1. Bandura's social learning theory emphasizes that behavior is learned through experiences with the environment and that cognitive factors influence learning.

2. Reciprocal determinism means that behavior, cognitive, and environmental influences operate interactively.

3. Observational learning, or modeling, is learning that occurs when a person observes and then repeats someone else's behavior.

4. One use of modeling is mentoring programs in which more experienced persons agree to develop a one-to-one relationship with a less experienced person and serve as a competent role model.

5. Self-efficacy is the belief that one can master a situation and produce positive outcomes.

D. Evaluating the Behavioral and Social Learning Perspectives
   1. This perspective emphasizes that environmental experiences and situations determine behavior patterns called personality.
   2. Social learning theory adds the influence of cognitions in explaining personality.
   3. This perspective can be viewed as reductionistic and as minimizing the role of enduring personality characteristics.

IV. The Phenomenological and Humanistic Perspectives
   A. The Perspectives
      1. The phenomenological perspective emphasizes on self-perceptions and perceptions of the world in understanding personality, therefore reality is what is perceived.
      2. The humanistic perspective emphasizes the person's capacity for personal growth, freedom, and positive qualities.
   B. Carl Rogers' Approach
      1. Rogers believed that most people have difficulty accepting their own true, innately positive feelings because they have dealt with conditioned positive regard, meaning that love and praise are dependent on conforming to parental or social standards.
      2. The self may become somewhat lost by mirroring what others want.
      3. Self-concept refers to individuals' overall perceptions of their abilities, behavior, and personality and is divided into the real self (who one actually is) and the ideal self (the self one wants to be).
      4. People can develop a more positive self-concept through unconditional positive regard, empathy, and genuineness.
      5. The fully functioning person is open to experience, not defensive, sensitive to the self and the external world, and has fairly harmonious relationships.
   C. Abraham Maslow's Approach
      1. Maslow developed a hierarchy of motives that reflects the order in which needs must generally be satisfied: physiological, safety, love and belongingness, self-esteem, cognitive and aesthetic needs, and self-actualization.
      2. Self-actualization is the motivation to develop one's full potential as a human being.
      3. Deficiency needs must be reasonably met first and then metaneeds (growth needs) can take precedence. Unfulfilled metaneeds can lead to alienation, weakness, or cynicism.
   D. Evaluating the Perspective
      1. This perspective emphasizes self-perceptions and perceptions of the world as key elements of personality.
      2. The perspective deals with the positive potential of the human being.
      3. Its concepts are difficult to research.
      4. The perspective is viewed by some as too optimistic and overestimating of its freedom and rationality of humans.

V. Trait Theory and Trait-Situation Interaction
   A. Personality Type Theory
      1. About 2400 years go, Hippocrates classified people's personalities based on body fluids.
      2. Sheldon developed a theory based on the three body types of endomorph, mesomorph, and ectomorph.

B. Trait Theories
   1. Trait theories state that personality consists of broad dispositions, called traits, that lead to characteristic responses.
   2. Gordon Allport defined personality using central traits (usually a person had fewer than ten) and secondary traits (more numerous, but less frequently observed).
   3. Eysenck believed that the dimensions of stability-instability and introversion-extraversion were the basic aspects of personality.
C. Recent Developments in Trait Psychology
   1. There may be five basic factors in personality: extraversion-introversion, friendly compliance versus hostile noncompliance, neuroticism, will to achieve, and intellect.
   2. Sensation seeking is the need for varied, novel, and complex sensations and experiences.
D. Individualism and Collectivism
   1. The most elaborate search for national traits has focused on the dichotomy of individualism-collectivism.
   2. Individualism involves personal goals over group goals with self-serving values such as feeling good, personal distinction, and independence.
   3. Collectivism emphasizes values of serving the group by subordinating personal goals to preserve group integrity, interdependence of members, and harmonious relationships.
   4. Individuals raised in one style can learn communication strategies that aid interacting with persons reared in the other style.
E. The Attack on Traits
   1. Mischel attacked the view of personality as consistent, broad, and internal traits.
   2. Instead, personality changes with the situation (situationalism).
   3. Instead, interactionists focus on a trait-situation interaction.

Learning Objectives

After reading and studying this chapter, students should be able to:

1. Know what psychologists mean when they refer to personality.
2. Identify and describe the central components to Freud's theory of personality structure.
3. Know what psychoanalytic defense mechanisms are, identify them, and know the purpose they serve.
4. Identify and describe the stages of Freud's theory of personality development.
5. Briefly describe how the theories of other psychoanalytic theorists principally differ from Freud.
6. Identify the key components of the Horney, Jung, and Adler theories of personality.
7. Explain how classical conditioning works and how it may form personality.
8. Describe the process of operant conditioning and how it may shape personality.
9. Know how social learning theory explains personality and the role that reciprocal determinism plays in personality formation.
10. Explain Rogers' approach to personality formation.
11. Identify Maslow's hierarchy of needs and the role they play in personality.
12. Identify Sheldon's personality type theory.
13. Define what traits are and how trait theories describe personality.
14. Identify the common dimensions found among all theories of personality.

15. Describe how traits interact with situations in relation to personality.
16. Contrast and compare the various theories of personality.
17. Know the chief limitations of psychoanalytic, behavioral, social learning, humanistic, and trait theories of personality.

Guided Review

After you have read the chapter one time, search through the chapter to find the appropriate words to complete these statements. Material is covered in the same order as the chapter.

1. Psychologists define _____ as enduring, distinctive thoughts, emotions, and behaviors that characterize the way an individual _____ to the world.
2. Freud believed that the _____ (conscious, unconscious) mind was more important because it was one way to reduce _____.
3. If Freud's personality structures are compared to rulers, the _____ is the monarch, the _____ is the prime minister, and the _____ is the high priest.
4. The _____ is the personality structure that consists of instincts and is totally _____. It is guided by the _____ principle and has the goal of seeking _____ _____ and the avoidance of _____.
5. The rational personality structure is the _____, which is guided by the _____ principle. Its goal is _____ achieved within the norms of society.
6. The ego is called the _____ branch of the personality because it houses our higher mental functions—reasoning, problem solving, and decision making.
7. The personality structure that deals with values and morals is the _____.
8. _____ _____ are _____ methods by which the ego distorts reality to protect itself from anxiety. The basic one is _____ in which threatening impulses are pushed out of conscious awareness.
9. In _____, cover motive rather than the real motive is accepted by the ego, while _____ involves shifting unacceptable feelings from one object to another, more acceptable object.
10. _____ is the defense mechanism that occurs when a useful course of action replaces an acceptable one, and _____ involves attributing our own shortcomings and faults to others.
11. _____ _____ is the defense mechanism that occurs when we express an unacceptable impulse by transforming it into its opposite, while _____ occurs when we behave in a way characteristic of a previous developmental level.
12. Freud believed that we went through _____ stages of _____ development, with each stage characterized by the focus on a different _____ _____.
13. Each psychosexual stage is characterized by conflicts that result in _____ if not resolved.
14. In the first psychosexual stage, the _____ stage, which lasts for about _____ months, the chief sources of pleasure are _____, _____, and _____.
15. The _____ stage is the second developmental stage and it ends around the age of _____ years.
16. Freud's third stage is the _____ stage, which lasts about _____ years; during this stage the child learns it is pleasurable to stimulate the _____.

17. The phallic stage is named for the Latin word for _____, which feminists view as symbolic of the _____-_____ of psychoanalytic theory. Indeed, Freud thought that since females lack a penis they develop less fully in _____ roles, _____, _____ _____, and _____.

18. During the phallic stage, boys experience the _____ _____, a process of falling in love with their _____, blocking this love, and _____ with the _____ of the father's gender role.

19. However, girls undergoing the _____ _____ fall in love with their _____, block this love and then love their _____, but because her _____ is not replaced, she eventually _____ with the _____ of the mother's gender role.

20. According to Freud, fixations in the _____ stage might result in smoking, kissing, chewing gum, sarcasm, or drinking while fixations in the _____ stage might include extreme messiness, interest in painting, great interest in statistics, or fear of dirt.

21. The last two psychosexual stages are _____ and _____.

22. Karen Horney placed less emphasis on _____ factors and more emphasis on _____ factors.

23. Horney countered Freud's concept of _____ _____ with the notion that both sexes envy the attributes of the other and proposed _____ _____ as men's coveting of women's reproductive capacities.

24. For Horney, the prime motive in human existence is the need for _____, which develops in three interpersonal strategies, that of _____ _____ people by seeking love and support, _____ _____ from people by becoming more independent, and _____ _____ people by becoming competitive and domineering.

25. Nancy Chodorow suggests women more than men define themselves in terms of their _____ and with more salient _____ while men use the defense mechanism of _____ more.

26. Jung's concept of the _____ _____ is equivalent to Freud's idea of the unconscious, while Jung's _____ _____ is shared by all human beings.

27. _____ are the primordial images in every individual's collective unconscious with two of them, the _____ and the _____, representing the feminine and masculine aspects within.

28. Another important archetype is the self, which is often expressed in art as a _____; the two aspects of the self are the "public mask" called the _____ and the "dark side" called the _____.

29. According to Jung, in the first part of our life the developmental task is doing well what comes _____, and later the task is to achieve _____.

30. While Jung called his theory _____ psychology, Adler named his _____ theory because he focused on each person's _____.

31. According to Adler, everyone strives for _____ to overcome feelings of _____ derived from interacting with bigger, more powerful people and from _____ _____.

32. The attempt to overcome imagined or real inferiorities or weaknesses by developing one's abilities is called _____, which Adler believed was a(n) _____ (abnormal, normal) process, while _____ is an exaggerated effort to conceal a weakness.

33. The two patterns of overcompensation are _____ _____, where one is overwhelmed by extreme feelings of inadequacy, and _____ _____, in which one has an exaggerated self-importance used to mask actual feelings of _____.

34. Important contributions of psychoanalytic theory include its emphasis on the importance of _____ experiences and looking at personality _____, the importance of _____ motivation, and its emphasis on _____ and anxiety.

35. Since it is difficult to conduct _____ on psychoanalytic concepts, it relies heavily on therapists' subjective evaluations of clients and recollections of early childhood.

36. The behavioral tradition of Pavlov and Watson suggest that personality is no more than _____ behavior.

37. _____ _____ occurs when a _____ stimulus acquires the ability to produce a response originally produced by another stimulus, called the _____ stimulus.

38. _____ are automatic stimulus-response connections, in which an UCS produces an _____ _____.

39. Skinner's _____ _____ is a form of learning in which the _____ of behavior produce changes in the _____ of the behavior's occurrence.

40. A reward or a _____ is a consequence that _____ the probability a behavior will occur, while _____ is a consequence that _____ the probability a behavior will occur.

41. A _____ _____ increases the frequency of a response because it is followed by a pleasant stimulus, while a negative reinforcement _____ the frequency of a response because an unpleasant stimulus is _____ or avoided.

42. Learning is more efficient when the interval between the stimulus and the response is _____ and operant learning is more efficient with _____ consequences.

43. _____ _____ theory, associated with Bandura and Mischel, emphasizes that behavior is learned through experiences with the environment and is affected by _____ factors.

44. The interaction among cognitions, behaviors, and environment is emphasized in the concept of _____ _____.

45. Observational learning, or _____, is learning that occurs when a person observes and then repeats someone else's behavior.

46. In a _____ relationship, a more experienced person works one-to-one with a less experienced person serving as a competent role model.

47. One way of improving coping skills is through _____-_____, the belief that one can master a situation and produce positive outcomes.

48. The behavioral perspective allows a psychologist to conduct _____, emphasizes control over one's _____, but is viewed by some as _____ and as minimizing the importance of _____ in personality.

49. According to the phenomenological perspective, reality is what is _____; a subset called the _____ perspective emphasizes personal growth, freedom, and positive qualities.

50. Rogers believed that _____ _____ _____ interferes with self-acceptance of one's own true, innately positive feelings, while _____ _____ _____, and _____ help in developing a positive self-concept.

51. One's _____-_____ is one's overall perceptions of one's abilities, behavior, and personality, and involves one's _____ _____, or the self as it really is, and the _____ _____, which is the self one would like to be. When these two aspects are discrepant, _____ occurs.

52. According to Rogers, a _____ _____ person is open to experience, sensitive to oneself and the external world, not very defensive, and fairly harmonious in relationships.

53. Maslow called the humanistic approach the "_____ _____" in psychology as an important alternative to _____ and _____ traditions.

54. In Maslow's hierarchy of motives, the first need to be satisfied is _____ and then _____, _____ and _____, _____-_____, cognitive and aesthetic needs, and _____-_____.

55. _____ _____ refer to Maslow's term for essential requirements, and _____, or growth needs, refer to higher self-actualized needs.

56. Realistic orientation, spontaneity, problem-centeredness, need for privacy, autonomy, democratic values, strong social interest, creativity, and philosophical humor are some of Maslow's characteristics of _____-_____ individuals.

57. Unlike the psychoanalytic perspective, this perspective emphasizes the _____ experience, and like the psychoanalytic perspective its concepts are difficult to _____.

58. The three body types in Sheldon's personality theory are the _____, the _____, and the _____.

59. Allport suggested that we have fewer than ten _____ traits and numerous _____ traits, while Eysenck views _____ dimensions to be primary personality descriptors.

60. Modern trait research suggests that there may be _____ basic dimensions of personality, which are _____-_____, _____ _____ versus _____ _____, _____, will to _____, and _____.

61. _____ _____ is the need for varied, novel, and complex sensations and experiences, and Farley suggests that thrill-seeking behavior can be either constructive or destructive.

62. _____ involves giving higher priority to personal goals than to group goals, while _____ emphasizes values that serve the group by subordinating personal goals.

63. The position of _____ attacks traits as enduring, consistent aspects across situations and time.

64. Interactionists value both _____ and _____ variables in understanding personality.

65. Three important issues that characterize personality are the degree to which personality is (1) _____ versus _____, (2) _____ versus _____, and (3) _____ versus _____.

66. _____ _____ involves testing individuals in order to more accurately describe their traits and characteristics.

Guided Review Answers

1. personality, adapts; 2. unconscious, conflict; 3. id, ego, superego; 4. id, unconscious, pleasure, immediate gratification, pain; 5. ego, reality, pleasure; 6. executive; 7. superego; 8. Defense mechanisms, unconscious, repression; 9. rationalization, displacement; 10. Sublimation, projection; 11. Reaction formation, regression; 12. five, psychosexual, erogenous zone; 13. fixations; 14. oral, eighteen, sucking, chewing, biting; 15. anal, three; 16. phallic, three, genitals; 17. penis, male-bias, gender, sexuality, sexual orientation, morality; 18. Oedipus complex, mother, identifying, strength; 19. Electra complex, mother, father, penis, identifies, weakness; 20. oral, anal; 21. latency, genital; 22. biological, sociocultural; 23. penis envy, womb envy; 24. security, moving toward, moving away, moving against; 25. relationships, emotions, denial; 26. personal unconscious, collective unconscious; 27. Archetypes, anima, animus; 28. mandala, persona, shadow; 29. easily, balance; 30. depth, individual, uniqueness; 31. superiority, inferiority, sibling rivalry; 32. compensation, normal, overcompensation; 33. inferiority complex, superiority complex, inferiority; 34. early, developmentally, unconscious, conflict; 35. research; 36. observable; 37. Classical conditioning,

neutral, unconditioned; 38. Reflexes, unconditioned response; 39. operant conditioning, consequences, probability; 40. reinforcement, increases, punishment, decreases; 41. positive reinforcement, increases, removed; 42. brief, immediate; 43. Social learning, cognitive; 44. reciprocal determinism; 45. modeling; 46. mentoring; 47. self-efficacy; 48. research, environment, reductionistic, cognitions; 49. perceived, humanistic; 50. conditioned positive regard, unconditioned positive regard, empathy; 51. self-concept, real self, ideal self, maladjustment; 52. fully functioning; 53. "third force," psychoanalytic, behavioral; 54. physiological, safety, love, belongingness, self-esteem, self-actualization; 55. Deficiency needs, metaneeds; 56. self-actualized; 57. conscious, research; 58. endomorph, mesomorph, ectomorph; 59. central, secondary, two; 60. five, extraversion-introversion, friendly compliance, hostile noncompliance, neuroticism, achieve, intellect; 61. Sensation seeking; 62. Individualism, collectivism; 63. situationalism; 64. trait (person), situation; 65. innate, learned, conscious, unconscious, internal, external; 66. Personality assessment.

Key Terms

For each term, briefly define the term in your own words and provide an example or situation (especially one you can visualize) that will help you retain the meaning of the concept. Key terms are presented in the order they are presented in the chapter.

1. personality (p. 31)

2. id (p. 32)

3. pleasure principle (p. 32)

4. ego (p. 32)

5. reality principle (p. 32)

6. superego (p. 32)

7. defense mechanisms (p. 33)

8. repression (p. 33)

9. rationalization (p. 33)

10. displacement (p. 33)

11. sublimation (p. 33)

12. projection (p. 33)

13. reaction formation (p. 33)

14. regression (p. 33)

15. erogenous zones (p. 33)

16. fixation (p. 33)

17. oral stage (p. 34)

18. anal stage (p. 34)

19. phallic stage (p. 34)

20. Oedipus complex (p. 34)

21. latency stage (p. 34)

22. genital stage (p. 34)

23. collective unconscious (p. 36)

24. archetypes (p. 36)

25. depth psychology (p. 37)

26. individual psychology (p. 37)

27. striving for superiority (p. 37)

28. sibling rivalry (p. 37)

29. compensation (p. 37)

30. overcompensation (p. 37)

31. inferiority complex (p. 37)

32. superiority complex (p. 37)

33. classical conditioning (p. 40)

34. reflexes (p. 40)

35. unconditioned stimulus (UCS) (p. 40)

36. unconditioned response (UCR) (p. 40)

37. conditioned stimulus (CS) (p. 40)

38. conditioned response (CR) (p. 40)

39. operant conditioning (instrumental conditioning) (p. 42)

62. trait theory (p. 50)

63. sensation seeking (p. 51)

64. individualism (p. 52)

65. collectivism (p. 52)

66. situationism (p. 53)

67. personality assessment (p. 57)

Study Aids

Students who do well on tests develop mnemonic aids to help them remember important terms and concepts. A few are suggested here, and you are encouraged to develop your own additional aids.

> **FREUD'S PERSONALITY STRUCTURES.** Use the word *pies* to help you remember that Freud's personality structures are: personality = id, ego, and superego. This word even reminds you of the order in which the personality structures develop. You can also remember the order of the psychosexual stages by using the sentence: Otto and Patty like giraffes. Using the first letters of each word (OAPLG) will correctly cue in the psychosexual stages: Oral, Anal, Phallic, Latency, Genital.

> **ANIMUS AND ANIMA.** You can remember the archetypes of anima and animus correctly by noting that aniMA, which is one's feminine aspects, ends in the word *MA*.

> **BODY TYPES.** If you need to remember Sheldon's three body types, remember that ENDomorphs have big ENDs, while Mesomorphs have MUSCLES, and finally ecTomorphs are THIN.

Understanding Concepts

Answer these questions to develop your understanding of the important ideas in this chapter.

1. Explain the similarities and differences between the id and the ego, and discuss how the ego must mediate between the id and the superego.

2. Since repression is part of all the other defense mechanisms, for each of the following defense mechanisms, describe (1) what is repressed and then (2) what is the distortion involved: rationalization, projection, regression, and displacement.

3. Explain why feminist psychologists believe that Freud's psychoanalytic theory is male-biased. Could the theory be altered to be non-sexist?

4. Compare the basic ideas of Sigmund Freud and Karen Horney and evaluate their contributions.

5. Compare Freud's and Jung's ideas about the unconscious.

6. Discuss the role of inferiority and superiority in Adler's theory. Include the following concepts: sibling rivalry, compensation, overcompensation, inferiority complex, and superiority complex.

7. Compare and contrast the psychoanalytic perspective, the behavioral perspective, and the humanistic perspective. Do you agree with Maslow that they are the "three forces" in psychology?

8. Distinguish among positive reinforcement, negative reinforcement, and punishment in terms of the type of stimulus and their effect on behavioral response rate.

9. Discuss Rogers' ideas about the self-concept and how to develop a positive one.

10. Compare Rogers' fully functioning person with Maslow's self-actualizing person. Are they identical?

11. Discuss the limitations of type theories such as Sheldon's theory.

12. Compare the ideas of trait theorists Allport and Eysenck.

13. Compare and contrast the concepts of extraversion and sensation seeking.

14. Describe individualism and collectivism and summarize how individuals in one style can learn to communicate with individuals in the other style.

Applying Concepts

Answer these questions to develop your ability to apply this chapter's material to your life and the world. Your own responses may differ from other students' in the class, and it is helpful to share your ideas with the other students.

1. How do the images of personality we use in our everyday conversations about people correspond to the way psychologists describe personality?

2. Write a brief description of your own personality. Do you tend to think in terms of the psychoanalytic, behavioral, phenomenological, or trait approach? Which perspective do you use the least? Why?

3. What advantages and what problems would occur for individuals whose id was much stronger than either the ego or the superego? If the superego was much stronger than either the id or the ego?

4. What advice would a psychoanalyst give parents for rearing psychologically healthy children? Would you be willing to follow this advice?

5. Assess yourself on your use of the three strategies suggested by Horney: moving toward people, moving away from people, and moving against people. Which of these strategies do you use most? Least? Are the strategies used in moderation and balance or do you use one or two of these strategies in an exaggerated fashion? Design a course of action that would increase your balance.

6. Discuss whether Jung's concept of collective unconscious is useful in understanding cultural aspects such as mythology, art, television characters, religion, folktales, and fortune-telling methods. Why or why not?

7. Take Self-Assessment 2.1 and evaluate your results. What is your need for uniqueness? Does your behavior reflect this need level?

8. Which primary motive do you prefer—Freud's sex drive, Horney's drive for security, or Adler's striving for superiority? Why?

9. Provide a personal example of classical conditioning, operant conditioning, and modeling.

10. Develop a set of self-efficacy thoughts that you could use to improve your performance as a college student (e.g., increasing class comments, improving study habits, increasing study time, starting term papers sooner in the semester).

11. Discuss the impact of having parents who express unconditioned positive regard versus conditioned positive regard toward their child. Would there be any drawbacks to parents who use unconditioned positive regard consistently?

12. Take Self-Assessment 2.2 on extraversion. Evaluate your results. Are you an extravert or an introvert? Are you comfortable with your orientation? Why or why not? Is one of the orientations better than the other?

13. Take Self-Assessment 2.3 on sensation seeking and evaluate your results. Are you a thrill seeker? Do your behaviors reflect your sensation seeking score?

Chapter Practice Tests

Answer these multiple-choice test questions to help you assess your understanding of the chapter's material. Evaluate your answers to determine which sections you need to further review.

Practice Test A

1. Psychologists use the word *personality* to refer to
   a. a person's ability to adapt in the world.
   b. the social and community aspects of a person.
   c. the distinctive aspects of a person.
   d. the adaptive and successful characteristics of a person.
   p. 31
2. For Freud, the struggle between meeting one's needs and caring for others is resolved by
   a. the id.
   b. the ego.
   c. the superego.
   d. fixations.
   p. 32
3. When a person reverts to an earlier stage of development to resolve unconscious conflicts, the person is using the psychoanalytic defense mechanism
   a. regression.
   b. rationalization.
   c. repression.
   d. displacement.
   p. 33
4. According to Freud's theory of personality development, which stage involves a repression of all sexual interest and a development of social interests?
   a. anal stage
   b. latency stage
   c. phallic stage
   d. genital stage
   p. 34

5. Karen Horney's theory of personality relied heaviest on the concept
   a. of striving for superiority.
   b. that anatomy is destiny.
   c. that people are primarily motivated by a need for security.
   d. of ego dominance.
   p. 36
6. Which psychoanalytic theorist referred to the inferiority complex?
   a. Freud
   b. Jung
   c. Adler
   d. Horney
   p. 37
7. Classical condition specifically involves
   a. a neutral stimulus being paired with a stimulus that produces a reflex.
   b. learning a new reflex.
   c. reinforcing old ways of behaving in new situations.
   d. replacing bad habits with good ones with unconditioned responses.
   p. 40
8. Which of the following is true about classical conditioning?
   a. A reflex can be conditioned to a previously neutral stimulus.
   b. Conditioning results from observation.
   c. Rewards are stronger than punishments.
   d. Reflexes are replaced by learned behaviors.
   p. 40

9. Skinner's theory of learning relies on the concept that
   a. behaviors are learned through observation.
   b. punishment is more powerful than rewards.
   c. behavior is influenced by the consequences that follow.
   d. negative reinforcement is more effective than punishment.
   p. 42

10. In social learning theory, another name for observational learning is
    a. modeling.
    b. classical conditioning.
    c. trial and error learning.
    d. imitation.
    p. 43

11. Which statement would Carl Rogers most likely support?
    a. Children develop personalities through a complex series of biological forces.
    b. Children develop personalities as a result of caring and nurturing relationships.
    c. Children develop personalities as a result of unconscious feelings for their parents.
    d. Children learn ways of behaving from peers that form the basis for what we call personality.
    p. 46

12. One of the central contributions of humanistic perspectives is that
    a. human beings develop through personal growth.
    b. childhood experiences are at the core of personality.
    c. experiences prevail over biological aspects.
    d. humans are driven by survival instincts.
    p. 48

13. Stan enjoys motor cross and bungy-jumping. Which of the following is a trait that characterizes Stan?
    a. neuroticism
    b. introversion
    c. sensation seeking
    d. mesomorphism
    p. 51

14. Traits best explain personality when
    a. the positive traits are focused on.
    b. situations are considered in combination with traits.
    c. the early childhood formation of traits is known.
    d. a person completes an MMPI.
    p. 53

15. Which theory emphasizes unconscious processes and internal determinants?
    a. psychoanalytic
    b. behavioral
    c. humanistic
    d. trait
    p. 54

Practice Test B

1. Freud's psychoanalytic theory states that the superego is primarily ____, while the ego is mostly ___.
   a. driven for pleasure, dissatisfying to the self
   b. consciously motivated, unconsciously motivated
   c. infantile, mature
   d. based in moral principles, based in reality
   p. 32

2. Freud's defense mechanisms function primarily to
   a. reduce anxiety.
   b. fool oneself into feeling better.
   c. revert back to earlier times.
   d. develop better social relationships.
   p. 33

3. Which of the following is a common criticism of Freud's psychoanalytic theory?
   a. The theory is outdated.
   b. Too much emphasis is placed on the family in development.
   c. Learning through observation is ignored.
   d. The theory cannot be scientifically tested.
   p. 37

4. Which psychoanalytic theorist referred to the coping strategy of moving toward others?
   a. Freud
   b. Jung
   c. Adler
   d. Horney
   p. 36

5. In classical conditioning, the conditioned stimulus
   a. produces a conditioned response.
   b. is similar to a conditioned response.
   c. acts as a powerful reinforcer.
   d. cannot be learned.
   p. 40

6. Giving a dog a biscuit for performing a trick will likely result in
   a. the conditioning of a salivary reflex.
   b. taming the dog.
   c. a greater probability that the trick will be performed again in the future.
   d. getting the dog's attention for observation.
   p. 40

7. Operant conditioning was founded by which theorist?
   a. Albert Bandura
   b. B. F. Skinner
   c. Abraham Maslow
   d. Carl Rogers
   p. 42

8. A person who feels confident that they can perform a complex task may be exhibiting
   a. overcompensation.
   b. a conditioned response.
   c. a superiority complex.
   d. self-efficacy.
   p. 44

9. Rogers emphasized which of the following?
   a. unconditioned positive regard
   b. a hierarchy of needs
   c. the interaction between traits and situations
   d. the scientific study of personality
   p. 45

10. According to Maslow, which of the following is a deficiency need?
    a. wholeness
    b. security
    c. truth
    d. justice
    p. 46

11. Which of Sheldon's personality types would be most likely to be an athlete?
    a. endomorphs
    b. ectomorphs
    c. mesomorphs
    d. They are all equally as likely.
    p. 49

12. Personality traits have their greatest influence on behavior when
    a. people are with others.
    b. situation influences are minimal.
    c. a person is provided with unconditional positive regard.
    d. situational influences are at their peak.
    p. 50

13. Which best describes personality assessment?
    a. a subspecialty of medicine
    b. a set of tools for trained professionals
    c. a way of determining what a person is all about
    d. a way to get into the unconscious without a person knowing it
    p. 57

14. Which theory emphasizes early innate tendencies, the unconscious and internal determinants of personality?
    a. psychoanalytic
    b. behavioral
    c. humanistic
    d. No theory emphasizes both of these.
    p. 54

15. Compared to behavioral theories,
psychoanalytic theories are more likely to
emphasize
   a. the unconscious.
   b. social relationships.
   c. criticism from parents and teachers.
   d. role models in a family.
   p. 55

Key for Practice Test A

1. Answer c; Personality consists of the distinctive characteristics related to how a person adapts to the world; page 31; Learning Objective 1
2. Answer b; The ego resolves unconscious conflicts between the id and superego; page 32; Learning Objective 2
3. Answer a; Regression involves reverting to an early developmental level in dealing with unconscious conflicts; page 33; Learning Objective 3
4. Answer b; The latency stage occurs when children reach school age and focus on developing socially expected skills and roles; page 34; Learning Objective 4
5. Answer c; Horney stressed social relations and their role in developing a sense of security, as opposed to Freud who stressed sexuality in development; page 36; Learning Objective 5
6. Answer c; Alfred Adler stated that people are primarily motivated by striving for superiority, and some may therefore develop an inferiority complex; page 37; Learning Objective 6
7. Answer a; Classical conditioning pairs a neutral stimulus, a conditioned stimulus, with a stimulus that naturally produces a response, an unconditioned stimulus; page 40; Learning Objective 7
8. Answer a; In classical conditioning, a naturally occurring response, or reflex, is learned to occur in the presence of a previously neutral stimulus; page 40; Learning Objective 7
9. Answer c; Operant conditioning stresses the role of what follows a behavior, or the behavior's consequences, which may either reward or punish the behavior; page 42; Learning Objective 8
10. Answer a; Modeling is when a behavior is learned by observing someone else observe its performance; page 43; Learning Objective 9
11. Answer b; Rogers held that unconditioned positive regard in social relationships provided the basis for adjustment and development; page 46; Learning Objective 10
12. Answer a; Humanistic perspectives share an emphasis on individuals and personal growth; page 48; Learning Objective 11
13. Answer c; Sensation seeking is a trait that is expressed when persons go after optimal levels of stimulation, such as in bungy jumping or motor cross; page 51; Learning Objective 13
14. Answer b; Traits and situations interact in behavioral expression; page 53; Learning Objective 15
15. Answer a; Psychoanalytic theory is based on unconscious conflicts and forces within the psychological makeup of the person; page 54; Learning Objective 15

Key for Practice Test B

1. Answer d; The superego is driven toward morally correct behavior, while the ego deals with the reality of situations; page 32; Learning Objective 2
2. Answer a; Anxiety results from unconscious conflicts, which are dealt with by defense mechanisms, and therefore reduce anxiety; page 33; Learning Objective 3
3. Answer d; Reliance on the unconscious makes psychoanalytic theory impossible to objectively study; page 37; Learning Objective 17
4. Answer d; Karen Horney discussed moving away from, toward, or against others; page 36; Learning Objective 6
5. Answer a; Conditioned responses result from the pairing of a conditioned stimulus with an unconditioned stimulus; page 40; Learning Objective 7
6. Answer c; According to operant conditioning, the biscuit will act as a positive reinforcement for the trick; page 40; Learning Objective 8
7. Answer b; B. F. Skinner founded operant conditioning; page 42; Learning Objective 8
8. Answer d; Self-efficacy is the social learning theory concept that involves a person believing that they have the skills to perform a specific task; page 44; Learning Objective 9
9. Answer a; Rogers stressed the role of unconditional positive regard in relationships as the foundation for developing an adjusted personality; page 45; Learning Objective 10
10. Answer b; Security needs, like safety, shelter, and food, is a deficiency as opposed to a metaneed; page 46; Learning Objective 11
11. Answer c; Mesomorphs are characterized by muscular and well-toned body types; page 49; Learning Objective 12
12. Answer b; Because situations and traits interact, traits will play a bigger role when situations play a lesser role; page 50; Learning Objective 15
13. Answer b; Personality tests are specialized tools for persons trained in their use, usually clinical and counseling psychologists; page 57; Learning Objective 13
14. Answer a; Psychoanalytic theory emphasizes the role of the unconscious, innate characteristics, and internal forces in personality development; page 54; Learning Objective 16
15. Answer a; Psychoanalytic theories stress the unconscious while behavioral theories only consider conscious aspects to be relevant; page 55; Learning Objective 16

Chapter Outline

I.   The Self
   A. Self-Understanding
      1. Over time, self-understanding becomes more internal and self-reflective, but always attached to the external world.
      2. Self-understanding is the individual's cognitive representation of the self—its rational underpinnings.
      3. Three dimensions of self-understanding are possible selves, self-discrepancies, and conscious and unconscious selves.
   B. Possible Selves
      1. Possible selves are what individuals might become, including what they would like to become, and what they are afraid of becoming.
      2. Each possible self is a personalized construction that may be articulated in considerable detail by the person.
      3. An important function of possible selves is self-evaluation.
      4. Self-defeating behavior patterns can keep us from becoming one or more of our positive selves.
      5. Gender influences our possible selves because boys and girls are usually given different messages about their possibilities.
   C. Self-Discrepancies
      1. Self-discrepancies can be viewed in terms of Rogers' ideal and real selves or in Higgins' actual, ideal, and ought selves.
      2. The actual self is one's representation of the attributes believed to be possessed.
      3. The ideal self is one's representation of what one ideally ought to possess—hopes, aspirations, and wishes.
      4. The ought self is one's representation of the attributes one should possess—duties, obligations, and responsibilities.
      5. In Higgins' self-discrepancy theory, problems occur when various selves are discrepant with each other.
      6. Discrepancies between actual and ideal selves lead to dejection-related emotions, such as sadness, disappointment, and shame.
      7. Discrepancies between actual and ought selves lead to agitated-related emotions, such as anxiety, fear, and guilt.
   D. Conscious and Unconscious Selves
      1. Psychologists differ in their views about how extensively the self is conscious or unconscious and whether the unconscious self is accessible to awareness.
      2. Freud and Jung emphasize the unconscious self; Skinner, Maslow, and Rogers do not.

3. Self-understanding may be restricted by cognitive limitations on accessing information and by defensive avoidance of painful self-knowledge.
4. Self-examination, self-exploration, and self-discovery are important to adjustment.
5. Narcissists are excessively self-centered and self-congratulatory and unaware of their actual self and how others perceive them. Authority, self-absorption, arrogance, and exploitiveness are key aspects of narcissistic personalities.
6. They have very low self-esteem at the unconscious level but present a false image of bloated self-esteem.

E. Self-Esteem
1. Self-esteem is the evaluative and affective dimension of self-concept.
2. It is also referred to as self-worth or self-image.
3. In addition to general self-worth, there are four domains of specific evaluations: general competence, moral self-approval, power, and love worthiness.
4. Four aspects of improving low self-esteem are: identifying the causes of low self-esteem and defining important domains of competence; emotional support and social approval; achievement; and coping.
5. Harter suggests that self-esteem enhancement programs that emphasize "feeling good" without attending to the causes of self-esteem fail.
6. Earlier studies showed that blacks had lower self-esteem and self-concept than whites, but recent studies do not find this, nor do Hispanic Americans have a more negative self-concept.
7. Emotional support and social approval that comes from being confirmed by others (family, spouses, friends, or teachers) is a powerful influence on a person's self-esteem.
8. Achievement can also improve an individual's self-esteem, including the direct teaching of skills such as self-efficacy.
9. Resolving problems and successful coping can increase self-esteem.

F. Can There Be Too Much Emphasis on the Self?
1. Collectivistic societies view the self differently than do individualistic ones.
2. Influenced by Zen Buddhism, Watts and Reynolds suggest that individuals in Western societies place too much emphasis on the past and on the future and forget to live their present self fully.
3. Reynolds suggests trying to live the present moment well by fully attending to the task at hand, even if trivial or painstaking.
4. He also suggests doing what needs to be done ("proper effort"), rather than doing only what is pleasant.
5. Baumeister suggests that Americans are so overconcerned with self-fulfillment and personal identity that they have become too self-critical, too pushed toward change, and too stressed.
6. When developing, maintaining, and enhancing a positive self-image becomes a burden, individuals try to escape the self.
7. Escapes from the self include leisure activities (e.g., reading, listening to music, dancing) as well as highly costly escapes such as substance abuse and radical cults.

II. Identity
A. Erikson's Eight Stages of the Human Life Span
1. Erikson's epigenetic principle is the process that guides development through the life cycle so that each time of life has a special focusing task until all parts have ascended to form a functioning whole.

2. The first stage of trust versus mistrust is aided by a feeling of physical comfort and a minimal amount of fear and apprehension and leads to a lifelong expectation that the world is a good and pleasant place to live.
3. From the first to third years, autonomy versus shame and doubt revolves around a developing sense of independence and will; it is made more difficult by restraint and harsh punishment.
4. The preschool stage of initiative versus guilt occurs with a sense of responsibility and initiative but is undermined by guilt and anxiety.
5. During the elementary school years, industry versus inferiority involves learning and imagination, but is hindered if children have feelings of incompetence and unproductiveness.
6. During adolescence, identity versus identity confusion involves finding out who one is and where one is heading, but the search for identity is hindered by being pushed and by not being exposed to many options.
7. In early adulthood, the task of intimacy versus isolation is to "find yet lose oneself in another."
8. During middle adulthood, generativity versus stagnation centers on assisting the younger generation to lead useful lives.
9. In integrity versus despair, older adults review their life and evaluate it.
10. The proper resolution of a stage crisis cannot be completely positive, but the positive resolution dominates.

B. Personality and Role Experimentation: Two Important Ingredients of Identity Development
1. A psychological moratorium is Erikson's term for the gap between childhood security and adult autonomy that occurs during identity exploration.
2. During a psychological moratorium, individuals try out different roles before achieving a stable sense of self.
3. This identity exploration is a deliberate and worthwhile effort to discover one's niche, but can be unsettling to the searcher and to those who know the individual.
4. Vocational roles are central to identity development especially in highly technical societies, and well-educated and trained persons experience the least stress in developing their identity.
5. Traditionally, more women than men have chosen career identities emphasizing nurturance rather than prestige or financial rewards.

C. Some Contemporary Thoughts on Identity
1. Identity development is a long process, more gradual than the term *crisis* implies.
2. Identity formation neither begins nor ends with adolescence.
3. Resolution of identity as a developmental task does not mean that identity will remain stable through the remainder of life, therefore it is best to be flexible and adaptable.
4. Identity formation does not happen neatly.

D. The Four Statuses of Identity
1. Marcia proposes that there are four possible statuses of identity, or ways of resolving the identity crisis.
2. Crisis is a period in which one is choosing among alternatives and commitment is when one has a personal investment in what one is doing.
3. In identity diffusion individuals have not yet experienced a crisis or a commitment.
4. With identity foreclosure individuals have made a commitment without experiencing a crisis.
5. Identity moratorium is being in the midst of a crisis with commitment absent or vague.

6. Identity achievement is the term for persons who have undergone a crisis and have made a commitment.

E. Developmental Changes: The Importance of College Experiences
   1. College upperclassmen are more likely to be identity achieved than college freshmen or high school students.
   2. College students are most likely to be identity achieved in vocational choice, less so in religious beliefs and political ideologies (where identity foreclosure or identity diffusion is more common).
   3. A common pattern in developing positive identities is "MAMA" cycles of moratorium-achiever-moratorium-achiever.

F. Gender
   1. Erikson proposed that males' aspirations were mainly oriented toward career and ideological commitments, while females' aspirations centered around marriage and child rearing.
   2. Research in the 1960s and 1970s supported Erikson but since then the sex differences have been diminishing.
   3. One possibility is that for many males identity formation precedes the stage of intimacy, but for many females the order is reversed.
   4. A study of adolescent females found that a clear sense of self was related to concerns about care and response in relationships.
   5. A study of college women found that a strong sense of self was associated with ability to solve problems of care in relationships while staying connected with both self and others.
   6. In today's world, the options for females have increased faster than males' options, and thus may at times be more confusing and conflicting.

G. Cultural and Ethnic Aspects of Identity
   1. A number of stages are involved in the development of ethnic identity. In Helms' modification of Cross's model of minority identity development, four stages are proposed: preencounter, encounter, immersion/emersion, and internalization/commitment.
   2. Preencounter is a stage in which ethnic minority individuals prefer dominant cultural values to those of their own culture.
   3. The encounter stage is usually a gradual process in which ethnic minority individuals begin to break through their denial, become aware that not all cultural values of the dominant group are beneficial to them, experience many conflicting attitudes about the self, and want to develop a minority identity but do not know how to do this.
   4. In stage 3, immersion involves completely endorsing minority views and rejecting the dominant society and the second phase of emersion involves developing notions of greater individual autonomy in deciding what to accept from one's own culture and the dominant culture.
   5. In stage 4, individuals experience greater self-control and flexibility and a sense of fulfillment regarding the integration of personal and cultural identities; internalization and commitment are key aspects.
   6. Helms also proposed a model of White ethnic identity in which individuals move from a stage of naivete about racial issues to a sophisticated state of multiculturalism or racial transcendence.
   7. The five stages of White ethnic identity are: contact, disintegration, reintegration, pseudo-independence, and autonomy.

Learning Objectives

After reading and studying this chapter, students should be able to:

1. Define what psychologists mean by self-understanding and its role in adjustment.
2. Describe the role of possible selves in adjustment.
3. Understand self-discrepancy theory.
4. Know what narcissistic personality is and the factors related to its development.
5. Define self-esteem and its role in adjustment.
6. Identify the major ways in which self-esteem may be increased.
7. Identify and describe each of Erikson's eight stages of development.
8. Know how role experimentation influences personality development and adjustment.
9. Identify and describe the four possible statuses of identity development.
10. Describe the role of a psychological moratorium in identity formation.
11. Know how gender may influence the development of identity.
12. Identify and describe the four stages of minority identity development.
13. Identify and describe the five stages of White ethnic identity development.

Guided Review

After you have read the chapter one time, search through the chapter to find the appropriate words to complete these statements. Material is covered in the same order as the chapter.

1. As we grow up, our self-understanding becomes more _____ and _____-_____, but remains influenced by the _____ contexts in which we live.
2. The definition of _____-_____ is the individual's _____ representation of the self, the substance and content of the person's self-conceptions.
3. _____ _____ are what individuals might become, including both our _____ for outcomes and our _____ outcomes.
4. It is psychologically _____ for possible selves to include both hoped for and dreaded outcomes because it can direct future positive states while also telling the individual what is to be _____ in the future.
5. An important function of possible selves is _____-_____, which involves deciding if one is doing well or poorly in one's life.
6. _____-_____ behavior patterns can keep us from becoming one or more of our positive possible selves.
7. Gender influences our possible selves with _____ typically receiving stronger, more definite messages about their possible selves, and _____ being exposed to more than one basic pattern.
8. Carl Rogers believed that a large discrepancy between _____ and real selves is a sign of _____.
9. Higgins distinguished among the _____ self, the _____ self, and the _____ self.

10. The individual's representation of one's real attributes makes up the _____ self; one's hopes, aspirations, and wishes are the _____ self; and the _____ self is one's duties, obligations, and responsibilities.

11. In Higgins's _____-_____ theory, problems occur when the different selves are _____ with each other; discrepancies between actual and _____ selves leads to _____-related emotions, such as sadness while discrepancies between actual and _____ selves leads to _____-related emotions, such as anxiety and guilt.

12. In a research study, actual self/ideal self-discrepancies were associated with _____, but not _____, and actual self/ought self-discrepancies were associated with _____, but not _____.

13. Both Freud and Jung believed the self is primarily _____, while Skinner, Maslow, and Rogers emphasized the _____ self.

14. Self-understanding is restricted by cognitive limitations on _____ _____ and by our _____ _____ of painful self-knowledge.

15. _____ individuals are unaware of their actual self and how others perceive them, and they are excessively _____-_____ and _____-_____ and may respond with rage and shame when others do not admire them.

16. Narcissistic persons are at their most _____ when their self-esteem is the most threatened.

17. _____-_____ is the evaluative and _____ dimension of self-concept, and it is also referred to as _____-_____ or _____-_____.

18. The four domains of self-esteem are general _____, moral _____-_____, _____, and _____ worthiness.

19. _____ suggests self-esteem enhancement programs of the 1960s were ineffective because the target was self-esteem itself but should have been the _____.

20. Individuals have the highest self-esteem when they perform _____ in domains that are important to the _____.

21. _____ support and _____ approval are powerful influences on a person's self-esteem.

22. The role of achievement in improving self-esteem has much in common with Bandura's concept of _____-_____.

23. Self-esteem also increases when individuals successfully _____ with problems.

24. Early attempts at comparing self-esteem and self-concept in Blacks and Whites found that _____ children had more negative self-concepts; in recent research, no differences were found for ethnic minorities except that some studies found lower self-esteem for _____ Americans.

25. It's somewhat _____ for persons to develop a positive sense of self in ethnic neighborhoods; there is _____ indication that acceptance within an ethnic group translates into prestige within mainstream American society.

26. Influenced by _____ _____, Watts and Reynolds have suggested that Western individuals place too much emphasis on the _____ and _____ when considering the self, thereby forgetting to live the _____ self fully.

27. Reynolds suggests living the present moment well by _____ _____ to the task at home even if it is _____ or painstaking.

28. The most comprehensive theory of identity development is that of _____ _____, who proposes _____ stages across the life span.

29. The _____ principle is the process that guides development through the life cycle so that each task has a time of ascendancy until all parts form a functioning whole.

30. _____ versus _____ is the first psychosocial stage, and good resolution requires _____ _____ and a minimal amount of _____ and _____.

31. _____ versus _____ and _____, the second psychosocial stage, involves toddlers discovering that their behavior is their _____, and they realize their _____.

32. During the preschool years, _____ versus _____ is a time of active, purposeful behavior, and a developing sense of _____ increases initiative.

33. _____ versus _____ occurs during the elementary school years and involves mastering knowledge and intellectual skills and expansive _____.

34. The stage during the _____ years is identity versus _____ _____ and involves individuals finding out who they are, what they are all about, and where they are going in life.

35. The three developmental stages in adulthood, in order, are _____ versus _____, _____ versus _____, and _____ versus _____.

36. Erikson's term for the gap between childhood security and adult autonomy is a _____ _____, during which there is identity _____.

37. Erikson believes that _____ roles are central to identity development, especially in highly technical societies, and training and education for appropriate careers is associated with achieving _____ self-esteem.

38. Identity formation neither begins nor ends with _____, but begins with the appearance of _____ in infancy and reaches its final phase with a _____ _____ and integration in old age.

39. _____ _____ believes Erikson's theory of identity development involves _____ possible statuses of identity.

40. _____ is defined as a period of identity exploration of meaningful alternatives, and _____ involves individuals showing a personal investment in what they are going to do.

41. Identity _____ involves no crisis and no commitment, with undecided and disinterested individuals fitting this status.

42. Individuals in identity foreclosure have made a _____ but have not experienced a _____.

43. Individuals in _____ _____ are in crisis but have not made a commitment, while those in _____ _____ have made a commitment without the crisis.

44. Individuals who have undergone a crisis and have made a commitment are in the status called _____ _____.

45. Compared to college freshmen, more college seniors are in the status called _____ _____, while those in _____ _____ have decreased.

46. Many individuals who develop positive identities follow "_____" cycles.

47. In the last couple of decades, the sex differences in identity development have _____, but some believe that for males _____ _____ is likely to precede the stage of _____ while for females the opposite order often takes place.

48. In comparing males and females, the task of identity exploration may be more complex for _____ because they try to establish identities in more domains.

49. Ethnic minority groups have struggled to maintain their _____ _____ while blending into the dominant culture, or to have an _____ identity.

50. _____ revised _____'s model of minority identity development to include _____ stages.

51. In the first stage called _____, ethnic minority individuals prefer _____ cultural values and may perceive their own physical features as _____.

52. In the second stage of _____, individuals realize they will never be a member of mainstream White America, and ethnic minority individuals begin to break through their _____; during this stage they see that not all dominant cultural values are beneficial to them and they want to identify with the minority group but don't know _____.

53. At the beginning of the third stage, which is called _____/_____, ethnic minority individuals completely _____ minority views and _____ the dominant society.

54. During the second phase of the third stage, individuals develop greater individual _____ and _____ level off.

55. The fourth stage is called _____/_____, and individuals experience a sense of fulfillment regarding the integration of their personal and _____ identities.

56. In Helms' _____ stages of _____ ethnic identity development, the first stage, called _____, is one in which White individuals are oblivious to ethnic/racial/cultural issues.

57. In stage 2, _____, Whites are caught between privileges of the "White culture" and humane desire to be fair.

58. In stage 3, _____, often characterized by the emotion _____, Whites _____ the White culture and _____ other cultures.

59. In stage 4, _____-_____, Whites recognize a personal responsibility to combat _____, and finally in stage 5, _____, Whites develop a _____ world view.

60. When we observe others' behavior, and the consequences which follow, we say that the other person is _____ behavior, and theorist _____ _____ has repeatedly shown that observations of others have a _____ impact on individual's behavior.

61. Role models have a greater influence on behavior when they are perceived to be _____ to the observer.

Guided Review Answers

1. interiorized, self-reflective, sociocultural; 2. self-understanding, cognitive; 3. Possible selves, hoped, dreaded; 4. healthy, avoided; 5. self-evaluation; 6. Self-defeating; 7. males, females; 8. ideal, maladjustment; 9. actual, ideal, ought; 10. actual, ideal, ought; 11. self-discrepancy, inconsistent, ideal, dejection, ought, agitated; 12. depression, anxiety, anxiety, depression; 13. unconscious, conscious; 14. accessing information, defensive avoidance; 15. Narcissistic, self-centered, self-congratulatory; 16. grandiose; 17. Self-esteem, affective, self-worth, self-image; 18. competence, self-approval, power, love; 19. Harter, causes; 20. competently, self; 21. Emotional, social; 22. self-efficacy; 23. cope; 24. Black, Anglo; 25. easier, no; 26. Zen Buddhism, past, future, present; 27. fully attending, trivial; 28. Erik Erikson, eight; 29. epigenetic; 30. Trust, mistrust, physical comfort, fear, apprehension; 31. Autonomy, shame, doubt, own, will; 32. Initiative, guilt, responsibility; 33. Initiative, guilt, responsibility; 34. adolescent, identity confusion; 35. intimacy, isolation, generativity, stagnation, integrity, despair; 36. psychological moratorium, exploration; 37. vocational, high; 38. adolescence, attachment life review; 39. James Marcia, four; 40. Crisis, commitment; 41. diffusion; 42. commitment, crisis; 43. identity moratorium, identity foreclosure; 44. identity achievement; 45. identity achievement, identity diffusion; 46. MAMA; 47. decreased, identity

formation, intimacy; 48. females; 49. cultural identity, inclusive; 50. Helms, Cross, four; 51. preencounter, dominant, undesirable; 52. encounter, denial, how; 53. immersion, emersion, endorse, reject; 54. autonomy, emotions; 55. internalization, commitment, cultural; 56. five, White, contact; 57. disintegration; 58. reintegration, anger, idealize, denigrate; 59. pseudo-independence, racism, autonomy, multicultural; 60. modeling, Albert Bandura, dramatic; 61. similar.

Key Terms

For each term, briefly define the term in your own words and provide an example or situation (especially one you can visualize) that will help you retain the meaning of the concept. Key terms are presented in the order they are presented in the chapter.

1. self-understanding (p. 64)

2. possible selves (p. 64)

3. actual self (p. 66)

4. ideal self (p. 66)

5. ought self (p. 66)

6. self-discrepancy theory (p. 66)

7. self-esteem (p. 67)

8. epigenetic principle (p. 73)

9. trust versus mistrust (p. 73)

10. autonomy versus shame and doubt (p. 73)

11. initiative versus guilt (p. 73)

12. industry versus inferiority (p. 73)

13. identity versus identity confusion (p. 74)

14. intimacy versus isolation (p. 74)

15. generativity versus stagnation (p. 74)

16. integrity versus despair (p. 74)

17. psychological moratorium (p. 75)

18. crisis (p. 76)

19. commitment (p. 77)

20. identity diffusion (p. 77)

21. identity foreclosure (p. 77)

22. identity moratorium (p. 77)

23. identity achievement (p. 77)

Study Aids

Students who do well on tests develop mnemonic aids to help them remember important terms and concepts. A few are suggested here, and you are encouraged to develop your own additional aids.

You can easily remember the actual, ideal, and ought selves by forming a vivid visual picture of each. For the actual self, you might picture a person seeing an accurate reflection in a mirror. For the ideal self, you might picture the mirror's reflection as having a crown on the head and holding a diploma saying "summa cum laude." For the ought self, you might picture the mirror's reflection as having a halo and holding a book titled *The Importance of Being Perfect.* These images accurately reflect the emphases on reality, being one's potential and dream, and being what one should be.

One of the hardest things to remember is the order of the eight psychosocial stages. First, remember the general order of TA-4Is-GI. The first two and last two stages become easier to cue using this model. Next, think about the 4I section. The correct order of the Is: initiative, industry, identity, and intimacy. Try to imagine a person of the "appropriate age" doing something indicative of the stage. The mnemonic and vivid visual images together will increase your abilities to remember all eight stages.

Spend a little time working with the labels of Marcia's four statuses of identity. Form word associations with each of these words: *diffusion* (e.g., scattered, undefined, rambling, disjoined, meandering, straggling, unconcentrated), *foreclosure* (e.g., cut off, finished, no longer open, unexplored), *moratorium* (e.g., putting off, exploring, gap, noncommitment), and *achievement* (e.g., accomplishment, fulfillment, realization, feat, mastery, consummation). In addition, remember which two involve a crisis: moratorium, achievement; and which two involve a commitment: foreclosure, achievement.

Understanding Concepts

Answer these questions to develop your understanding of the important ideas in this chapter.

1. Discuss the relationship between self-understanding and self-esteem. Are they fairly independent, or do changes in one aspect influence the other?

2. How do possible selves affect our attitudes and behaviors? Why are both positive and negative selves useful?

3. How does one's gender influence possible selves? Why does the text say that understanding female possible selves is more complex and more confusing?

4. Compare and contrast the roles of the actual self, ideal self, and the ought self in our lives, including how discrepancies affect emotions.

5. What is the impact on self-understanding if the self is mostly unconscious or mostly conscious?

6. Describe the narcissistic personality and what behaviors typically result from this personality pattern.

7. Discuss the general domains that are part of self-esteem.

8. What aspects would be good to include in a self-esteem enhancement program? Why would you include these aspects? Would self-efficacy play a role?

9. Compare individualistic and collectivistic societies on how individuals view the self. Do individualistic societies place too much emphasis on the self? Do you agree with Baumeister that overconcern with self-fulfillment contributes to stress problems and substance abuse?

10. Describe the main tasks of infancy, childhood, adolescence, and adulthood according to Erikson's psychosocial stages. Evaluate how well you think psychosocial theory describes the major crises of life.

11. Compare and contrast the main features (especially in terms of the presence or absence of crisis and commitment) of each of Marcia's four identity statuses.

12. Describe Helms' models for both ethnic identity and White ethnic identity development.

13. Compare how psychoanalytic perspective and phenomenological perspective would suggest gaining insight into one's personal sense of self.

14. What is the role of modeling in identity development?

Applying Concepts

Answer these questions to develop your ability to apply this chapter's material to your life and the world. Your own responses may differ from other students' in the class, and it is helpful to share your ideas with the other students.

1. The preview discusses a man who "put up a false front" to impress a woman because of his fears that she couldn't like "the real me." Is this typical dating behavior? Why? Can you relate an incident where you had the same response?

2. As the text states, we all have an idea of how we are unique from each other. Write a paragraph of your own unique self-description.

3. Discuss how modern society affects self-understanding. What aspects increase one's self-understanding? What aspects make self-understanding harder or more elusive?

4. Do psychology courses affect self-understanding? Self-esteem? Self-identity? How?

5. How do schools influence students' possible selves? How should they influence students' possible selves? Would you change the curriculum or the methods of teaching to influence possible selves?

6. How do you think messages from family members and social networks impact your actual self, ideal self, and ought self? Do different people impact one more than the other?

7. How could counselors help their clients using Higgins' self-discrepancy theory?

8. Take Self-Assessment 3.1 and measure yourself on narcissism. How narcissistic are you? Do you agree with the psychologists who propose that narcissism is more common in our society than it used to be? Why or why not?

9. Take Self-Assessment 3.2 and evaluate your self-esteem level. What is your general level of self-esteem? Consider your self-esteem in the four domains of the self (general competence, moral self-approval, power, and love worthiness). Where is your self-esteem the highest? The lowest? What could you do to improve weak areas?

10. Pick a trivial task and try Reynolds' suggestion (based on morita therapy) that you fully attend to each detail of the task. Afterwards, describe what the experience was like.

11. Evaluate your personal resolution of the psychosocial stages that you have been through. Which ones were successfully resolved? Least successfully resolved? With which crises are you currently dealing?

12. Do you think that elementary school curriculum and methods should be constructed in ways that help youngsters better resolve their current and previous psychosocial stages? Why, or why not? How could schools aid resolution of the psychosocial crises?

13. How might the high rates of suicide among adolescents be related to identity development in adolescence? What aspects of contemporary society may be related to adolescent suicide?

14. In what ways do you think the emergence of youth gangs may be related to identity development? How might life in the city contribute to roles that gangs play in the lives of youth?

15. Describe your personal experiences with each of Marcia's identity statuses: identity diffusion, identity foreclosure, identity moratorium, and identity achievement. Discuss the impact of your gender and your ethnic identity in your personal identity development.

Chapter Practice Tests

Answer these multiple-choice test questions to help you assess your understanding of the chapter's material. Evaluate your answers to determine which sections you need to further review.

Practice Test A

1. Which of the following is true about a person's sense of self?
   a. The self is unconscious and unknown.
   b. A sense of who one is plays many important roles in many aspects of human life.
   c. A sense of self develops only in childhood.
   d. Psychologists have not been able to define what the self is.
   p. 64

2. The rational side of identity is provided by
   a. the views held by people close to you.
   b. the degree to which one has hobbies.
   c. one's self-understanding.
   d. the unconscious components identity.
   p. 64

3. Possible selves include
   a. all things a person has ever done.
   b. all those aspects of the self that others view.
   c. all of what a person might become.
   d. the hierarchy of unmet needs.
   p. 65

4. Steven would like to be more musical and creative than he feels he has been. This is an example of his
   a. ideal self.
   b. real self.
   c. actual self.
   d. ought self.
   p. 65

5. When is a person likely to experience feelings of guilt, fear, and anxiety?
   a. discrepancies between ought and ideal selves
   b. discrepancies between real and actual selves
   c. discrepancies between actual and ideal selves
   d. discrepancies between ought and actual selves
   p. 66

6. If Raymond has a narcissistic personality, which of the following is most likely to be true about him?
    a. He often thinks about himself and his relationships with others.
    b. He has an enlarged self-esteem at all levels of his personality.
    c. He believes others view him the same as he views himself.
    d. He has a deep sense of who he is.
    p. 67

7. Which of the following is not one of the four domains of self-esteem?
    a. general competence
    b. power
    c. self-discrepancy
    d. moral self-approval
    p. 67

8. Self-esteem is most likely to be influenced by
    a. performing a routine task a person dislikes.
    b. successfully avoiding a dreaded task.
    c. doing well on a disliked job.
    d. performing competently at a task that a person values.
    p. 71

9. According to Erikson, a crisis occurs when
    a. development is stifled.
    b. a catastrophe in life happens.
    c. development reaches a major turning point.
    d. a challenge most people would not face arises.
    p. 73

10. As a toddler, Paula was allowed to go off on her own and explore her environment. According to Erikson, which of the following is most likely to be true of Paula?
    a. She will tend to require assistance with complex problems.
    b. She will work well on her own and not doubt her abilities.
    c. She will start tasks but not finish them.
    d. She will take lots of time getting to know someone before she confides in them.
    p. 73

11. The opportunity to try out different roles and aspects of the personality is offered by
    a. intimate relationships.
    b. the churches and temples of traditional religion.
    c. psychological moratoriums.
    d. psychosexual fixations.
    p. 75

12. David is in his fourth year of college and has declared a major and belongs to several social clubs and honor societies. Which is the most likely status of David's identity?
    a. identity diffusion
    b. identity foreclosure
    c. identity moratorium
    d. identity achievement
    p. 77

13. By their senior year, college students are most likely to achieve identity in which area?
    a. career and vocational choice
    b. religious beliefs
    c. family values
    d. political ideologies
    p. 78

14. Joe and Betty are both seventeen years old. Which of the following is most likely true about Joe but not Betty?
    a. Intimacy is more important than autonomy.
    b. Intimacy and autonomy are equally important.
    c. Emotional bonds play a major role in identity achievement.
    d. Autonomy plays a major role in identity achievement.
    p. 78

15. At which stage of ethnic identity development do individuals completely endorse minority views and reject dominant society?
    a. preencounter
    b. encounter
    c. immersion/emersion
    d. internalization/commitment
    p. 79

Practice Test B

1. Which of the following will provide the best description of a person's unique self?
    a. one's own self-description
    b. the projected views one holds of other people
    c. the results of psychological testing
    d. the unconscious view of the self disclosed by dreams
    p. 65

2. What a person might become, would like to become, and may even be afraid of becoming constitutes their
    a. possible selves.
    b. probable selves.
    c. self-discrepancies.
    d. levels of unconsciousness.
    p. 65

3. When might a person be most likely to utilize an aspect of possible selves?
    a. when joining a retirement plan
    b. when making a major life decision, such as planning a family
    c. when choosing a new car
    d. when relaxing and enjoying the company of others.
    p. 65

4. Joseph feels that he should volunteer time at a nursing home. This is an example of his
    a. actual self.
    b. ought self.
    c. ideal self.
    d. real self.
    p. 65

5. A person is likely to experience agitated-related feelings, such as anxiety, fear, and guilt when there are
    a. discrepancies between ought and ideal selves.
    b. discrepancies between real and actual selves.
    c. discrepancies between actual and ideal selves.
    d. discrepancies between actual and ought selves.
    p. 66

6. A person with a narcissistic personality will be unlikely to
    a. make far-reaching statements about themselves.
    b. have a low sense of self-esteem on an unconscious level.
    c. tend to be unaware of how others actually perceive them.
    d. engage in frequent self-reflection.
    p. 66

7. How persons view themselves and feel about themselves composes which dimension of the self-concept?
   a. actual self
   b. ideal self
   c. self-respect
   d. self-esteem
   p. 67

8. Self-esteem is likely to be influenced most strongly by which of the following?
   a. doing well on most any task
   b. winning an argument
   c. receiving support and approval from others
   d. none of the above
   p. 69

9. An evaluation of one's life to determine if a change in lifestyle is needed in order to achieve life goals occurs in which of Erikson's stages?
   a. intimacy versus isolation
   b. generativity versus stagnation
   c. integrity versus despair
   d. introspection versus projection
   p. 74

10. Psychological moratoriums serve the purpose of
    a. teaching social rules and laws.
    b. causing epigenetic crises.
    c. experimenting with a variety of social roles.
    d. reviewing life in late adulthood.
    p. 75

11. Experimentation is important in identity development because
    a. variety brings about balance.
    b. society values diversity.
    c. learning is best through trial and error.
    d. it is a way to cope with emerging conflicting identities.
    p. 76

12. Identity foreclosure occurs when a person
    a. forms an intimate relationship.
    b. has not sufficiently experimented.
    c. has made a commitment and not experienced a crisis.
    d. has either made a commitment or experienced a crisis.
    p. 77

13. Which of the following is an example of a psychological moratorium?
    a. becoming an uncle or an aunt
    b. a sorority or fraternity
    c. joining a religious temple or church
    d. voting in an election
    p. 78

14. An outcome of the sequence of Erikson's stages for female identity development is that
    a. females may wrongly appear developmentally delayed.
    b. female superiority cannot be realized.
    c. males and females appear more alike than they are.
    d. the role of autonomy is underemphasized in development.
    p. 78

15. Manny prefers that his friends be American rather than to share his Italian heritage, and does not practice any of the traditional Italian holidays. Which of the following best represents Manny's cultural identity development?
    a. preencounter
    b. encounter
    c. immersion/emersion
    d. internalization/commitment
    p. 79

Key for Practice Test A

1. Answer b; The sense of self and identity are expressed across decisions and behaviors; page 64; Learning Objective 1
2. Answer c; Self-understanding provides a rational aspect to the self; page 64; Learning Objective 1
3. Answer c; The possible selves relate to those aspects of the self that can be potentially achieved in the future; page 65; Learning Objective 2
4. Answer a; A person's aspirations to become what they view as the best they can be is referred to as the ideal self; page 65; Learning Objective 3
5. Answer d; The ought self is what we believe we "should be" and the actual self is how we view ourselves to be. Not meeting the expectations of the how we "should be" creates feelings of guilt, fear, and anxiety; page 66; Learning Objective 3
6. Answer c; Narcissistic persons distort their view of themselves and believe others share in this distortion; page 67; Learning Objective 4
7. Answer c; Self-discrepancy concerns the actual, ideal, and ought aspects of the self rather than self-esteem; page 67; Learning Objective 5
8. Answer d; Achieving in areas of personal importance is one way to build self-esteem; page 71; Learning Objective 6
9. Answer c; Developmental crises occur when a person faces a critical point in achieving the task of a specific developmental stage; page 73; Learning Objective 7
10. Answer b; Toddlers experience Erikson's stage of autonomy versus doubt and shame, and independent exploration facilitates developing a sense of autonomy; page 73; Learning Objective 7
11. Answer c; Psychological moratoriums are provided to experiment with a range of social roles and other aspects of identity; page 75; Learning Objective 8
12. Answer d; Both commitment and crisis are apparent in this description, therefore suggesting identity achievement; page 77; Learning Objective 9
13. Answer a; College offers most opportunities for defining one's career and vocational identity; page 78; Learning Objective 10
14. Answer d; Males and females differ in the roles that autonomy and intimacy play in identity, with autonomy being more important in male development; page 78; Learning Objective 11
15. Answer c; Stage 3 of ethnic minority identity development is characterized by immersion/emersion; page 79; Learning Objective 12

Key for Practice Test B

1. Answer a; Persons' self-perceptions can be highly accurate, and are more accurate than the other choices; page 65; Learning Objective 1
2. Answer a; Possible selves encompass future prospects of the self; page 65; Learning Objective 2
3. Answer b; Possible selves function in major life decision making; page 65; Learning Objective 2
4. Answer b; The ought self dictates what one "should" do in terms of right and wrong; page 65; Learning Objective 3
5. Answer d; Conflicts between actual and ought selves create discomfort for the individual because of the values imposed by the ought self; page 66; Learning Objective 3
6. Answer d; Narcissistic personality interferes with self-reflection insofar as there is no need to be self-critical; page 66; Learning Objective 4

7. Answer d; Self-esteem involves a feeling about the self as well as how persons think about themselves; page 67; Learning Objective 5

8. Answer c; Self-esteem is often built through social acknowledgement for accomplishments; page 69; Learning Objective 6

9. Answer b; Generativity involves producing for the next generation and becomes a developmental task of middle adulthood; page 74; Learning Objective 7

10. Answer c; Social roles are tested in socially sanctioned contexts called psychological moratoriums, such as college, clubs, and job programs; page 75; Learning Objective 8

11. Answer d; Experimenting with new roles and behaviors is central to identity development and must involve some level of experimentation; page 76; Learning Objective 8

12. Answer c; Identity foreclosure is a committed acceptance to an aspect of identity without experiencing a crisis; page 77; Learning Objective 9

13. Answer b; Colleges provide numerous opportunities to experiment with career paths as well as social relationships, as is the case for fraternities and sororities; page 78; Learning Objective 10

14. Answer a; Like many early theories, Erikson's stages are based on models of male development and may apply differently to women and young girls; page 78; Learning Objective 11

15. Answer a; The preencounter stage lacks any integration of cultural backgrounds with current social structures; page 79; Learning Objective 12

Chapter Outline

I.   The Nature of Stress
   A. What Is the Relationship between Illness and Stress?
      1. Two-thirds of office visits to family doctors are for stress-related symptoms.
      2. Stress contributes to many of the leading causes of death.
   B. What Is the Definition of Stress?
      1. The word stress was initially borrowed from physics, but the comparison of pressure on physical objects to pressure on human beings is limited since only humans can think and reason.
      2. Stress is the response of individuals to stressors, the circumstances and events that threaten individuals and tax their coping abilities.
II. Physical and Biological Factors in Stress
   A. The Autonomic Nervous System
      1. The autonomic nervous system (ANS) takes messages to and from the body's internal organs, monitoring such processes as breathing, heart rate, and digestion.
      2. The sympathetic division arouses the body, and the parasympathetic division complementarily calms the body.
   B. The Endocrine System—Glandular Information Processing
      1. The ANS acts upon the endocrine glands producing a number of important body reactions.
      2. Endocrine glands manufacture hormones which are directly released into the blood stream.
      3. The endocrine glands are the hypothalamus, pituitary, thyroid, parathyroid, adrenal, pancreas, ovaries (female) and testes (male).
      4. The adrenal glands, located just above the kidneys, secrete the quick-moving epinephrine and norepinephrine that play important roles in coping with stress, influencing moods, and affecting energy levels.
   C. The General Adaptation Syndrome
      1. Selye, who first used general adaptation syndrome (GAS), defined stress as "the wear and tear on the body due to the demands placed on it."
      2. GAS consists of three stages: alarm, resistance, and exhaustion.
      3. In the alarm stage, the body temporarily is in shock (loss of muscle tone, lowered body temperature, drop in blood pressure) and then has a rebound, or countershock period.
      4. The resistance stage is a no-holds-barred effort to combat stress.
      5. If the all-out effort to combat stress fails and stress persists, the individual moves into the exhaustion stage.
      6. GAS applies to both short-term and long-term stressors, with long-term stressors often leading to health and emotional problems.

7. Negative aspects of stress are called distress, while the positive features of stress are called eustress.

8. Individuals should respect their "race horse" or "tortoise" nature.

D. Illness and the Immune System

1. Psychoneuroimmunology explores connections between psychological factors and the nervous and immune system.

2. The immune system recognizes foreign materials such as bacteria, viruses, and tumors, and having white blood cells of the lymph system destroy them.

3. With occurrence of breast cancer, women who are angry and agitated had stronger immune systems than those who felt helpless and passively accepting.

4. Researchers are looking at the psychoneuroimmunological factors that influence AIDS.

III. Emotional Factors in Stress

A. What Is Emotion?

1. Stress is associated with a display of negative emotions.

2. Emotion is feeling (or affect) that involves a mixture of physiological arousal, conscious experience, and overt behavior.

B. Range and Classification of Emotions

1. More than 200 emotions are named in the English language.

2. Robert Plutchik classifies emotions by positive or negative, primary or mixed, and by intensity, and emotions have polar opposites.

3. Positive emotions enhance self-esteem while negative emotions lower self-esteem.

4. The primary emotions are happiness, disgust, surprise, sadness, anger, and fear, and they can be combined to form the other emotions (e.g., jealousy is composed of love and anger).

5. Plutchik believes you cannot simultaneously experience emotions that are polar opposites (e.g., love and remorse, optimism and disappointment), but they can both be experienced by shifting attention to different aspects of a situation.

C. Happiness

1. Diener's review of happiness research found that factors contributing to happiness were self-esteem, a good marriage or love relationship, social contacts, regular exercise, sleeping well, and meaningful religion.

2. Age, gender, race, education, intelligence, and children were not related to happiness.

3. Winners and nonwinners of a lottery did not affect general happiness, but nonwinners were happier doing life's mundane things. Likewise, people in wealthy countries are not happier than people in poor countries.

4. Positive emotions like happiness are associated with increased generosity, eagerness, expansiveness, and free-flowing use of one's resources.

5. Optimal experiences of emotions are feelings of deep enjoyment and happiness, and Csikszentmihalyi calls these experiences flow.

6. Flow is most likely to occur when people develop a sense of mastery and involves a state of concentration in which an individual becomes absorbed while engaging in an activity.

7. Opportunities for flow can be increased by setting challenges involving tasks that are neither too difficult nor too simple for our abilities.

D. Anger

1. The powerful emotion of anger occurs when one feels like one has not been treated fairly or when expectations have been violated.

71

2. Catharsis is the release of anger by directly or vicariously engaging in anger or aggression.
3. Psychoanalytic theory proposes that catharsis reduces anger while social learning theory (which has more research support) suggests that vicarious anger actually increases feelings of anger.
4. According to Carol Tavris, ventilating anger often follows this cycle: a precipitating event, an angry outburst, shouted recriminations or crying, a furious peak (may include physical assault), exhaustion, and a sullen apology.

IV. Personality Factors in Stress
  A. Type-A Behavior Pattern
    1. Research by Friedman and Rosenman led to the concept of Type-A behavior pattern, characterized by excessively competitive, hard-driven, impatient, and hostile behavior, which they thought was related to heart disease.
    2. However, it is the specific aspect of hostility which is related to heart disease risk.
  B. Hardiness
    1. Hardiness is a personality style characterized by a sense of commitment, control, and a perception of problems as challenges.
    2. Hardiness coupled with exercise and social support is associated with lower levels of illness.

V. Cognitive Factors in Stress
  A. Individual Differences
    1. Stress results from environmental events that place demands on our lives.
    2. However, not everybody sees the same events as stressful.
  B. Lazarus' Cognitive Appraisal Theory
    1. Cognitive appraisal is an individual's interpretation of events in life as harmful, threatening, or challenging, and the determination of one's resources to effectively cope with the event.
    2. In primary appraisal, individuals interpret whether an event involves harm or loss that has already occurred, a threat of some future danger, or a challenge to be overcome.
    3. In secondary appraisal, individuals evaluate their resources and determine how effectively they can be used to cope with the event.
    4. Lazarus believes that an individual's experience of stress is a balance of primary and secondary appraisal.

VI. Environmental Factors in Stress
  A. Overload, Conflict, and Frustration
    1. Burnout, a hopeless, helpless feeling brought on by relentless work-related stress, results in a state of physical and emotional exhaustion marked by chronic fatigue and low energy.
    2. Burnout affects up to 25 percent of college students, and it is the most frequent reason students leave school before earning their degrees. It can be combatted by reducing overload, modifying coping strategies, or "stopping out" for a semester or two.
    3. Conflict occurs when we must decide between two or more incompatible stimuli.
    4. The approach/approach conflict is a conflict in which the individual must choose between two attractive stimuli or circumstances.
    5. The avoidance/avoidance conflict is a conflict in which the individual must choose between two unattractive stimuli or circumstances.
    6. The approach/avoidance conflict is a conflict involving a single stimulus or circumstance that has both positive and negative characteristics.
    7. Frustration refers to any situation in which a person cannot reach a desired goal.

B. Life Events and Daily Hassles
1. Significant life events are a major source of stress.
2. Research with the Holmes and Rahe Social Readjustment Rating Scale indicates that persons with many significant life events are more likely than others to experience future health problems.
3. The Sarason, Johnson, and Siegel Life Experiences Survey measures a greater number of life events and also takes into account that events seen as having a negative impact cause more stress.
4. Daily hassles and daily uplifts may play an even larger role in stress.

VII. Sociocultural Factors in Stress
A. Acculturation and Acculturative Stress
1. Acculturation refers to cultural change that results from continuous, first-hand contact between two distinctive cultural groups.
2. Acculturative stress refers to the negative consequences of acculturation.
3. Acculturation occurs in phases, of which the first is precontact phase, during which two cultural groups remain distinct.
4. In the contact phase, the groups meet, interact, and new stressors appear; in practice, the balance of cultural flow is from the larger, more dominant culture to the smaller, less dominant group, which therefore experiences more stress.
5. There can be a conflict phase, in which the smaller cultural group is pressured to change its way of life; intergroup conflict creates threats to person and property, while psychological conflict creates confusion and uncertainty.
6. A crisis phase may evolve in which conflict peaks and a resolution is required.
7. If an adaptation phase follows, the cultural relations are stabilized in some way.
8. A person facing acculturation can experience four kinds of change pressures: assimilation (merge into the "mainstream"), integration (maintenance of cultural identity and being part of the larger culture), separation (withdrawal from the larger culture), and marginalization (alienation from both cultures).
B. Socioeconomic Status
1. Poverty imposes considerable stress on individuals and families.
2. Ethnic minority families are disproportionately among the poor; Blacks and female heads of household are especially at risk for persistent poverty.
3. Poverty is related to threatening and uncontrollable life events.
C. Gender
1. In almost all studies, employed women are healthier than nonemployed women.
2. Women experience more conflict between roles and more overload than men do, especially in family responsibilities.
3. Roles with time constraints, irregular schedules, and little autonomy may jeopardize health.
4. Poor women face the double jeopardy of poverty and sexism; some have the triple jeopardy of poverty, racism, and sexism.
5. Feminization of poverty refers to the fact that far more women than men live in poverty.
6. Harriet Lerner suggests that many women are socialized to respond to stress and anger in one of two styles—the "nice lady" syndrome or the "bitchy woman" syndrome.

Learning Objectives

After reading and studying this chapter, students should be able to:

1. Understand the nature of stress as studied by psychologists.
2. Know the structures and functions of the autonomic nervous system.
3. Know the structures and functions of the endocrine system.
4. Identify the stages of the general adaption syndrome and its relationship to stress.
5. Know the relationship between the immune system and illness.
6. Define what emotions are.
7. Understand the role of specific emotions in reacting to stress.
8. Know what Type-A behavior is and how it is related to stress.
9. Understand the concept of hardiness.
10. Identify cognitive factors involved in stress.
11. Describe how overload, conflict, and frustration are related to stress.
12. Identify and describe daily hassles and major life events related to stress.
13. Understand the relationship between acculturation, socioeconomic status, gender and stress.

Guided Review

After you have read the chapter one time, search through the chapter to find the appropriate words to complete these statements. Material is covered in the same order as the chapter.

1. Two-thirds of office visits to family doctors are for _____-related symptoms, and _____ is believed to be a factor in coronary heart disease, cancer, lung problems, accidental injuries, cirrhosis of the liver, and suicide.
2. Stress was loosely borrowed from the field of _____, but unlike metal, humans can _____ so the human experience of stress is more complex.
3. _____ is the response of individuals to _____, circumstances and events that threaten them and tax their _____ abilities.
4. The _____ _____ _____ takes messages to and from the body's internal organs, monitoring such processes as breathing, heart rate, and digestion.
5. The ANS is divided into two divisions—the _____ nervous system that arouses the body, and the _____ nervous system that calms the body—which _____ function to keep the bodily systems both in balance and responsive to the environment.
6. The _____ _____ release chemicals called _____, which they manufacture, directly into the _____.
7. The endocrine glands are the _____ and the _____ gland in the brain, the _____ and _____ glands at the front of the neck, the _____ glands just above the kidneys, the _____ in the abdomen, the _____ in females, and the _____ in males.
8. The adrenal glands secrete _____ (which acts on smooth muscles, the heart, the stomach, the intestines, and sweat glands) and _____, (which interacts with the _____ gland and the _____). These hormones travel _____ _____ than other hormones.

9. _____, founder of stress research, defined _____ as the wear and tear on the body due to the demands placed on it.

10. The _____ _____ _____ describes the common effects on the body when demands are placed on it, and it consists of the three stages of _____, _____, and _____.

11. The alarm stage, which is _____ in length, can be divided into an initial reaction of _____ which is followed by _____.

12. The _____ stage involves total effort to combat stress, and if this effort fails to control the stress, the individual moves into the _____ stage, and vulnerability to _____ increases.

13. _____ involves negative aspects of stress, and _____ is Selye's concept to describe the positive features of stress.

14. _____ explores connections among psychological factors, the nervous system, and the _____ system.

15. In the _____ system, the _____ _____ _____ recognize and destroy foreign materials such as _____, _____, and _____.

16. Women with breast cancer who reacted with _____ had stronger immune systems than those who _____ _____ the disease.

17. _____ is feeling (or _____) involving a mixture of _____ arousal, _____ experience, and overt _____.

18. _____ developed an _____ wheel to demonstrate how _____ emotions work, including how adjacent ones mix to produce other emotions.

19. Positive emotions enhance _____-_____ and improve _____, while negative emotions do the opposite.

20. Plutchik believes you cannot simultaneously experience emotions that are _____ _____, and to experience both emotions you have to shift your attention to different aspects of the situation and alternate between the emotions.

21. In a review of research on happiness, the factors found to contribute to happiness were _____-_____, a _____ _____ or _____ relationship, _____ contacts, regular _____, _____ well, and meaningful _____ _____.

22. Age, gender, race, education, intelligence, wealth, and children were not related to _____.

23. According to Diener, happiness boils down to the _____ of positive emotions and the _____ of negative emotions.

24. _____ has been studying the optimal experiencing of emotion, which he calls _____.

25. We make optimal experiencing of emotion happen by setting _____ for ourselves that are neither too difficult nor too simple, developing a sense of _____, and being fully _____ while engaging in an activity.

26. _____ is an emotional response to unfair treatment or violated expectations, and is especially strong when we perceive another's behavior as _____, _____, and _____.

27. _____ is the release of anger or aggressive energy by directly or _____ engaging in anger or aggression, and psychoanalytic theory supports the _____ _____, that behaving angrily or watching anger reduces subsequent anger, while research findings support _____ _____ theory's position that anger would be increased.

28. Countries at war have _____ rates of domestic violence, and compared with nations that remained at peace, postwar nations had a(n) _____ in homicide rates.

29. _____ in her book *Anger: The Misunderstood Emotion* proposes an escalating cycle when anger is ventilated.

30. Two cardiologists named _____ and _____ studied the impatience of cardiac patients and after eight years of research described a _____-_____ behavior pattern, characterized as excessively _____, _____-_____, _____, and _____.

31. Recent research suggests that persons most likely to develop heart disease are _____ or consistently turn _____ inward, and that, possibly, developing ability to control _____ and develop more _____ will reduce risk for heart disease.

32. _____ is a personality style characterized by a sense of _____ (rather than alienation), _____ (rather than powerlessness), and a perception of problems as challenges (rather than _____).

33. Hardiness, along with _____ and _____ _____, reduced illness in executives' lives.

34. _____ _____ is _____'s term to describe individuals' interpretations of events in their lives as harmful, threatening, or challenging and how to effectively cope with the event.

35. In _____ appraisal, individuals interpret whether an event involves _____ that has already occurred, a _____ of some future danger, or a _____ to be overcome.

36. _____ appraisal is a _____ process that people use to evaluate their resources and determine how effectively they can be used to _____ with the event.

37. Lazarus believes that an individual's experience of _____ is a balance of primary and secondary _____, and stress is _____ when harm and threat are high and challenge and resources are low.

38. Burnout is a hopeless, helpless feeling brought on by relentless _____-_____ stress, and results in physical and emotional _____ including chronic _____ and low energy.

39. The most frequent reason students leave school before earning their degrees is _____, and "_____-_____" for a while can be helpful, but so can reducing _____ and adopting different _____ strategies.

40. _____ occurs when one must decide between two or more incompatible stimuli.

41. The _____/_____ conflict is one in which the individual must choose between two attractive stimuli or circumstances, and it is the _____ stressful of the _____ kinds of conflict.

42. The _____/_____ conflict is one in which the individual must choose between two unattractive stimuli or circumstances, and in this type of conflict a _____ in decision making is likely.

43. The _____/_____ conflict involves a(n) _____ stimulus or circumstances with both positive and negative characteristics, so this conflict is characterized by _____.

44. _____ refers to any situation in which a person cannot reach a desired goal.

45. The Social Readjustment Rating Scale developed by _____ and _____ measures _____ _____ to predict future _____.

46. Daily _____ may play a larger role than life events in our stress level and physical health.

47. _____ refers to cultural change that results from continuous, firsthand contact between two distinctive cultural groups, with its negative consequences called _____ _____.

48. The phase in which two cultural groups remain distinct is called the _____ phase, and when the two groups meet and interact causing new stressors to appear they are in the _____ phase.

49. In the contact phase more culture exchange moves from the _____ group to the _____ group, who ends up stressed and pressured to change its way of life in a _____ phase.

50. There may be a highly stressful _____ phase when conflict comes to a head and a(n) _____ is required, hopefully leading to a(n) _____ phase.

51. _____ suggests that a person facing acculturation can adapt to the pressures of change in four different ways _____, _____, _____, and _____.

52. When individuals relinquish their cultural identity and move into the larger society it is called _____, and when individuals withdraw from the larger culture and maintain their cultural identity it is called _____, or _____ if imposed by the larger society.

53. _____ is the process in which individuals feel out of psychological contact with both traditional society and the dominant society, while _____ is when cultural integrity is maintained as well as being an integral part of the larger culture.

54. _____ and _____ are the least adaptive responses to acculturation.

55. Families headed by _____ _____ are ten times more likely to live in poverty than families headed by _____ _____.

56. _____ is related to being a crime victim and a victim of violence, marital unhappiness, and perception of _____.

57. According to almost all studies, employed women are _____ than nonemployed women; women with many roles and women who have job authority and autonomy are _____ likely to have a sense of well-being.

58. Of the sexes, _____ experience more role conflict and overload, with important gender differences occurring in the area of _____ _____.

59. The _____ _____ _____ refers to the fact that far more women than men live in poverty, with low _____ and _____ being two major causes.

60. According to Harriet Lerner, men and women often deal differently with stressful situations that produce _____ and _____, with men dealing more directly and assertively but also poorly venting, while some women have only the styles of the "_____ _____" syndrome and the "_____ _____" syndrome.

61. In a study of people living near a landfill that affected community drinking water, _____ _____ and _____ _____ played significant roles in reducing the stress of individuals.

1. stress, stress; 2. physics, think; 3. Stress, stressors, coping; 4. autonomic nervous system; 5. sympathetic, parasympathetic, complementarily; 6. endocrine glands, hormones, bloodstream; 7. hypothalamus, pituitary, thyroid, parathyroid, adrenal, pancreas, ovaries, testes; 8. epinephrine, norepinephrine, pituitary, liver, more quickly; 9. Selye, stress; 10. general adaptation syndrome, alarm, resistance, exhaustion; 11. short, shock, countershock; 12. resistance, exhaustion, disease; 13. Distress, eustress; 14. Psychoneuroimmunology, immune; 15. immune, white blood cells, bacteria, viruses, tumors; 16. anger, passively accepted; 17. Emotion, affect, physiological, conscious, behavior; 18. Plutchik, emotion, primary; 19. self-esteem, relationships; 20. polar opposites; 21. self-esteem, good marriage, love, social, exercise, sleeping, religious faith; 22. happiness; 23. frequency, infrequency; 24. Csikszentmihalyi, flow; 25. challenges, mastery, absorbed; 26. Anger, unjustified, avoidable, willful; 27. Catharsis, vicariously, catharsis hypothesis, social learning; 28. higher, increase; 29. Tavris; 30. Friedman, Rosenman, Type-A, competitive, hard-driven, impatient, hostile; 31. hostile, anger, anger, trust; 32. Hardiness, commitment, control, threats; 33. exercise, social support; 34. Cognitive appraisal, Lazarus; 35. cognitive, harm, threat, challenge; 36. Secondary, cognitive, cope; 37. stress, appraisal, high; 38. work-related, exhaustion, fatigue; 39. burnout, "stopping out," overload, coping; 40. Conflict; 41. approach, approach, least, three; 42. avoidance, avoidance, delay; 43. approach, avoidance, single, vacillation; 44. Frustration; 45. Holmes, Rahe, life events, health; 46. hassles; 47. Acculturation, acculturative stress; 48. precontact, contact; 49. dominant, smaller, conflict; 50. crisis, resolution, adaptation; 51. Berry, assimilation, integration, separation, marginalization; 52. assimilation, separation, segregation; 53. Marginalization, integration; 54. Separation, marginalization; 55. Black women, White men; 56. Poverty, powerlessness; 57. healthier, more; 58. women, family responsibilities; 59. feminization of poverty, income, divorce; 60. frustration, anger, "nice lady," "bitchy woman"; 61. social support, community organizations.

Key Terms

For each term, briefly define the term in your own words and provide an example or situation (especially one you can visualize) that will help you retain the meaning of the concept. Key terms are presented in the order they are presented in the chapter.

1. stress (p. 91)

2. autonomic nervous system (ANS) (p. 92)

3. sympathetic nervous system (p. 92)

4. parasympathetic nervous system (p. 92)

5. endocrine glands (p. 92)

6. hormones (p. 92)

7. adrenal glands (p. 93)

8. general adaptation syndrome (GAS) (p. 93)

9. distress (p. 94)

10. eustress (p. 94)

11. psychoneuroimmunology (p. 94)

12. emotion (p. 95)

13. flow (p. 98)

14. catharsis (p. 98)

15. Type-A behavior pattern (p. 99)

16. hardiness (p. 99)

17. cognitive appraisal (p. 100)

18. primary appraisal (p. 100)

19. secondary appraisal (p. 100)

20. burnout (p. 101)

21. approach/approach conflict (p. 101)

22. approach/avoidance conflict (p. 102)

23. avoidance/avoidance conflict (p. 102)

24. frustration (p. 102)

25. acculturation (p. 105)

26. acculturative stress (p. 105)

27. assimilation (p. 105)

28. integration (p. 105)

29. separation (p. 105)

30. marginalization (p. 105)

31. feminization of poverty (p. 107)

Study Aids

Students who do well on tests develop mnemonic aids to help them remember important terms and concepts. A few are suggested here, and you are encouraged to develop your own additional aids.

Sympathetic and Parasympathetic. To keep from confusing the two divisions of the autonomic nervous system, remember both SYMPATHETIC and STRESS start with S and both PARASYMPATHETIC and PEACEFUL start with P. Now you'll be able to remember that the sympathetic division is responsible for arousal and the parasympathetic division calms one down.

General Adaptation Syndrome. It's easier to remember the three stages in order by remembering the word ARE—arousal, resistance, exhaustion. Then, you can very easily describe the effects of each stage just by thinking about the label.

The HITCH with Type-A. You can remember the traits of Type-A behavior by using the word HITCH.

*H*urrying
*I*mpatient
*T*ime urgency
*C*ompetitive
*H*ostile

Acculturation AIMS. Berry suggests that there are four different ways in which people can adapt to acculturation. Arrange these four in an order that allows you to use the word AIMS to help you recall these ways, in other words—assimilation, integration, marginalization, separation.

Understanding Concepts

Answer these questions to develop your understanding of the important ideas in this chapter.

1. Compare and contrast the three stages of Selye's general adaptation syndrome, and discuss GAS's role in "being sick."

2. Distinguish between distress and eustress.

3. Explain the major features of Robert Plutchik's emotion wheel.

4. List the factors that seem to be associated with happiness, and another list of factors that do not seem to be related to happiness.

5. Compare the psychoanalytic catharsis hypothesis and the social learning theory view of catharsis. Which does research support?

6. Discuss the concept of Type-A behavior pattern, and summarize how research findings have modified initial beliefs.

7. Describe the hardy personality, and discuss its role as a stress buffer.

8. Compare and contrast the definition and roles of primary appraisal and secondary appraisal.

9. Describe and compare each of the three types of conflict: approach/approach, avoidance/avoidance, approach/avoidance. Give an example of each that you have experienced.

10. Describe the phases of acculturation and the four ways by which individuals can adapt to acculturation.

11. Describe who makes up the poor, and discuss the general effects of poverty.

Applying Concepts

Answer these questions to develop your ability to apply this chapter's material to your life and the world. Your own responses may differ from other students' in the class, and it is helpful to share your ideas with the other students.

1. Take Self-Assessment 4.1 to find out your vulnerability to stress. How vulnerable are you? What could you do to reduce your vulnerability?

2. You are a psychologist writing a letter to a health insurance company trying to convince them that if they cover stress and emotional-problems counseling in their policies they will eventually save money on medical bills. Compose this letter.

3. What role has stress played in your health? Are stomachaches, getting a cold, headaches, and trouble sleeping more of a problem during stressful times? Has stress created more serious health problems for you?

4. How important is research on psychoneuroimmunology in the field of AIDS research? Why?

5. Why do you think psychologists have done more research on anxiety and anger than on happiness?

6. Describe an experience you have had with flow, or optimal experiencing of emotion.

7. Take Self-Assessment 4.2 on anger, and compare your levels of state and trait anger. What do the results say about your emotional style? What do you like about your approach to anger? What would you change? Why?

8. How might belief or non-belief in the catharsis hypothesis affect someone who is in charge of television programming? Someone in charge of children's playground activities?

9. How might you help others to develop a hardy personality style? Do you think hardiness should be developed in the schools? Do you think it is often a goal in counseling?

10. Some people bounce a check and they become completely stressed out about it. Other people bounce a check and they don't worry about it at all. What factors might explain such vast differences in responding to potentially stressful events?

11. Design a workshop dealing with overload and burnout in the classroom. What topics would you cover? What would be the goals of such a workshop?

12. Take the Holmes and Rahe Social Readjustment Rating Scale in Self-Assessment 4.3, and score and evaluate your results. According to the scale, what is your risk for physical illness?

13. Why are employed women healthier than nonemployed women? If women experience more role conflict and role overload, why do research findings suggest that the more roles a woman juggles the healthier she seems to be?

14. Are women socialized to be too nice ("nice at any price")? If so, how does this affect their ability to handle and express anger? Do you agree with the text material on "nice lady" syndrome and "bitchy woman" syndrome? How could this effectively change?

Chapter Practice Tests

Answer these multiple-choice test questions to help you assess your understanding of the chapter's material. Evaluate your answers to determine which sections you need to further review.

Practice Test A

1. Situations may be ____ that cause a person ____.
   a. stress, stressor
   b. stressors, fear
   c. stressors, stress
   d. stress, fear
   p. 91

2. While working at his job, Manny nearly sliced his hand off. Which of the following is most likely true?
   a. Manny's parasympathetic nervous system was activated.
   b. Manny's sympathetic nervous system was activated.
   c. Neither Manny's parasympathetic nor sympathetic nervous systems were activated.
   d. Manny passed out because of his autonomic nervous system.
   p. 92

3. Frank just found out that he is going to be fired from his job. Which of the following is likely to be part of his response?
   a. activation of the parasympathetic nervous system
   b. release of epinephrine
   c. exhaustion
   d. All of these are likely reactions.
   p. 92

4. The stage of the general adaptation syndrome characterized by a temporary state of shock is referred to as
   a. shock.
   b. initiation.
   c. resistance.
   d. alarm.
   p. 93

5. Renne is under a lot of stress at home. In order to keep from becoming physically ill, it is necessary that she
   a. adapt to her home life.
   b. move out.
   c. take a vacation to recover and decrease stress.
   d. talk with a friend about the problems at home.
   p. 93

6. AIDS is a disease of the immune system, therefore, people who have AIDS and are depressed may
   a. further suppress the immune system.
   b. cause a person to be cured.
   c. increase the person's resistance.
   d. help establish resistance in AIDS patients.
   p. 95

7. Emotions are difficult to define because
   a. there is such a wide range of them.
   b. they involve physical responses.
   c. it is not apparent when a person is in an emotional state.
   d. emotions are like feelings.
   p. 95

8. A happy person is more likely to experience
   a. a healthy digestion system.
   b. greater self-esteem.
   c. easier expression of angry feelings.
   d. greater intelligence.
   p. 97

9. Doing something that is constructive for others when you are angry can result in
   a. greater anger.
   b. less destructive anger.
   c. more angry people.
   d. a state of exhaustion.
   p. 98

10. Michael is a very competitive person and is impatient with others. Which of the following probably best characterizes him?
    a. hardiness
    b. anger-prone personality
    c. Type-A behavior pattern
    d. all of these
    p. 99

11. Research on hardiness has shown that
    a. any given buffer is effective in coping with stress.
    b. multiple buffers may have more power than any single buffer.
    c. health has little to do with stress buffers.
    d. a sense of control is unrelated to health.
    p. 100

12. Charles bounced a check and has no money to cover it. Which of the following will most influence the level of stress he experiences over this event?
    a. his bank's reaction
    b. how he appraises the situation
    c. whether or not he discusses it with a close friend
    d. the number of checks he has bounced in the past
    p. 100

13. Situations that involve not being able to reach a desired goal result in
    a. burnout.
    b. conflict.
    c. frustration.
    d. secondary appraisal.
    p. 101

14. Situations that result in stress share what common characteristics?
    a. good things
    b. bad things
    c. change
    d. things that happen to others
    p. 102

15. Women who take on varied roles and new challenges are likely to benefit by increasing their
    a. self-esteem.
    b. attitudes toward men.
    c. physical strength.
    d. role in the community.
    p. 107

Practice Test B

1. Bob was mugged by a man with a gun who stole his wallet and all of his money. In this situation, the robber can be referred to as
    a. a strain.
    b. a stressor.
    c. a stress.
    d. a social stressor.
    p. 91

2. When faced with a threatening situation, the sympathetic nervous system will influence
    a. the heart.
    b. breathing.
    c. digestion.
    d. All of these are influenced.
    p. 92

3. Of the following, which is not an endocrine gland?
    a. adrenals
    b. testes
    c. thyroid
    d. salivary
    p. 92

4. The general adaptation syndrome explains reactions to stressors for
    a. people who experience certain types of problems.
    b. certain types of people.
    c. people under a wide range of situations.
    d. people with strong endocrine systems.
    p. 93

5. In the general adaptation syndrome, an all out effort to combat stress is referred to as
   a. alarm.
   b. reactive.
   c. resistance.
   d. exhaustion.
   p. 93
6. The immune system seems to be stronger in persons who are
   a. accepting of their illness.
   b. angered by their illness.
   c. depressed about being ill.
   d. none of these
   p. 94
7. Psychoneuroimmunologists have learned that
   a. people who are angry about their disease have stronger immune systems.
   b. depression worsens the condition of people with AIDS.
   c. animals and humans are very different in their response to stress.
   d. the immune system does not involve emotional responses.
   p. 94
8. Psychologists define emotions on the basis of
   a. physiological arousal.
   b. conscious experience.
   c. overt behavior.
   d. all of these
   p. 95
9. Which of the following has been related to happiness?
   a. age
   b. race
   c. education
   d. exercise
   p. 96
10. People who are angry, impatient, competitive, and irritated are characterized by
    a. anger-prone personality.
    b. Type-A behavior pattern.
    c. hardiness.
    d. loneliness.
    p. 99

11. Debbie has a sense of commitment and control over her world. She is probably best characterized by
    a. hardiness.
    b. naivete.
    c. Type-A behavior pattern.
    d. a neurotic personality.
    p. 100
12. According to theories of coping, stress is most likely to be lowest when
    a. threat, harm, and challenge are all high.
    b. threat and harm are low and challenge is high.
    c. threat, harm, and challenge are all low.
    d. there is a balance in threat, harm, and challenge.
    p. 100
13. Which of the following is most similar to Selye's exhaustion stage of general adaptation syndrome?
    a. burnout
    b. conflict
    c. frustration
    d. secondary appraisal
    p. 101
14. Indexes of stress that rely on situations or events to define are subject to problems because
    a. such events happen so rarely.
    b. these events provide no information about the person's reactions to them.
    c. some events occur for some people but not others.
    d. situations are more alike than different.
    p. 102
15. Women and men are likely to differ in which of the following?
    a. self-esteem
    b. reactions to frustrating events
    c. immune system responses
    d. roles that decrease the effects of stress
    p. 107

Key for Practice Test A

1. Answer c; Stressors are situations that result in feelings of psychological stress; page 91; Learning Objective 1
2. Answer b; The sympathetic nervous system is activated under stressful conditions; page 92; Learning Objective 2
3. Answer b; Epinephrine is released during periods of stress in conjunction with activation of the sympathetic nervous system; page 92; Learning Objective 3
4. Answer d; Alarm is the immediate response to extreme stress in the general adaptation model of stress reactions; page 93; Learning Objective 4
5. Answer c; Prolonged stress has the greatest effects on the body and relief gives the body a chance to recover; page 93; Learning Objective 4
6. Answer a; Depression and other negative emotional states have been shown to affect the immune system; page 95; Learning Objective 5
7. Answer c; Emotions are physical reactions and internal responses that cannot be easily observed but must be described by a person; page 95; Learning Objective 6
8. Answer b; General happiness in life increases persons' sense of personal satisfaction and their view of themselves; page 97; Learning Objective 7
9. Answer b; Positive emotional states offset negatives, therefore doing something positive can relieve anger; page 98; Learning Objective 7
10. Answer c; Type-A behavior involves a high level of competition and impatience, in addition to other characteristics; page 99; Learning Objective 8
11. Answer b; Multiple buffers against stress, such as social supports and means for relieving tension, will add up and be more effective than any one alone; page 100; Learning Objective 9
12. Answer b; Events themselves do not cause stressful reactions. It is the person's perceptions and appraisal that influence responses to events; page 100; Learning Objective 10
13. Answer c; Frustration is the result of a desired goal being blocked from being achieved; page 101; Learning Objective 11
14. Answer c; Changes, such as getting married, having a baby, a death, divorce, are all considered stressful life events and are all characterized by change; page 102; Learning Objective 12
15. Answer a; Self-esteem is enhanced through success at new challenges and diversifying roles; page 107; Learning Objective 13

Key for Practice Test B

1. Answer b; Events are stressors when they produce a stress response; page 91; Learning Objective 1
2. Answer d; Multiple organ systems are influenced by the sympathetic nervous system; page 92; Learning Objective 2
3. Answer d; Endocrine glands release substances into the blood stream. Salivary glands do not do this; page 92; Learning Objective 3
4. Answer c; The GAS is applied to most animals and can occur under many stressful situations; page 93; Learning Objective 4
5. Answer c; Resistance occurs when the body utilizes reserves to fight off the effects of stress; page 93; Learning Objective 4

6. Answer b; Research has shown that fighting back does have positive effects on responses to illnesses; page 94; Learning Objective 5

7. Answer a; Anger appears to result in increased immune responses among people who suffer a disease; page 94; Learning Objective 5

8. Answer d; Because emotions are internal responses, psychologists use a number of aspects of the person to define emotions, including behavior, descriptions of experiences, and bodily reactions; page 95; Learning Objective 6

9. Answer d; Exercise has many positive affects on a person that can increase general life satisfaction; page 96; Learning Objective 7

10. Answer b; Type-A behavior pattern includes anger, competitiveness, impatience, and irritability; page 99; Learning Objective 8

11. Answer a; Hardiness is a general personality style that prepares people for coping with potentially stressful situations; page 100; Learning Objective 9

12. Answer b; Challenge motivates responding while threat can diminish efforts to cope; page 100; Learning Objective 10

13. Answer a; Burnout occurs after long efforts to resist stressful situations; page 101; Learning Objective 11

14. Answer b; Events alone do not define stress, but rather interpretations of events define the occurrence of stress; page 102; Learning Objective 12

15. Answer b; Emotional reactions for men and women differ, and frustration is one example of such a difference; page 107; Learning Objective 13

Chapter Outline

I. The Nature of Coping
    A. What Is Coping?
        1. There are individual differences in how people adjust to stress.
        2. Coping is an extremely important part of adjustment.
        3. Coping is the process of managing taxing circumstances, expending effort to solve personal and interpersonal problems, and seeking to master, minimize, reduce, or tolerate stress and conflict.
    B. Cognitive Appraisal, Problem-Focused Coping, and Emotion-Focused Coping
        1. Cognitive appraisal occurs in two stages—primary appraisal (interpretation of an event's harm, threat, or challenge) and secondary appraisal (evaluation of one's resources and how to cope).
        2. Lazarus distinguishes between two general types of coping efforts: problem-focused coping and emotion-focused coping.
        3. Problem-focused coping is squarely facing one's troubles and trying to solve them.
        4. Emotion-focused coping is responding to stress in an emotional manner, especially using defensive appraisal.
        5. Emotion-focused coping is adaptive when a defense mechanism allows people to cope with a flood of feelings, but continual use is usually maladaptive.
        6. Over the long-term, problem-focused coping leads to better adjustment than emotion-focused coping.
        7. Most individuals use both problem-focused and emotion-focused coping when adjusting to stressful circumstances.
    C. Active-Cognitive, Active-Behavioral, and Avoidance Coping Strategies
        1. Active-cognitive strategies are coping responses in which individuals actively think about a situation in an effort to adjust more effectively.
        2. Active-behavioral strategies are coping responses in which individuals take some type of action to improve their problem situation.
        3. Avoidance strategies are responses that individuals use to keep stressful circumstances out of awareness so they do not have to deal with them.
        4. Of these three strategies, active-cognitive and active-behavioral coping are the more adaptive strategies.
    D. More Ways to Cope
        1. A study by Folkman and others found that married couples use eight different coping strategies.
        2. Confrontative coping is aggressive effort to change the situation.
        3. Seeking social support is effort expended to obtain emotional comfort and feedback from others.

4. Planful problem-solving is deliberate problem-focused efforts to reduce stress and manage the conflict.
5. Self-control is effort made to regulate one's feelings and behavior.
6. Distancing is effort in detaching one's self from the stressful circumstance.
7. Positive reappraisal involves trying to find positive meaning in the experience by emphasizing how it can be used to grow as a person.
8. Accepting responsibility is acknowledging one's role in the problem.
9. Escape/avoidance is invoking wishful thinking or making efforts to escape or avoid the situation by eating, drinking, smoking, or using drugs.
10. Self-efficacy, an optimistic outlook, and seeking social support are all helpful coping methods.
11. Traditionally, women have been more likely than men to use social support coping strategies.
12. Other coping strategies include a change in surroundings, engaging in enjoyable activities, using humor, and trying stress management techniques.
   E. Multiple Coping Strategies
      1. Multiple coping strategies are usually superior to just a single strategy.
      2. In addition to effective coping strategies, regular exercise, sensible eating, reduced drinking, and practicing relaxation can be useful.
II. Developing Self-Efficacy
   A. What Is Self-Efficacy's Role in Coping?
      1. Self-efficacy is the belief that one can master a situation and produce positive outcomes.
      2. Self-efficacy affects problem-solving behavior.
      3. Self-efficacy influences whether people try to develop healthy habits, how much effort is expended in coping, how long one will persist in efforts, and how much stress is experienced.
   B. How can a sense of self-efficacy be increased?
      1. Initially select something that you think you can accomplish; as your sense of self-efficacy is developed you can try harder tasks.
      2. Distinguish between your past performance and your present project.
      3. Keep good records so you can be concretely aware of your successes.
      4. Pay close attention to your successes.
      5. Make a list of the specific kinds of situations in which you expect to have the most difficulty and the least difficulty; if possible, begin with the easier situations and tasks.
III. Thinking Positively and Optimistically
   A. Thinking Positively
      1. A positive mood improves our ability to process information efficiently, increases altruism, and raises self-esteem.
      2. Usually an optimistic attitude is superior to a pessimistic one.
      3. Optimism enhances our sense of controlling the environment.
   B. Cognitive Restructuring and Positive Self-Talk
      1. Cognitive restructuring is modifying the thoughts, ideas, and beliefs that maintain an individual's problems.
      2. Self-talk is the soundless, mental speech used when one thinks about something, plans, or solves problems.
      3. Positive self-talk can build the confidence needed to allow using talents to the fullest.

4. Negative thinking can decrease self-confidence, discourage behavioral attempts, and block one's perception of improved circumstances.

5. In fine-tuning self-talk, the first step is to notice what one does say to oneself.

6. Another step is looking at the thought connection with one's feelings—thoughts about "loss" are associated with sadness or depression, while thoughts that center on "future threats" are associated with anxiety and thoughts of "being attacked" are connected with anger.

7. Thoughts about anticipated situations also influence feelings and behaviors.

8. Persons can identify and modify common flaws in self-talk such as all-or-nothing thinking, overgeneralization, jumping to conclusions, magnification and "should" statements.

C. Positive Self-Illusion

1. Researchers have found evidence that maintaining some positive illusion about one's self and the world is healthy.

2. An optimal margin of illusion of viewing oneself as slightly above average seems to be the ideal overall orientation.

3. Seeing things accurately can produce depression, and seeing suffering as without meaning can hinder moving forward.

4. On the other hand, imagining potential problems can allow one to develop relevant strategies.

D. Developing An Optimistic Outlook

1. Seligman believes that cognitive therapy offers the best tools for overcoming chronic pessimism.

2. One strategy is to avoid rumination and wallowing in self-pity when a bad event occurs.

3. Another strategy is to dispute negative thoughts.

4. One benefit of having an optimistic outlook is increased resistance to physical disease.

IV. Increasing Self-Control

A. A Five-Step Self-Control Program

1. Step 1. Specify the problem you want to control more effectively in a concrete way.

2. Step 2. Make a commitment to change, including requiring yourself to do things that will increase the likelihood of sticking to your project.

3. Step 3. Collect data about your behavior.

4. Step 4. Design a program that includes cognitive restructuring.

5. Step 5. Maintain your gains and improvement using post-checks, renewed course of action when needed, and a buddy system.

B. Thought-Stopping

1. Thought-stopping is a specific self-control and cognitive restructuring strategy in which the individual says "Stop!" when an unwanted thought occurs.

2. Then immediately substitute another idea—a pleasant one that is the opposite of your original unwanted thought.

C. Empowerment

1. Empowerment is a concept that refers to the importance of assisting individuals to develop skills they need to control their own lives.

2. One way to improve empowerment is to develop more community-based services.

3. Mental health professions are involved in empowerment programs with diverse groups including economically floundering farmers, victims of rape and domestic violence, and gay liberation groups.

V. Seeking Social Support
   A. What Is the Value of Social Support?
      1. Social support is information and feedback from others that one is loved and cared for, esteemed and valued, and part of a network of communication and mutual obligation.
      2. The benefits of social support include tangible assistance, information, and emotional support.
   B. Is Social Support Effective?
      1. Researchers consistently have found that social support helps individuals cope with stress.
      2. Depressed persons had fewer and less supportive relationships with family members, friends, and co-workers than did nondepressed persons.
      3. Prognosticators of cancer, mental illness, and suicide included a lack of closeness to one's parents and a negative attitude toward one's own family.
      4. Widows die at a rate that is three to thirteen times higher than married women for every known cause of death.

VI. Increasing Disinhibition, Engaging in Enjoyable Activities, and Using Humor
   A. Increasing Disinhibition
      1. Actively inhibiting our emotions and behaviors is associated with a variety of health problems.
      2. Research by Pennebaker found that individuals who write about a traumatic experience for fifteen minutes a day for just three or four consecutive days had increased health and well-being for several months.
      3. Writing may work because the silence increases illness risk, and/or writing may help to reorganize thoughts and feelings and lead to increased sense of survival or self-confidence and/or may lead to better coping strategies.
      4. Sometimes inhibition is positive (e.g., curbing alcohol drinking, inhibiting violent tendencies).
   B. Engaging in Enjoyable Activities
      1. Some people become immobilized by stress and become immersed in their sorrows and anxieties.
      2. It helps to participate in activities that you enjoy.
   C. Using Humor
      1. Laughter reduces inhibition, releases pent-up emotions, and aids redefinition of a stressful circumstance in a less threatening way.
      2. It is useful to look for humor in everyday occurrences.
      3. Humor can help us from taking ourselves and our problems too seriously, allowing us to be "human rather than perfect."
      4. The use of sexist, racist, or ageist humor is not a recommended coping strategy—base humor on the shared elements of the absurd in life rather than basing humor on aggression and superiority.

VII. Stress Management
   A. What Are Stress Management Programs?
      1. Stress management programs teach individuals how to appraise stressful events, how to develop skills for coping with stress, and how to put these skills into use in their everyday lives.
      2. Programs can be broad in scope or teach one specific skill.

B. Meditation and Relaxation
   1. Meditation is the system of thought that incorporates exercises to attain bodily or mental control and well-being, as well as enlightenment.
   2. Meditation either is clearing the mind to have new experiences or increasing one's focused concentration.
   3. Transcendental meditation (TM) is the most popular form of meditation in the United States, and it uses a mantra, a resonant sound that is repeated to focus attention.
   4. Physiologically, meditation results increases alpha brain waves, lowers oxygen consumption, slows heart rate, and increases blood flow to the arms and forehead.
   5. Meditation and relaxation both lower body arousal.
C. Biofeedback
   1. Biofeedback is the process in which people's muscular or visceral activities are monitored by instruments which provide feedback to individuals so they can learn to voluntarily control their physiological activities.
   2. Biofeedback can be used to lower blood pressure, but it is just easier to raise blood pressure.
   3. Relaxation training is as effective as biofeedback in reducing blood pressure.
D. Assertiveness Training
   1. Assertiveness training involves teaching individuals to act in their own best interests, to stand up for their legitimate rights, and to express their views directly and openly.
   2. Non-assertive behavior is submissive, self-denying and inhibited, and involves allowing others to choose options in one's own life.
   3. Aggressive behavior is hostile, often angry, deprecating of others, and self-enhancing at others' expense.
   4. Assertive behavior involves acting in one's own best interest, standing up for one's legitimate rights, and making self-choices, but doing these things without hurting others.
   5. In most cultures, women have been more likely to be socialized to be too nonassertive and men to be too aggressive.
E. Time Management
   1. Time management involves developing skills for learning how to use one's time more effectively to accomplish one's goals.
   2. The daily To-Do list is a technique that identifies and ranks activities to be accomplished each day.
   3. Be realistic when estimating the time needed for the tasks on your list.
   4. A time log on a daily and weekly basis is another useful technique.

Learning Objectives

After reading and studying this chapter, students should be able to:

1. Define coping.
2. Identify and describe the various cognitive models of coping.
3. Define self-efficacy and understand how it is developed.
4. Understand cognitive restructuring and the role of self-talk in coping.
5. Describe the positive self-illusion.

6. Understand how an optimistic outlook is developed.
7. Identify and define the steps to self-control.
8. Know what thought-stopping is and how it can be used.
9. Define empowerment.
10. Understand the role of social support in coping.
11. Understand what it means to increase disinhibition.
12. Know how enjoyable activities and humor are involved in coping.
13. Define what stress management programs are and how they work.
14. Understand the basic mechanisms of various stress reduction techniques and their limitations.

Guided Review

After you have read the chapter one time, search through the chapter to find the appropriate words to complete these statements. Material is covered in the same order as in the chapter.

1. _____ is the process of managing taxing circumstances, expending effort to solve personal and interpersonal problems, and seeking to master, minimize, reduce, or tolerate stress and conflict.
2. According to _____, cognitive appraisal involves the two stages of _____ appraisal, in which individuals interpret whether an event involves _____, _____, or _____, and _____ appraisal, in which individuals evaluate their _____ and determine how to effectively _____ with the stressful event.
3. Squarely facing one's troubles and trying to solve them is called _____-_____ coping.
4. _____-_____ coping is responding to stress in an emotional manner, especially using _____ appraisal.
5. Over the long term, _____-focused coping leads to better adjustment then _____-focused coping, but most individuals use both kinds.
6. _____-_____ strategies are coping responses in which individuals actively think about a situation in an effort to adjust more effectively.
7. _____-_____ strategies are coping responses in which individuals take some type of action to improve their problem situation.
8. _____ strategies are responses that individuals use to keep stressful circumstances out of awareness so they do not have to deal with them.
9. In the two classification systems, the least adaptive coping styles are _____-_____ coping and _____ strategy.
10. Among the _____ strategies married couples use to cope with a stressful event, _____ _____ involves an aggressive effort to change the situation, while _____ _____ _____ involves expending effort to obtain emotional comfort and feedback from others.
11. Effort to regulate one's feelings and behaviors is coping by _____-_____, while detaching oneself from the stressful circumstance is called _____.
12. The other strategies are _____ _____-_____, positive _____, accepting _____, and _____/_____.

13. Traditionally, women have been more likely than men to use _____ _____ coping strategies.

14. Multiple coping strategies are usually _____ to using just a single strategy.

15. _____'s concept of _____-_____ is the belief that one can master a situation and produce positive outcomes.

16. The first step in increasing your sense of self-efficacy is to select a task that you can _____, the second step is to _____ between your past performance and your present project, and the third step is to keep good _____ so you can be concretely aware of your _____.

17. The fourth step is to pay close attention to your _____, and the fifth step is to begin with easier tasks and deal with more difficult situations later.

18. Thinking _____ and avoiding _____ thoughts is generally a good coping strategy when trying to handle stress more effectively.

19. _____ _____ is modifying the thoughts, ideas, and beliefs that maintain an individual's problems.

20. _____-_____ (also called _____-_____) is the soundless, mental speech we use when we think about something, plan, or solve problems.

21. _____ self-talk can build the confidence needed to use talents to one's fullest; unaltered _____ self-talk can decrease self-confidence, discourage _____ changes, and block one's _____ of improved circumstances.

22. Thoughts that center on "_____" are associated with feelings of sadness or _____, thoughts that center on "future threats" are associated with feelings of _____, and thoughts of "_____ _____" are associated with feelings of _____.

23. It is useful to compare your self-talk _____ with what actually took place, and to _____ your self-talk to fit reality.

24. An optimal margin of illusion exists when individuals see themselves as slightly _____ _____.

25. A negative outlook can increase the emotions of _____ and _____, and even highly accurate perceptions is associated with _____, yet a strategy of _____ _____ can help at times in handling stress.

26. Seligman believes that _____ therapy offers the best tools for overcoming chronic pessimism, and developing a positive thinking pattern can often be accomplished in _____ to _____ counseling sessions.

27. Part of becoming optimistic is merely to do less _____ _____, and another aspect is to _____ negative thoughts.

28. A series of studies by Peterson showed that an optimistic outlook is associated with _____ to physical _____.

29. In the five-step control program, the first step involves _____ the problem you want to control more effectively, and the second step is to make a _____ to change.

30. The third step is to collect _____ about your _____ and this is followed by _____ a program using modification of self-talk among other strategies.

31. The fifth step involves _____ your gains and improvement with _____-_____ and a renewed course of action if necessary.

32. _____-_____ is a specific strategy in which a person says "_____!" to end an unwanted idea and then _____ a more pleasant idea that is the _____ of the original unwanted thought.

33. _____ is a concept that refers to the importance of assisting individuals to develop skills they need to control their own lives, and one way is to develop more _____-_____ services by involving natural caregivers in the community.

34. To meet the needs of Hispanic Americans, _____ _____ _____ centers can serve as multipurpose centers with staff that can speak Spanish as well as English.

35. _____ _____ is information and feedback from others that one is loved and cared for, esteem and valued, and part of a network of _____ and _____ _____.

36. The benefits of social support fall into three categories: _____ _____, _____, and _____ _____.

37. Researchers find that social support helps individuals cope with _____, and those with social support have lower rates of _____, _____ _____, and suicide.

38. Actively _____ our emotions and behaviors is associated with a variety of health problems, and even _____ about a traumatic experience for fifteen minutes daily for a few days is associated with long-term health benefits.

39. _____ can be positive when it comes to self-restraint of violent tendencies or drug usage, but on the whole, _____ is preferred.

40. _____, or being able to _____ at yourself, is beneficial because it releases _____ and allows oneself to be "human rather than _____," but it should be based on shared elements of life's absurdity rather than based on _____ and _____.

41. _____ _____ programs teach individuals how to _____ stressful events and how to develop and apply _____ for coping with stress.

42. _____ is the system of thought that incorporates exercises to attain bodily or mental control and well-being, as well as _____, and the most popular form in the United States is _____ _____, which utilizes a _____, which is repeated to focus attention.

43. Both meditation and _____ have similar physiological effects, which includes _____ oxygen consumption, _____ heart rate, _____ blood flow to the arms and forehead, and EEG patterns that are predominantly _____ waves.

44. In _____, muscular or visceral activities are monitored by instruments which provide information to individuals so that they can learn to _____ control their physiological activities.

45. _____ _____ involves teaching individuals to act in their own best interest, to stand up for their _____ _____, and to express their views directly and openly.

46. _____-_____ behavior is submissive, self-denying, and inhibited; _____ behavior is hostile, angry, deprecating of others, and self-enhancing at others' expense; and _____ behavior is being direct and open and making self-choices but without hurting others.

47. In most cultures, women are more likely to be socialized to be too _____-_____ and men to be too _____. But changing gender roles in Western countries are resulting in more _____ behaviors from both women and men.

48. _____ _____ involves developing skills for learning how to use one's time more effectively to accomplish one's goals, with one skill being a daily _____-_____ and a periodic _____ _____.

49. Compared to sadness, _____ is more serious and complex and persists for an extended time period.

50. _____ _____, the innovator of _____ _____ Therapy, suggests that depressed persons identify their self-defeating thoughts and dispute them, especially their tendencies to do "_____" of situations by emphasizing the negative and minimizing the positive.

Guided Review Answers

1. Coping; 2. Lazarus, primary, harm, threat, challenge, secondary, resources, cope; 3. problem-focused; 4. Emotion-focused, defensive; 5. problem, emotion; 6. Active-cognitive; 7. Active-behavioral; 8. Avoidance; 9. emotion-focused, avoidance; 10. eight, confrontative coping, seeking social support; 11. self-control, distancing; 12. planful problem-solving, reappraisal, responsibility, escape/avoidance; 13. social support; 14. superior; 15. Bandura, self-efficacy; 16. accomplish, distinguish, records, successes; 17. successes; 18. positively, negative; 19. Cognitive restructuring; 20. Self-talk, self-statements; 21. Positive, negative, behavioral, perception; 22. "loss," depression, anxiety, "being attacked," anger; 23. predictions, modify; 24. above average; 25. anger, guilt, depression, defensive pessimism; 26. cognitive, six, twelve; 27. negative thinking, dispute; 28. resistance, disease; 29. specifying, commitment; 30. data, behavior, designing; 31. maintaining, post-checks; 32. Thought-stopping, "stop," substitutes, opposite; 33. Empowerment, community-based; 34. community mental health; 35. Social support, communication, mutual obligation; 36. tangible assistance, information, social support; 37. depression, cancer, mental illness; 38. inhibiting, writing; 39. Inhibition, disinhibition; 40. Humor, laugh, anxiety, perfect, aggression, superiority; 41. Stress management, appraise, skills; 42. Meditation, enlightenment, transcendental meditation, mantra; 43. relaxation, lowered, slowed, increased, alpha; 44. biofeedback, voluntarily; 45. Assertiveness training, legitimate rights; 46. Non-assertive, aggressive, assertive; 47. non-assertive, aggressive, assertive; 48. Time management, To-Do list, time log; 49. depression; 50. Albert Ellis, Rational Emotive, "catastrophizing."

Key Terms

For each term, briefly define the term in your own words and provide an example or situation (especially one you can visualize) that will help you retain the meaning of the concept. Key terms are presented in the order they are presented in the chapter.

1. coping (p. 114)

2. problem-focused coping (p. 114)

3. emotion-focused coping (p. 114)

4.   active-cognitive strategies (p. 115)

5.   active-behavioral strategies (p. 115)

6.   avoidance strategies (p. 115)

7.   cognitive restructuring (p. 119)

8.   self-talk (self-statements) (p. 119)

9.   thought-stopping (p. 123)

10. empowerment (p. 123)

11. social support (p. 125)

12. stress management programs (p. 127)

13. meditation (p. 127)

14. transcendental meditation (p. 127)

15. mantra (p. 127)

16. biofeedback (p. 128)

17. assertiveness training (p. 128)

18. non-assertive behavior (p. 128)

19. aggressive behavior (p. 129)

20. assertive behavior (p. 129)

21. time management (p. 130)

22. To-Do list (p. 130)

Study Aids

Students who do well on tests develop mnemonic aids to help them remember important terms and concepts. A few are suggested here, and you are encouraged to develop your own additional aids.

Kinds of Coping. Remember the different kinds of coping (problem-focused and emotion-focused; active-cognitive, active-behavioral, and avoidance) by visualizing an example of each in your own life. For example, how have you used each as a college student?

The Thought & Emotion Connection. When remembering what thoughts are typically associated with different emotions, keep it as simple as possible rather than memorizing long sentences. For example, it's enough to remember:

LOSS = SAD

THREAT = ANXIETY

ATTACKED = ANGER

And, because you can remember these without much effort, you have <u>gained</u> some time— and that's the key for thoughts associated with an emotion not discussed in this chapter, gain = joy.

The Five-Step Self-Control Program. This is another concept that is best to learn using the briefest descriptions possible. You can enhance the descriptions by visualizing someone going through the five steps.

1. Specify problem.
2. Commitment to change.
3. Collect behavioral data.
4. Design and use a strategy.
5. Maintain the gains.

Assertive, Non-assertive, and Aggressive Behaviors. Easily remember the different effects of these three behaviors by remembering: *non-assertive* behaviors are unfair to oneself, *aggressive* behaviors are unfair to others, and *assertive* behaviors are fair to all.

Understanding Concepts

Answer these questions to develop your understanding of the important ideas in this chapter.

1. Distinguish between problem-focused coping and emotion-focused coping.

2. Compare and contrast the three coping strategies proposed by Billings and Moos—active-cognitive, active-behavioral, and avoidance coping. Which ones are compatible with problem-focused coping? With emotion-focused coping?

3. How well do self-efficacy, optimistic thinking, and problem-focused coping interact with each other?

4. Summarize the benefits of optimistic thinking.

5. How do cognitive and behavioral coping strategies differ from psychoanalytic defense mechanisms (see chapter 2)?

6. How does empowerment differ from traditional counseling programs?

7. Describe the major benefits of social support.

8. While under challenging conditions, a person may be too stressed to be able to identify and employ coping strategies. What might they have done to prepare themselves for better coping? Make several suggestions.

9. Compare the relative effectiveness of meditation, relaxation training, and biofeedback? What are the typical physiological results?

10. Distinguish among non-assertive, aggressive, and assertive behavior.

11. What social influences shape the development of assertiveness in children? How are boys and girls taught differently about acceptable assertive behavior?

12. Suggest several ways to help combat depression.

Applying Concepts

Answer these questions to develop your ability to apply this chapter's material to -1e and the world. Your own responses may differ from other students' in the class, and it is helpful to share your ideas with the other students.

1. Come up with a college student example for the five types of coping strategies mentioned in this chapter: problem-focused, emotion-focused, active-cognitive, active-behavioral, and avoidance coping. How effective was each strategy? Which ones do you think are most important for college students to use?

2. Look at the eight coping strategies used by married couples and described in figure 5.2. Which ones do you use the most in your relationships? Do you use certain ones mostly with females? With males? Do you use different ones with older or younger individuals? Do you use the same or different strategies with family members and with friends?

3. Choose a specific behavior you would like to work on and improve, such as better study habits, increased optimism, or a regular exercise program. Work out a self-efficacy strategy with this behavior.

4. Review the negative aspects of self-talk given in figure 5.4. Which ones do you use often? Give an example of how you have used three of these flaws.

5. Assess your optimism and pessimism tendencies. Would you benefit from increasing your optimism? How might you go about becoming more optimistic?

6. Describe a situation in which a counselor might encourage a client to use a thought-stopping technique.

7. Do you believe that students need empowerment programs in the college community? Design the basic components of a possible student empowerment program. Alternatively, you can investigate and summarize the main features of an empowerment program already on your campus.

8. Currently women do more social support coping than do men. How might counselors (and others) encourage men to comfortably use social support more often?

9. Make a concerted effort to increase disinhibition (perhaps by a 15-minute-a-day journal), enjoyable activities, or humor for one week. Summarize the results of your efforts. Did it improve your coping? Your mood?

10. Since women are more likely to exhibit non-assertive responses and men are more likely to exhibit aggressive responses, would you design assertiveness training programs differently for women and men? Why?

11. Take Self-Assessment 5.2 on assertiveness and evaluate yourself. Would you benefit from an assertiveness training program or from reading a book on assertiveness? List specific deficiencies that you need to work on.

12. Try using a daily To-Do list for a week. Afterwards, evaluate it as a time management aid. Did you actually use it? Did you find it easy or difficult to rank your daily priorities?

Chapter Practice Tests

Answer these multiple-choice test questions to help you assess your understanding of the chapter's material. Evaluate your answers to determine which sections you need to further review.

Practice Test A

1. Coping primarily functions to
   a. eliminate all stressors.
   b. help others.
   c. improve relationships.
   d. minimize or reduce stress and conflict.
   p. 114

2. Social support as a coping strategy
   a. is less effective than most other strategies.
   b. is more often used by women than men.
   c. is at the core of all other ways of coping.
   d. relies on a person's self-esteem.
   p. 125

3. It can be said that using more than one coping strategy in a stressful situation is
   a. less efficient than using just the right one.
   b. often a waste of energy.
   c. usually superior to using a single strategy.
   d. not usually possible.
   p. 117

4. Self-efficacy is a
   a. behavior.
   b. belief.
   c. dependance on others.
   d. social demand.
   p. 118

5. The concept of self-talk is based on the notion
   a. of talking oneself into a mental illness.
   b. that internal messages impact behavior.
   c. that thoughts are greater than actions.
   d. that emotions, thoughts, and behaviors all work together.
   p. 119

6. Which of the following is not a possible outcome of defensive pessimism?
   a. A person can become prepared for stressful life events.
   b. Relevant strategies for coping can be developed.
   c. Motivations for positive future outcomes can be increased.
   d. All of these are possible outcomes.
   p. 121

7. Cognitive therapists would be least likely to encourage
   a. self-talk.
   b. reflecting back on one's childhood.
   c. self-efficacy.
   d. establishing socially supportive relationships.
   p. 122

8. Buddies in self-control programs serve to
   a. encourage reciprocal disinhibition.
   b. keep a check on progress.
   c. help others.
   d. increase social relationships.
   p. 122

9. A cognitive therapist may tell someone that they should say "stop" to themselves every time
   a. they think something negative.
   b. they have a dream that confirms low self-esteem.
   c. they set goals that are out of range.
   d. an unmet need surfaces.
   p. 122

10. Community-based centers that assist persons in developing specific skills to regain control of their lives aim to increase their
    a. self-control.
    b. empowerment.
    c. income.
    d. jobs.
    p. 123

11. Stanley gives his brother a percent of his income to help him out now and then. What kind of social support would this be considered?
    a. tangible support
    b. needed support
    c. emotional support
    d. global support
    p. 125

12. Dave does not express his feelings and does not tell anyone about the pain he is experiencing. One potential outcome of this type of inhibition is
    a. complications of heart disease.
    b. mental illness.
    c. chronic colds and other physical complaints.
    d. All of these are potential outcomes.
    p. 125

13. Which is not a purpose of humor in coping?
    a. redefine stress as less threatening
    b. release pent-up emotions
    c. disinhibit stress-related feelings
    d. increase emotional social support
    p. 126

14. Groups that effectively deal with reducing stress that has physical effects will usually include which of the following?
    a. humor
    b. dream interpretation
    c. learning new skills for coping
    d. discussion of new medical drug trials
    p. 126

15. Om Mani Padme Hum is a
    a. meditation master.
    b. system of transcendental meditation.
    c. mantra.
    d. Zen Buddhist master.
    p. 127

Practice Test B

1. Coping is defined as
   a. any means of eliminating all stressors.
   b. avoiding stressful life events.
   c. process of managing taxing circumstances.
   d. developing socially supportive relationships.
   p. 114

2. Which of the following is true of positive thinking as a coping strategy?
   a. It is less effective than most other strategies.
   b. Women are more likely to use it than men.
   c. It is at the core of all other ways of coping.
   d. It is one of many adaptive mechanisms for coping.
   p. 115

3. Multiple coping strategies in stressful situations
   a. are likely to confuse the issues.
   b. are the least effective.
   c. can be superior to using a single strategy.
   d. add to a complex situation.
   p. 117

4. The belief that one can master a situation and produce positive outcomes is called
   a. narcissism.
   b. self-esteem.
   c. self-efficacy.
   d. the coping illusion.
   p. 118

5. Positive self-talk can function to
   a. talk oneself into a mental illness.
   b. replace negative internal messages.
   c. reduce maladaptive coping.
   d. focus nearly everyone's emotions on their thoughts.
   p. 119

6. Low self-esteem is most likely to
   a. create maladaptive coping strategies.
   b. result in loss of self-control.
   c. be related to negative self-illusions.
   d. occur among people who get everything they desire.
   p. 120

7. Cognitive therapists almost always
   a. focus on feelings.
   b. encourage wallowing in self-pity.
   c. focus on thoughts.
   d. focus on establishing supportive relationships.
   p. 120

8. Developing a program to increase your self-control almost always includes which of the following?
   a. learning to express anger
   b. self-punishment
   c. self-talk
   d. disinhibition
   p. 122

9. The purpose of thought-stopping is to
   a. self-monitor.
   b. enhance self-thought control.
   c. increase social support.
   d. increase self-esteem.
   p. 123

10. A basic premise of empowerment is that
    a. disenfranchised persons cannot take care of themselves.
    b. strategies for self-help are lacking among poor people.
    c. people in poverty can regain control with specific skills.
    d. nothing changes without outside help.
    p. 123

11. Which of the following is not a type of social support?
    a. information
    b. tangible assistance
    c. emotional
    d. structural
    p. 125

12. A disinhibiting experience that a therapist may use may involve
    a. getting naked and running about the house.
    b. going without sleep for extended periods of time.
    c. writing about feelings.
    d. exercising regularly.
    p. 126

13. For stress to not demobilize a person, the text suggests
    a. doing something enjoyable.
    b. buying self-help books.
    c. getting counseling.
    d. disinhibiting feelings.
    p. 126

14. Which of the following is not a component of stress management programs?
    a. appraisal of stressful events
    b. developing coping skills
    c. strategies for including others as social support agents
    d. plan for putting skills into action
    p. 128

15. Assertive behavior is different from aggressive behavior mostly in terms of
    a. effort.
    b. consideration of others.
    c. moral reasoning.
    d. specific skills related to empowerment.
    p. 128

1. Answer d; Effective coping reduces stress and resolves conflict; page 114; Learning Objective 1
2. Answer b; Women are more effective than men at developing supportive relationships; page 125; Learning Objective 2
3. Answer c; Coping strategies can have added effects, making multiple strategies better than any one alone; page 117; Learning Objective 2
4. Answer b; Self-efficacy is the belief that one has the skills to effectively perform a behavior; page 118; Learning Objective 3
5. Answer b; Self-talk involves developing internalized statements that guide coping behavior; page 119; Learning Objective 4
6. Answer d; Defensive pessimism does not involve mechanisms of effective coping; page 121; Learning Objective 5
7. Answer b; Cognitive therapists would not find reflection on past experiences as effective as dealing with present thoughts and perceptions; page 122; Learning Objective 6
8. Answer b; Self-monitoring and an external check on progress play critical roles in self-control; page 122; Learning Objective 7
9. Answer a; Thought-stopping is one of the techniques that cognitive therapists use; page 122; Learning Objective 8
10. Answer b; Empowerment allows people to take control of their own development and progress; page 123; Learning Objective 9
11. Answer a; Tangible support involves actually giving something material for assistance; page 125; Learning Objective 10
12. Answer d; Keeping negative emotions locked up and hidden can have a number of negative effects on a person's health and well-being; page 125; Learning Objective 11
13. Answer d; Humor may or may not make new friends, but it does increase personal sense of well-being; page 126; Learning Objective 12
14. Answer c; Coping skills training groups are the most widely used types of groups to reduce stress; page 126; Learning Objective 13
15. Answer c; Mantras are chants that accompany meditations; page 127; Learning Objective 14

Key for Practice Test B

1. Answer c; Coping mechanisms are invoked in response to potentially stressful situations; page 114; Learning Objective 1
2. Answer d; There are several coping strategies that can be used at any given time. Some are more effective for some people and their effectiveness usually varies with different situations; page 115; Learning Objective 2
3. Answer c; Coping strategies can have additive effects, making a combination more effective than any one alone; page 117; Learning Objective 2
4. Answer c; Self-efficacy is the belief that one can effectively perform a coping response; page 118; Learning Objective 3
5. Answer b; Self-talk can act to counter the negative messages we regularly send ourselves on a regular basis; page 119; Learning Objective 4
6. Answer c; Self-esteem is directly tied to one's view of him or herself; page 120; Learning Objective 5

7. Answer c; Cognition is another word for thoughts, and therefore, cognitive therapists focus on thoughts in their treatment; page 120; Learning Objective 6

8. Answer c; Self-talk is effective in guiding behavior and is used to promote and inhibit behaviors, bringing them under personal control; page 122; Learning Objective 7

9. Answer b; Thought-stopping is a self-control technique to inhibit negative thoughts that may lead to negative emotions; page 123; Learning Objective 8

10. Answer c; Empowerment results in personal control and directedness, and is often achieved by learning new skills; page 123; Learning Objective 9

11. Answer d; Social support can be given through information, emotional sharing, and materials; page 125; Learning Objective 10

12. Answer c; Writing out one's thoughts and feelings can be an effective means of releasing stress; page 126; Learning Objective 11

13. Answer a; Doing something pleasurable is incompatible with demobilization due to stress; page 126; Learning Objective 12

14. Answer c; Although social support can be useful in dealing with stress, most programs focus on independent skills for reducing stress that do not rely on others; page 128; Learning Objective 13

15. Answer b; Assertive responses include acknowledging the other person's feelings and still meeting one's own needs; page 128; Learning Objective 14

Chapter Outline

I. What Is Gender?
   A. Gender is the sociocultural dimension of being female or male.
   B. Gender Identity
      1. The part of self-concept involving one's sense of being male or female.
      2. It is acquired by two or three years old.
   C. Gender role is a set of expectations that prescribe how females and males should think, act, and feel.

II. Biological Influences on Gender
   A. Sex Chromosomes
      1. During the 1920s, researchers confirmed the existence of human sex chromosomes.
      2. Humans have 46 chromosomes arranged in pairs, with the 23rd pair having two X chromosomes (females) or one X and one Y (male).
      3. One gene called the TDF (the testes determining factor) on the sex chromosome determines biological sex.
      4. The genetic difference between men and women is 1 in 150,000 genes (or 99.8% genetically the same).
   B. Prenatal Hormones
      1. All embryos start out the same, then male sex organs start to differ from female sex organs when the TDF gene triggers secretion of androgens.
      2. Insufficient androgens in the male embryo or excessive androgens in the female embryo results in ambiguous genitals, a condition called pseudohermaphroditism.
      3. With genetically female (XX) chromosomes, masculine-looking genitals can be adjusted with surgery. They often are "tomboys" until puberty and then appropriate levels of estrogen are produced.
      4. Most genetic males (XY) with ambiguous genitals are reassigned as females; at puberty must be given estrogen and progesterones.
   C. Genital Differences
      1. Freud believed the sex drive influenced human behavior and that gender and sexual behavior were essentially unlearned and instinctual.
      2. Erikson said genital differences contributed to males being more intrusive and aggressive and to females being more inclusive and passive.
      3. Erikson modified his view to say that females are now transcending their biological heritage.

III. Social Influences on Gender
   A. Cultural Discrimination of the Sexes
      1. Different baby colors, hair cuts, clothing, and toys from early on.
      2. Both adults and peers reward gender differences throughout childhood and adolescence.
      3. Observational learning also teaches gender differences, including effects of the media.

B. Identification Theory
  1. Stems from Freud's view that the preschool child develops a sexual attraction to the opposite-sex parent, then renounces this attraction and identifies with the same-sex parent.
  2. Freud thought this happened around the age of five or six, but gender-typing occurs earlier than this.
C. Social Learning Theory of Gender
  1. Emphasizes children's gender development through observation and imitation of gender-related behaviors, and through rewards and punishments children experience for gender appropriate and inappropriate behavior.
  2. Rather than sexual attraction, the major factor is behavioral consequences.
  3. In addition to parents, other adults, television characters, and peers are gender role models.
  4. Elementary school playgrounds have been called "gender schools."

IV. Cognitive Influences on Gender
A. Cognitive Developmental Theory of Gender
  1. Children's gender typing occurs after acquiring gender constancy.
  2. After gender constancy, children often organize their world on the basis of gender.
  3. Kohlberg based his ideas on Piaget's cognitive developmental theory.
  4. Preschool children rely on physical features to determine gender, and believe people can change gender by changing dress or hair length.
  5. In elementary school, people have gender constancy so the task is to be the "proper" boy or girl.
B. Gender Schema Theory
  1. Schema is a mental framework that organizes and guides an individual's perceptions.
  2. This theory states that an individual's attention and behavior are guided by an internal motivation to conform to gender-based sociocultural standards and stereotypes.
  3. Children use a lot of energy developing appropriate schemas, or scripts, for their gender.
  4. Children actively construct mental concepts of gender, but society determines to a large extent the concepts of gender that are most important.

V. Gender Stereotypes, Similarities, and Differences
A. Gender Role Stereotyping
  1. Gender role stereotypes are broad categories that reflect our impressions and beliefs about females and males.
  2. All stereotypes are images of the typical member of a particular social category.
  3. Stereotypes simplify the complex world so that individuals are not overwhelmed, but can lead to wrong assumptions and poor conclusions.
  4. In Broverman's study, the description of competent adult women was different from that of the competent adult male and competent adult.
  5. Women are seen for more counseling sessions than are men and are given stronger prescriptive medications by psychiatrists.
  6. The "masculine" and "feminine" stereotypes often mean different characteristics across the socioeconomic spectrum.
  7. In a study in thirty countries, men were viewed as dominant, independent, aggressive, achievement-oriented, and enduring, while women were viewed as nurturant, affiliative, less confident and more helpful in times of distress.

8. Women and men in developed countries perceived themselves as more similar to one another than women and men who lived in less-developed countries.
   B. Gender Similarities and Differences
      1. Differences between the sexes have often been exaggerated, by overemphasizing small percentage differences, by focusing on average score differences rather than overlap, by overassuming a biological cause, and by overrelating animal research to humans.
      2. On average, females live longer than males and are less likely to develop physical disorders, due to advantages of female hormones and disadvantages of male hormones.
      3. Females have more body fat and males have more height.
      4. In the last two decades, verbal differences between the sexes have virtually disappeared, though the math and spatial differences still exist.
      5. Males do outperform females in math, but only among the gifted.
      6. The only consistent sex differences in visual-spatial tasks are in rotating objects mentally and in disembedding figures.
   C. Social Differences
      1. Males are more active and aggressive than females.
      2. Gilligan suggests that female preteens become aware that their intense interest in intimacy is not prized by the male-dominated culture, even though society values women as caring and altruistic, and they experience a dilemma of choosing to be selfish (independent and self-sufficient) or selfless (remain responsive to others).
      3. Eagly and Crowley suggest that female helping is nurturant and caring while male helping is heroic and chivalrous.
      4. In the American culture, girls exhibit more caregiving behavior than boys as early as elementary school; in sibling-care societies, the sex difference in nurturant behaviors is very small.
   D. Gender and Emotion
      1. Males and females are more alike than different in their experience of emotion, often using the same facial expression, same language, and same emotional descriptions.
      2. Men are more likely to show anger toward strangers when challenged, and more likely to turn anger into aggressive action.
      3. Female-male differences in emotion are more likely to occur in contexts that highlight social roles and relationships.
      4. Females are more likely to express fear and sadness than males.
      5. Emotion beliefs affect our comments about our own emotional experiences.
VI. How Can Gender Roles Be Classified?
   A. Well-Adjusted Males and Females
      1. Traditionally, well-adjusted males were independent, aggressive, and power-oriented.
      2. Well-adjusted females were expected to be dependent, nurturant, and uninterested in power.
      3. Masculine characteristics were considered more desirable.
   B. Instrumental and Expressive Traits
      1. Instrumental traits paralleled the male's roles.
      2. Expressive traits paralleled the female's roles.
      3. Instrumental was more valued than expressive.

C. Androgyny
　　1. Feminists argued that people could show both expressive and instrumental traits.
　　2. This led to the concept of androgyny, the presence of desirable feminine and masculine characteristics in the same individual.
　　3. Androgyny is measured by the Bem sex-role inventory, and classifies individuals as feminine, masculine, androgynous, or undifferentiated.
　　4. In relationships, a feminine or androgynous gender role may be more desirable; a masculine or androgynous gender role more desirable in work and academic settings.
D. Traditional Masculinity and Problem Behaviors in Adolescent Males
　　1. According to Pleck, male adolescents perceive they are more masculine if they engage in premarital sex, drink alcohol and take drugs, and participate in illegal delinquent activities.
　　2. The National Survey of Adolescent Males found strong evidence for the relationship of adolescent males' attitudes toward masculinity and problem behaviors.
E. Gender Role Transcendence
　　1. Pleck argues that the concept of androgyny should be replaced with gender role transcendence.
　　2. Gender role transcendence is the belief that when an individual's competence is at issue, it should be conceptualized on a person basis rather than by femininity, masculinity, or androgyny.
VII. The Feminist Perspective on Gender
A. Historical Perspectives
　　1. Psychology has portrayed human behavior with a male dominant theme.
　　2. In politics, women have been treated as burdens rather than assets, and their roles have been limited.
　　3. Many women have been uneducated, experience physical and psychological abuse, and are depressed.
　　4. Women in male-dominated societies often have low self-esteem.
B. Need to Examine Psychological Issues from a Female Perspective
　　1. Miller and Gilligan suggest society needs to more highly value connectedness.
　　2. Miller suggests that women must not only maintain their competency in relationships but to be self-motivated, too.
　　3. Lerner emphasizes that women need to be strong, assertive, independent, and authentic in their relationships.
VIII. Men's Issues
A. The Men's Movement
　　1. An emotional, spiritual movement reasserts masculinity and resists being "soft" males.
　　2. A need to be less violent and more nurturant but retain "masculine identity."
B. An Armor of Masculinity
　　1. According to Goldberg, the critical difference between men and women is that women can sense and articulate their feelings and men can not.
　　2. Being "true" men kills men.
C. Need to Get in Touch with Their Emotions and Their Bodies
　　1. Recognizing and avoiding the suicidal "success" syndrome.
　　2. Becoming aware of their body's needs, and not being alarmed by occasional impotence.
　　3. Elude the binds of masculine role playing.

4. Relate to liberated women as their equal rather than serving as their guilty servant or hostile enemy.
5. Develop male friendships.
D. Bly's 1990s Men's Movement
1. Men as "soft," having bonded with their mother because their father was unavailable.
2. Missing a deep masculine identity.
3. Emphasizes separateness of the sexes.
IX. Ethnicity and Gender
A. Women of Color
1. Women of color are a varied group with many differences.
2. The term is popular among Asian, Hispanic, African, and Native American women.
B. Ethnic Minority Females
1. The nature and focus of psychological research on African American females has begun to change.
2. African American women remain underrepresented in all areas of psychology and in other academic disciplines.
3. Asian American women's roles have deep roots in Asian culture.
4. In Mexican families, women traditionally have assumed the role of homemaker and caretaker of children.
5. For Native Americans, the amount of social and governing control exhibited by women and men depends on tribal customs.
C. Ethnic Minority Males
1. They have experienced considerable discrimination.
2. African American males are often poor, often die young, and earn less.
3. Only recently have psychologists done research on positive dimensions of African American males.
4. Asian cultural values are reflected in traditional patriarchal Chinese and Japanese families.
5. In Mexican families, men traditionally assume the instrumental role of provider and protector of the family.
6. Native American tribes vary in their gender roles.

Learning Objectives

After reading and studying this chapter, students should be able to:

1. Define gender.
2. Identify and describe the biological influences on gender.
3. Identify and describe the social influences on gender.
4. Identify and describe the cognitive influences on gender.
5. Know the cognitive theories of gender and the differences between them.
6. Understand gender role stereotyping.
7. Identify and describe the differences and similarities related to gender.
8. Understand the relationship gender and emotion.
9. Know the methods for classifying gender.

10. Describe the feminist perspective on gender.
11. Identify and describe men's gender issues.
12. Understand the relationship between ethnicity and gender.

Guided Review

After you have read the chapter one time, search through the chapter to find the appropriate words to complete these statements. Material is covered in the same order as the chapter.

1. _____ refers to the sociocultural dimension of being female or male with two aspects being _____ _____, which is the sense of being male or female, and _____ _____, which is a set of expectations that prescribe how females and males should think, act, and feel.

2. Humans normally have _____ chromosomes arranged in pairs, with the _____ pair being the sex chromosomes.

3. When the sex chromosome pair is two X-shaped chromosomes, a _____ is produced, while one X-shaped and one _____-shaped chromosome produce a _____.

4. Biological sex is determined by _____ gene(s) called the _____ _____ _____ (or TDF); therefore the genetic difference between men and women is _____ in _____ genes.

5. Initially, female and male embryos are identical, but different sex organs develop when the TDF gene triggers secretion of _____, the main class of male sex hormones.

6. _____ androgens in the male embryo or _____ androgens in the female embryo results in an individual with ambiguous genitals, a condition called _____.

7. A female with ambiguous genitals receives _____ to achieve a genital/genetic match, and then at puberty _____, the main class of female sex hormones, to continue proper development.

8. Genetic males with ambiguous genitals are usually _____ to the female sex, requiring taking _____ and _____ at puberty to develop in a feminine way.

9. _____ theorists Sigmund Freud and Erik Erikson believed that an individual's genitals play a pivotal role in gender behavior, with Erikson suggesting that genital differences contribute to males being more _____ and _____ and to females being more _____ and _____.

10. _____ theory stems from Freud's view that the preschool child develops a _____ attraction to the _____-_____ parent, then by _____ years of age, renounces this attraction because of _____ feelings and subsequently _____ with the _____-_____ parent.

11. Two problems with Freud's identification theory is that gender typing occurs much _____ than five years old and gender roles develop regardless of the presence of a _____-_____ parent in the family.

12. The _____ _____ theory of gender emphasizes that children's gender development occurs through observation and _____ of gender-related behaviors and through _____ and punishments children experience for gender appropriate and inappropriate behavior.

13. _____ are important models of gender roles, as are other _____, television characters, and, increasingly with age, _____ become increasingly important.

14. The segregation of the sexes during _____ is so evident that researchers who have observed elementary school children have characterized playgrounds as "_____ _____."

15. The social learning view is sometimes criticized for its emphasis on the _____ acquisition of gender roles, and the _____ _____ theory states that individuals actively construct their gender world.

16. According to _____'s cognitive developmental theory of gender, children's gender typing occurs after the development of _____ _____.

17. Preschool children rely on _____ features such as dress and hairstyle to decide who falls into each gender category, and until in _____'s _____ _____ stage, when children understand _____ _____, they may believe that people can change their own gender by changing appearance.

18. _____ is a mental framework that organizes and guides an individual's perceptions, therefore, a _____ _____ organizes the world in terms of female and male.

19. _____ _____ theory states that an individual's attention and behavior are guided by an _____ motivation to _____ to gender-based sociocultural standards and stereotypes.

20. The key to gender schema theory is a general _____ to respond to and _____ information on the basis of _____-defined gender _____.

21. To summarize, children _____ construct mental concepts of gender, but _____ determines to a large extent the concepts of _____ that are most important.

22. Gender role _____ are broad categories that reflect our impressions and beliefs about females and males.

23. A study by Broverman found that professional _____ were influenced by their attitudes toward men and women, with descriptions of mature and competent adult _____ being different than other mature and competent adults.

24. _____ are seen for more counseling sessions and are given _____ prescriptive medications by psychiatrists.

25. Gender stereotypes are often modified in the face of _____ and _____ changes, and "masculine" and "feminine" stereotypes often mean different characteristics across the _____ spectrum.

26. In a thirty-country study of female and male stereotypes, males were typically viewed as _____, _____, _____, _____-_____, and _____, while women were viewed as _____, _____, less _____, and more _____ in times of distress.

27. Women and men in _____ countries perceived themselves as more similar to one another than those living in other countries, and _____ are the more likely to perceive similarity between the sexes.

28. In gender research, the differences between the sexes have often been _____, and sometimes statements about female-male comparisons forget that they deal with _____ difference.

29. Most sex differences are due to an interaction between _____ and _____ factors.

30. _____ live longer and are less likely to develop _____ disorders, primarily because _____ strengthens the _____ system making them more resistant to infection and also producing more "good" _____.

31. Male _____ triggers the production of low-density _____, which clogs blood vessels, resulting in twice the risk of _____ disease.

32. Adult females have twice the _____ _____ of their male counterparts, and for females it is more concentrated around the _____ and _____, and for males around the _____.

33. Since 1974, sex differences in _____ abilities have virtually disappeared, but _____ and _____ differences still exist.

34. Only among the _____ do males outperform females in math.

35. The two spatial tasks in which males consistently do better than females are in the ability to _____ _____ _____ and in performance on tasks of _____ _____.

36. Males are more _____ and _____ than females, a difference that is apparent by the age of two years.

37. _____ believes adolescence may be a critical juncture in girls' and women's development, and around twelve years, girls become aware that their intense interest in _____ is not prized by the male-dominated culture.

38. According to Gilligan, girls have the dilemma of appearing selfish if they become _____ and _____-_____, or selfless if they remain _____ to others, and many young adolescents "_____" their distinctive voice, becoming less _____ and more _____ in offering their opinions.

39. Female adolescent and adult self-doubt and ambivalence may translate into _____ and _____ disorders.

40. With regard to _____ behavior, Eagly and Crowley suggest that the female gender role emphasizes choices that are _____ and _____ while the male gender role emphasizes choices that are _____ and _____.

41. In the American culture, _____ exhibit more caregiving behavior by elementary school, but this gender difference is small in _____-_____ societies.

42. When it comes to emotions, females and males are similar in facial _____, emotional _____, and descriptions of their emotional experiences, but men are more likely to show _____ toward strangers, and are more likely to turn anger into _____ action.

43. Females are more likely to express _____ and _____ than males, especially when communicating with their friends and family.

44. _____ traits paralleled the male's purposeful, competent entry into the outside world, and _____ traits paralleled the female's responsibility to be warm and emotional in the home.

45. Characteristics assigned to males are more _____ by society than those assigned to women.

46. _____ is the negative treatment of women because of their sex.

47. Persons with both instrumental and expressive traits express _____; those who are only instrumental are _____; those who are only expressive are _____; and one who is neither high on instrumental or expressive aspects is called _____.

48. Bem suggested that _____ individuals are the most flexible and mentally healthy, and _____ individuals are the least flexible and healthy, although _____ roles influence which gender roles are most adaptive.

49. In the male adolescent culture, males will perceive that they are _____ masculine if they engage in premarital sex, drink alcohol and take drugs, and participate in illegal delinquent activities.

50. Joseph Pleck would replace the concept of androgyny with _____ _____ _____, so that competence would be based on the person rather than femininity, masculinity, or androgyny.

51. Feminists believe that psychology has historically portrayed human behavior with a _____ dominant theme.

52. Most women have been socialized to center their life around _____, _____, and _____, and now some are labeled as "_____" because they "love too much."

53. Goldberg suggests that men's problems with sensing and articulating their feelings and problems results in an _____ of _____ that is defensive and powerful in maintaining _____-_____ patterns.

54. Robert Bly, a disciple of _____'s ideas, believes that today's males are "_____," having bonded with their _____ because their _____ was unavailable.

55. "_____ of _____" is especially popular among Asian, Hispanic, African, and Native American _____ who fundamentally disagree with the White, middle-class women's movement.

Guided Review Answers

1. Gender, gender identity, gender role; 2. 46, 23rd; 3. female, Y, male; 4. one, testes determining factor, 1, 150,000; 5. androgens; 6. Insufficient, excessive, pseudohermaphroditism; 7. surgery, estrogen; 8. reassigned, estrogens, progesterones; 9. Psychoanalytic, intrusive, aggressive, inclusive, passive; 10. Identification, sexual, opposite-sex, 5/6, anxious, identifies, same-sex; 11. earlier, same-sex; 12. social learning, imitation, rewards; 13. Parents, adults, peers; 14. play, "gender school"; 15. passive, cognitive developmental; 16. Kohlberg, gender constancy; 17. physical, Piaget, concrete operational, gender constancy; 18. Schema, gender schema; 19. Gender schema, internal, conform; 20. readiness, categorize, culturally, roles; 21. actively, society, gender; 22. stereotypes; 23. counselors, women; 24. Women, stronger; 25. cultural, historical, socioeconomic; 26. dominant, independent, aggressive, achievement-oriented, enduring, nurturant, affiliative, confident, helpful; 27. developed, women; 28. exaggerated, average; 29. biological, environmental; 30. Females, physical, estrogen, immune, cholesterol; 31. testosterone, lipoprotein, coronary; 32. body fat, breasts, hips, abdomen; 33. verbal, math, spatial; 34. gifted; 35. rotate objects mentally, disembedding figures; 36. active, aggressive; 37. Gilligan, intimacy; 38. independent, self-sufficient, responsive, "silence," confident, tentative; 39. depression, eating; 40. helping, nurturant, caring, heroic, chivalrous; 41. girls, sibling-care; 42. expression, language, anger, aggressive; 43. fear, sadness; 44. Instrumental, expressive; 45. valued; 46. Sexism; 47. androgyny, masculine, feminine, undifferentiated; 48. androgynous, undifferentiated, cultural; 49. more; 50. gender role transcendence; 51. male; 52. relatedness, caring, support, "codependent"; 53. armor, masculinity, self-destructive; 54. Jung, "soft," mother, father; 55. "Women, color," feminists.

Key Terms

For each term, briefly define the term in your own words and provide an example or situation (especially one you can visualize) that will help you retain the meaning of the concept. Key terms are presented in the order they are presented in the chapter.

1. gender (p. 142)

2. gender identity (p. 142)

3. gender role (p. 142)

4. androgen (p. 143)

5. estrogen (p. 143)

6. identification theory (p. 144)

7. social learning theory of gender (p. 144)

8. cognitive developmental theory of gender (p. 145)

9. schema (p. 145)

10. gender schema (p. 145)

11. gender schema theory (p. 145)

12. gender role stereotypes (p. 146)

13. sexism (p. 151)

14. androgyny (p. 151)

15. gender role transcendence (p. 152)

Study Aids

Students who do well on tests develop mnemonic aids to help them remember important terms and concepts. A few are suggested here, and you are encouraged to develop your own additional aids.

> **Gender Theories.** To learn the different theories, remember the following "telegraphic bits."
> *Identification Theory:* Freud. Sexual attraction to opposite-sex parent.
> *Social Learning Theory:* Rewards & punishments. imitation. passive.
> *Cognitive Developmental Theory:* Kohlberg. Gender consistency before gender typing. active.
> *Gender Schema Theory:* Bem. Mental frameworks. scripts. categorizing information by culturally-defined gender roles.
>
> **Gender Descriptions.** Remember various labels.
> "I'M Ever Faithful."
> Instrumental—Masculinity   Expressive—Femininity
> *And*rogynous = masculine *and* feminine, or, instrumental *and* expressive
> *Un*differentiated = *un*-masculine & *un*-feminine

Understanding Concepts

Answer these questions to develop your understanding of the important ideas in this chapter.

1. Distinguish between gender identity and gender role, the two aspects of gender.

2. Explain why there are more difficulties with an XY-pseudohermaphrodite than with an XX-pseudohermaphrodite.

3. Summarize Erik Erikson's position on "anatomy is destiny" including his original position and his modified view.

4. Describe Freud's identification theory and evaluate the validity of this position.

5. Compare and contrast the social learning theory of gender and the cognitive developmental theory of gender.

6. Distinguish between cognitive developmental theory of gender and gender schema theory.

7. Summarize how gender differences have been misinterpreted in the past and discuss what we now know about actual gender differences.

8. Discuss Gilligan's position about early adolescence being a "critical juncture in female development."

9. Describe the basic characteristics of an androgynous individual, an instrumental (masculine) individual, an expressive (feminine) individual, and an undifferentiated individual. How would they differ in flexibility, mental health, relationships, and achievement settings?

10. Discuss the relationship between traditional masculinity and problem behaviors in adolescent males.

11. Why does Pleck prefer the term gender role transcendence to androgyny?

12. What does Goldberg mean by the armor of masculinity? What suggestions does Goldberg make to help men live physically and psychologically healthy lives?

13. What are the similarities and the differences in the women's movement and the men's movement?

14. Discuss whether gender-related attitudes and behaviors are similar across different ethnic groups.

Applying Concepts

Answer these questions to develop your ability to apply this chapter's material to your life and the world. Your own responses may differ from other students' in the class, and it is helpful to share your ideas with the other students.

1. What are your reactions to the scientific evidence that all embryos start out identical and then male embryos differentiate when TDF triggers androgens? Is this information consistent with traditional religious beliefs? How might it explain the higher rate of birth defects in male babies?

2. After having a genital birth defect corrected through reconstructive surgery and other corrective techniques, should a child be told about the birth defect? If so, at what age should they be told? How would it be best to handle the situation of telling them?

3. Using ideas from social learning theory, cognitive developmental theory, and gender schema theory, explain how you would design a preschool day care center to promote either traditional or androgynous gender roles.

4. Make a list of characteristics and behaviors describing (1) masculinity and (2) femininity that have changed during your lifetime.

5. What are the practical implications of the Broverman study of professional counselors' gender role stereotyping? You might want to include ideas from Sociocultural Worlds 6.1.

6. Take Self-Assessment 6.1 on the attitudes toward women, and evaluate your responses. What is your general attitude toward women? Has it changed recently? Do you think it is likely that it will change much in the future?

7. Keeping in mind gender cognitive differences and social differences, how would you structure school curricula to benefit both boys and girls? Would you make any changes to help early adolescent girls deal with the "critical juncture in their development"?

8. As masculine and feminine gender roles merge and gender differences continue to recede, how will male and female relationships adapt and change? Will there be positive and negative consequences of these changes?

9. Take Self-Assessment 6.2 from the Bem Sex-Role Inventory, and write about your own gender role orientation. How does your gender role orientation influence your daily and life choices (e.g., favorite activities, friendships, career and family goals)?

10. Discuss the impact of the feminist perspective on the field of psychology.

11. As women's gender roles change, how have men adjusted their expectations of women? Have men adjusted their gender roles to compensate for women's changes?

12. Write out your advice for Leon and Mary and for Katie and Mickey, whose situations are described in Critical Thinking about Adjustment.

Chapter Practice Tests

Answer these multiple-choice test questions to help you assess your understanding of the chapter's material. Evaluate your answers to determine which sections you need to further review.

Practice Test A

1. Social expectations that prescribe how males and females should think, feel, and act is referred to as
   a. gender role.
   b. gender identity.
   c. gender.
   d. gender scripts.
   p. 142

2. The TDF gene
   a. causes the development of the male genitals.
   b. stops the development of female genitals.
   c. triggers secretion of androgens.
   d. triggers secretion of estrogen.
   p. 143

3. Genetic males born with ambiguous genitals are usually
   a. surgically reconstructed to be correct males.
   b. surgically reconstructed to be females.
   c. left alone to develop as males.
   d. left alone to develop as females.
   p. 144

4. According to social learning theory, peers are important in the development of gender roles because
   a. they provide feedback on gender-related behavior.
   b. they act against parents.
   c. peers are more powerful social agents than parents.
   d. peers all desire their own opposite-sex parents.
   p. 144

5. Which of the following plays a role in gender development?
   a. biology
   b. social context
   c. environment
   d. a combination of all of these
   p. 145

6. Which theory suggests that very young children have a great deal of knowledge about gender roles?
   a. identification theory
   b. social learning theory
   c. gender schema theory
   d. cognitive developmental theory
   p. 145

7. Gender role stereotypes are most different from
   a. gender schema.
   b. social expectations.
   c. gender identity.
   d. ethnic stereotypes.
   p. 146

8. Which of the following is not true of gender stereotypes?
   a. They tend to become more extreme as countries develop.
   b. They are often consistent across various cultures.
   c. They are images of the typical member of each gender.
   d. They are similar in many ways from stereotypes of ethnic groups.
   p. 146

9. A well-established gender difference is that
   a. females are more advanced in motor control.
   b. females live longer than males.
   c. females are better in language.
   d. males are far more advanced in mathematics.
   p. 148

10. For males and females, emotions differ most regarding
    a. feelings of sadness.
    b. physical processes.
    c. the context of emotions.
    d. positive and negative feelings.
    p. 151

11. Androgyny is characterized by
    a. low masculinity and high femininity.
    b. high femininity and low masculinity.
    c. low masculinity and low femininity.
    d. high masculinity and high femininity.
    p. 151

12. Which of the following contemporary social problems is probably related to gender roles?
    a. pollution
    b. violence
    c. poverty
    d. AIDS
    p. 152

13. Feminists adhere closest to which of the following concepts?
    a. Masculine traits are more socially valuable and should be adopted by women.
    b. People should be considered as people regardless of gender.
    c. Gender roles are a male-derived concept that keep women at a lower social level.
    d. Masculinity and femininity are outdated concepts to be replaced by gender transcendence.
    p. 154

14. The men's movement has focused on helping men achieve
    a. higher levels of masculinity.
    b. greater emotional expression.
    c. better success in sexual settings.
    d. better adjustment in family and career life.
    p. 156

15. Asian American males have been observed to have
    a. become more rigid and traditional in their gender roles than the Chinese.
    b. become less rigid and traditional in their gender roles than the Chinese.
    c. become very patriarchal.
    d. not varied in their cultural views on gender.
    p. 158

Practice Test B

1. The internal sense of being males or females is
    a. gender.
    b. gender role.
    c. gender identity.
    d. gender scripts.
    p. 142

2. Males have the sex chromosome pair ___, while females have ___.
    a. XY, YX
    b. YX, XO
    c. XX, XY
    d. XY, XX
    p. 143

3. Females with XX chromosomes who are born with ambiguous genitals are usually
    a. left alone to develop as males.
    b. left alone to develop as females.
    c. surgically altered to be males.
    d. surgically altered to be females.
    p. 144

4. Which theory places an emphasis on a child's sexual attraction to a parent in developing gender roles?
    a. social learning theory
    b. gender schema theory
    c. Erikson's theory "anatomy is destiny"
    d. identification theory
    p. 145

5. Social learning theory states that peers are most likely to contribute to the development of gender roles by
    a. sharing opposite-sex parents.
    b. punishing opposite-sex behavior.
    c. modeling interactions with parents.
    d. guiding internal motivations for gender behavior.
    p. 145

6. Cognitive influences on gender roles primarily involve
    a. information conveyed by others.
    b. differences in the brains of males and females.
    c. observations of others in the environment.
    d. the mental processes that organize information.
    p. 145

7. Gender constancy is
   a. when a child can recognize that their gender does not change.
   b. acting out the behavior of either sex.
   c. a label for boys and girls to apply to themselves and others.
   d. knowledge of gender-related behavior.
   p. 145

8. Gender role stereotypes are most closely related to which of these other concepts?
   a. gender schema
   b. gender constancy
   c. gender identity
   d. androgyny
   p. 146

9. Research has shown that males are better than females in navigating through environments. This really means
   a. that the researcher was male.
   b. that the study was slanted against females.
   c. that males and females are more alike than they are different.
   d. that the law of averages is male biased.
   p. 147

10. The stereotype that females are more emotional than males can result in
    a. attitudes that are harmful to males.
    b. attitudes that are harmful to females.
    c. attitudes that are harmful to males and females.
    d. males actually becoming more emotional.
    p. 151

11. That males and females are emotionally different is usually a product of
    a. hormone differences.
    b. the situation.
    c. genetics.
    d. family values
    p. 151

12. Phil's friends all say that he is androgynous. If they are correct, this means that Phil can be characterized as
    a. low masculinity and high femininity.
    b. high femininity and low masculinity.
    c. low masculinity and low femininity.
    d. high masculinity and high femininity.
    p. 152

13. Which theoretical perspective states that the entire concept of gender roles was developed to increase oppression of women?
    a. the men's movement
    b. social cognitive theory
    c. masculinism
    d. feminism
    p. 154

14. The men's movement has emphasized that differences between men and women involve
    a. physical strength.
    b. coping resources.
    c. emotional expression.
    d. adjustment to family life.
    p. 155

15. Ethnic minority women have been among the most underrepresented groups in
    a. feminism.
    b. social sciences.
    c. research studies.
    d. all of the above.
    p. 157

1. Answer a; Gender roles set up expectations that can establish standards for behavior; page 142 Learning Objective 1

2. Answer a; Gonads develop into testes only with the signal given by the TDF gene; page 143; Learning Objective 2

3. Answer b; Medical technology is more able to reconstruct the female systems than the male systems; page 144; Learning Objective 2

4. Answer a; Peers quickly tell children their behavior is outside of that which is socially expected, including gender-related behaviors; page 144; Learning Objective 3

5. Answer d; Gender development is complex and involves several interacting factors; page 145; Learning Objective 4

6. Answer c; Gender schema theory states that knowledge structures related to gender are developed at a young age through a combination of biological and social forces; page 145; Learning Objective 5

7. Answer c; Gender identity is a part of one's internalized view of the self, or self-concept; page 146; Learning Objective 6

8. Answer a; Developed countries provide greater diversity in cross gender behavior; page 146; Learning Objective 6

9. Answer b; On average, women live longer than men, and this seems to be the result of several factors; page 148; Learning Objective 7

10. Answer c; The experiences and processes involved in emotions do not differ for males and females, but the situational factors associated with emotional responses do differ; page 151; Learning Objective 8

11. Answer d; Having strong masculine and feminine traits is referred to as androgyny, and this is different from being low in the two types of characteristics; page 151; Learning Objective 9

12. Answer b; Violence, as it is related to aggression, is connected to social gender roles; page 152; Learning Objective 9

13. Answer c; Because gender roles prescribe behaviors that are more closely linked to social success, such as independence, competitiveness, and assertiveness, socially constructed gender roles may place women at a disadvantage under certain circumstances; page 154; Learning Objective 10

14. Answer b; Men are socialized to hold their feelings in and this can be a negative attribute in relationships, health, and satisfaction; page 156; Learning Objective 11

15. Answer b; Gender expectancies and behavior are driven by social and cultural forces; page 158; Learning Objective 12

Key for Practice Test B

1. Answer c; Gender identity is the internal sense of being male or female that is a central part of the self-concept; page 142; Learning Objective 1

2. Answer d; While males and females both possess an X chromosome, females have an additional X and males have a Y; page 143; Learning Objective 2

3. Answer d; Medical technology can alter the ambiguous genitals to match the XX chromosomes, although the case is different from an XY male with ambiguous chromosomes; page 144; Learning Objective 2

4. Answer d; Identification theory states that gender-related behaviors are learned through observation of parent behavior; page 145; Learning Objective 3

5. Answer b; Peers quickly let children know when their behavior is outside of those that are socially expected; page 145; Learning Objective 3

6. Answer d; Gender schema are one of the mental processes that organize information in the development of gender roles; page 145; Learning Objective 4

7. Answer a; Gender constancy occurs when a child realizes that sex is a fixed part of a person that does not change; page 145; Learning Objective 5

8. Answer a; Stereotypes and gender schema involve the expectation for males and females to behave a certain way; page 146; Learning Objective 6

9. Answer c; Sex differences in mental abilities refers to average differences. The overlap between males and females is greater than the differences between them; page 148; Learning Objective 7

10. Answer c; Expectations set up by stereotypes can be harmful to both men and women. Men are expected to be less expressive and women become expected to be irrational; page 151; Learning Objective 8

11. Answer b; Context plays a great role in emotional expression, and men and women vary differently across different situations; page 151; Learning Objective 8

12. Answer d; Androgyny is a mix of both high masculine and high feminine traits, as opposed to having low characteristics of both; page 152; Learning Objective 9

13. Answer d; Feminist theories hold that gender roles set up expectations for females to respond in socially disadvantaged ways as compared to males; page 154; Learning Objective 10

14. Answer c; The men's movement has focused on developing more acceptance for men to express their feelings across a variety of situations; page 155; Learning Objective 11

15. Answer d; Women of color have been under-represented across all facets of the social sciences, including as theorists, scientists, and research participants; page 157; Learning Objective 12

Chapter Outline

I.   The Human Sexual Response
    A. Sexual Arousal
        1. Both biological and psychological factors are involved in our sexual arousal.
        2. The pituitary gland controls all of the hormones including estrogens, the main class of female sex hormones, and androgens (including testosterone), the main class of male sex hormones.
        3. At puberty, males experience a great increase in testosterone levels resulting in more sexual thoughts and fantasies, masturbation, and nocturnal emissions.
        4. The higher the male adolescent testosterone level, the more preoccupied with sexuality and the more sexual activity.
        5. The testes secrete consistent levels of androgens, so human males can engage in sexual behavior at any time, although with aging the level gradually declines.
        6. At puberty, ovaries begin to produce estrogen, but the levels vary with the highest levels during ovulation.
        7. In many non-human female animals, high-estrogen periods are the only time that there is sexual activity; this is not the case for human females.
        8. What "turns people on" is influenced by their sociocultural background, their individual preferences, and their cognitive interpretations.
        9. Cultural values and behaviors vary from the very sexually repressed people of Ines Beag to the very sexually liberated people of the Mangaian culture; these cultural differences point out the importance of environmental experiences in determining sexual arousal.
      10. Sexual fantasies are a common sexual stimulant for both men and women, with the most common fantasies being oral-genital sex, and being found irresistible; males are more likely to fantasize sex with an imaginary lover and having others give in after resistance.
      11. Non-obsessive, voluntary fantasies serve as a way of fulfilling sexual desires, of imagining what one would like, and of rehearsing behaviors one wants to perform.
      12. Men are more aroused by visual stimulation, and women are more sexually aroused through tender, loving touches coupled with verbal expressions of love.
      13. Men become aroused quickly, while women have a more gradual building of arousal.
    B. The Human Sexual Response Cycle
        1. William Masters and Virginia Johnson measured the physiological responses of female and male volunteers as they masturbated or had sexual intercourse.
        2. The human sexual response cycle consists of four phases: excitement, plateau, orgasm, and resolution.
        3. The excitement phase, which can last minutes or hours, is the beginning of erotic responsiveness and involves the two processes of engorgement of blood vessels and muscle tension.
        4. Erection and vaginal lubrication are part of the excitement phase.

5. The plateau phase is a continuation and heightening of arousal with increases in breathing, pulse rate, and blood pressure.
6. Orgasm lasts from three to fifteen seconds and consists of an explosive discharge of neuromuscular tension and an intense pleasurable feeling.
7. During the resolution phase, blood vessels return to their normal state.
8. For males, the refractory period, part of the resolution phase, is a period of time when orgasm cannot be achieved; the refractory period increases with age.
9. Aphrodisiacs are natural and artificial substances believed to enhance sexual arousal and responsiveness, but only a few actually do increase sexual responsiveness.
10. Sexual aids are normal devices used to enhance or intensify sexual arousal and responsiveness usually by application on the genitals or in the genital area.

II. Sexual Attitudes and Behavior
   A. Heterosexual Attitudes and Behavior
      1. During the twentieth century, college students showed an increase in sexual intercourse and the gap between the number of sexually active males and sexually active females has narrowed.
      2. There is a shift at all adult ages away from the double standard of viewing sexual activity among unmarried males acceptable but not for unmarried females.
      3. Other twentieth century trends have been lengthened foreplay and greater variety of sexual techniques, including oral-genital sex.
      4. Couples are more likely to have intercourse at least three times a week in the first two years of being together.
      5. Decrease in sexuality during middle and late adulthood for married couples can be due to a decrease in sexual desire, but other reasons include involvement in other activities (e.g., career, family).
      6. Among older male adults, orgasm occurs less frequently and more direct stimulation is usually needed for erection.
      7. Among older adults, the major predictors of continuing sexuality are good health, available partner, and a belief that sexuality is lifelong.
      8. There is much variation in sexual attitudes and behaviors among college students with one-quarter regularly engaging in intercourse and one-quarter identifying themselves as virgins.
      9. The majority of college students believe that premarital sex is not wrong and that it is okay for single people to live together.
     10. A sexual script is a stereotyped pattern of role prescriptions for how individuals should sexually behave, and two influential scripts are the traditional religious script and the romantic script.
     11. Females learn to link sexual intercourse with love more than males do.
     12. The double standard script encourages women to deny their sexuality and do minimal planning for safe sexual decisions, as well as leading females to think that males are more sexual and less in control of their sexual behaviors.
     13. Although decreasing in impact, the double standard is still at work in extramarital relations.
   B. Homosexual Attitudes and Behavior
      1. Sexual orientation may best be described as a continuum from exclusively heterosexual to exclusively homosexual, as proposed by Kinsey.
      2. Bisexuals are sexually attracted to people of both sexes; it is not very common.

3. Although the majority of people are heterosexual, a sizeable minority have engaged in some homosexual behavior.
4. Lesbians are more likely to be involved in intimate, enduring relationships, have fewer sexual partners, and have fewer "one night" stands than are homosexual men.
5. Homosexual couples have more frequent sex during the first two years than later in their relationship.
6. For the last few decades, attitudes toward homosexuality were becoming more permissive, at least until recently.
7. Individuals who have negative attitudes toward homosexuals also are likely to favor severe controls for AIDS, such as excluding AIDS carriers from the workplace and schools.
8. Irrational and negative feelings against homosexuals is called homophobia.
9. Homosexuals and heterosexuals have similar physiological responses during sexual arousal and seem to be aroused by the same types of tactile stimulation.
10. There may be a biological basis for homosexuality based on twin studies.
11. The critical period hypothesis suggests that the second to fifth months after conception may play a role in sexual orientation.
12. LeVay found that an area of the hypothalamus that governs sexual behavior is twice as large in heterosexual than in homosexual males.
13. Sexual orientation is most likely determined by a combination of genetic, hormonal, cognitive, and environmental factors.
14. Children raised by homosexual parents are no more likely to be homosexual than are children raised by heterosexual parents.
15. There is no evidence that parental dominance or weakness contributes to homosexuality.

III. Psychosexual Disorders
   A. Psychosexual Dysfunctions
      1. Psychosexual dysfunctions are disorders that involve impairments in the sexual response cycle, either the desire for gratification or the ability to achieve it.
      2. Disorders include low sex drive, inability to maintain an erection, premature ejaculation, and inhibited female orgasm.
      3. Therapy proposed by Masters and Johnson included focusing directly on the sexual problem, involving one's sexual partner in therapy, and having both a male and a female therapist.
      4. Sex therapy is highly successful in dealing with psychosexual dysfunctions.
      5. Kaplan pointed out that often sexual difficulties are directly related to inhibitions in sexual desires.
      6. Therapists have been able to help spinal cord injured persons be sexual.
   B. Incest
      1. A universal taboo is incest, a sexual relationship between two relatives.
      2. The most common form is brother-sister, with father-daughter sexual relationship being second most common.
      3. In general, the greater the age discrepancy of the individuals involved, the greater the resultant problems.
      4. Incest is psychologically harmful for immediate family relationships and also for the future relationships of a child involved in incest.

C. Paraphilias
1. Paraphilias are psychosexual disorders in which the source of an individual's sexual satisfaction is an unusual object, ritual, or situation.
2. Fetishism is a psychosexual disorder in which an individual relies on inanimate objects or a specific body part for sexual gratification.
3. Transvestism is a psychosexual disorder in which an individual obtains sexual gratification by dressing up as a member of the opposite sex.
4. Exhibitionism is a psychosexual disorder in which individuals expose their sexual anatomy to others to obtain sexual gratification.
5. Voyeurism is a psychosexual disorder in which individuals derive sexual gratification by observing the sex organs or sex acts of others, often from a secret vantage point.
6. Sadism is a psychosexual disorder in which individuals derive sexual gratification from inflicting pain on others.
7. Masochism is a psychosexual disorder in which individuals derive sexual gratification from being subjected to physical pain, inflicted by others or themselves.
8. Pedophilia is a psychosexual disorder in which the sex object is a child and the intimacy usually involves manipulation of a child's genitals.

D. Disorder of Gender Identity or Transsexualism
1. Transsexualism is a psychosexual disorder in which an individual has an overwhelming desire to become a member of the opposite sex; in other words, gender identity is at odds with their anatomical features.
2. Some transsexuals decide to undergo surgery to change sex.

IV. Forcible Sexual Behavior
A. Rape
1. Rape is forcible sexual intercourse with a person who does not give consent.
2. Legal definitions differ from state to state.
3. Nearly 200,000 rapes are reported annually, but actual rapes are much larger.
4. Rape may be prevalent because males are socialized to be sexually aggressive, view women as inferior, and place personal pleasure as the most important goal.
5. Rapists use aggression to enhance sense of power or masculinity. They are angry at women and wish to hurt their victims.

B. Acquaintance Rape
1. Acquaintance rape is coercive sexual activity directed at someone with whom the individual is at least casually acquainted.
2. Two-thirds of college men admitted that they fondled women against their will and one-half admitted to forced sexual activity.
3. Males who coerce females tend to believe misconceptions, such as women wanting to be raped and men being unable to control their sexual behavior.

C. The Rape Victim
1. Rape is traumatic to the victim and those close to her.
2. The initial reaction is often shock, numbness, and disorganization.
3. Later the victim experiences depression, fear, anxiety, and a need to return to normal.
4. About half experience sexual dysfunctions and about one-fifth make a suicide attempt.

5. Recovery is affected by prior psychological adjustment, coping abilities, social support, and professional counseling and empowerment through prosecution.
6. Most victims are females, but male rape does occur.

V. Sexual Harassment
   A. Defining Sexual Harassment
      1. Sexual harassment comes in many forms from sexist remarks and covert physical contact to blatant propositions and sexual assaults.
      2. Millions of women experience sexual harassment each year in work and educational settings.
      3. Sexual harassment is a manifestation of power and domination of one person over another and can result in serious psychological consequences for the victim.
   B. Elimination of Sexual Harassment
      1. Elimination requires work and academic environments compatible with the needs of women workers and students.
      2. There is a need for equal opportunities to develop a career and obtain an education in a sexual harassment free climate.
      3. There needs to be social intolerance and non-acceptance of sexual harassment.

VI. Pornography and Violence against Women
    A. Feminists and Pornography
       1. Feminists campaigned against pornography beginning in the late 1970s.
       2. Feminists objected to how pornography demeans women and how it glorifies violence against women.
    B. Pornography Research
       1. Erotic films and slides influence sexual behavior for brief time periods.
       2. Viewing or reading about sexual violence increases sexual and other aggression toward females, and Donnerstein argues it is the violence and not the erotism that causes negative attitudes toward women.
    C. Rape and Pornography
       1. Rapists report below average exposure to erotic magazines and movies during adolescent years.
       2. When Denmark stopped censoring pornographic materials, sex-related crimes actually decreased.
       3. There is no evidence that sexual content without aggression stimulates negative feelings toward woman.

VII. Sexually Transmitted Diseases
     A. Definition and Incidence
        1. Sexually transmitted diseases (STDs) are diseases that are contracted primarily through sex—intercourse as well as oral-genital and anal-genital sex.
        2. STDs have also been referred to as venereal diseases (VDs).
        3. STDs are an increasing health problem, especially for adults in their late teens and early twenties.
     B. Gonorrhea
        1. Gonorrhea ("drip," "clap") is caused by a bacterium from the gonococcus family, and it thrives in the moist mucous membranes lining the mouth, throat, vagina, cervix, urethra, and anal tract.

2. Males have a ten percent chance and females have a forty percent chance of infection with each exposure.
3. Symptoms in males (appear three days to a month after contact) include penile discharge, burning during urination, blood in the urine, aching pain or pressure in the genitals, and swollen and tender lymph glands in the groin.
4. Except for pelvic inflammation, females have no symptoms in the early stages, but if not treated, the disease causes infection in the reproductive and pelvic regions within two months with possible scarring of the fallopian tubes and infertility resulting.
5. Gonorrhea can be successfully treated in its early stages with penicillin or other antibiotics.
6. Up to two million cases of gonorrhea occur annually in the United States.

C. Syphilis
1. Syphilis is caused by the bacterium Treponema pallidum of the spirochete family.
2. It is transmitted by penile-vaginal, oral-genital, or anal contact and also can be transmitted to the fetus after the fourth month of pregnancy.
3. In the primary stage, a sore or chancre appears for up to six weeks at the site of infection.
4. Untreated, it moves to the six-week secondary stage—rash, fever, sore throat, headache, swollen glands, joint pain, poor appetite, and hearing loss.
5. Penicillin can successfully treat syphilis in both the primary and secondary stages.
6. If untreated, it enters the latency stage and spirochetes can spread throughout the body; it can infect others in sexual contact for two years and after that still be transmitted to the fetus.
7. Thirty to fifty percent of those in the latent stage enter the tertiary stage where syphilis causes paralysis, insanity, or even death
8. Syphilis is on the rise in the United States.

D. Chlamydia
1. Chlamydia is the most common of all sexually transmitted diseases with about four million Americans infected each year (about ten percent of all college students).
2. It is highly contagious, and difficult for women to get treatment because they are asymptomatic.
3. Untreated chlamydia in women can cause pelvis inflammatory disease (PID) and result in infertility or ectopic pregnancies.
4. Chlamydia is the number one cause of preventable female infertility.

E. Herpes Genitalis
1. Herpes can be caused by a large family of viruses with many different strains, and two forms exist.
2. Type I is characterized by cold sores and fever blisters and Type II includes painful sores on the lower body, but they can be transmitted to either lower or upper body.
3. Approximately 75 percent of individuals exposed to an infected partner will develop herpes.
4. Three to five days after contact, itching and tingling can occur followed by sores and blisters lasting up to three weeks and recurring later in more mild attacks.
5. Transmission through the nervous system can cause encephalitis and blindness, increases the risk of cervical cancer, and it can also be transmitted from a pregnant woman to her offspring at birth.
6. Herpes cannot be cured but symptoms can be alleviated, and at least one million American have each type of herpes.

F. AIDS
    1. AIDS is caused by the human immunodeficiency virus (HIV) which destroys the body's immune system.
    2. Well over one million Americans are now asymptomatic carriers of AIDS; the incidence is higher among Hispanics and Blacks in the United States but no one is immune.
    3. AIDS can be transmitted only by sexual contact, sharing of needles, or blood transfusion (which are now tightly monitored).
    4. The only safe behavior is sexual abstinence, but safe sex is the second best option.
    5. When HIV^+ is in stage 1, individuals are asymptomatic but can transmit the disease to others.
    6. In stage 2, HIV^+ individuals have symptoms such as swollen lymph glands, fatigue, weight loss, diarrhea, fever, and sweats.
    7. In the AIDS stage a person has symptoms and at least one disease; diseases become fatal because of a vulnerable immune system.

VIII. Sexual Knowledge
  A. How Good Is Our Sexual Knowledge?
    1. Both American adults and adolescents lack basic sexual knowledge.
    2. One reason is that misinformation is nearly as common as correct knowledge.
  B. Sex Education
    1. Some sex education teachers are poorly trained.
    2. The majority of American adolescents say they cannot talk freely about sex with their parents, and a majority of parents want the schools to conduct sex education.
    3. But sex education in the schools is controversial, because some believe the education is a "license to have sex and be promiscuous."
    4. Researchers have found that sex education classes do improve adolescents' knowledge about human sexuality but do not always change their behavior.
    5. Good sex education and readily available condoms does reduce teen pregnancy rates.
    6. Swedish adolescents are sexually active earlier than American adolescents, see more explicit sex on television, yet have a complete sex education.
  C. Contraception
    1. Inadequate knowledge about contraception and inconsistent use of effective methods have resulted in this country's highest adolescent pregnancy rate among industrialized countries.
    2. A majority of adolescents do not use contraception during their first sexual intercourse experience.
    3. The two most important factors in choosing methods of contraception are safety and effectiveness.
    4. Without contraception, 90 percent of women who are sexually active would become pregnant in the first year.

Learning Objectives

After reading and studying this chapter, students should be able to:

1. Understand the process of human sexual arousal.
2. Identify and describe the male and female sexual response cycles.

3. Know the sexual attitudes related to heterosexuality.
4. Know the sexual attitudes related to homosexuality.
5. Identify and describe sexual dysfunctions and sex therapy.
6. Understand what is currently known about incest.
7. Identify and understand the various paraphilias.
8. Describe transsexualism and its relationship to gender identity.
9. Know the current thinking on forcible sexual behavior.
10. Know what sexual harassment is and the harm it does.
11. Understand the relationship between pornography and violence against women.
12. Identify the various sexually transmitted diseases and their symptoms.
13. Recognize the common deficits in sexual knowledge.
14. Identify and be ready to explain the available methods of contraception.

Guided Review

After you have read the chapter one time, search through the chapter to find the appropriate words to complete these statements. Material is covered in the same order as the chapter.

1. Instead of viewing sex as a _____ skill, sex is best conceptualized as a form of _____ within a relationship.
2. Both _____ and _____ factors are involved in our sexual arousal.
3. _____, subtle and powerful chemicals in the bloodstream, are controlled by the _____, which is located in the _____.
4. _____ are the main class of sex hormones in females while _____ (with _____ being the most important one) are the main class of sex hormones in males.
5. Males experience a dramatic increase in _____ levels at _____ resulting in an increase in sexual thoughts and behaviors.
6. The males' _____ secrete androgens in fairly _____ amounts with a gradual _____ as they age, while the females' _____ produce _____ whose levels vary over an approximately _____-long cycle.
7. Although not true of female humans, in many species females are _____ to male initiatives to mate only in _____-estrogen periods.
8. Postmenopausal women who are given _____ experience an increase in sexual interest and pleasure.
9. Among the _____ _____ of Ireland, sex is quite _____ with lack of knowledge, limited experiences, and belief that sex is bad for one's health.
10. In the _____ culture of the South Pacific, boys are encouraged to _____, and, when they turn thirteen, they are instructed about sexual strategies including how to aid their female partner in having _____ as well as having intercourse with an _____ woman.
11. Sexual _____ are a common sexual stimulant for both men and women, and the two most common ones are _____-_____ sex and being found _____ by others.
12. A common sexual fantasy for both men and women is thinking about sex with a(n) _____ lover while more men than women think about sex with a(n) _____ lover and more _____ think about sex with a member of the same sex.

13. As long as sexual fantasies do not become _____, fantasy can enhance development of an intimate sexual relationship.

14. _____ are more aroused by what they see, while _____ become sexually aroused through tender, loving touches coupled with _____ expressions of love.

15. _____ can become aroused quickly, while arousal for _____ is more typified as a gradual building of arousal.

16. _____ and _____ observed and measured the _____ responses of adult volunteers as they _____ or had sexual intercourse and identified the _____ _____ _____ _____ consisting of four phases—_____, _____, _____, and _____.

17. The _____ phase can last several minutes to several hours and involves two processes, that of _____ of blood vessels and muscle _____.

18. The most obvious signs of the excitement phase are partial _____ of the _____ and _____ _____.

19. The second phase, the _____ phase, is a continuation and heightening of arousal with increases in _____, _____ rate, and _____ _____ and complete penile _____.

20. The _____ phase only lasts from three to _____ seconds and involves an explosive discharge of neuromuscular _____ and an intense _____ feeling.

21. For males but not females, part of the _____ phase is the _____ period during which they cannot achieve another _____; this period _____ in length as men age.

22. Men have _____ pattern(s) of sexual response while females have _____ pattern(s).

23. _____ are natural and artificial substances believed to enhance sexual arousal and responsiveness, and _____ _____ are items used to enhance or intensify sexual arousal and responsiveness usually by application on or near the genitals.

24. _____ _____ include vibrators, massage creams, oils, lotions, _____ (penis-shaped objects), _____ _____ _____ (an oriental method for female _____), and _____ _____ (used to extend the length of _____), and they are considered _____ devices to increase sexual pleasure.

25. Gathering accurate information about sexual attitudes and behavior is hindered by the _____ _____ (not all individuals are willing to be part of this kind of research) and by reluctance of some to give candid responses.

26. During the twentieth century, both college students and other adults increased in having _____ _____ and shifted away from the _____ _____.

27. Since the 1940s, adults have increased the average length of _____ and also use more variety of _____ _____, with a big increase in _____-_____ sex.

28. For both cohabitating and married couples, sex is _____ frequent in the first two years of being together, and _____ adults have more sex than other adults.

29. Among older males, _____ may only occur in every second or third act of intercourse and more _____ _____ is usually needed for an erection.

30. For elderly females, the most common reason for cessation of sexuality is not having a(n) _____.

31. Among college students, _____-_____ identified themselves as regularly engaging in sexual intercourse and about _____-_____ identified themselves as virgins.

32. _____ of college students have had more than one sexual partner, and about _____-_____ have had at least five partners.

33. A(n) _____ _____ is a stereotyped pattern of role prescriptions for how individuals should sexually behave.

34. In the _____ _____ script, sex is accepted only within _____ and both _____ and _____ sex are taboo, especially for _____.

35. In some forms of the religious script, sex is positively viewed only for its _____ value and sexuality is often a source of _____.

36. In the _____ script, sex is synonymous with _____.

37. Females learn to link sexual intercourse with _____ more than males do.

38. The _____ _____ script is the belief that many sexual activities are acceptable for males but not females, which results in women _____ their sexuality and doing little planning for safe sexual decisions.

39. The _____ _____ script encourages males to devalue their female partner's values as well as puts pressure on them to be as _____ _____ as possible.

40. In Kinsey's research, about _____-_____ of husbands and _____-_____ of wives have had extramarital affairs; now, the figure for husbands is about the same and has _____ for females.

41. The majority of men and women _____ of extramarital sex.

42. Kinsey was one of the first to view sexual orientation as a _____ rather than either-or heterosexuality and homosexuality.

43. Some individuals are _____, being sexually attracted to people of both sexes.

44. Kinsey found that 37 percent of men and 13 percent of women had participated in some _____ acts to orgasm between adolescence and old age with _____ being more likely to be in enduring relationships than their male counterparts.

45. For the last few decades, attitudes toward homosexuality were becoming more _____, at least until recently.

46. Individuals who had negative attitudes toward homosexuals were more likely to favor severe controls for those with _____.

47. Irrational and negative feelings against homosexuals is called _____.

48. Homosexual and heterosexual individuals have _____ physiological responses during sexual arousal and seem to be aroused by _____ tactile stimulation.

49. In one study, when one identified twin was homosexual, over half of the time the other twin was _____.

50. It is possible that in the second to fifth months after _____, a fetus's exposure to characteristic female levels of _____ may result in male homosexuality.

51. In one study, LeVay found that the area of the _____ that governs sexual behavior was _____ as large in heterosexual as homosexual men, while the area was about the same for homosexual men and _____ females.

52. _____ _____ are sexual problems caused mainly by psychological problems, while _____ _____ involve impairments in the sexual response cycle.

53. In psychosexual dysfunctions associated with the _____ phase, individuals show little sexual drive while not being able to maintain an erection is associated with the _____ phase.

54. A problem with the orgasmic phase may be that men may have _____ _____, or rapid orgasm, while women are more likely to experience _____ orgasm.

143

55. There is a _____ success rate in treating psychosexual dysfunctions.
56. The techniques proposed by _____ and _____ formed the basis for modern psychological treatments of sexual problems, and center on treating the actual problem and using the context of a sexual relationship.
57. _____ built upon these techniques and especially worked with sexual difficulties directly related to _____ in sexual desires.
58. Males with spinal cord injuries may not be capable of typical erections, but some can have _____ erections achieved by direct stimulation of areas around the penis and still others use a "_____ _____."
59. _____ is a sexual relationship between two relatives, and it is virtually a _____ _____.
60. The most common form of incest is a _____-_____ sexual relationship with the second most common form _____-_____ sexual relationship.
61. In general, the greater the _____ discrepancy the more problems result, but any incest victim may have future problems.
62. _____ are psychosexual disorders in which the source of an individual's sexual _____ is an unusual object, ritual, or situation.
63. _____ is when an individual relies on _____ objects or a specific body part for sexual gratification.
64. In _____ or _____-_____, individuals obtain sexual gratification by dressing up as a member of the opposite sex.
65. In _____ individuals expose their _____ _____ to others to obtain sexual gratification and in _____ derive sexual gratification by observing the sex organs or sex acts of others, usually secretly.
66. _____ involves deriving sexual gratification from inflicting pain on others and _____ involves deriving sexual gratification from being subjected to physical pain.
67. _____ is when the sex object is a _____ and the intimacy usually involves manipulation of the child's genitals.
68. _____ is when an individual has an overwhelming desire to become a member of the opposite sex, and sometimes the individual undergoes _____ to reassign one's sex.
69. _____ is forcible sexual intercourse with a person who does not give _____, and legal definitions differ from state to state.
70. About _____ rapes are reported annually in the United States, and the actual number of rapes is much higher.
71. _____ or _____ _____ is coercive sexual activity directed at someone with whom the individual is at least casually acquainted, and these rapes are a problem on college campuses.
72. Initial reactions to rape includes _____, _____, and _____ and they may experience depression, fear, and anxiety for a long time.
73. About half of rape victims experience _____ _____, such as reduced sexual desire or inhibited orgasm, and one-fifth make a _____ _____.
74. _____ _____ ranges from sexist remarks to sexual assaults in work and educational settings.
75. Feminists suggest that _____ demeans women and glorifies violence against women.

76. When sexual content is combined with _____, male aggression toward females may increase, but there is no evidence that sexual content alone stimulates _____ feelings toward women.

77. _____ _____ _____ are diseases that are contacted primarily through sex, and include bacteria-caused diseases of _____, _____, and _____, which is the most common STD.

78. Although men experience a discharge and pain from _____, most women show no symptoms, yet with time may experience scarring of the _____ _____ resulting in _____.

79. Syphilis is caused by _____ _____, a member of the _____ family and the primary stage involves a _____ at the site of infection.

80. The _____ stage of syphilis includes a rash, fever, and swollen glands among other symptoms, but still can be treated with _____.

81. During the _____ stage spirochetes spread throughout the body and for those who reach the _____ stage, syphilis can cause paralysis, insanity, or death.

82. _____ is the number one cause of preventable female infertility.

83. The STDs _____ _____ and _____ _____ _____ _____ are incurable because they are caused by _____.

84. Herpes simplex has two varieties called _____ _____ and _____ _____, with a million Americans having each type.

85. AIDS is caused by _____ _____ _____ that destroys the body's _____ system, and it can only be contracted through _____ contact, sharing of _____, and unmonitored _____ _____.

86. American adolescents and adults have _____ sexual knowledge, yet school sex education remains controversial.

87. _____ knowledge about contraception and _____ use of effective methods has produced this country's _____ adolescent pregnancy rate in the industrialized world.

88. Without using contraceptives, _____ percent of women who are sexually active would become pregnant in the first year.

Guided Review Answers

1. performance, communication; 2. biological, psychological; 3. Hormones, pituitary, brain; 4. Estrogens, androgens, testosterone; 5. testosterone, puberty; 6. testes, consistent, decline, ovaries, estrogens, month; 7. receptive, high; 8. estrogen; 9. Ines Beag, repressed; 10. Mangaian, masturbate, orgasms, experienced; 11. fantasies, oral-genital, irresistible; 12. former, imaginary, women; 13. obsessive; 14. Men, women, verbal; 15. Men, women; 16. Masters, Johnson, physiological, masturbated, human sexual response cycle, excitement, plateau, orgasm, resolution; 17. excitement, engorgement, tension; 18. erection, penis, vaginal lubrication; 19. plateau, breathing, pulse, blood pressure, erection; 20. orgasm, fifteen, tension, pleasurable; 21. resolution, refractory, orgasm, increases; 22. one, three; 23. Aphrodisiacs, sexual aids; 24. Sexual aids, dildos, ben wa balls, masturbation, cock rings, erection, normal; 25. volunteer bias; 26. sexual intercourse, double standard; 27. foreplay, sexual techniques, oral-genital; 28. more, young; 29. orgasm, direct stimulation; 30. partner; 31. one-quarter, one-quarter; 32. Half, one-quarter; 33. sexual script; 34. traditional religious, marriage, premarital, extramarital, women; 35. reproductive, sin; 36. romantic, love; 37. love; 38. double standard, denying; 39. double standard, sexually active; 40. one-half, one-quarter, increased; 41. disapprove; 42. continuum; 43. bisexual; 44. homosexual, lesbians; 45. permissive; 46. AIDS;

47. homophobia; 48. similar, similar; 49. homosexual; 50. conception, hormones; 51. hypothalamus, twice, heterosexual; 52. Psychosexual disorders, psychosexual dysfunctions; 53. desire, excitement; 54. premature ejaculation, inhibited; 55. high; 56. Masters, Johnson; 57. Kaplan, inhibitions; 58. reflex, "stuffing technique"; 59. Incest, universal taboo; 60. brother-sister, father-daughter; 61. age; 62. Paraphilias, satisfaction; 63. Fetishism, inanimate; 64. transvestism, cross-dressing; 65. exhibitionism, sexual anatomy, voyeurism; 66. Sadism, masochism; 67. Pedophilia, child; 68. Transsexualism, surgery; 69. Rape, consent; 70. 200,000; 71. Date, acquaintance rape; 72. shock, numbness, disorganization; 73. sexual dysfunctions, suicide attempt; 74. Sexual harassment; 75. pornography; 76. violence, negative; 77. Sexually transmitted diseases, gonorrhea, syphilis, chlamydia; 78. gonorrhea, fallopian tubes, infertility; 79. Treponema pallidum, spirochete, chancre; 80. secondary, penicillin; 81. latent, tertiary; 82. Chlamydia; 83. herpes genitalis, acquired immune deficiency syndrome, viruses; 84. Type I, Type II; 85. human immunodeficiency virus, immune, sexual, needles, blood transfusion; 86. inadequate; 87. Inadequate, inconsistent, highest; 88. ninety

Key Terms

For each term, briefly define the term in your own words and provide an example or situation (especially one you can visualize) that will help you retain the meaning of the concept. Key terms are presented in the order they are presented in the chapter.

1. human sexual response cycle (p. 171)

2. aphrodisiacs (p. 171)

3. sexual aids (p. 171)

4. sexual script (p. 174)

5. traditional religious script (p. 174)

6. romantic script (p. 174)

7. double standard (p. 175)

8. bisexual (p. 175)

9. psychosexual disorders (p. 179)

10. psychosexual dysfunctions (p. 179)

11. incest (p. 180)

12. paraphilias (p. 180)

13. fetishism (p. 180)

14. transvestism (p. 180)

15. exhibitionism (p. 180)

16. voyeurism (p. 180)

17. sadism (p. 180)

18. masochism (p. 180)

19. pedophilia (p. 181)

20. gender identity disorder (transsexualism) (p. 181)

21. rape (p. 181)

22. date or acquaintance rape (p. 181)

23. sexually transmitted diseases (STDs) (p. 183)

24. gonorrhea (p. 184)

25. syphilis (p. 184)

26. chlamydia (p. 184)

27. herpes (p. 184)

28. AIDS (p. 185)

Study Aids

Students who do well on tests develop mnemonic aids to help them remember important terms and concepts. A few are suggested here, and you are encouraged to develop your own additional aids.

The Human Sexual Response Cycle. Remember EPOR to help you recall the four phases in their proper order: Excitement, Plateau, Orgasm, and Resolution.

The Paraphilias. Be able to remember the various paraphilias by taking the time to differentiate them by the source of their sexual gratification, as in the following list:

Fetishism—inanimate objects, body parts
Transvestism—cross-dressing
Exhibitionism—exposing one's genitals
Voyeurism—secretly see another's genitals or sexuality
Sadism—inflicting pain
Masochism—receiving pain
Pedophilia—child

Sexually Transmitted Diseases. You can more easily remember the effects of various STDs by remembering the general rule that STDs caused by bacteria can be successfully treated and those that are caused by viruses cannot be cured. Therefore, of the STDs discussed in this chapter, the curable ones are: gonorrhea, syphilis, and chlamydia; the noncurable ones are: herpes genitalis and AIDS.

Understanding Concepts

Answer these questions to develop your understanding of the important ideas in this chapter.

1. Discuss the roles of hormones in sexual arousal and describe how hormonal levels change during puberty.

2. What roles do sexual fantasies play in people's lives?

3. Describe each of the four phases of the human sexual response cycle and give any sex differences in the phases.

4. Distinguish between aphrodisiacs and sexual aids.

5. Summarize the similarities and differences between heterosexual and homosexual attitudes and behavior.

6. Why does intercourse frequency decrease in long-term relationships?

7. Explain the traditional religious script, the romantic script, and the double standard script and how these scripts affect sexual expression.

8. Discuss what is known or hypothesized about the cause of sexual orientation.

9. Be able to provide the source of sexual gratification for the various paraphilias, e.g., fetishism, transvestism, exhibitionism, voyeurism, sadism, masochism, and pedophilia.

10. Distinguish between transvestism and transsexualism.

11. Summarize what researchers know about pornography's effects.

12. Discuss why many adolescents do not properly or consistently use contraceptives.

Applying Concepts

Answer these questions to develop your ability to apply this chapter's material to your life and the world. Your own responses may differ from other students' in the class, and it is helpful to share your ideas with the other students.

1. After reading the descriptions of the Ines Beag and Mangaian cultures, write a description of the sexual values and behaviors of American culture (perhaps describe the sexual culture of your college campus).

2. What is the cultural impact of males being more sexually aroused by visual stimuli than are females?

3. Because Masters and Johnson's research was based on observations of volunteers, do their results reflect the sexual functioning of the average person? Could the volunteers who agreed to be observed be different in their sexual/physical functioning from most other people who would not be comfortable in such contexts? Do you believe the volunteer bias plays a smaller role in physiological studies than in attitudinal studies about sex?

4. Discuss sexual problems that might occur because of the traditional religious sexual script, the romantic script, and the double standard script.

5. Take Self-Assessment 7.1 on the level of your sexual satisfaction and discuss your results.

6. What aspects of society do you think influence whether people are permissive toward homosexuality? Assess your own attitudes in Self-Assessment 7.2 and discuss your position here.

7. Why is sex therapy so successful?

8. What could be done to reduce the incidence of acquaintance rape on your college campus?

9. What could be done to reduce the incidence of sexual harassment on your college campus?

10. What might be different about American culture that has resulted in it having the highest rate of sexual violence against women and children in the world?

11. How can erotic art and pornography be distinguished? How can researchers define pornographic materials as being different from works of art that involve nudity?

12. Develop an educational program that would help reverse the trend of increasing numbers of sexually transmitted diseases in this country.

13. Discuss the societal effects of the AIDS epidemic. How has AIDS changed your life and your sexual choices?

14. Present your argument for whether schools should have a sex education curriculum. What topics would you cover in elementary school, middle school, and high school? What guidelines did you use to determine when different topics should be presented?

Chapter Practice Tests

Answer these multiple-choice test questions to help you assess your understanding of the chapter's material. Evaluate your answers to determine which sections you need to further review.

Practice Test A

1. Which of the following influences personal sexual excitement and arousal?
   a. alcohol and drugs
   b. sociocultural background
   c. body smells called pheromones
   d. specific mechanisms in the male and female brain
   p. 168

2. The body returns to pre-arousal during which phase of the sexual response cycle?
   a. excitement
   b. plateau
   c. orgasm
   d. resolution
   p. 171

3. Elderly people have a tendency to
   a. hate sex.
   b. have sex only slightly less frequently.
   c. not change at all in terms of sexuality.
   d. explore new sexual acts.
   p. 174

4. Sexual scripts have been found to result in females
   a. being more aggressive in sexual relationships.
   b. having more sex than ever before.
   c. having to rationalize their sexual behavior.
   d. becoming more equal with males in their relationships.
   p. 174

5. The sexual relationships and sexual response patterns experienced by homosexuals are
   a. perverse.
   b. abnormal, but not a mental illness.
   c. more similar than different from heterosexuals.
   d. similar to an antisocial life style.
   p. 175

6. The sexual dysfunction characterized by being unable to maintain sexual activity for very long because the male climaxes too quickly is referred to as
   a. rapid orgasm.
   b. inhibited sexual desire.
   c. male-inhibited orgasm.
   d. erectile failure.
   p. 179

7. Which of the following is true of incest?
   a. The closer the ages of the persons involved the more problematic.
   b. The greater the age disparity of the persons involved the more problematic.
   c. It is taboo only in Western cultures.
   d. It has become less taboo as double standards have diminished.
   p. 180

8. Lew cannot satisfy himself sexually without first placing clothespins on his genitals in a sexual ritual. Lew probably has which paraphilia?
   a. sadism
   b. fetishism
   c. masochism
   d. inhibited male orgasm
   p. 180

9. Which of the following would most likely say, "I have always thought I was a man even though I was born a girl. Now I just want my body to match my feelings."
   a. a homosexual woman
   b. a bisexual woman
   c. a person with gender roles at odds with their anatomical features
   d. a person with a gender identity at odds with their anatomical features
   p. 181

10. Victims of sexual violence are very likely to experience
   a. a strengthening in their current relationships.
   b. a sense of empowerment.
   c. thoughts of suicide.
   d. emotional inhibitions.
   p. 182

11. Situations where men and women experience a differential in power and the possibility for domination often lead to
   a. reverse discrimination.
   b. rape.
   c. sexual harassment.
   d. acts of perversion.
   p. 182

12. According to feminist theorists, which of the following is not one of the problems with pornography?
   a. It demeans women.
   b. It perpetuates cultural rape myths.
   c. It glorifies violence against women.
   d. It causes men to have rape fantasies they act out.
   p. 183

13. Sexually active college students are most likely to contract which sexually transmitted disease?
   a. syphilis
   b. chlamydia
   c. gonorrhea
   d. herpes genitalis
   p. 184

14. Most people get their knowledge about sex from
   a. their doctor.
   b. their parents.
   c. the schools.
   d. their friends and personal experiences.
   p. 186

15. Which of the following is most true about contraceptive use?
   a. Young people are well informed about contraception.
   b. Older adults are well informed about contraception.
   c. It is most likely that a first sexual experience will not involve contraception.
   d. It is difficult to become pregnant, even without using contraception.
   p. 187

Practice Test B

1. Which of the following is true of sexual fantasies?
   a. They are an unhealthy way of fulfilling desires.
   b. They can cause sexually violent behavior.
   c. Actions can be rehearsed through them.
   d. They can lead to deviant behavior.
   p. 169

2. The sexual response cycle consisted of which two bodily processes?
   a. engorgement of blood vessels, tightening of the skin
   b. surges of hormones, muscle tension
   c. surges of hormones, tightening of the skin
   d. engorgement of blood vessels, muscle tension
   p. 171

3. Sexual energy begins to mount and then becomes increasingly more intense during which phase of the sexual response cycle?
   a. excitement
   b. plateau
   c. orgasm
   d. resolution
   p. 171

4. Sexual double standards are harmful to men because they
   a. allow women more behavioral options.
   b. restrict their behavior in several new situations.
   c. place pressure on men to be sexually active.
   d. place the responsibility for birth control on men.
   p. 172

5. Homosexuals have been even more discriminated against in recent years because of
   a. a changing social climate.
   b. a lack of tolerance.
   c. AIDS.
   d. all of the above.
   p. 175

6. Which of the following is a sexual dysfunction?
   a. abnormal female orgasm
   b. homosexuality
   c. rapid orgasm
   d. false male orgasm
   p. 179

7. Incest occurs when
   a. a step-father touches his step-son in a sexual way.
   b. a brother and step-sister fondle each other.
   c. a father has sexual intercourse with his daughter.
   d. all of the above.
   p. 180

8. Most children who are sexually abused grow up to
   a. have sexual and relationship problems.
   b. abuse children themselves.
   c. have problems that are incurable.
   d. accept their abuse and forgive the abuser.
   p. 180

9. When a person has an overwhelming desire to become a member of the opposite sex, they are suffering from
   a. homosexuality.
   b. transsexualism.
   c. bisexuality.
   d. sexual dimorphism.
   p. 181

10. Reporting rape can have which effect on a rape victim?
    a. increasing the "victim role"
    b. empowering the victim
    c. increasing a sense of helplessness
    d. reducing self-esteem through humiliation
    p. 181

11. Sexual harassment is the result of
    a. male-female differences in gender roles.
    b. differential power and domination of one person over another.
    c. women getting into career "fast tracks."
    d. the threat of unemployment among men.
    p. 182

12. Studies suggest watching pornographic films that contain no acts of violence against women result in
    a. aggressive behavior toward women.
    b. aggressive behavior toward men as well as women.
    c. no changes in aggressive behavior.
    d. an increase in tendencies to rape.
    p. 183

13. Which of the following sexually transmitted diseases is not caused by a virus?
    a. AIDS
    b. chlamydia
    c. herpes genitalis
    d. none of the above
    p. 184

14. In the United States, sex education is
    a. widely available to young adults.
    b. highly controversial.
    c. the best in the world.
    d. not acceptable to most parents.
    p. 186

15. Which of the following is true about contraceptive use?
    a. Most young people rely on the pill.
    b. Most older adults use condoms.
    c. About 90% of women would become pregnant without contraception.
    d. All of the above.
    p. 188

Key for Practice Test A

1. Answer b; Cultural attitudes and social expectations play a key role in personal perceptions and expectations regarding sexual arousal; page 168; Learning Objective 1

2. Answer d; Resolution is when the changes that occurred in the sexual response cycle, namely in terms of blood pressure and muscle tension become resolved and return to normal levels; page 171; Learning Objective 2

3. Answer b; Just as most bodily functions slow down during aging, so too does sexual functioning and response; page 174; Learning Objective 3

4. Answer c; Sexual scripts dictate that females be uninterested in sexual exploration, and therefore must rationalize their sexual feelings; page 174; Learning Objective 3

5. Answer c; Human sexual relations are more alike than different regardless of the combination of sexes involved; page 175; Learning Objective 4

6. Answer a; Rapid orgasm in the male used to be called premature ejaculation; page 179; Learning Objective 5

7. Answer b; Incestuous contact between an adult and a child is more psychologically harmful than sex play between two same-age children; page 180; Learning Objective 6

8. Answer b; Fetishes involve ritualistic involvement of inanimate objects as a part of sexual activity; page 180; Learning Objective 7

9. Answer d; When a person feels that their self-concept as a man or woman (gender identity) does not match their biological sex, their difficulty has been labeled transsexualism; page 181; Learning Objective 8

10. Answer c; Rape and other acts of sexual violence leave victims with several serious psychological difficulties that persist for long periods of time and may include thoughts of suicide as well as suicide attempts; page 182; Learning Objective 9

11. Answer c; Sexual harassment results from situations which allow power plays and domination; page 182; Learning Objective 10

12. Answer d; Feminist theories claim that pornography may promote attitudes that foster rape, but do not state that fantasies are the cause of rape; page 183; Learning Objective 11

13. Answer b; Chlamydia is the most frequently occurring sexually transmitted disease on college campuses; page 184; Learning Objective 12

14. Answer d; Western society has not yet instituted means for ongoing and open sex education, leaving more informal channels responsible for education about sexual matters; page 186; Learning Objective 13

15. Answer c; First sexual experiences rarely involve contraception and therefore run a very high risk for unwanted pregnancy; page 187; Learning Objective 14

1. Answer c; Fantasies provide a private, normal, healthy outlet for sexual energy; page 169; Learning Objective 1

2. Answer d; Sexual response consists of changes in blood flow and muscle tension. These changes occur throughout the whole body as well as the genital regions; page 171; Learning Objective 2

3. Answer a; Excitement is the first phase of the sexual response cycle and results in increased sexual arousal; page 171; Learning Objective 2

4. Answer c; Sexual double standards set up expectations that men will be aggressive and women passive in sexual encounters, a damaging and limiting situation for both sexes; page 172; Learning Objective 3

5. Answer d; Prejudice against homosexuals continues to increase while other groups gain more civil liberties. Social intolerance and irrational fears associated with AIDS have contributed to recent increases in discrimination against homosexuals; page 175; Learning Objective 4

6. Answer c; Rapid orgasm occurs in men and women when the experience of orgasm occurs too soon after sexual contact is initiated for sexual gratification, and it is a recurrent problem; page 179; Learning Objective 5

7. Answer d; Incest occurs when family members have sexual contact with each other; page 180; Learning Objective 6

8. Answer a; Child sexual abuse leaves many psychological wounds, with some of the most profound being in the areas of interpersonal trust and sexual relationships; page 180; Learning Objective 7

9. Answer b; Transsexualism is when one's gender identity is not consistent with their biological sex; page 181; Learning Objective 8

10. Answer b; Victims can increase their sense of control and regain power over their situation by reporting the rape to the police; page 181; Learning Objective 9

11. Answer b; Sexual harassment occurs when a person in a position of power takes advantage of a person in less power; page 182; Learning Objective 10

12. Answer c; It is the combination of sex and violence that research has shown to have negative effects; page 183; Learning Objective 11

13. Answer b; Herpes genitalis is caused by herpes simplex virus II, and AIDS is caused by human immunodeficiency virus; page 148; Learning Objective 12

14. Answer b; Sex education in the U.S. is apparently needed, but many people feel, without any evidence, that education will promote promiscuous behavior; page 186; Learning Objective 13

15. Answer d; Contraceptive use varies at different ages and without the use of contraception most women will become pregnant; page 188; Learning Objective 14

Chapter Outline

I. Attitudes and Persuasion
   A. Attitudes and Behavior
     1. Attitudes do not always agree with one's behavior.
     2. LaPiere's 1934 study showed more prejudicial attitudes toward the Chinese than prejudicial behaviors toward a Chinese couple.
     3. It may be harder to behaviorally carry out an attitude than to state an attitude.
     4. Changes in behavior precede changes in attitude.
     5. One explanation is that individuals have a strong need for cognitive consistency and a second view is that observing one's own behavior clarifies one's attitudes.
     6. Festinger's cognitive dissonance refers to an individual's motivation toward consistency and away from inconsistency, or justifying one's actions to experience less discrepancy.
     7. Consistent with cognitive dissonance, George Kelly suggested that "no person need be a victim of his own autobiography" and one should reinterpret one's past to reinforce one's behavioral changes.
     8. Bem's self-perception theory emphasizes that individuals make inferences about their attitudes by perceiving their behavior.
   B. Persuasion and Attitude Change
     1. The four key components of persuasion are the source, the communication, the channel, and the target.
     2. The source is more effective if the communicator is an expert, competent, and trustworthy, and if the communicator has power, attractiveness, likability, and similarity.
     3. Negative messages appeal to our emotions, while positive messages appeal to our rational, logical thinking.
     4. With all other aspects being equal, the more frightened we are the more we will change our attitude.
     5. Because it presents live images, television is considered the most powerful medium for changing attitudes.
     6. Younger people are more likely to change their attitudes than older ones, and females are more susceptible to persuasion than males.
     7. The foot-in-the-door technique involves asking another person to initially agree to a small request, and this is followed by a larger request.
     8. The door-in-the-face technique starts with an initial major request that is typically turned down and then the person is asked to comply with a smaller request.
II. Social Perception and Attribution
   A. Social Perception
     1. Social perception is our judgment about the qualities of individuals.
     2. Impressions of others are cognitively organized to be unified and integrated.

3. The primacy effect refers to the enduring quality and importance of initial impressions.
4. Social comparison is the process by which individuals evaluate their thoughts, feelings, behaviors, and abilities in relation to other people.
5. People prefer to compare themselves with others who are similar than with those who are dissimilar.
6. Impression management is the process in which individuals strive to present themselves in a favorable light.
7. Impression management strategies include using behavioral matching, conforming to situational norms, showing appreciation of others and flattering them, and using positive nonverbal cues.
8. Self-monitoring describes individuals' awareness of the impressions they make on others and the degree to which they fine-tune their performances accordingly.
9. High self-monitoring individuals seek information about appropriate ways to present themselves and invest considerable time in trying to "read" and understand others.

B. Attribution
1. Attribution theory states that individuals are motivated to discover the underlying causes of behavior as part of their interest in making sense out of the behavior.
2. We can attribute behaviors to internal or external causes.
3. In general, males attribute successes to internal causes and failures to external causes and females are more likely to attribute successes to external causes and failures to internal causes.
4. The fundamental attribute error states that observers overestimate the importance of traits and underestimate the importance of situations when they explain another person's behavior.

III. Conformity
A. Conforming in a Variety of Circumstances
1. Conformity occurs when individuals adopt the attitudes or behavior of others because of real or imagined pressure from others.
2. Asch's classic experiment on conformity found that subjects conformed 35 percent of the time in a simple perceptual judgment situation.
3. Zimbardo did a study showing how subjects conformed to the roles of prisoners and guards.

B. Obedience
1. Obedience is behavior that complies with the explicit demands of the individual in authority.
2. Milgram did a classic study in obedience in which a "teacher" supposedly gave shocks to a "learner" and results indicated that about two-thirds of subjects obeyed and delivered 450 volts.
3. Psychologists debate the ethical nature of Milgram's obedience experiment.

C. Resisting Social Influence
1. Individuals may try to control us, but we can exert personal control over our actions and influence others in turn.
2. Responses to a request from an authority include compliance, pretending to comply, public dissent but still following directives, open disregard and refusal to comply, challenging authority, and intervention from higher authorities or an organized group of people.

IV. Group Relations
   A. Motivation for Group Behavior and the Structure of Groups
      1. Groups satisfy personal needs, reward us, provide information, raise self-esteem, and give an identity.
      2. Norms are rules that apply to all members of a group.
      3. Roles are rules and expectations that govern certain positions in the group, and roles define how people should behave in a particular position in the group.
   B. Deindividuation
      1. Deindividuation is the loss of identity as an individual and the development of group identity in group situations that promote arousal and anonymity.
      2. In 1895, LeBon observed how groups can foster uninhibited behavior, including mob behavior.
      3. Anonymity may be an important aspect promoting deindividuation.
   C. Groupthink
      1. Groupthink is the motivation of group members to maintain harmony and unanimity in decision making, suffocating differences of opinion in the process.
      2. Groupthink can result in disastrous decisions, as in the Bay of Pigs incidence, the Watergate cover-up, and the escalation of the Vietnam War.
      3. Leaders can avoid groupthink by encouraging dissident opinions.
   D. Leadership
      1. The great person theory says that individuals have certain traits that are best suited for leadership positions.
      2. Those with leadership qualities are considered to be assertive, cooperative, decisive, dominant, energetic, self-confident, tolerant of stress, willing to assume responsibility, diplomatic and tactful, and persuasive.
      3. The situational view of leadership argues that the needs of the group change from time to time influencing who will be a leader.
   E. Majority-Minority Influence
      1. The majority exerts both normative and informational pressure on the group and usually determines decision making.
      2. Consistent minority views have a greater effect than if less consistent.
V. Prejudice, Ethnocentrism, and Conflict
   A. Prejudice
      1. Prejudice is an unjustified negative attitude toward an individual based on the individual's membership in a group.
      2. Prejudice can be based on any detectable difference, such as race, sex, sexual orientation, age, religion, or nationality.
      3. A stereotype is a generalization about a group's characteristics, which does not take into account any variation from one individual to the next.
   B. Ethnocentrism
      1. Ethnocentrism is the tendency to favor one's own group over other groups.
      2. The positive side of ethnocentrism is the fostering of a sense of pride.
      3. Two forms of racism are aversive racism and symbolic racism.

C. Conflict
   1. Tajfel's social identity theory states that when individuals are assigned to a group they invariably think of the group as an in-group for them.
   2. This process occurs because individuals want to have a positive self-image, but also helps to explain prejudice and conflict between groups.
   3. Just being assigned to a group creates a "we" and "they."

Learning Objectives

After reading and studying this chapter, students should be able to:

1. Identify the relationships between attitude and behavior.
2. Understand the processes of persuasion and attitude change.
3. Know the mechanisms of social perception.
4. Understand theories of attribution.
5. Describe the process of conformity.
6. Understand obedience and the role it plays in behavior.
7. Identify how persons can resist the influence of social forces.
8. Understand how behavior is influenced by groups.
9. Describe deindividuation.
10. Explain what groupthink is and how it can be avoided.
11. Identify and describe qualities of leadership.
12. Understand the influence of majority and minority.
13. Understand how prejudice, ethnocentrism, and conflict occur.

Guided Review

After you have read the chapter one time, search through the chapter to find the appropriate words to complete these statements. Material is covered in the same order as the chapter.

1. _____ are beliefs and opinions that can predispose individuals to behave in certain ways.
2. More than fifty years ago, _____ toured the United States with a _____ couple and found little prejudicial _____ toward the couple, while responses to written inquiries indicated _____ prejudicial positions indicating that what we say and what we can be _____.
3. Ample evidence exists that changes in behavior _____ changes in attitude.
4. Developed by _____, _____ _____ is a concept that refers to an individual's motivation toward consistency and away from _____.
5. Cognitive dissonance is about trying to _____ tension by cognitively _____ things that are unpleasant.
6. Therapist _____ proposed that "no person need be a victim of his own _____," suggesting that _____ your past and viewing it in a new way is a good way to reinforce _____ _____ you have made.

162

7. Bem believes that cognitive dissonance relies too heavily on _____ factors, which are difficult to measure.

8. _____-_____ theory is Bem's theory of the _____-_____ connection, and it emphasizes that individuals make inferences about their attitudes by perceiving their _____.

9. "I hate my job. I need to develop a better attitude toward it, or I could quit and be a beach bum" reflects _____ _____ theory, while "I am spending all of my time thinking about how much I hate my job. I really must not like it" reflects _____-_____ theory.

10. Social psychologists believe that the four key components of _____ are: who conveys the message (the _____), what the message is (the _____), what medium is used (the _____), and for whom the message is intended (the _____).

11. One factor involved in believing a source is _____, which depends on qualifications, and another factor is _____, which is whether the source is viewed as honest.

12. Four important characteristics that add to a communicator's ability to change people's attitudes are _____, _____, _____, and _____.

13. _____ is an important characteristic for the communicator because it is associated with the ability to impose _____ or control _____ and _____.

14. _____ is widely used in advertising, and researchers have shown that people are more likely to buy products that are advertised by persons of their own _____.

15. In addition to similarity, products can be promoted by appealing to our _____ _____.

16. An additional influential communicator factor is the _____ of the communicator.

17. Researchers have found that _____ voters discriminate against female candidates, seeing them as less qualified.

18. Attractiveness was less consistently an asset for _____ political candidates than for the other sex.

19. Negative strategies appeal to our _____, while positive approaches appeal to our _____ _____.

20. In addition, with all other aspects being equal, the more frightened we are the _____ we will change our attitude.

21. _____ appeals can be positive as well as negative, such as how music is used in advertising messages.

22. _____ is considered the most powerful medium for changing attitudes.

23. Younger people are _____ likely to change their attitudes than older people, and females are _____ likely to change their attitudes than males.

24. Another factor is the _____ of the audience's attitude.

25. The _____-_____-_____-_____ technique involves asking another person to initially agree to a small request and later getting compliance with a _____ request.

26. The _____-_____-_____-_____ technique begins with a major request that will likely be _____ _____ and later asking the person to comply with a _____ request.

27. One way to resist foot-in-the-door technique and the door-in-the-face technique is to build up your _____ and to realize that such requests often play on your vulnerability.

163

28. _____ _____ is our judgment about the qualities of individuals, which involves how we form _____ of others, how we gain _____-_____ from our perception of others, and how we present ourselves to others to _____ their perceptions of us.

29. As we form impressions of others, we cognitively organize the information so that the impressions are _____ and _____.

30. The _____ _____ refers to the enduring quality and importance of initial impressions.

31. We gain self-knowledge by observing others through _____ _____.

32. According to _____, who proposed the theory of social comparison, people prefer to compare themselves with others who are _____.

33. _____ _____ is the process in which individuals strive to present themselves in a favorable light.

34. Four "impression management" strategies are using _____ matching, _____ to situational _____, showing _____ to others and _____ them, and using _____ _____ cues.

35. _____-_____ is a term that describes individuals' awareness of the impressions they make on others and the degree to which they fine-tune their performance accordingly.

36. _____ self-monitoring individuals seek information about appropriate ways to present themselves and invest considerable time in trying to "read" and understand others.

37. _____ _____ states that individuals are motivated to discover the underlying _____ of behavior as part of their interest in making sense out of behavior.

38. Causes of behavior can be _____, such as traits or motive, or _____, such as situational factors.

39. Attributing a low test score to difficult test items is an _____ attribution, while saying it was due to studying too little is an _____ attribution.

40. In general, males attribute success to _____ causes and females attribute success to _____ causes, but men attribute failures to _____ causes and women attribute failure to _____ causes.

41. We often attribute our own behavior to _____ causes and other people's behavior to _____ causes.

42. The _____ _____ _____ is that an observer overattributes internal causes and underattributes causes in another's behavior.

43. _____ occurs when individuals adopt the attitudes or behavior of others because of real or imagined _____ from others.

44. _____ conducted the classic experiment on conformity and found that participants conformed to _____ answers about 35 percent of the time.

45. In another study, _____ found that college student volunteers quickly conformed to the roles of _____ and _____ in a mock prison.

46. _____ is behavior that complies with the explicit demands of the individual in _____.

47. _____ predicted that few subjects would deliver 450 volts in _____'s obedience to authority experience, but a _____ did.

48. Because the subjects in Milgram's obedience to authority experience felt anguish and were very disturbed about "harming" another individual, some psychologists question whether the study was _____, but Milgram felt that _____ the subjects about the _____ was adequate and that the results revealed a lot about human nature.

49. An important current ethical guideline of the _____ _____ _____ is that researchers obtain _____ _____ from their volunteers.

50. _____ are rules that apply to all members of a group.

51. _____ are rules and expectations that govern certain _____ in the group and define how people should behave in a particular position.

52. _____ is the loss of identity as an individual and the development of _____ _____ in group situations that promote _____ and _____.

53. _____ is the motivation of group members to maintain harmony and _____ in decision making, suffocating differences of opinion in the process.

54. The _____ _____ _____ says that individuals have certain traits that are best suited for leadership positions, however, the _____ view of leadership argues that the needs of a group change from time to time.

55. The majority exerts both _____ and _____ pressure on the group.

56. The minority cannot win through _____ pressure but it can use _____ pressure, and the majority is most likely to listen when the minority is _____ and _____.

57. _____ is an unjustified _____ attitude toward an individual based on the individual's membership in a group.

58. A(n) _____ is a generalization about a group's characteristics, which does not take into account any variation from one individual to the next.

59. _____ is the tendency to favor one's own group over other groups.

60. _____ proposed the _____ _____ theory which states that when individuals are assigned to a group they invariably think of the group as a(n) _____-_____.

61. The conflict White Americans experience between their genuinely _____ values and their own _____ feelings toward Black Americans is called _____ racism.

62. The attitude that Black Americans are pushing too hard, too fast for equality, and making unfair demands is an example of _____ racism.

Guided Review Answers

1. Attitudes; 2. LaPiere, Chinese, behavior, strong, different; 3. precede; 4. Festinger, cognitive dissonance, inconsistency; 5. reduce, justifying; 6. Kelly, autobiography, reinterpreting, behavioral changes; 7. internal; 8. Self-perception, attitude-behavior, behavior; 9. cognitive dissonance, self-perception; 10. persuasion, source, communication, channel, target; 11. expertise, trustworthiness; 12. power, attractiveness, likableness, similarity; 13. Power, sanctions, rewards, punishments; 14. Similarity, ethnicity; 15. personal ideals; 16. sex; 17. male; 18. female; 19. emotions, logical thinking; 20. more; 21. Emotional; 22. Television; 23. more, more; 24. strength; 25. foot-in-the-door, larger; 26. door-in-the-face, turned down, smaller; 27. assertiveness; 28. Social perception, impressions, self-knowledge, influence; 29. unified, integrated; 30. primary effect; 31. social comparison; 32. Festinger, similar; 33. Impression formation; 34. behavioral, conforming, norms, appreciation, flattering, positive nonverbal; 35. Self-monitoring; 36. High; 37. Attribution theory, causes; 38. internal, external; 39. external, internal; 40. internal, external, external,

internal; 41. external, internal; 42. fundamental attribution error; 43. Conformity, pressure; 44. Asch, incorrect; 45. Zimbardo, prisoners, guards; 46. Obedience, authority; 47. Psychiatrists, Milgram, majority; 48. ethical, debriefing, deception; 49. American Psychological Association, informed consent; 50. Norms; 51. Roles, positions; 52. Deindividuation, group identity, arousal, anonymity; 53. Groupthink, unanimity; 54. great person theory, situational; 55. normative, informational; 56. normative, informational, consistent, confident; 57. Prejudice, negative; 58. stereotype; 59. Ethnocentrism; 60. Tajfel, social identity, in-group; 61. egalitarian, negative, aversive; 62. symbolic

Key Terms

For each term, briefly define the term in your own words and provide an example or situation (especially one you can visualize) that will help you retain the meaning of the concept. Key terms are presented in the order they are presented in the chapter.

1. attitudes (p. 199)

2. cognitive dissonance (p. 199)

3. self-perception theory (p. 200)

4. foot-in-the-door technique (p. 203)

5. door-in-the-face technique (p. 203)

6. social perception (p. 204)

7. primacy effect (p. 204)

8. social comparison (p. 204)

9. impression management (p. 205)

10. self-monitoring (p. 205)

11. attribution theory (p. 206)

12. fundamental attribution error (p. 206)

13. conformity (p. 208)

14. obedience (p. 209)

15. norms (p. 211)

16. roles (p. 211)

17. deindividuation (p. 211)

18. groupthink (p. 212)

19. great person theory (p. 212)

20. prejudice (p. 213)

21. stereotypes (p. 213)

22. ethnocentrism (p. 213)

23. social identity theory (p. 214)

Study Aids

Students who do well on tests develop mnemonic aids to help them remember important terms and concepts. A few are suggested here, and you are encouraged to develop your own additional aids.

Behavior and Attitude. Sometimes figures are more useful than long descriptions in being able to remember important concepts. Figure 8.1 is useful in distinguishing between cognitive dissonance theory and self-perception theory. In addition, remember just key words instead of memorizing long definitions to understand new concepts. For example:

COGNITIVE DISSONANCE THEORY
justification   reduce tension   internal consistency

SELF-PERCEPTION THEORY
make inferences   observe one's behavior

Key Components of Persuasion. Remember "Silly Chipmunks Can Talk" and use the first letter of each word to help you recall the four components of persuasion: Source, Communicator, Channel, and Target.

Attribution for Self and Others. Remember that in making attributions about the *self* we overemphasize *situational* factors, both of which begin with *S*. Then remember that the *opposite* (i.e., trait) factors are overestimated with *others* (both start with *O*).

Understanding Concepts

Answer these questions to develop your understanding of the important ideas in this chapter.

1. Summarize the relationship between attitudes and behaviors.

2. Distinguish between cognitive dissonance theory and self-perception theory.

3. People can change their views and opinions simply by discussing issues with others. What aspects of a conversation can bring about such changes? How can a conversation affect the opinions and attitudes of others?

4. What characteristics of the source affects persuasiveness?

5. Compare and contrast the foot-in-the-door technique and the door-in-the-face technique.

6. Describe how we develop impressions of others.

7. Why do most individuals do social comparison with similar others? Do you think one's sense of confidence might affect this tendency?

8. What are useful strategies for impression management?

9. Summarize the differences in attributing causes for our own behavior and for the behavior of others. Be sure to explain the fundamental attribution error.

10. Distinguish between compliance due to conformity and compliance due to obedience.

11. What role does conformity play in groupthink and deindividuation?

12. Explain the majority's and the minority's influence on normative and informational pressure on the group.

13. What is the relationship between prejudice and stereotypes?

14. Use social identity theory to explain ethnocentrism.

Applying Concepts

Answer these questions to develop your ability to apply this chapter's material to your life and the world. Your own responses may differ from other students' in the class, and it is helpful to share your ideas with the other students.

1. Do you agree with John Locke's statement that "The actions of men are the best interpreters of their thoughts"? How does Locke's statement fit with cognitive dissonance theory and self-perception theory?

2. Provide examples of cognitive dissonance theory and self-perception theory from your own experiences this semester.

3. Kelly was one therapist who used ideas consistent with cognitive dissonance in his counseling practice. How might counselors use this theory in helping clients? For example, would it be a useful approach with a client who wants to quit smoking?

4. Based on what the chapter says about persuasion, list ten things that you would consider doing if you were running a campaign for a political candidate. Explain your choices.

5. According to Sociocultural Worlds 8.1, male voters discriminate against female candidates while female voters tend to vote evenly between male and female candidates. Why do you think this pattern exists? Do you think it will be changing? What could be done to help bring about changes?

6. You are in charge of getting volunteers for your organization's annual bazaar. How might you use the foot-in-the-door technique and the door-in-the-face technique to get volunteers? Give a specific example for each technique.

7. Why should someone who writes reference letters be aware of the primacy effect? How could a person increase or decrease the chances for someone to get accepted at a college or a job? How does the primacy effect influence our dating behaviors?

8. How might social comparison theory be useful to a counselor working with a youngster with low self-confidence when this youngster has a sibling who gets excellent grades and another who is excellent in sports?

9. Take and evaluate Self-Assessment 8.1 on self-monitoring and evaluate your style. If a person's natural tendency is to self-monitor a lot, changing his or her behavior to fit particular situations, can this person be considered genuine and honest?

10. What is the impact of the female-male differences in attributions concerning successes and failures? Is this difference consistent with socialization of females and males?

11. Discuss the role of conformity with peers among adolescents. What are its positive and negative aspects?

12. Are there some people who would be more likely to give the maximum levels of shock in Milgram's studies? Do some people naturally tend to be more aggressive than others, despite specific situations?

13. How can deindividuation and groupthink influence political movements and political decisions? What could be done to reduce their effects?

14. Explore your stereotypes of faculty and students based on group characteristics such as age, gender, and ethnicity. What stereotypical impressions of students do you make based on their college major? How useful are these stereotypes?

15. Using Critical Thinking about Adjustment, evaluate how television advertisements affect your attitudes and behaviors. Summarize your conclusions here.

Chapter Practice Tests

Answer these multiple-choice test questions to help you assess your understanding of the chapter's material. Evaluate your answers to determine which sections you need to further review.

Practice Test A

1. How a person says they feel and what they do
   a. is always consistent.
   b. often differs.
   c. are controlled by different areas of the brain.
   d. none of the above.
   p. 199

2. When people have established themselves to know a great deal about a subject they may be considered to have
   a. expertise.
   b. credibility.
   c. trustworthiness.
   d. all of the above.
   p. 200

3. Negative political campaign ads appeal to voters'
   a. rational thinking.
   b. emotions.
   c. trustworthiness.
   d. cognitive dissonance.
   p. 201

4. How people form judgments about others and how these judgments are related to race relations is studied by which area of research?
   a. social persuasion theories
   b. social perception
   c. attribution theories
   d. groupthink
   p. 204

5. Accurate self-perceptions are most likely to develop when we
   a. compare ourselves to others who are very different.
   b. compare ourselves to others who are very similar.
   c. do not compare ourselves to others.
   d. solicit comments from others about ourselves.
   p. 204

6. Sally claims that she won the contest because she is so lucky. If Josh won, he would more likely attribute his success to
   a. luck.
   b. skill.
   c. chance.
   d. the person who taught him to play.
   p. 206

7. Stan just joined a group of people who all agreed on a solution to the problem. It is more likely that Stan will agree with the group
   a. unless there is evidence to the contrary.
   b. even when there is evidence to the contrary.
   c. when they have friends in the group.
   d. unless they have friends in the group.
   p. 208

8. Behavior that complies with the explicit demands of authority is referred to as
   a. conformity.
   b. groupthink.
   c. obedience.
   d. deindividuation.
   p. 208

9. Keith was told by his boss to turn in his co-workers if he saw them stealing. Keith chose to resist the social pressure exerted by his boss but was not sure how to do so. The text may advise him to
   a. begin stealing himself.
   b. turn in the names of other students who did not cheat.
   c. turn himself in as cheating.
   d. none of the above.
   p. 208

10. Ken has adopted the standards that have been set for all persons in his community. One could say that he has adopted the community
    a. roles.
    b. norms.
    c. rules.
    d. none of the above.
    p. 208

11. The process by which persons lose their own identity when in a group that takes on an identity of its own is called
    a. groupthink.
    b. conformity.
    c. normative drift.
    d. deindividuation.
    p. 211

12. Groupthink can happen when
    a. a leader is highly authoritative.
    b. people conform to the opinion of others.
    c. people do not give differing opinions.
    d. there are rewards for conformity.
    p. 212

13. The great person theory states that
    a. leaders can only lead the weak.
    b. only people who possess specific traits can be leaders.
    c. members of the majority can lead only after a popular vote.
    d. leadership is genetic.
    p. 212

14. Members of a minority can win in a democracy by
    a. overturning the power at the top.
    b. abandoning their ideals.
    c. being consistent about expressing their opinions.
    d. failing to conform with majority decisions.
    p. 212

15. The tendency to favor one's own group over other groups is called
    a. discrimination.
    b. racism.
    c. groupthink.
    d. ethnocentrism.
    p. 213

Practice Test B

1. When people do something that does not match their attitudes, they are most likely to
    a. justify their attitudes.
    b. force themselves to change their attitudes.
    c. justify their behavior.
    d. place a greater emphasis on their past and future behavior.
    p. 199

2. Lenny views himself as a popular person at work because he has gone to every volunteer meeting held. His interpretation is based on which theory?
    a. attribution theory
    b. cognitive dissonance
    c. self-perception theory
    d. great person theory.
    p. 200

3. Which of the following is true about television as medium for persuasion?
    a. Television is not as powerful as any other media.
    b. Experts disagree about how powerful television is.
    c. Anything can be persuaded if presented on television.
    d. Television can only target certain people.
    p. 203

4. For a television message to be successful, it is important that the
    a. source be identified with by the audience.
    b. source be an expert.
    c. source sends an honest message.
    d. message be succinct.
    p. 203

5. A student who wishes to make a positive impression on a professor, bringing the textbook to class and asking lots of questions during lectures, is most likely
    a. conforming to situation norms.
    b. showing appreciation of others.
    c. using positive nonverbal cues.
    d. using behavioral matching.
    p. 205

6. Attributions about behavior serve the function of
    a. establishing a balance between attitudes and behavior.
    b. finding the causes of behavior.
    c. making people feel better about themselves.
    d. persuading others that behavior is appropriate.
    p. 206

7. Brutality can occur
    a. only with brutal people.
    b. when there is good reason.
    c. under circumstances that demand conformity.
    d. in most any prison.
    p. 209

8. The fact that so many people administered shock in the Milgram studies illustrates that
    a. people can be driven to madness.
    b. people are all Nazis.
    c. ordinary people can become Nazilike.
    d. World War II was based on false information.
    p. 209

9. Challenging and confronting authority figures is referred to as
    a. antisocial behavior.
    b. resisting authority.
    c. unreasoned action.
    d. all of the above.
    p. 210

10. Standards set for all members of a group are called
    a. procedures.
    b. roles.
    c. norms.
    d. policies.
    p. 211

11. A military school that demands the identity of the group far supersedes that of the individual is directly related to the process of
    a. normative drift.
    b. conformity.
    c. deindividuation.
    d. groupthink.
    p. 211

12. A corporation where the Chair of the Board surrounds herself with yes persons is very suspectable to
    a. deindividuation.
    b. conformity.
    c. normative drift.
    d. groupthink.
    p. 212

13. The great person theory states that
    a. most people can be a great leader if they think they can.
    b. there are specific traits related to leadership.
    c. only the few can lead.
    d. that people want to be led if there is a certain person to lead.
    p. 212

14. For the most part majority rules, but the minority can win by
    a. persistently making its point.
    b. joining the majority.
    c. subverting democracy.
    d. failing to conform with majority decisions.
    p. 212

15. Stereotypes include which of the following?
    a. broad generalizations
    b. focus on group characteristics
    c. mental images of persons
    d. all of the above.
    p. 213

Key for Practice Test A

1. Answer b; What people say and how they feel often does not match their behavior; page 199; Learning Objective 1

2. Answer a; Expertise is the result of a breadth of knowledge on a narrow subject; page 200; Learning Objective 2

3. Answer b; Negative ads draw out emotional reactions against opponents; page 201; Learning Objective 2

4. Answer b; Social perception is the area of social psychology that studies how persons view others and how these views affect behavior; page 204; Learning Objective 3

5. Answer b; Social comparison involving others similar to ourselves results in a more accurate self-perception; page 204; Learning Objective 3

6. Answer b; Males are more likely to make internal attributions for their successes; page 206; Learning Objective 4

7. Answer b; Social conformity research shows that people go along with a group despite evidence to the contrary; page 208; Learning Objective 5

8. Answer c; Obedience results in behavior that follows an authoritative rule; page 208; Learning Objective 6

9. Answer d; The text does not provide any direct advice for such a problem; page 208; Learning Objective 7

10. Answer b; Norms are the socially set expectations and standards for the behavior of community members; page 208; Learning Objective 8

11. Answer d; Deindividuation occurs when the identity of individuals is relinquished and replaced by a group identity; page 211; Learning Objective 9

12. Answer c; Groupthink occurs when there is complacent agreement among group members, in the absence of critical thinking; page 212; Learning Objective 10

13. Answer b; The great person theory holds that specific qualities form the basis of leadership and that only some people have this combination of traits; page 212; Learning Objective 11

14. Answer c; Opinions expressed consistently by a minority can have a strong influence on the behavior of the majority; page 212; Learning Objective 12

15. Answer d; Ethnocentrism is when a group member holds their own group in a more positive position than other groups without any sound basis; page 213; Learning Objective 13

Key for Practice Test B

1. Answer c; Behavior is justified to bring a match between behavior and beliefs; page 199; Learning Objective 1

2. Answer c; Self-perception theory states that we develop a view of ourselves through interpretations of our own behavior; page 200; Learning Objective 1

3. Answer b; The research has thus far not been conclusive on the exact means by which television is or is not persuasive; page 203; Learning Objective 2

4. Answer a; Identification with the message sender is the key to a successful persuasive message; page 203; Learning Objective 2

5. Answer a; The student's behavior matches the norms or expectations of the classroom situation; page 205; Learning Objective 3

6. Answer b; Attributions about behavior allow a person to perceive specific things to cause the occurrence of the behavior; page 206; Learning Objective 4

7. Answer c; Brutality is one of several aspects of conformity at its extreme; page 209; Learning Objective 5

8. Answer c; Conformity to authority occurs among most persons, not just among the weak or mentally imbalanced; page 209; Learning Objective 6

9. Answer b; Resisting authority results in non-conformity; page 210; Learning Objective 7

10. Answer c; Norms set a standard and expectations for group members; page 211; Learning Objective 8

11. Answer c; Deindividuation occurs when a person loses their own identity in place of a group identity; page 211; Learning Objective 9

12. Answer d; Groupthink occurs when group members do not challenge the status quo and do not offer conflicting solutions; page 212; Learning Objective 10

13. Answer b; The great person theory focuses on specific qualities of leadership and states that persons with such traits can be effective leaders; page 212; Learning Objective 11

14. Answer a; Minorities can win in a democracy by persistently pointing to weaknesses in the opposing views; page 212; Learning Objective 12

15. Answer d; Stereotypes involve a focus on groups rather than individuals, a mental image of group members that fit a mold, and broad sweeping generalizations across individuals; page 213; Learning Objective 13

Chapter 9 Interpersonal Communication

Chapter Outline

I. What Is Interpersonal Communication?
   A. Interpersonal Communication Involves Content and Relationship Dimensions
      1. Messages include a content dimension and a relationship dimension.
      2. Many communication problems occur because of relationship implications, especially power aspects of the relationship.
   B. The Components of Interpersonal Communication
      1. The message is the information being delivered from the sender to the receiver.
      2. Communication involves encoding, the act of producing messages, and decoding, the act of understanding messages.
      3. The noise dimension is environmental, physiological, and psychological factors that decrease the likelihood that a message will be expressed or understood accurately.
      4. Transactional means that communication is an ongoing process between sender and receiver that unfolds across time.
      5. Social communication always occurs in a context, the environment in which messages are sent and received.
      6. Interpersonal communication is a transactional process that is ongoing over time. This process involves a sender and a receiver, who often send and receive messages simultaneously. These messages are sent through verbal or nonverbal channels. As a message is conveyed, the receiver attempts to decode it, although noise can restrict the accuracy of a message.
II. Verbal Interpersonal Communication
   A. The Denotative and Connotative Meanings of Words and Messages
      1. Denotation is the word's and message's objective meaning.
      2. Connotation is the word's and message's subjective, emotional, or personal meaning.
      3. Words and messages with connotative meaning can be labeled on a good-bad scale.
      4. The more concrete our word choices and the messages we deliver the more people are likely to agree on their meaning; abstract words can deliver many connotative messages and communication becomes unclear.
   B. Speaking Skills
      1. Speaking is expressing thoughts and feelings in words and behavior with accuracy and clarity so that the other person (or people) understands what you mean.
      2. To communicate effectively speakers need to take into account the background characteristics, needs, and abilities of the listeners.
      3. Messages are more effectively conveyed when it is simple, concrete, and specific.
      4. Messages that are abstract, general, or complex are best accompanied by examples, especially ones that relate to the personal experiences of the listeners.
      5. Good speakers have consistent verbal and nonverbal messages.

179

C. Listening Skills
   1. The majority of communication activity is listening.
   2. About 60 percent of listening is to communication media and 40 percent is face-to-face listening.
   3. Hearing is a physiological sensory process in which auditory sensations are received by the ears and transmitted to the brain.
   4. Listening describes the psychological process of interpreting and understanding the significance of what someone says.
   5. Good listening may involve talking less than we usually do and listening more.
   6. Good listening means paying careful attention to the person who is talking.
   7. Reflective listening occurs when the listener restates the feelings and/or content of what the speaker has communicated and does so in a way that reveals understanding and acceptance.
   8. Paraphrasing is a concise response to the speaker that states the essence of the speaker's content in the listener's own words.
   9. A good reflective listener periodically pulls together a summative reflection of the main themes and feelings the speaker has expressed over a reasonably long conversation or even over several conversations.
   10. Good listening means giving feedback in a competent manner.
   11. Feedback involves sending a message back to the speaker regarding the listener's reaction to what is said or the effect the message has on the listener.
D. Self-Disclosure
   1. Self-disclosure is communication of intimate details about ourselves to someone else.
   2. The Johari Window is a model of self-disclosure with four basic quadrants: the open self, the blind self, the hidden self, and the unknown self.
   3. The open self is known to yourself and to others, the blind self is known to others but not yourself, the hidden self is known to yourself but not shared, and the unknown self is not known to yourself or to others.
   4. As relationships endure, more self-disclosure occurs, including self-disclosures involving psychological risk.
   5. Risky self-disclosures involves giving away power and being vulnerable, but also brings strength and protection by generating intimacy.
   6. Trust, privacy, a nonjudgmental ear, empathic understanding, and a common bond all increase the likelihood an individual will engage in self-disclosure.
E. Barriers to Effective Verbal Communication
   1. The specific barriers in interpersonal communication are judging, sending solutions, and avoiding the other's concerns.
   2. Judging is a barrier to effective communication that includes criticizing, name-calling, and labeling, and praising evaluatively.
   3. Sending solutions are ineffective communication patterns that can be transmitted caringly as advice, indirectly by questioning, authoritatively as an order, aggressively as a threat, or with a halo around it as moralizing.
   4. Moralizing often includes words like "should" and "ought," and moralizing often demoralizes by fostering anxiety, arousing resentment, and inviting pretense.

5. Avoiding the other's concerns is an ineffective communication technique that involves diverting or logical solutions, which are especially good at getting conversations derailed.

6. Arguments express oppositional views rather than open dialogue.

G. Gender Differences in Conversation

1. Tannen analyzed the talk of women and men and found that women do more rapport talk and men do more report talk.

2. Rapport talk is the language of conversation and a way of establishing connections and negotiating relationships, and it involves discussing similarities and matching experiences.

3. Report talk is public speaking and includes story telling, joking, or imparting information, and it serves as a way of getting and keeping attention.

4. For men, talk is for information; for women, talk is for interaction and a way to show caring and interest.

5. Women are more comfortable talking when they feel safe and close, among friends and equals, while men feel comfortable talking when there is a need to establish and maintain their status in a group.

III. Nonverbal Interpersonal Communication

A. What Is Nonverbal Communication?

1. Nonverbal communication refers to messages that are transmitted from one person to another by means other than linguistic.

2. Nonverbal communication includes body communication (gestures, facial expressions, eye communication, and touch), space communication, silence, and paralanguage (e.g., tone of a person's voice).

B. Characteristics of Nonverbal Communication

1. Nonverbal communication may occur in clusters or packages with other nonverbal behaviors.

2. Nonverbal behavior always communicates.

3. Nonverbal communication is influenced by sociocultural contexts, with cultures varying in how close they stand to another, amount of appropriate eye contact, and other aspects.

4. Black Americans and Hispanic Americans engage in less eye contact than White Americans; Hispanic Americans stand closer than White Americans; Asian American use quieter voices and smile differently than White Americans; and Native Americans speak softer and slower and avoid firm handshakes compared to White Americans. Understanding cultural meanings of nonverbal behavior improves communication between them.

5. There are also gender differences in nonverbal communication.

6. Nonverbal communication is often spontaneous and ambiguous.

7. Nonverbal behavior may be discrepant from verbal behavior.

C. Body Communication

1. A gesture is a motion of the limbs or body made to convey a message to someone else.

2. Facial expressions can communicate important messages.

3. Eye contact serves four functions: (1) monitoring feedback; (2) signaling a conversational turn; (3) signaling the nature of a relationship; and (4) compensating for physical distance.

4. Touch is among our first pleasant experiences, not only the rewarding feelings of touch from others, but our own touching of objects.

5. Among the functions of touch are sexual expression, consolation and support, and power and dominance.

6. Higher-status people are more often allowed to touch lower-status people than vice versa.
7. Generally, women touch more and are touched more than are men.
8. Touching patterns vary considerably from one culture to another.

    D. Space Communication
1. Proxemics, a term coined by Edward Hall, is the study of the communicative function of space, especially how people unconsciously structure their space.
2. The four space zones are intimate distance, personal distance, social distance, and public distance.
3. Territoriality is the possessive or ownershiplike reaction to an area of space or particular objects.

    E. Silence and Paralanguage
1. Silence can communicate via body posture, eyes, facial expressions, and gestures, and can indicate that one is thinking about what the other person is communicating.
2. Silences establish and maintain order between talking people.
3. Silences or lack of silences can change our sense of being allowed to say what we want or of being so rushed we can't get our points across.
4. Paralanguage refers to the nonlinguistic aspects of verbal expression, such as the rapidity of speech, the volume of speech, and the pitch of speech.

Learning Objectives

After reading and studying the chapter, students should be able to:

1. Identify and describe the dimensions of interpersonal communication.
2. Know the various components of interpersonal communication.
3. Distinguish between denotative and connotative meanings.
4. Understand the basic principles of speaking skills.
5. Understand the basic principles of listening skills.
6. Know what self-disclosure is and how it is used in communication.
7. Identify and describe the barriers to effective communication.
8. Define nonverbal communication.
9. Identify and describe the characteristics of nonverbal communication.
10. Know what body communication is and how it is used.
11. Know what space communication is and how it is used.
12. Understand how silence and paralanguage are used in communication.

Guided Review

After you have read the chapter one time, search through the chapter to find the appropriate words to complete these statements. Material is covered in the same order as the chapter.

1. A message includes both a _____ dimension and a _____ dimension.
2. The _____ is the information being delivered from the sender to the receiver.

3. Communication involves _____, the act of producing messages, and _____, the act of understanding messages.

4. Another important dimension of interpersonal communication is _____—environmental, _____, and psychological factors that decrease the likelihood that a message will be expressed or understood accurately.

5. That communication is _____ means that communication is an ongoing process between _____ and _____ unfolding across time.

6. Social communication always occurs in a _____, the environment in which messages are sent and received.

7. When people from different cultural and _____ groups interact, they may follow different _____ of communication.

8. _____ _____ is a _____ process that is ongoing over _____, involving a _____ and a _____, who often send and receive messages _____ through both _____ and _____ channels with _____ restricting the accuracy of a message.

9. _____ is the word's and message's objective meaning and _____ is the word's and message's subjective, emotional, or personal meaning.

10. Words and messages that have connotative meaning can usually be placed on a _____-_____ scale.

11. _____ is expressing thoughts and feelings in words and behavior with _____ and _____ so that the other person understands what you mean.

12. Messages are more effective when they are _____, _____, and _____.

13. Abstract, general, or complex messages are best accompanied by appropriate _____ to illustrate the _____.

14. In communication, the most time is spent in _____.

15. The majority of listening is listening to the _____ _____ with the remainder being _____-_____-_____ listening.

16. _____ is a physiological _____ _____ in which auditory sensations are received by the ears and transmitted to the brain, while _____ describes the _____ process of interpreting and understanding the significance of what someone says.

17. Strategies for good listening include: (1) stop _____ the conversation; (2) pay _____ _____ to the person who is talking; (3) use _____ skills; and, (4) give _____ in a competent way.

18. _____ listening is an effective communication strategy in which the listener restates the _____ and/or _____ of what the speaker has communicated and does so in a way that reveals understanding and acceptance.

19. _____ is a concise response to the speaker that states the essence of the speaker's _____ in the _____'s own words.

20. A good reflective listener periodically pulls together a _____ _____ of the main _____ and _____ the speaker has expressed over a reasonably long conversation or even several conversations that span several meetings.

21. _____ involves sending a message back to the speaker regarding the listener's _____ to what is said or the effect the message has on the listener.

22. _____-_____ is the communication of intimate details about ourselves to someone else.

23. The _____ _____ is a model of self-disclosure that helps us understand the proportion of information about ourselves that we and others know about.

24. The _____ self reflects information about yourself known to you and to others, while the _____ self is made up of information that others know about you but you do not.

25. The _____ self is what you know about yourself but others do not, and the _____ self includes information not known by yourself or others.

26. _____ _____-_____ give away power and increase vulnerability but at the same time bring strength by generating _____.

27. Privacy, a _____ ear, _____ understanding, and a common bond all increase the likelihood an individual will engage in self-disclosure.

28. The specific barriers that can harm our interpersonal communication fall into three main categories: _____, _____ _____, and _____ the other's concerns.

29. _____ is a barrier to effective communication that includes _____, _____-_____ and _____, and _____ _____.

30. _____ is rarely constructive because it implies a lack of confidence and intelligence in the other person.

31. _____ are sent coercively and forcefully, and _____ are solutions that are sent with the message that punishment will be forthcoming if the solution is not implemented.

32. _____ often includes words like "should" and "ought," and often demoralizes by fostering _____, arousing _____, and inviting _____.

33. One way to avoid the other's concern is to use _____, which is especially good at getting conversations derailed, and another is to use _____ _____, thereby ignoring the other's feelings.

34. _____ are characterized as conversation spoilers because they express _____ views rather than _____ dialogue.

35. Tannen suggests that women engage in more _____ _____ and men in more _____ _____.

36. Lack of communication is more often given by _____ as a reason for divorce.

37. For men, talk is for _____; for women, talk is for _____.

38. _____ _____ refers to messages that are transmitted from one person to another by means other than linguistic.

39. Perhaps as much as _____ percent of communication is nonverbal.

40. The general characteristics of nonverbal communication includes that it: (1) may occur in _____; (2) always _____; (3) is influenced by _____ contexts; (4) is often _____ and _____; and, (5) may be _____ from verbal behavior.

41. _____ Americans are more likely to make eye contact than other ethnic groups.

42. Compared to Hispanic Americans, White Americans stand _____ apart and do not tend to _____ while communicating.

43. White Americans view a firm handshake as a sign of strength and power, but _____ Americans view a firm handshake as aggressive and disrespectable.

44. _____ are motions of the limbs or body to convey messages to someone else.

45. _____ _____ can communicate important messages including disclosing specific _____.

46. _____ contact can serve four functions: (1) monitoring _____; (2) signaling a _____ turn; (3) signaling the _____ of a relationship; and, (4) compensating for _____ _____.

47. _____ is among our first pleasant experiences, both in receiving it from others but also in exploring objects.

48. Among the functions of touch are _____ _____, _____ and _____, and _____ and _____.

49. Higher-status people are _____ often allowed to touch lower-status people than vice versa.

50. _____ is the study of the communicative function of space, especially how people unconsciously structure their space.

51. According to _____, the four distinct zones in which we interact are _____ distance, _____ distance, _____ distance, and _____ distance.

52. _____ is the possessive or ownershiplike reaction to an area or space or particular objects.

53. _____ is an important part of interpersonal communication in that it establishes and maintains order between talking people.

54. _____ refers to the _____ aspects of verbal expression such as rapidity of speech and volume of speech.

55. A monotone voice means _____ while a slow speed, low-pitch voice means _____.

Guided Review Answers

1. content, relationship; 2. message; 3. encoding, decoding; 4. noise, physiological; 5. transactional, sender, receiver; 6. context; 7. ethnic, rules; 8. Interpersonal communication, transactional, time, sender, receiver, simultaneously, verbal, nonverbal, noise; 9. Denotation, connotation; 10. good-bad; 11. Speaking, accuracy, clarity; 12. simple, concrete, specific; 13. examples, ideas; 14. listening; 15. communication media, face-to-face; 16. Hearing, sensory process, listening, psychological; 17. dominating, careful attention, reflective, feedback; 18. Reflective, feelings, content; 19. Paraphrasing, content, listener's; 20. summative reflection, themes, feelings; 21. Feedback, reaction; 22. Self-disclosure; 23. Johari Window; 24. open, blind; 25. hidden, unknown; 26. Risky self-disclosures, intimacy; 27. nonjudgmental, empathic; 28. judging, sending solutions, avoiding; 29. Judging, criticizing, name-calling, labeling, praising evaluatively; 30. Advice; 31. Orders, threats; 32. Moralizing, anxiety, resentment, pretense; 33. diverting, logical solutions; 34. Arguments, oppositional, open; 35. rapport-talk, report talk; 36. women; 37. information, interaction; 38. Nonverbal communication; 39. 93; 40. clusters, communicates, sociocultural, spontaneous, ambiguous, discrepant; 41. White; 42. further, touch; 43. Native; 44. Gestures; 45. Facial expressions, emotions; 46. Eye, feedback, conversational, nature, physical distance; 47. Touch; 48. sexual expression, consolation, support, power, dominance; 49. more; 50. Proxemics; 51. Hall, intimate, personal, social, public; 52. Territoriality; 53. Silence; 54. Paralanguage, nonlinguistic; 55. boredom, depression

Key Terms

For each term, briefly define the term in your own words and provide an example or situation (especially one you can visualize) that will help you retain the meaning of the concept. Key terms are presented in the order they are presented in the chapter.

1. message (p. 223)

2. encoding (p. 223)

3. decoding (p. 223)

4. noise (p. 223)

5. transactional (p. 223)

6. interpersonal communication (p. 224)

7. denotation (p. 225)

8. connotation (p. 225)

9. speaking (p. 225)

10. hearing (p. 226)

11. listening (p. 226)

12. reflective listening (p. 227)

13. paraphrasing (p. 227)

14. self-disclosure (p. 227)

15. Johari Window (p. 227)

16. judging (p. 229)

17. sending solutions (p. 229)

18. avoiding the other's concerns (p. 229)

19. nonverbal communication (p. 231)

20. gesture (p. 235)

21. proxemics (p. 236)

22. territoriality (p. 237)

23. paralanguage (p. 237)

Study Aids

Students who do well on tests develop mnemonic aids to help them remember important terms and concepts. A few are suggested here, and you are encouraged to develop your own additional aids.

Components of Interpersonal Communication. Use MENTion to help you remember that components include the Message, Encoding, Noise, and Transaction.

Denotation and Connotation. In order to keep the right definitions with each word, remind yourself that both *d*enotation and *d*efinition begin with a *d*—therefore it is denotation which is a word's objective definition or meaning. Therefore connotation involves the *personal* meaning (you can think of your personal computer and personal connotation as a further mnemonic aid).

Proxemics. To keep the four personal space distances in the proper order remember the sentence, "INdividual PEople SOmetimes PUsh." Using the first two letters of each word will help you recall these categories from closest to farthest: INtimate, PErsonal, SOcial, and PUblic, including being able to remember the correct order of personal and public.

Understanding Concepts

Answer these questions to develop your understanding of the important ideas in this chapter.

1. Define interpersonal communication.

2. List and provide an example of each of the components of interpersonal communication.

3. Show that you understand denotative and connotative meanings of words and messages by providing an example of each.

4. Distinguish between hearing and listening.

5. Describe reflective listening and discuss the role that paraphrasing and summative reflection play in good communication.

6. What is self-disclosure? What are the advantages and disadvantages of self-disclosure? How is the Johari Window useful in understanding one's self-disclosure style?

7. List and discuss the three main barriers to effective verbal communication.

8. Compare and contrast the typical female and male patterns of communication. Describe both rapport talk and report talk.

9. What are the main aspects of nonverbal communication?

10. When a person's nonverbal expressions do not seem to match the words they are saying, which are you more likely to believe expresses their actual feelings?

11. Describe and discuss the important aspects of body communication.

12. Summarize the power differences in verbal and nonverbal communication.

13. What is proxemics, and what is the role that distance between two people plays in communication?

14. What is paralanguage? What aspects indicate different emotions?

Applying Concepts

Answer these questions to develop your ability to apply this chapter's material to your life and the world. Your own responses may differ from other students' in the class, and it is helpful to share your ideas with the other students.

1. Given that you often communicate in noisy environments, how is it that you can filter out noise to listen to the other person? Is the filtering accomplished through a conscious choice or an unconscious process?

2. Do we sometimes increase noise so that we do not communicate as much to some individuals, or in some situations?

3. Analyze the main problems that occur in your important communications with others. What could you do to minimize these effects?

4. Show that you understand how to use concrete examples to get across ideas that are abstract by writing a paragraph that addresses the topic of "being in love."

5. Review the section on listening skills and try to do "your best listening" for a few hours. Summarize here the effects of practicing good listening skills. Did the speaker react to your efforts?

6. Discuss how the difference between hearing and listening is important in discussing parent-teenage offspring communication.

7. Discuss your approach to self-disclosure using the model of the Johari Window. How risky is it for you to self-disclose early in a relationship? Are some private thoughts so private that you would not disclose them to anyone?

8. Choose someone with whom you would like to be on closer terms. In an appropriate situation, try telling something personal about yourself to the individual. After you have gone back to your room, write down a brief summary of what you said, how the person responded, how you felt during the conversation, and whether you believe it is something you can do more of to strengthen the bond between you and the other person. Remember to proceed slowly in your self-revelations because if you don't, you may overwhelm the person.

9. Discuss the roles that judging, sending solutions, and avoiding the other's concern have played in hindering your verbal communication in an important relationship. Which barrier is the most trouble for you?

10. Take and score Self-Assessment 9.1 on argumentativeness. Interpret the results. Do you tend to approach or avoid arguments? How does this affect your communication? Your own well-being? What would you like to change?

11. Review the material in Sociocultural Worlds 9.1. How might a marriage/relationship counselor use this information when working with a couple who is having difficulties in their relationship?

12. If a friend of yours plans to join the Peace Corps or to work overseas, what would you tell your friend about cross-cultural communications? Is there a way to teach cultural nonverbal communication as well as the foreign language? Would you include these aspects in language and cultural courses?

13. Read Sociocultural Worlds 9.2. Were you already familiar with the ideas presented? Have you personally misjudged other people because of these ethnic differences? Have you been misperceived because of these differences? What might help to correct these problems?

14. Describe the messages that you learn about touch from your family. Have you made any modifications to these messages? How comfortable are you with touch?

15. How might you use the different space zones to be an effective teacher? An effective business manager?

16. Describe the role that territoriality plays in your life. For example, how do you react to a roommate? Or someone sitting next to you in the library or school cafeteria?

17. Experiment with using more silence in your communication. What are the results? How did you feel when remaining silent?

Chapter Practice Tests

Answer these multiple-choice test questions to help you assess your understanding of the chapter's material. Evaluate your answers to determine which sections you need to further review.

Practice Test A

1. That a child communicates differently to a parent than a parent does to a child illustrates the _____ dimension in communication.
   a. nonverbal
   b. skill
   c. relationship
   d. message
   p. 223
2. Transactional refers to which dimension in communication?
   a. encoding process
   b. decoding process
   c. the effects a message has on the receiver
   d. the ongoing process between sender and receiver
   p. 223
3. Communication between persons always involves a
   a. source of conflict.
   b. transactional analysis.
   c. context.
   d. problem and solution.
   p. 223

4. The meaning of concrete words tends to be
   a. denotative.
   b. connotative.
   c. double.
   d. abstract.
   p. 225
5. Good speakers tend to
   a. look away from the listener.
   b. use common, jargon-type phrases.
   c. use intelligent sounding words.
   d. use verbal and nonverbal messages consistently.
   p. 225
6. When a listener restates feelings or content of the speaker, they are using
   a. paraphrasing.
   b. restating.
   c. reflective listening.
   d. summary statements.
   p. 226

7. Frank self-disclosed that he was a part-time chef; in doing so he shared which aspect of self-disclosure?
   a. shared self
   b. unknown self
   c. hidden self
   d. open self
   p. 227

8. Self-disclosing a lot early in a relationship may have the effect of
   a. gaining sympathy.
   b. increasing the speed that a relationship develops.
   c. overwhelming the listener.
   d. running out of things to say prematurely.
   p. 227

9. When I told Hannah that I found her to be selfish, which communication barrier was likely set up?
   a. fighting
   b. stereotyping
   c. threatening
   d. judging
   p. 229

10. Giving advise may actually
    a. solve many problems.
    b. help the other person to open up.
    c. undermine your communication.
    d. establish a close friendship.
    p. 229

11. Nonverbal behaviors are
    a. any nonlinguistic behavior.
    b. expressions that match spoken words.
    c. the basis of interpersonal communication.
    d. the same as context.
    p. 231

12. Which of the following is true of nonverbal behaviors?
    a. Men and women are similar in their use of nonverbal behaviors.
    b. They are always consistent with verbal behavior.
    c. They constitute as much as 93% of our communication.
    d. They always occur in the context of verbal behavior.
    p. 233

13. Touch as a part of communication can carry any of the following functions except
    a. sexual interest.
    b. power.
    c. support.
    d. appropriate distance.
    p. 235

14. Possessive reactions to area of space are called
    a. proxemics.
    b. territoriality.
    c. distancing.
    d. paralanguage.
    p. 236

15. Tony became silent at a break in the discussion. Because he is a good listener, it is likely that he
    a. was thinking about what I was trying to communicate.
    b. formulating a question.
    c. thinking of a conversation we had last week.
    d. all of the above.
    p. 237

Practice Test B

1. The relationship dimension of interpersonal communication includes apparent distinction of
   a. gender.
   b. status.
   c. fluency.
   d. courtesy.
   p. 223

2. The flowing process between sender and receiver is what makes communication
   a. interpersonal.
   b. transactional.
   c. reciprocal.
   d. intimate.
   p. 224

3. A person's meaning is more likely to be clear to a listener if the person uses words that are
   a. common.
   b. connotative.
   c. strict.
   d. denotative.
   p. 225

4. Abstract words are more likely to have meanings that are
   a. denotative.
   b. connotative.
   c. double.
   d. understood.
   p. 225

5. Good speakers tend to
   a. use a lot of head nods.
   b. use informal language, like "pretty good."
   c. use a lot of examples.
   d. also be good listeners.
   p. 225

6. Good listeners are characterized by
   a. paying careful attention.
   b. overcoming communication barriers.
   c. using paraphrasing.
   d. self-disclosing.
   p. 226

7. Which of the following is not a listening skill discussed in the text?
   a. reflective listening
   b. eye scanning
   c. feedback
   d. paraphrasing
   p. 226

8. A prerequisite of self-disclosure is that the listener be
   a. well skilled.
   b. reflective.
   c. trusted.
   d. a long-established friend.
   p. 227

9. Solutions that are sent with an emphasis on forthcoming punishments are called
   a. threats.
   b. orders.
   c. judgments.
   d. aggressive.
   p. 227

10. Avoidance of others' feelings is likely to result in
    a. self-disclosure.
    b. not allowing others to self-disclose.
    c. a breakdown of communication.
    d. causing someone to become maladjusted.
    p. 229

11. Nonverbal behaviors include which of the following?
    a. winking
    b. gesturing
    c. silence
    d. all of the above
    p. 230

12. Different cultures differ markedly in terms of their
    a. acceptance of gestures.
    b. use of nonverbal behaviors.
    c. reliance on nonverbal behaviors.
    d. none of the above.
    p. 233

13. Which of the following is true about touching as a part of communication?
    a. Touching is almost always sexually motivated.
    b. Touching occurs with the same frequency across cultures.
    c. Touching can signify status.
    d. Men touch more than women.
    p. 233

14. Space and area often communicate
    a. status.
    b. intimacy.
    c. comfort.
    d. all of the above.
    p. 236
15. Silence offers the opportunity to
    a. take a rest from a conversation.
    b. end a conversation.
    c. increase intimacy in the conversation.
    d. all of the above.
    p. 237

Key for Practice Test A

1. Answer c; The relationship dimension in communication involves the rules for how language is used differently in social contexts and for persons of differing statuses; page 223; Learning Objective 1
2. Answer d; The dynamic exchange between message senders and receivers constitutes the transactional characteristics of communication; page 223; Learning Objective 2
3. Answer c; Context includes all factors within which communication is embedded; page 223; Learning Objective 2
4. Answer a; Concrete words have a clear meaning without necessary references for understanding; page 225; Learning Objective 3
5. Answer d; Inconsistencies between verbal and nonverbal messages result in unclear communications; page 225; Learning Objective 4
6. Answer c; Reflective listening provides feedback feelings and content to a speaker as a check on understanding as well as a signal to the speaker that what is being said is understood; page 226; Learning Objective 5
7. Answer d; Different levels of self-disclosure occur in communications with others. Readily accessible information about a person is a part of the open self; page 227; Learning Objective 6
8. Answer c; Getting too close too soon can cause a listener to feel overwhelmed with the level of intimacy; page 227; Learning Objective 6
9. Answer d; Judgmental statements about another person can cause extreme barriers in communication; page 229; Learning Objective 7
10. Answer c; Advice can cause a listener to devalue suggestions offered even in addition to the advice itself; page 229; Learning Objective 7
11. Answer a; Nonverbal communications consist of the gesture, facial expressions, vocal qualities, and other features outside of but in conjunction with words spoken; page 231; Learning Objective 8
12. Answer c; Nonverbal communications have multiple sources that simultaneously accompany words; page 233; Learning Objective 9
13. Answer d; Touch implies close distancing that may actually be inside one's comfort zone; page 235; Learning Objective 10

14. Answer b; Many animals exhibit territoriality, including humans, which results in clear reactive communications regarding intrusions into personal space; page 236; Learning Objective 11

15. Answer a; One characteristic of good listener is not thinking about things other than the immediate message received; page 237; Learning Objective 12

Key for Practice Test B

1. Answer b; Status distinctions between message senders and receivers sets the rules and guidelines for communication within a relationship; page 223; Learning Objective 1

2. Answer b; Transactional characteristics of communication represents the flow of information; page 224; Learning Objective 2

3. Answer d; Denotative meanings lack ambiguity and necessary references to other objects for understanding; page 225; Learning Objective 3

4. Answer b; Connotative words carry more subtle meanings; page 225; Learning Objective 3

5. Answer c; Examples help clarify points for listeners and provide an illustration for what the speaker means; page 225; Learning Objective 4

6. Answer a; A good listener is highly attentive to both verbal and nonverbal communications; page 226; Learning Objective 5

7. Answer b; Active listening involves feedback and information flow back to the speaker about the message they sent; page 226; Learning Objective 5

8. Answer c; A lack of trust in a listener strongly influences a speaker not to self-disclose; page 227; Learning Objective 6

9. Answer a; Threats are based on the possibility of actual punishment; page 227; Learning Objective 7

10. Answer c; Open communication is directly related to the open expression of feelings as well as thoughts; page 229; Learning Objective 7

11. Answer d; Any behavior that accompanies words in the context of communication is considered nonverbal communication; page 230; Learning Objective 9

12. Answer b; Similar to the differences in verbal language across cultures, there are marked differences in nonverbal expressions; page 233; Learning Objective 9

13. Answer c; It is generally more acceptable for people of a higher status in a relationship to more freely touch people of a lower status; page 233; Learning Objective 10

14. Answer d; The distance and positioning of persons in interpersonal communication act to communicate several relevant dimensions; page 236; Learning Objective 11

15. Answer a; Silence is a break in the communication flow for both the speaker and listener. Silence, therefore, allows both speaker and listener to formulate a perspective of where they are in the communication process; page 237; Learning Objective 12

Chapter Outline

I.   Tomorrow's Jobs and the Changing Faces and Places of Organizations
    A.   Tomorrow's Jobs
        1.   There is a long-term shift from goods-producing to service-producing employment.
        2.   By 2000, nearly four of every five jobs will be in service industries.
        3.   The fastest growing careers will be those that require the most educational preparation.
        4.   Much growth will occur for technicians and related support occupations, with paralegals being the fastest growing career.
        5.   The greatest decrease will be in agriculture, forestry, fishing, and related occupations.
    B.   The Changing Faces and Places of Organizations
        1.   Workers are becoming more culturally diverse and more women are entering the workforce.
        2.   Failures, down-scaling, and mergers are part of the workplace, partly due to the shift from manufacturing to service.
        3.   Businesses are increasingly becoming international organizations.
        4.   With knowledge increasing, workers need to engage in continuing education.
        5.   Some employers are promoting health and other issues among their employees.
II.   Career Development Across the Life Span
    A.   Childhood
        1.   Ginzberg, Super, and Roe propose stage theories in career development.
        2.   The fantasy stage is Ginzberg's label for the childhood years during which careers are perceived in an unrealistic manner.
        3.   The growth stage is Super's label during which children move from no vocational interest (birth to 3 years), to extensive career fantasies (4 to 10 years) to career interests based on likes and dislikes (10 to 12 years) to beginning to take ability into account in career choices (13 and 14 years).
        4.   Roe emphasizes that parent-child relationships affect occupational selection.
    B.   Adolescence
        1.   Ginzberg's tentative stage (11 to 17 years) is a transition period between the novice fantasy stage and the realistic stage (18 to 25 years) when pragmatic decisions are made.
        2.   Super's exploration stage (15 to 24 years) is when individuals explore and evaluate the work world in a general way.
        3.   Parents have impact, both positive and negative, on their offsprings' career decisions.
        4.   Schools can play a major role in career exploration, although limited budgets, too few counselors, and the Back to Basics movement may hinder this role.

5. Many hold their first jobs during adolescence, and these jobs may teach responsibility and provide spending money but may lower grades, interfere with social life, and teach unrealistic money concepts or misuse of money.

6. Up until 16 years of age, more than ten hours of work weekly is associated with more negative than positive outcomes.

C. Early Adulthood

1. Most college students cannot accurately chart their adult career path and experts differ on whether a liberal education or a specific focused course of study is better.

2. Career entry involves need for high competence and many personal demands.

3. In Super's establishment stage (25 to 45 years) individuals pursue a permanent career and attain a pattern of stable work in a particular career.

4. According to Levinson, individuals develop a distinct occupational identity and establish themselves in the occupational world, and this is accomplished in a myriad of ways.

5. A college degree is associated with earlier and greater career advancement.

6. Most career advancement occurs early in adulthood.

D. Middle Adulthood

1. This time period often includes career and life reflection.

2. Super called this period the maintenance stage, which is most appropriate for those who remain in the same career.

3. Levinson suggests that people adjust to realistic possibilities about what can be done in the time left in an occupation, and some choose to make career or other life changes.

4. About 10 percent make a career change, which may temporarily produce imbalance but usually produces rejuvenation.

E. Late Adulthood

1. Super's decline stage (65 and older) is when individuals' career activity declines and retirement takes place.

2. Not all older workers fit Super's model, but for many retirement is an important event, with today's workers spending 10 to 15 percent of their lives in retirement.

3. The Social Security System of 1935 allowed retirement and the turn away from mandatory retirement at 65 allowed others to continue working.

4. Good health, adequate income, being active, having an education, and having an extended social network are associated with satisfactory retirement.

5. The fewer choices older adults have regarding their retirement, the less satisfied they are with their lives.

6. In a typical life course the first third emphasizes education, the second third emphasizes work, and the last third emphasizes leisure; this is becoming more blended.

III. Career Exploration, Planning, and Decision Making

A. Developing a Personal, Individualized Career Plan

1. Most experience changes that require modifications in their careers, with the average worker now making five or six job transitions.

2. Bolles emphasizes that individuals need to use change to become wiser, and that even mistakes can result in positive change.

3. The three important components of a successful career plan are: (1) goals, hopes, and wishes; (2) marketable skills; and (3) personal fit.

B. Holland's Personality Type Theory
  1. Holland's personality type theory emphasizes that it is important to develop a match or fit between an individual's personality type and the selection of a particular career.
  2. When careers fit one's personality, workers enjoy their work more and stay longer in these jobs.
  3. Holland proposes six basic career-related personality characteristics: realistic, investigative, artistic, social, enterprising, and conventional.
  4. Most people reflect a combination of two or three types.
C. Vocational Tests
  1. Both the Strong-Campbell Interest Inventory and the Self-Directed Search incorporate Holland's personality theory.
  2. The *Myers-Briggs Type Indicator (MBTI)* is another useful test for career exploration.
  3. It is important to have these tests accurately interpreted and to see them as one part of a larger inquiry process.
IV. Job Satisfaction and Stress
A. Job Satisfaction
  1. Organizational factors include pay, promotion opportunities, nature of the work, policies and procedures, and working conditions.
  2. Job satisfaction is influenced by coworkers and supervisors.
  3. Individual needs and aspirations also influence job satisfaction.
  4. Job dissatisfaction affects turnover and absenteeism.
  5. Older workers tend to have higher levels of job satisfaction.
B. Just Manageable Difficulty
  1. Brim's "just manageable difficulty" is the optimal level of effort in one's life.
  2. The goal is to be neither overloaded or underloaded.
  3. Job satisfaction is highest when one's position involves problems that can be solved with a comfortable amount of effort and work.
C. Personal Doubting—Fear of Success and the Imposter Phenomenon
  1. Horner's fear of success refers to how some individuals sabotage their own performance or avoid success to avoid expected negative consequences of success.
  2. The imposter phenomenon, often caused by perfectionism, is the haunting fear of competent, successful people that their successes will be overturned and they will be revealed as frauds.
D. Work-Related Stress
  1. In Moos' comprehensive model, the association between the environmental system (Panel I) and individual adaptation (panel V) is influenced by the personal system (panel II), as well as by cognitive appraisal and coping (panels III and IV).
  2. The bidirectional path of the model suggests that all of these factors can influence each other and that reciprocal feedback can occur at any point.
  3. Four main aspects of work settings are associated with employee stress and health problems: high job demands, inadequate participation in decision making, high supervisor control, and role ambiguity.
  4. Stress is most likely in low-autonomy, high-control situations.

5. Work and family settings compete for scarce personal resources, and stressors in one area affects the other.

6. Although there can be role overload, employment, marriage, and parenthood are associated with good physical health among both women and men.

E. Dysfunctional Workplaces

1. Many psychologists see problems with workplace structure, organization, and personnel as a major cause of stress.

2. Schaef and Fassel compare dysfunctional workplaces with addictive persons, and they recommend that dysfunctional workplaces adopt a twelve-step approach to become healthier.

3. Dysfunctional workplaces encourage workaholism, miscommunication, office politics, ambiguous roles, frequent reorganizations, and dishonesty.

4. Other dysfunctional workplaces are caused by powerful workers who are arrogant, alone, adventuresome, and adulterers, and whose only source of self-esteem is getting ahead at work, even at the expense of others.

V. Work and Leisure

A. Work Addiction—Workaholics

1. Workaholics are persons who are seemingly addicted to work, and they can be described as having a calm, collected obsession with their work and productivity.

2. On the other hand, Type-A personality individuals are highly aggressive and impatient with their work.

3. Despite the benefits of leisure activities on health, workaholics are less likely to take the time for rest and relaxation.

B. Leisure

1. Leisure refers to the pleasant times after work when individuals are free to pursue activities and interests of their own choosing, such as hobbies, sports, and reading.

2. At the beginning of the twentieth century, the average work week was 72 hours; only in the last half of the century did the average become 40 hours.

3. Much of the gain in leisure time is spent watching television, but sports and other activities are more common, too.

4. Middle-aged adults need to prepare financially and psychologically for retirement, and one area for preparation is developing leisure activities that can continue during old adulthood.

C. Balancing Multiple Roles—Trying to Be Superwomen and Supermen

1. Attempts at "superhuman-ness" have been increasing for the last few decades, especially for women.

2. There has been a shift toward expecting women to have careers rather than being full-time stay-at-home mothers; in different eras, career women and full-time mothers have felt devalued.

3. Although married women's careers are still viewed by many as secondary to their husbands, more now believe that women will stay employed after marriage and after parenthood.

4. Improved reproductive technologies have allowed women more control over when and if to have children, but also create dilemmas about their "biological clock."

5. Gradually, work organizations are providing options such as computer terminals at home, job sharing, part-time careers, and day-care at the workplace.

6. The "superman" trend began in the 1980s.
7. Women's greater comfort and expertise in domestic and parenting tasks can make it hard for husbands to take on a bigger role.

VI. Gender and Ethnicity in the Workplace
   A. Increases in Labor Force Participation by Females and Ethnic Minority Individuals
      1. In 1985, white males were almost half of the labor force, but by 2000 they will represent only 15 percent.
      2. The increase in women, ethnic minorities, and immigrants in the workforce suggests the need for a multiethnic, gender-comfortable workplace.
   B. The Glass Ceiling in Management
      1. The glass ceiling describes the subtle barrier that prevents women and ethnic minorities from moving up in the management hierarchy.
      2. Although women have nearly one-third of all management positions, only 2 percent of senior executives are women.
      3. Female and male managers are much more similar than dissimilar on many different personality, motivational, and intellectual factors.
      4. Many in the dominant group have a bias that women and people of color are less suited for management positions.
      5. Tension results when organization group membership changes but identity group membership does not.
      6. Tokenism is being treated as a representative of a group rather than as an individual.

Learning Objectives

After reading and studying the chapter, students should be able to:

1. Discuss how careers and the job market has changed in recent years.
2. Describe the development of career interests and careers over the course of the life span.
3. Know how one would go about developing a personalized career plan.
4. Identify and describe the components of Holland's personality type theory.
5. Identify and describe the key vocational tests.
6. Define job satisfaction.
7. Know what the "just manageable difficulty" level is and how it relates to job satisfaction.
8. Understand fear of success and the imposter syndrome.
9. Discuss what work-related stress is and how it may impact health.
10. Know what a dysfunctional workplace is and its effects.
11. Define the common characteristics of workaholics.
12. Define leisure and its role at different points in the life span.
13. Understand how contemporary society requires the balancing of multiple roles.
14. Know how the labor force has changed with respect to the role of women and ethnic minorities.
15. Define the glass ceiling effect in management and how it can affect careers.

Guided Review

After you have read the chapter one time, search through the chapter to find the appropriate words to complete these statements. Material is covered in the same order as the chapter.

1. An important workplace shift is from _____-producing to _____-producing employment, and by 2000, nearly _____ of every five jobs will be in these industries.
2. The greatest growth in jobs will be for _____ and related support occupations, with the fastest growing occupation being _____.
3. _____, _____-_____, and _____ will continue with the shift from the manufacturing sector to the service sector.
4. Because jobs are more complex and cognitively demanding, workers will require considerable _____ _____ through workshops, short courses, individualized training, and other formats.
5. The three stages in Eli Ginzberg's theory are _____, _____, and _____.
6. According to Ginzberg, until the age of _____, the fantasy stage is one in which careers are perceived in an _____ manner.
7. Donald Super proposes five stages in career development: _____, _____, _____, _____, and _____.
8. Super's first stage, called _____ stage, moves one from vocational interest to extensive career _____, to career interests based on _____ and _____, and finally to beginning to consider _____ in their career choices.
9. Anne Roe emphasized _____-_____ relationships in shaping occupational selection.
10. In Ginzberg's theory, ages 11 to 17 are in the _____ stage when individuals are in a transition between the _____ stage and the more mature _____ stage.
11. According to Ginzberg, during the _____ stage, individuals from age _____ to about _____ years make pragmatic career decisions; the comparable stage in Super's theory is the _____ stage.
12. In the exploration stage, individuals consider their _____, _____, _____, _____, and _____ in considering career choices.
13. Parents' _____ and pressures influence their offsprings' career decisions.
14. One place where adolescents can get advice about career choices is their _____, but the _____ to _____ movement, tight budgets, and too few _____ hinder this process.
15. Typically, an adolescent holds at least one _____ _____ before high school graduation.
16. The positive benefits of employment during adolescence include enjoying the _____ of working, liking having one's own _____ _____, and learning how to be _____; the negative aspects include pitfalls of teenage _____, such as buying _____ or _____, getting lower _____, and giving up much of their _____ life.
17. Until the age of sixteen, all the benefits of a job can be acquired by working up to _____ hours a week; more than that is associated with more _____ outcomes.

18. In the latter part of Super's _____ stage, individuals often begin their entry into an occupation.

19. During Super's _____ stage, which lasts from age _____ to _____ years, individuals pursue a _____ career and attain a pattern of _____ work in a particular career, and Levinson believes that during this time individuals develop a distinct

_____ _____.

20. Most career advancement occurs in _____ adulthood, typically by the time people are in their early _____; a _____ _____ is associated with earlier and greater career advancement.

21. Since the majority of middle-aged adults remain in the same career, Super's label of the _____ stage is very appropriate.

22. Levinson's research found that many middle-aged men felt _____ by their bosses, their wives, and their children, and sometimes these feelings produced _____.

23. About _____ percent of middle-aged Americans change careers.

24. Super's fifth career stage is called the _____ stage because career activity lets up and _____ often takes place.

25. Although retirement occurs at many different ages, retiring at age _____ is called early retirement and at _____, standard retirement.

26. Retirement is a twentieth-century phenomenon largely affected by the establishment of the

_____ _____ _____ in 1935.

27. Individuals who have inadequate _____, poor _____, and additional _____ have difficult retirement adjustments, and _____ and _____-_____ also affect adjustment.

28. The typical life course pattern has been to emphasize _____, _____, and _____ respectively in one-third of one's life; this formula is becoming more unsatisfactory and persons are blending each aspect throughout their lives.

29. The average worker now makes five or six job _____.

30. It is useful to develop the expectation that change cannot be _____ and to assume that change can usually be turned to your _____.

31. Richard Bolles wrote a popular book on job hunting and careers called _____ _____ _____ _____ _____, a book that emphasizes that change can be used to increase wisdom.

32. The three important components of a successful career plan are: (1) _____, _____, and _____; (2) _____ _____; and (3) _____ _____.

33. When addressing goals, it is useful to begin with _____ goals and move toward _____ ones as well as to think about _____ categories.

34. Both *Motivated Skills Card Sort* and *SkillScan* are used to help individuals compile a list of _____ skills and they often provide good information for one's _____.

35. John _____'s _____ _____ theory emphasizes developing a _____ between an individual's personality type and career selection.

36. Holland's six basic career-related personality characteristics are: _____, _____, _____, _____, _____, and _____.

37. _____ individuals, such as farmers, truck drivers, and construction workers, like the _____ and enjoy working in manual activities, and they are _____ _____, _____, and often _____-_____.

38. The investigative type is interested in _____ more than people, and is the type with the highest _____ level and _____ level.

39. The artistic type has a _____ orientation, and these individuals often have a distaste for _____, value _____ and _____, and sometimes have difficulty in _____ _____.

40. The _____ type is oriented toward working through and with other people, and they enjoy _____ and developing others as well as assisting others in need.

41. The _____ style is more oriented toward _____ than things or ideas, but these individuals seek to _____ others, especially when they want to reach specific goals.

42. _____ types function best in well-structured circumstances and are skilled at working with _____.

43. Holland's personality types are incorporated into the _____-_____ _____ _____ and his own _____-_____ _____.

44. _____ _____ should be used as one part of a larger inquiry process that includes an _____ about the person's life interests and goals.

45. _____ are at the heart of job satisfaction.

46. _____ factors contributing to job satisfaction include pay, _____ opportunities, the nature of the work, _____ and _____ of the organization, and _____ conditions.

47. Employees have higher job satisfaction if they get along with fellow _____-_____ and if they perceive their _____ to be warm, understanding, and have a high degree of _____.

48. Job satisfaction affects _____ and _____.

49. Typically, with age, job satisfaction _____.

50. According to Gilbert Brim, "_____ _____ _____," is the optimal level of effort in one's life, and the goal is to arrange one's life to avoid both _____ and _____.

51. Matina Horner proposed the term _____ _____ _____ to describe how some individuals _____ their own performance because they expect success to produce _____ consequences, and it is a term best applied to _____ situations.

52. The _____ _____ is a haunting fear experienced by _____, _____ people who expect their successes to be overturned and themselves to be revealed as _____.

53. The _____ of successful individuals and about _____-_____ of mental health professions report feelings of the imposter phenomenon at some point in their careers.

54. The major cause of the imposter phenomenon is _____, and when experiencing this phenomenon it is important to remember: your _____ do not necessarily reflect objective reality, try to accept _____, learn to be more _____ in daily routines, and become more tolerant of _____ _____.

55. In the Moos model of work-related stress and coping, the association between the _____ _____ (Panel I) and _____ (Panel V) is influenced by the _____ _____ (Panel II) as well as by _____ _____ and _____ (Panels III and IV).

56. A work climate involving high _____ and _____ produces more positive coping and cognitive appraisals than one that is oriented toward _____ control.

57. The _____ path of Moos' model suggests that all of these factors can influence each other and that _____ feedback can occur at any point.

58. There can be both positive and negative connections between _____ and _____, and these settings often compete for scarce _____ resources.

59. Schaef and Fassel call dysfunctional workplaces _____ organizations and characterize these places as encouraging workaholism, _____, office _____, _____ roles and responsibilities, frequent _____, and _____.

60. Berglass suggests that _____ in the workplace create many problems in the workplace, and these individuals have three of the following characteristics: (1) _____, (2) a sense of _____, (3) the need to seek _____, and (4) _____.

61. The success syndrome involves individuals who seem _____ and _____, but who have a basic _____ of underlings and the belief that problems are resolved by making more _____ and having more _____.

62. _____ seem to be addicted to work, but this lifestyle is not always stressful.

63. Unlike workaholics, the _____-_____ personalities are highly aggressive and impatient with their work, and their _____ with work is more stressful.

64. _____ refers to the pleasant times after work when individuals are free to pursue activities and interests of their own choosing—hobbies, sports, or reading, for example.

65. Having multiple roles can make people feel like they have to be "_____" and "_____."

66. Belief that women's careers are _____ to men's has remained the majority position, while _____ numbers support the women's career continuing after motherhood.

67. Accurate _____ _____ allows women to continue their careers but creates crises surrounding their "_____."

68. The trend for "_____" who handle the home, work, and parenting began in the 1980s.

69. The "_____ _____" in management refers to the subtle barrier that prevents _____ and _____ _____ from moving up in the management hierarchy.

70. A special concern for women and ethnic minorities in organizations is _____, which means being treated as a representative of a group rather than as an _____.

Guided Review Answers

1. goods, service, four; 2. technicians, paralegals; 3. Failures, down-scaling, mergers; 4. continuing education; 5. fantasy, tentative, realistic; 6. eleven, unrealistic; 7. growth, exploration, establishment, maintenance, decline; 8. growth, fantasies, likes, dislikes, abilities; 9. parent-child; 10. tentative, fantasy, realistic; 11. realistic, 18, 25, exploration; 12. needs, interests, capacities, values, opportunities; 13. expectations; 14. school, Back, Basics, guidance counselors; 15. paying job; 16. status, spending money, responsible, affluence, alcohol, drugs, grades, social; 17. 10, negative; 18. exploration; 19. establishment, 25, 45, permanent, stable, occupational identity; 20. early, forties, college degree; 21. maintenance;

22. constrained, rebellion; 23. 10; 24. decline, retirement; 25. 62, 65; 26. Social Security System; 27. income, health, stresses, choice, self-determination; 28. education, work, leisure; 29. transitions; 30. avoided, advantage; 31. *What Color Is Your Parachute;* 32. goals, hopes, wishes, marketable skills, personal fit; 33. general, specific, multiple; 34. employable, resume; 35. Holland's personality type, match; 36. realistic, investigative, artistic, social, enterprising, conventional; 37. Realistic, outdoors, physically robust, practical, anti-intellectual; 38. ideas, education, prestige; 39. creative, conformity, freedom, ambiguity, interpersonal relations; 40. social, nurturing; 41. enterprising, people, dominate; 42. Conventional, details; 43. Strong-Campbell Interest Inventory, *Self-Directed Search;* 44. Vocational tests, interview; 45. Interests; 46. Organizational, promotion, policies, procedures, working; 47. co-workers, boss, integrity; 48. turnover, absenteeism; 49. increases; 50. "just manageable difficulty," overload, underload; 51. fear of success, sabotage, negative, specific; 52. imposter phenomenon, competent, successful, frauds; 53. majority, two-thirds; 54. perfectionism, feelings, compliments, flexible, personal errors; 55. environmental system, adaptation, personal system, cognitive appraisal, coping; 56. involvement, autonomy, external; 57. bidirectional, reciprocal; 58. family, work, personal; 59. addictive, miscommunication, politics, ambiguous, reorganizations, dishonesty; 60. narcissists, arrogance, aloneness, adventure, adultery; 61. healthy, loyal, mistrust, money, power; 62. Workaholics; 63. Type-A, obsession; 64. Leisure; 65. "superwomen," "supermen"; 66. secondary, increasing; 67. reproductive technology, "biological clocks"; 68. "supermen"; 69. "glass ceiling," women, ethnic minorities; 70. tokenism, individual

Key Terms

For each term, briefly define the term in your own words and provide an example or situation (especially one you can visualize) that will help you retain the meaning of the concept. Key terms are presented in the order they are presented in the chapter.

1. fantasy stage (p. 250)

2. growth stage (p. 250)

3. tentative stage (p. 250)

4. realistic stage (p. 250)

5. exploration stage (p. 250)

6. establishment stage (p. 252)

7. maintenance stage (p. 252)

8. decline stage (p. 253)

9. personality type theory (p. 255)

10. just manageable difficulty (p. 259)

11. fear of success (p. 260)

12. the imposter phenomenon (p. 260)

13. workaholic (p. 265)

14. leisure (p. 266)

15. glass ceiling concept (p. 267)

16. tokenism (p. 268)

Study Aids

Students who do well on tests develop mnemonic aids to help them remember important terms and concepts. A few are suggested here, and you are encouraged to develop your own additional aids.

> **Stage Theories.** You can use mnemonics to help you remember the order of stages in both Ginzberg's and Super's theory. For Ginzberg, use the consonants in the work FuTuRe to remember the order Fantasy, Tentative, and Realistic. You can remember the order in Super's theory by using, GEE, M.D, or Growth, Exploration, Establishment, Maintenance, and Decline.

> **Personality Type Theory.** Holland purposively labeled his six personality types (Realistic, Investigative, Artistic, Social, Enterprising, and Conventional) so that their initials form RIASEC, which can easily be said and remembered. You can also remember the six types by using the sentence "Realistic Investigators Artfully Socialize Entrepreneurs at Conventions." Finally, for each of the six types, visualize a career that represents qualities associated with the type.

Understanding Concepts

Answer these questions to develop your understanding of the important ideas in this chapter.

1. Describe the changes that are expected to occur in the workplace by the twenty-first century.

2. Compare and contrast the stage career development theories of Eli Ginzberg and Donald Super.

3. Discuss the advantages and disadvantages of being an employed adolescent.

4. Explain Levinson's ideas about the young adult's establishment of an occupational identity and the middle-aged adult's struggle with career stability versus rebellion.

5. What factors are associated with a satisfactory retirement?

6. List and explain the three important components of a successful career plan.

7. Describe each of Holland's six career-personality types: realistic, investigative, artistic, social, enterprising, and conventional.

8. Summarize the primary factors that contribute to job satisfaction.

9. Explain how "just manageable difficulty," fear of success, and the imposter phenomenon affect your work.

10. Explain Moos' comprehensive model of work-related stress, coping, and adaptation.

11. How do work settings impact one's health? One's family?

12. Describe the characteristics of a dysfunctional workplace.

13. Compare and contrast the characteristics of a workaholic and a Type-A personality.

14. Define the glass ceiling in management and discuss its impact on the workforce. What are the possible causes of its existence?

Applying Concepts

Answer these questions to develop your ability to apply this chapter's material to your life and the world. Your own responses may differ from other students' in the class, and it is helpful to share your ideas with the other students.

1. Considering the changes that are expected in the workplace in the next couple of years, would you make any changes in school curriculum to help adjust to these changes?

2. Considering the ideas of Ginzberg's and Super's stage theories, how would you discuss career options with your child and adolescent offspring?

3. Anne Roe emphasized that the parent-child relationship and also parental expectations have an important impact on occupational selection. Summarize the major effects of your parents on your career goals.

4. How do developmental theories of career adjustment account for people who just fall into a career, almost as if it were by accident of some quirk of fate? An example might be someone who gets married and then just starts working for their in-laws' business.

5. For you, what would be the ideal age to retire? Would you gradually taper off your work hours, or just retire completely? How would you like to spend your retirement years?

6. Do Self-Assessment 10.1 on career goal-setting, and summarize your twenty-year, ten-year, and five-year goals here. Evaluate the difficulty level of this task.

7. Evaluate yourself on each of Holland's six career-personality types: realistic, investigative, artistic, social, enterprising, and conventional. Which is most like you? Least like you? Are your college major and career goals a "fit" with your personality type(s)?

8. Thinking back to what you read about personality theories in chapter 2, what theories most closely resemble Holland's career development theory? Could theories of personality be used to make Holland's views about career development even stronger?

9. What would you say to an employer who asks you, "Why should I even care if my workers like their job? What possible difference could their job satisfaction mean to me?"

10. Explain how you might take the concept of "just manageable difficulty" into consideration in your career plans.

11. Take the imposter test in Self-Assessment 10.2 and evaluate your results. Do you fit the imposter phenomenon? Can you provide a specific example of when you experienced it?

12. If an employer wanted to do things to reduce the levels of stress for her employees, would she have to worry about their productivity going down? Is it possible that their productivity could increase?

13. If you were a career counselor, what would you suggest to a client who was employed in a dysfunctional workplace or who had a narcissistic boss?

14. Discuss your personal balance among education, work, and leisure.

15. How well do you manage the multiple roles of modern society? Are you, or do you expect to be, a "superwoman" or "superman"?

16. Reread Critical Thinking about Adjustment: How to Be a Successful Job Hunter. Discuss your ability to follow these suggestions. What marketable skills, education, and experience will you include in your resume?

Chapter Practice Tests

Answer these multiple-choice test questions to help you assess your understanding of the chapter's material. Evaluate your answers to determine which sections you need to further review.

Practice Test A

1. A person who wants to secure an outdoor job that has a definite future would be safest to consider being a
   a. building engineer.
   b. farmer.
   c. game warden.
   d. park service ranger.
   p. 248

2. Ginzberg's tentative stage and Super's exploration stage both occur during
   a. childhood.
   b. puberty.
   c. adolescence.
   d. young adulthood.
   p. 250

3. With respect to the career paths that people take, which of the following is true?
   a. Most people choose one career in a lifetime.
   b. Most people change careers several times.
   c. Most people fall into a career regardless of their plans.
   d. Career selection processes are universal, the same for everyone.
   p. 254

4. Ken finds himself most interested in dealing with people, but he is also interested in science. According to Holland's theory, which types may characterize him?
   a. social, investigative
   b. conventional, social
   c. interpersonal, investigative
   d. conventional, interpersonal
   p. 256

5. Vocational tests can be characterized by the fact that
   a. they can purchased and used in self-assessment.
   b. their results are rarely inaccurate.
   c. their results are often inaccurate.
   d. they cannot be taken by everyone.
   p. 257

6. Job satisfaction among older workers appears to
   a. decline as retirement approaches.
   b. be lower than among their younger counterparts.
   c. be relatively high.
   d. vary between extremes from day to day.
   p. 258

7. A job that is challenging and difficult but involves problems that require work and do eventually get solved is likely to result in job satisfaction that is
   a. low.
   b. high.
   c. unknowable based on this information.
   d. lower than management's.
   p. 259

8. A factor strongly associated with the imposter phenomenon is
   a. perfectionism.
   b. minimizing the role of effort.
   c. work-related stress.
   d. mental illness.
   p. 260

9. Which of the following is not a factor in coping with work-related stress?
   a. personal characteristics
   b. job morale
   c. cognitive appraisal
   d. factors in the environment
   p. 261

10. An agency that has a great deal of internal strife and conflict may conclude that
    a. the situation cannot be attributed to just one person.
    b. the situation can be attributed to one person, but not any other single person below management.
    c. the situation is irreversible with the present staff.
    d. the situation can be attributed to one person.
    p. 263

11. Workaholics can find satisfaction in others outside their work by
    a. involving others in their work.
    b. taking time off.
    c. developing ties with co-workers.
    d. giving up some of their work investment.
    p. 265

12. Leisure takes on a great importance during
    a. young adulthood.
    b. the start of retirement.
    c. the middle years.
    d. none of the above.
    p. 266

13. As men and women's social roles change, which of the following is true?
    a. More is expected of women but not men.
    b. More is expected of men but not women.
    c. Less is expected of men and more of women.
    d. Both men and women have higher expectations.
    p. 267

14. A business that hires a large number of women and minorities for the first time and has trouble adjusting to the change would be advised to
    a. segregate the workers and slowly phase them together.
    b. require some mandatory training in diverse cultures.
    c. integrate familiarity with diverse cultures into existing work activities.
    d. fire all majority workers and hire only minorities and women.
    p. 267

15. The fact that there are so few women and minorities in upper management in most large companies signifies the existence of
    a. basement effects.
    b. glass ceilings.
    c. false expectations.
    d. poorer education among those groups.
    p. 267

Practice Test B

1. If a person wanted to select a career that will most likely be in demand in the future, they would not choose to be
    a. a nurse.
    b. a lawyer.
    c. an engineer.
    d. park service ranger.
    p. 248

2. Childhood career dreams give way during which stage of career development?
    a. tentative
    b. exploration
    c. realistic
    d. pragmatic
    p. 250

3. Changes in development are likely to have
    a. predictable effects on career paths.
    b. no effects on career paths.
    c. inevitable, although not necessarily predictable effects on career paths.
    d. negative effects on career paths.
    p. 251

4. A person who is characterized by Holland's theory as enterprising is most likely to fit which type of career?
    a. scientist
    b. clerk
    c. nurse
    d. none of the above
    p. 257

5. When a person goes for career counseling, they are most likely to take which of the following tests?
    a. Holland's *Self-Directed Search*
    b. Strong-Campbell Interest Inventory
    c. *Motivated Skills Card Sort*
    d. the MMPI
    p. 257

6. Which of the following is most true about job satisfaction?
    a. People tend to be either satisfied or not satisfied over the course of a career.
    b. A single factor usually determines satisfaction.
    c. Satisfaction is complex and involves many factors.
    d. Satisfaction is derived from one's core interests.
    p. 259

7. People are most likely to experience job satisfaction when
   a. there is a great deal to do and pressure to do it.
   b. there is enough idle time to waste.
   c. they fear failure.
   d. there is a balance between effort and productivity.
   p. 259

8. It is very common for people who fear success to
   a. not excel in most areas of their life.
   b. have experienced many failures as a child.
   c. avoid opportunities to excel in specific areas.
   d. set high expectations they cannot achieve.
   p. 260

9. Coping with work-related stress is primarily a matter of
   a. balancing work and leisure.
   b. increasing self-efficacy.
   c. adapting to existing conditions.
   d. none of the above.
   p. 261

10. A dysfunctional workplace has been thought to be similar to
    a. a family with alcoholic parents.
    b. a low income neighborhood.
    c. a disease.
    d. a faulty computer system.
    p. 263

11. Which is most likely true about workaholics?
    a. They dislike what they do.
    b. They have Type-A personalities.
    c. Their work is like a hobby.
    d. They experience stress on the job.
    p. 265

12. Americans are very likely to include which of the following leisure activities?
    a. travel
    b. reading
    c. sports
    d. social activities
    p. 266

13. The trend for men to handle a career and child-raising responsibilities started in the
    a. 1920s.
    b. 1940s.
    c. 1960s.
    d. 1980s.
    p. 267

14. Workplaces can adjust to the influx of women and ethnic minorities, but it may be necessary to
    a. hire diverse management.
    b. prepare manuals on work relations.
    c. familiarize themselves with diverse cultures.
    d. enforce anti-discrimination laws.
    p. 267

15. Management can deal better with the influx of women and ethnic minorities by
    a. receiving special training.
    b. not engaging in tokenism.
    c. not hiring diverse groups.
    d. decreasing their own work loads.
    p. 268

Key for Practice Test A

1. Answer a; Engineering careers appear secure now while jobs connected to agriculture and the environment are less secure; page 248; Learning Objective 1
2. Answer c; Developmental theories of career development view puberty as an early trial period for interest; page 250; Learning Objective 2

3. Answer b; Career development is a lifelong, dynamic process that includes the possibility of multiple changes; page 254; Learning Objective 3

4. Answer a; Social interests are reflected in dealing with people and investigative interests include science and analytic thinking; page 256; Learning Objective 4

5. Answer c; Like all tests, vocational tests are not perfect and involve an element of effort; page 257; Learning Objective 5

6. Answer c; Older workers often experience increases in job satisfaction as other pressures in their lives subside; page 258; Learning Objective 6

7. Answer b; High job satisfaction is a product of personal challenges that are met with success; page 259; Learning Objective 7

8. Answer b; Effort accounts for much of success and the imposter phenomenon underplays the role of effort; page 260; Learning Objective 8

9. Answer b; Overall morale is less important in dealing with job-related stress than are personality, environment, and cognitive influences; page 263; Learning Objective 9

10. Answer d; One person in an agency can cause conflict and turmoil among staff. This problem is most difficult to manage when the person is in an upper-level position; page 265; Learning Objective 10

11. Answer a; Persons who join into the world of the workaholic can become a part of what is most important to them; page 266; Learning Objective 11

12. Answer c; Leisure activities increase in middle adulthood as career achievement levels off; page 267; Learning Objective 12

13. Answer d; Changes in social roles for men and women have resulted in a broader range of expectations for both; page 267; Learning Objective 13

14. Answer c; Exposure to new groups require acclimation and a business can do programming to facilitate this process; page 267; Learning Objective 14

15. Answer b; Glass ceilings place unspoken limitations on how far members of a certain group can excel into upper management; page 267; Learning Objective 15

Key for Practice Test B

1. Answer d; Personal service and engineering careers appear to be on a steady increase in demand; page 248; Learning Objective 1

2. Answer c; The realistic phase of career development brings aspirations into check with real abilities and opportunities; page 250; Learning Objective 2

3. Answer c; Development theories of career development state that changes and experiences throughout the life span impact the course that career paths take; page 251; Learning Objective 3

4. Answer d; Enterprising characteristics most closely relate to business, management career; page 257; Learning Objective 4

5. Answer b; The Strong-Campbell Interest Inventory is the most widely used career interest test; page 257; Learning Objective 5

6. Answer c; Numerous factors related to one's personality, lifestyle, work environment, and work responsibilities affect job satisfaction; page 259; Learning Objective 6

7. Answer d; Job satisfaction is directly related to the challenges and successes and their balance; page 259; Learning Objective 7

8. Answer c; Fears of success, as is the case with other fears, results in behavior that avoids challenging situations; page 260; Learning Objective 8

9. Answer d; Coping with work-related stress involves using skills in both personal and environmental systems; page 261; Learning Objective 9
10. Answer a; Dysfunctional families and dysfunctional work places share many things in common, including conflict and poor problem solving; page 263; Learning Objective 10
11. Answer c; Workaholics are driven by the pleasure they get from their job; page 265; Learning Objective 11
12. Answer c; Sports, both participating and observing, are among the most frequent leisure activities in American culture; page 266; Learning Objective 12
13. Answer d; The 1980s saw an increased role of men in child rearing as well as the pursuit of their career; page 267; Learning Objective 13
14. Answer c; Increases in familiarity with unfamiliar groups increases tolerance and acceptance, while reducing conflict; page 267; Learning Objective 14
15. Answer a; Training in ethnic and gender affairs results in increased familiarity and, therefore, understanding; page 268; Learning Objective 15

Chapter Outline

I.   What Attracts Us to Each Other?
   A.   Similarity
      1.   Familiarity is necessary for a close relationship to develop.
      2.   We like to associate with people who are similar to us.
      3.   Depressed persons preferred to meet unhappy others and nondepressed persons preferred to meet happy others.
      4.   According to consensual validation, we are attracted to similar others because the other persons support our attitudes and behaviors.
   B.   Physical Attraction
      1.   In a computer dating study, physical attractiveness determined how much one was attracted to the date.
      2.   Physical attraction affects popularity, teachers' evaluations, and selection of a marital partner.
      3.   It is rewarding to be around physically attractive persons.
      4.   According to the matching hypothesis, while we may prefer a more attractive person in the abstract, in the real world we end up choosing someone who is close to our own level of attractiveness.
      5.   In an intimate partner, women rate considerateness, honesty, dependability, kindness and understanding as most important, and men first list good looks, cooking skills, and frugality.
      6.   As relationships endure, physical attraction assumes less importance.
      7.   Physical attractiveness varies across cultures and within a culture over time.
      8.   Overweightness remains a sign of female beauty in most underdeveloped countries, but not in economically developed countries.
   C.   Personality Characteristics
      1.   Personality characteristics also affect attractiveness levels.
      2.   Highly likeable traits include: sincere, honest, understanding, loyal, truthful, trustworthy, intelligent, dependable, thoughtful, considerate, good-natured, reliable, mature, kind-hearted, friendly, earnest, warm, kind, happy.
II.   The Faces of Love
   A.   Altruism
      1.   Altruism is an unselfish interest in helping someone.
      2.   Egoism is when one gives to another to ensure reciprocity, to gain self-esteem, to control impression management, or to avoid social and self-censure.
      3.   In altruism, any benefits to the giver are unintended.
      4.   Reciprocity is a universal aspect of altruism, involving mostly trust, but also guilt and anger.
      5.   According to social exchange theory, individuals should benefit those who benefit them, and when a benefit is received, an equivalent benefit should be returned at some point.

6. In social exchange theory, it is the individual who decides what are the costs and rewards and how much weight goes to each factor.
7. Feelings of responsibility and an ability to empathize affect altruistic motives, but the situational characteristics are a strong influence, too.
8. The bystander effect states that individuals who observe an emergency help less when others are present than when they are alone.
9. Bystander intervention is less likely in the following circumstances: possible retaliation, much time required, ambiguous situation, related individuals struggling, victim is drunk, victim from a different race, little prior knowledge about or skill to intervene.

B. Friendship
1. Friendship is a close relationship involving enjoyment, acceptance, trust, respect, mutual assistance, openness, understanding, and spontaneity.
2. According to Rubin, liking involves similarity and a positive evaluation, while loving involves being close, dependent, absorbed, and exclusive.
3. According to Davis, friends and romantic partners share acceptance, trust, respect, confiding, understanding, spontaneity, mutual assistance, and happiness, but romantic relationships also have fascination and exclusiveness.
4. Females exchange more intimate self-disclosures with same-sex friends than do males, except androgynous males do as much self-disclosing.
5. A male typically discloses more initially to female stranger than a female to a male stranger.

C. Romantic or Passionate Love
1. Romantic love (also called passionate love or Eros) has strong components of sexuality and infatuation and often predominates in the early part of a love relationship.
2. Romantic love is the main reason people choose to marry, and more than ever "being in love" is a reason both men and women give for marriage and "not being in love" as a sufficient reason to get a divorce.
3. Berscheid suggests that romantic love is about 90 percent sexual desire.

D. Affectionate or Companionate Love
1. Affectionate love (or companionate love) occurs when individuals desire to have the other person near and have a deep, caring affection for the person.
2. As love matures, passion tends to give way to affection and secure attachment or distress takes place; in this transition, deficiencies in the other person are more easily noticed.
3. In Sternberg's triangular theory of love, love has the three forms of passion, intimacy, and commitment, and affectionate love has intimacy and commitment.
4. Infatuation involves only the element of passion; fatuous love has only passion and commitment. Affectionate love has mostly intimacy and commitment, while consummate love has all three components.

III. Destructive Elements in Close Relationships
A. Anger
1. Driscoll suggests there are three cyclic anger patterns in relationships—"anger justifies itself" pattern, passivity and outburst pattern, and a catharsis-perceived injustice pattern.
2. According to Tavris, the first step in breaking an anger cycle is to stop focusing on the partner and trying to rescue or change the other.
3. Instead, focus on your own options, given the choices the other person chooses to make, and work on controlling your anger.

B. Jealousy
1. Jealousy is the perceived fear of losing someone's exclusive love.
2. Individuals with low self-esteem and feelings of insecurity are especially prone to become jealous, and jealous persons often idealize their partner while underestimating their own self-worth.
C. Excessive Dependency
1. Some close relationships involve an extreme degree of unhealthy dependency on the part of one partner.
2. Making excessive dependency demands may result in a resentful and hostile partner.
3. Excessively dependent persons are characterized by low self-esteem and feelings of insecurity.

IV. Falling Out of Love
A. Destructive elements can become so great that individuals fall out of love.
B. Falling out of love can lead to depression, obsessive thoughts, sexual dysfunction, poor work, difficulty in meeting new friends, and self-condemnation.
C. Getting Out of Destructive Relationships
1. Communicate honestly about conflicting feelings about the relationship to a close friend.
2. Develop your own identity and increase your self-esteem.
3. Recognize and stop self-defeating thoughts that prevent taking effective actions to leave the relationship.
4. When emotionally ready, fall in love with someone else.

V. Loneliness
A. Factors of Loneliness
1. Loneliness is common due to society's emphasis on self-fulfillment, the importance placed on commitment, and the decline in stable close relationships.
2. Both men and women who lack female companions have a greater risk of being lonely.
3. Lonely people often have had poor relationships with their parents.
4. Low self-esteem, self-blaming, and poor social skills are associated with loneliness.
B. Attributions about Loneliness
1. Men are more likely to blame themselves, women are more likely to blame external factors.
2. Men are socialized to initiate relationships while traditionally women are not, therefore men may conclude that they should do something about their loneliness.
C. Reducing Loneliness
1. Change your actual social relationships by forming new ones, using existing ones better, or by creating "surrogate" relationships.
2. Change your social needs and desires by reducing the desire for social contact, such as by choosing more solitary activities.
3. A poor coping strategy is to use substance abuse or workaholism to distract yourself from loneliness.

VI. Intimacy
A. Identity and Intimacy
1. According to Erikson, identity versus identity confusion is the most important issue of adolescence, and intimacy versus isolation is the task of early adulthood.
2. Intimacy is finding yourself yet losing yourself in another person.

B. Styles of Intimate Interaction
   1. Orlofsky identified five styles of intimate relationships: intimate, preintimate, stereotyped, pseudointimate, and isolated.
   2. The intimate style involves at least one deep, long-lasting love relationship while the preintimate style is more ambivalent about commitment. The pseudointimate style involves maintaining long-lasting attachment with little or no depth or closeness.
   3. The stereotyped style involves maintaining a long-lasting attachment with little or no depth or closeness, and with the isolated style the individual generally withdraws from social encounters.
   4. Intimate and preintimate individuals are more sensitive to partners' needs and more open in friendships.
C. Levels of Relationship Maturity
   1. White proposes three levels of relationship maturity: self-focused, role-focused, and individuated-connected.
   2. The self-focused level is being concerned only with how a relationship affects oneself.
   3. Perceiving others as individuals in their own right begins to develop in the role-focused level, but the perspective is stereotypical and emphasizes social acceptability.
   4. In the adult individuated-connected level, there is both self-understanding and consideration of others' motivation and anticipation of their needs.
D. Intimacy and Independence
   1. Development in early adulthood often involves balancing intimacy and commitment with independence and freedom.
   2. The extent to which autonomy develops affects early adulthood maturity.

Learning Objectives

After reading and studying the chapter, students should be able to:

1. Understand the role of similarity in interpersonal attraction.
2. Know how much of a factor physical attraction is in attraction.
3. Know how much of a factor personality is in attraction.
4. Understand altruism and how it relates to love relationship.
5. Define friendship an understand how it is different from love.
6. Identify the characteristics of romantic and passionate love.
7. Identify the characteristics of affectionate and companionate love.
8. Know how anger and jealousy can be destructive in relationships.
9. Understand excessive dependency in relationships.
10. Understand how people fall out of love relationships.
11. Know what loneliness is and how it affects people.
12. Know how identity and intimacy are related.
13. Identify and describe the various styles of intimate interaction.
14. Understand different levels of relationship maturity.
15. Understand the relationship between intimacy and independence.

Guided Review

After you have read the chapter one time, search through the chapter to find the appropriate words to complete these statements. Material is covered in the same order as the chapter.

1. _____ is a condition that is necessary for a close relationship to develop.
2. We like to associate with people who are _____ to us.
3. Depressed college students preferred to meet _____ others while nondepressed college students preferred to meet _____ others.
4. One explanation of why we are attracted to similar others is _____ _____.
5. In a computer dating study, the positive evaluation of a date was most related to the other person's _____ _____.
6. According to the _____ _____, in the abstract we prefer a more _____ person, but in the real world we choose someone who is _____ to our own level of attractiveness.
7. In an intimate partner, women view the most important traits as _____, _____, _____, _____, and _____, while men emphasize _____ _____, _____ _____, and _____.
8. The "ideal" beauty _____ across cultures and across times.
9. _____ is a sign of female beauty in most underdeveloped countries but not in economically developed countries.
10. _____ is an unselfish interest in helping someone, while _____ is helping for self-serving reasons.
11. _____ is a fundamental tenet of every widely practiced religion in the world, and _____ is the most important principle involved in it.
12. According to _____ _____ theory, individuals should _____ those who benefit them.
13. In social exchange theory, it is the _____ who decides what are the costs and rewards and how much _____ goes to each factor.
14. A person may choose to stay in a costly relationship with few rewards because it seems to be the best _____, and another might leave a rewarding relationship because there seems to be a different relationship that would have more _____ and fewer _____.
15. Altruistic motivations are affected by one's ability to _____ or to feel a sense of _____ for another's welfare.
16. Research on bystander intervention was stimulated by the brutal murder of New Yorker _____ _____, whose murder was witnessed by thirty-eight neighbors and no one called the police.
17. The _____ _____ states that individuals who observe an emergency help _____ when others are present than when they are alone.
18. Studies by Darley and Latane indicated that when alone, a person will help _____ percent of the time; with the presence of another person, a person helps _____ percent of the time.
19. Bystander intervention is less likely when there is a possibility of _____, when helping takes _____, when the situation is _____, when the struggling individuals are _____, when the victim is _____, or when the person who needs help is from a different _____.

20. _____ is a form of close relationship that involves enjoyment, acceptance, trust, respect, mutual assistance, openness, understanding, and spontaneity.

21. _____ involves taking friends as they are without trying to change them; _____ is assuming our friends will act in our best interest; and _____ involves thinking our friends make good judgments.

22. According to Rubin, _____ involves our belief that someone is similar to us and _____ involves being close to someone.

23. Rubin believes that loving includes _____, a more _____ orientation toward the individual, and qualities of _____ and _____.

24. Compared to friend relationships, Davis suggests that our love relationships are more likely to involve _____ and _____.

25. Compared to the other sex, _____ are more likely to disclose intimate information about themselves to same-sex friends.

26. _____ males do more self-disclosure than other males.

27. Compared to the other sex, _____ did more self-disclosure to opposite-sex strangers.

28. Eros, _____ love, or _____ love has strong components of _____ and _____ and often predominates in the _____ part of a love relationship.

29. _____ love is the main reason persons get married, especially for the _____ gender.

30. _____ love, also called _____ love, involves desiring nearness and a deep, caring affection for another person, and, according to Sternberg, involves the two components _____ and _____.

31. _____ are twice as likely than their spouses to initiate a divorce.

32. According to Sternberg's _____ theory of love, the three components of love are _____, _____, and _____.

33. In _____, passion is the only element, while in _____ love there is mostly intimacy and commitment and in _____ love there is mostly passion and commitment.

34. When all three components are present, a person is experiencing _____ love.

35. According to Driscoll, three cyclic anger patterns in close relationships are (1) an "_____ _____ _____" pattern, (2) a _____ and _____ pattern common among those who fear anger or conflict expression, and (3) a _____-_____ _____ pattern of too willing expression of angry feelings.

36. According to Tavris, the first step in breaking a destructive cycle of anger in close relationships is to drop the dream of _____ or _____ your partner.

37. Tavris describes the importance of _____ in keeping anger controlled and _____ is not an effective way of handling anger; sometimes it is best to do nothing and let anger _____.

38. Jealousy is the _____ fear of losing someone's _____ love.

39. Persons with low _____-_____ and feelings of _____ are especially prone to becoming jealous.

40. A third destructive element in close relationships is excessive _____.

41. Some situations in which it may be wise to "fall out of love" are when we are _____ with a person who betrays our _____ repeatedly, when we are involved with someone who drains us _____ and _____, and when we desperately love someone who does not love us.

42. A main cause of getting into and staying with destructive relationships is our feeling of being _____ and _____ by ourselves.

43. Steps to getting out of a destructive relationship include: (1) having or developing a close
_____ or supportive network; (2) developing our own _____ and increasing our
_____-_____; (3) stopping _____-_____ thoughts that
prevent us from leaving a bad relationship; and (4) allow ourselves in time, to fall in love with someone
else.

44. Reasons for _____ include feeling isolated, and overemphasis on self-fulfillment and
_____, and the importance attached to _____ in relationships while there is a
_____ in stable close relationships.

45. Both men and women who lack _____ companions have a greater risk of loneliness, as do
those with a history of poor relationships with their _____.

46. Lonely people often have low _____-_____, tend to _____ themselves
more than they deserve, and have poor _____ _____.

47. One study found that two weeks after the school year began _____ percent of college freshmen
felt lonely at least part of the time since arriving on campus.

48. When it comes to attributing their loneliness, _____ are more likely to blame themselves, and
_____ are more likely to blame external factors; perhaps the gender difference is due to how
we are socialized to _____ relationships.

49. The two recommendations for reducing loneliness are to change your _____ _____
or to change your _____ _____ and _____, and a poorer way to resolve
loneliness is to _____ yourself through work or alcohol and drugs.

50. According to Erikson, during adolescence the most important issue is _____ versus
_____ _____.

51. The main task of early adulthood is _____ versus _____.

52. According to Orlofsky, the five intimate styles are _____, _____,
_____, _____, and _____.

53. In the _____ style, the individual forms and maintains one or more deep and
_____-_____ love relationships; the preintimate style, by contrast, shows mixed
emotions about _____.

54. In the _____ style, a long-lasting attachment has little depth or closeness, and in the
_____ style, the individual withdraws from social encounters and has little or no
_____.

55. The _____-_____ level is the first level of relationship maturity, in which one's
relationship is viewed only in how it affects the self.

56. The _____-_____ level involves perception of others as individuals but is
_____ and emphasizes _____ _____.

57. The highest level of relationship _____ is the _____-_____ level, in
which there is understanding of one's self and others' motivation and needs.

58. Development in early adulthood often involves an intricate balance of _____ and
_____ on one hand, and _____ and _____ on the other.

Guided Review Answers

1. Familiarity; 2. similar; 3. unhappy, happy; 4. consensual validation; 5. physical attractiveness;
6. matching hypothesis, attractive, close; 7. considerateness, honesty, dependability, kindness, understanding,
good looks, cooking skills, frugality; 8. varies; 9. Overweightness; 10. Altruism, egoism; 11. Reciprocity,

trust; 12. social exchange, benefit; 13. individual, weight; 14. available, rewards, costs; 15. empathize, responsibility; 16. Kitty Genovese; 17. bystander intervention, less; 18. 75, 50; 19. retaliation, time, ambiguous, related, drunk, race; 20. Friendship; 21. Acceptance, trust, respect; 22. liking, loving; 23. dependency, selfless, absorption, exclusiveness; 24. fascination, exclusiveness; 25. females; 26. Androgynous; 27. males; 28. romantic, passionate, sexuality, infatuation, early; 29. Romantic, male; 30. Affectionate, companionate, intimacy, commitment; 31. Wives; 32. triangular, passion, intimacy, commitment; 33. infatuation, affectionate, fatuous; 34. consummate; 35. "anger justifies itself," passivity, outburst, catharsis-perceived injustice; 36. rescuing, changing; 37. civility, catharsis, subside; 38. perceived, exclusive; 39. self-esteem, insecurity; 40. dependency; 41. obsessed, trust, emotionally, financially; 42. incomplete, inadequate; 43. friend, identity, self-esteem, self-defeating; 44. loneliness, achievement, commitment, decline; 45. female, parents; 46. self-esteem, blame, social skills; 47. 75; 48. men, women, initiate; 49. social relations, social needs, desires, distract; 50. identity, identity confusion; 51. intimacy, isolation; 52. intimate, preintimate, stereotyped, pseudointimate, isolated; 53. intimate, long-lasting, commitment; 54. stereotyped, isolated, attachment; 55. self-focused; 56. role-focused, stereotypical, social acceptability; 57. maturity, individuated-connected; 58. intimacy, commitment, independence, freedom.

Key Terms

For each term, briefly define the term in your own words and provide an example or situation (especially one you can visualize) that will help you retain the meaning of the concept. Key terms are presented in the order they are presented in the chapter.

1. consensual validation (p. 277)

2. matching hypothesis (p. 278)

3. altruism (p. 279)

4. egoism (p. 279)

5. social exchange theory (p. 280)

6. bystander intervention (p. 281)

7. friendship (p. 282)

8. romantic love (p. 283)

9. affectionate love (p. 284)

10. triangular theory of love (p. 285)

11. jealousy (p. 286)

12. intimate style (p. 292)

13. preintimate style (p. 292)

14. stereotyped style (p. 292)

15. pseudointimate style (p. 292)

16. isolated style (p. 292)

17. self-focused level (p. 292)

18. role-focused level (p. 292)

19. individuated-connected level (p. 292)

Study Aids

Students who do well on tests develop mnemonic aids to help them remember important terms and concepts. A few are suggested here, and you are encouraged to develop your own additional aids.

Social Exchange Theory. Picture a set of scales—on the left side an individual places all the costs of a relationship, and on the right side all the benefits. Which way the scale tips influences whether one keeps the relationship or not. Of course, this depends on whether one believes the "scale's reading" is at least minimally acceptable and also is compared to other possibilities.

Friendship. If you wish to remember the eight aspects of friendship, you can help remember the first letter of each word by using the mnemonic: SOUR MEAT.

Spontaneity	Mutual assistance
Openness	Enjoyment
Understanding	Acceptance
Respect	Trust

Triangular Theory. Just remember that "people PIC their friends and lovers" to help you remember Sternberg's three components of love: **Passion, Intimacy,** and **Commitment.**

Understanding Concepts

Answer these questions to develop your understanding of the important ideas in this chapter.

1. Discuss the roles of similarity, physical attraction, and personality characteristics in attraction to other persons.

2. Defend or refute the phrase "familiarity breeds contempt."

3. Explain the consensual validation explanation of why similarity is important in interpersonal attraction.

4. Compare and contrast altruism and egoism.

5. Summarize the social exchange theory and provide an example.

6. What personal and situational characteristics influence helping behavior? What is the bystander effect?

7. What are the primary characteristics of friendships?

8. How is friendship different from love?

9. Are the friendships of women and men different?

10. Compare and contrast romantic (passionate) love and affectionate (companionate) love.

11. What are the components of Sternberg's triangular theory? How do they combine into different forms of love?

12. What are the three cyclic anger patterns that occur in close relationships, and how can these patterns be broken?

13. What conditions increase jealousy? How can a person successfully cope with jealousy?

14. Describe loneliness and its causes, and then discuss how to decrease lonely feelings.

15. List and describe Orlofsky's five styles of intimate relationships.

16. Compare and contrast White's three levels of relationship maturity.

Applying Concepts

Answer these questions to develop your ability to apply this chapter's material to your life and the world. Your own responses may differ from other students' in the class, and it is helpful to share your ideas with the other students.

1. The chapter cites a study that suggests that "misery loves company." Does your own experience agree—when you are sad or depressed do you prefer to avoid happy people and stick to other miserable persons? Give some examples.

2. Take the sample computer dating questionnaire items in Self-Assessment 11.1. What are your reactions to the items? To the possibility of trying computer dating?

3. How can researchers who study the matching hypothesis show that people match on physical attractiveness when this is such a subjectively interpreted aspect of a person? Can you think of ways that researchers could attempt to measure physical attractiveness?

4. Explain the differences in attractiveness for female body weight in developing and developed countries.

5. Using table 11.1 as a guide, what are the top five personality traits that you like in people, and what are the five traits that you most dislike?

6. Analyze one of your personal relationship experiences using the social exchange theory. What do you like and dislike about this theory?

7. Use the bystander effect to explain why many people think that small-town people are friendlier than city people.

8. Take Self-Assessment 11.2 on passionate love and evaluate your results. Summarize the role that passionate love and companionate love play in your intimate relationships. Also label these relationships in terms of Sternberg's triangular theory.

9. Is it possible that a person always loves in the same way, or do people love differently in different relationships?

10. Assess whether anger, jealousy, and excessive dependency have ever significantly affected your close relationships. How did you handle it?

11. Anger, jealousy, and dependency are closely related because they tend to occur together in relationships. What is the link among these negative emotions? Is there any particular order in which they are likely to occur?

12. Have you ever made yourself "fall out of love"? What were the circumstances? If no, under what circumstances might you find it important to disengage from a relationship?

13. Take Self-Assessment 11.3 to assess your vulnerability in a close relationship. Evaluate your results.

14. Why is loneliness a common experience among college students?

15. What elements of modern life actually increase the loneliness that individuals experience? What elements of modern life help to decrease loneliness?

16. Evaluate yourself in terms of Orlofsky's intimate relationship styles and in terms of White's levels of relationship maturity. What do the styles say about your typical relationships? Are there any changes you would like to work toward?

17. Describe your personal balance between intimacy and independence.

Chapter Practice Tests

Answer these multiple-choice test questions to help you assess your understanding of the chapter's material. Evaluate your answers to determine which sections you need to further review.

Practice Test A

1. Similarity between partners in terms of values and attitudes in a relationship can serve to
   a. reduce the pressure to diversify.
   b. validate our own attitudes and behavior.
   c. increase conflict.
   d. reduce relationship stress.
   p. 277

2. Keeping the company of attractive people will usually
   a. make you feel less good about yourself.
   b. increase your sense of inadequacy.
   c. increase your sense of self-esteem.
   d. decrease your sense of self-esteem.
   p. 278

3. Studies have identified specific personality characteristics that people prefer to find in others. Which of the following is true about these findings?
   a. They are only positive characteristics.
   b. The personality characteristics do not differ for different people.
   c. They tend to be a mix of positive and negative characteristics.
   d. They are characteristics we see in ourselves.
   p. 278

4. During which situation is diffusion of responsibility most likely?
   a. Several people offer to help in a crisis.
   b. A person singly witnesses a crisis.
   c. Several people witness a crisis.
   d. Several people are trapped in a life-threatening situation.
   p. 281

5. Friendships and love relationships share much in common, but friendships are more likely to be perceived as
   a. unstable.
   b. stable.
   c. accepting.
   d. trusting.
   p. 282

6. Romantic love is most likely to involve
   a. trust.
   b. self-disclosure.
   c. sexual attraction.
   d. anxiety.
   p. 283

7. According to Robert Sternberg, fatuous love occurs when there is
   a. passion and commitment but not intimacy.
   b. passion and intimacy but not commitment.
   c. intimacy and commitment but not passion.
   d. passion, commitment, and intimacy.
   p. 285

8. Jealousy is primarily driven by the
   a. perceived fear of losing someone's exclusive love.
   b. anger over an ending relationship.
   c. frustration over trying to keep a person to oneself.
   d. threat of a person leaving.
   p. 286

9. People in relationships with excessively dependant partners will often
   a. feel flattered.
   b. experience hostility.
   c. not notice it.
   d. lose their commitment.
   p. 288

10. Falling out of love with someone is often accomplished by
   a. falling in love with someone else.
   b. refusing to think about the person.
   c. concentrating on positive things about oneself.
   d. all of the above.
   p. 288

11. Changing desires for social relationships can result in
   a. becoming more introspective.
   b. feeling more romantic.
   c. feeling less lonely.
   d. none of the above.
   p. 288

12. A clear sense of who we are and what we are about should occur
   a. after we develop intimate relationships.
   b. before we develop intimate relationships.
   c. during the course of developing intimate relationships.
   d. as a part of the same Erikson stage as intimacy.
   p. 291

13. The intimacy style that involves a long-lasting attachment with little or no depth is referred to as
    a. preintimate.
    b. pseudointimate.
    c. isolate.
    d. stereotyped.
    p. 292

14. The highest level of relationship maturity is
    a. individuated-connected.
    b. self-focused.
    c. role-focused.
    d. intimate-stereotyped.
    p. 292

15. Intimate relationships involve a solid commitment to each other, but adults in relationships must also establish their
    a. financial means.
    b. personal leisure time.
    c. identity.
    d. none of the above.
    p. 293

Practice Test B

1. The process by which persons with similar interests and values confirm each other's attitudes and behaviors is called
    a. consensual validation.
    b. the similarity factor.
    c. matching characteristics.
    d. assimilation.
    p. 276

2. A person who dates an attractive person will
    a. look better than they do.
    b. feel they look better than they do.
    c. have a consensual relationship.
    d. increase their potential to look better.
    p. 277

3. There are specific qualities that people desire in those they date, most of which involve
    a. physical attributes.
    b. hobbies and interests.
    c. personality characteristics.
    d. none of the above.
    p. 278

4. Most religious of the world hold which of the following as a central tenet?
    a. reciprocity
    b. altruism
    c. sanctity
    d. egoism
    p. 279

5. Like openness, the willingness to share private aspects of the self with others is referred to as
    a. self-disclosure.
    b. personal acceptance.
    c. trust.
    d. mutual assistance.
    p. 282

6. Love relationships are sexually first characterized by
    a. liking.
    b. openness.
    c. affection.
    d. passion.
    p. 283

7. Affectionate love characterizes
    a. new couples.
    b. family relationships.
    c. long-term love relationships.
    d. none of the above.
    p. 284

8. Anger in close relationships is often the result of
    a. trying to change the other person.
    b. not getting your way.
    c. being deceived and lied to.
    d. physical violence.
    p. 286

9. Jealousy and excessive dependency share which features in common?
   a. anger
   b. low self-esteem
   c. fear
   d. addiction
   p. 287

10. Falling out of love will be most difficult for people who have experienced feelings of
    a. infatuation.
    b. anger.
    c. excessive dependance.
    d. jealousy.
    p. 288

11. A lonely man is more likely to attribute his loneliness to
    a. other people.
    b. a past relationship.
    c. himself.
    d. his childhood.
    p. 290

12. An inability to develop intimate relationships
    a. can stifle identity development.
    b. can be harmful to the personality.
    c. can promote introspection.
    d. all of the above.
    p. 291

13. Which style of intimate relationships is characterized by mixed emotions and ambiguous feelings about commitment?
    a. stereotyped
    b. pseudointimate
    c. preintimate
    d. isolated
    p. 292

14. Mark is concerned about how Diane is feeling about him and whether or not she feels as much for him as he does for her. Which level of relationship maturity does this seem like?
    a. self-focused
    b. role-focused
    c. individuated
    d. dependency
    p. 292

15. Adults strive to achieve a healthy level of intimacy and maintain their
    a. identity.
    b. independence.
    c. autonomy.
    d. all of the above.
    p. 292

Key for Practice Test A

1. Answer a; Shared values and attitudes in a relationship serve as a source of support and confirmation; page 277; Learning Objective 1
2. Answer d; Research in social comparison shows that comparing ourselves to persons perceived as more desirable can serve to decrease our personal sense of satisfaction; page 278; Learning Objective 2
3. Answer a; People prefer positive qualities in others, and preferences are variable for different people; page 278; Learning Objective 3
4. Answer c; Diffusion of responsibility occurs when several people witness a crisis and none takes personal responsibility for providing assistance; page 281; Learning Objective 4
5. Answer b; Friendships are perceived as more stable than love relationships; page 282; Learning Objective 5
6. Answer c; Romantic love includes a strong component of sexual desire for the other person. This is a part of the passionate dimension to romance; page 283; Learning Objective 6
7. Answer a; Fatuous love lacks intimacy with respect to mutual sharing, although it is characterized by commitment and passion; page 285; Learning Objective 7

8. Answer a; Jealousy is most closely related to fear because jealous responses work to reduce the fear-causing threat, although usually ineffectively; page 286; Learning Objective 8

9. Answer b; Hostile responses are likely when a person begins to feel trapped or closed in on, as can happen with an excessively dependent partner; page 286; Learning Objective 9

10. Answer d; Falling out of love can take several paths, but always involves placing the focus of positive attention on something or someone other than the ex-partner; page 288; Learning Objective 10

11. Answer c; Adjusting one's expectations and desires can result in reduced negative feelings, including loneliness; page 288; Learning Objective 11

12. Answer b; In order to share one's personal self with another person in an intimate relationship, they must first have a clear sense of self to share; page 291; Learning Objective 12

13. Answer d; Stereotyped intimacy has the quality of lasting a long time but lacks the depth and sharing that characterizes other styles of intimacy; page 292; Learning Objective 13

14. Answer a; The highest level of intimacy is characterized by a person being committed and connected to another but remaining separate in terms of their personal individuality and identity; page 292; Learning Objective 14

15. Answer c; Adults in intimate relationships must establish and maintain their personal identity as well as remaining open and sharing with their partners; page 293; Learning Objective 15

Key for Practice Test B

1. Answer a; Consensual validation occurs when two people share similar values and attitudes and serve to reflect each others' positions; page 276; Learning Objective 1

2. Answer b; Affiliating with persons perceived as more attractive can have the effect of increasing a personal sense of attractiveness; page 277; Learning Objective 2

3. Answer c; Specific personality characteristics are among the qualities most preferred in dating partners; page 278; Learning Objective 3

4. Answer b; Altruism, the selfless giving to others, is reflected in all humanitarian and religious doctrines; page 279; Learning Objective 4

5. Answer a; Self-disclosure is most similar to openness in friendships; page 282; Learning Objective 5

6. Answer d; Passion and romance are the early qualities of most love relationships; page 283; Learning Objective 6

7. Answer c; Affectionate love develops over long periods of time in long-standing love relationships; page 284; Learning Objective 7

8. Answer a; Attempts to change someone will likely result in anger and resentment, as well as frustration on the part of the person trying to make the changes; page 286; Learning Objective 8

9. Answer b; Feelings of low self-worth can lead to both jealousy and excessive dependence in relationships; page 287; Learning Objective 9

10. Answer c; Excessive dependence involves the loss of self and personal identity into the relationship, making loss of the relationship extremely threatening; page 288; Learning Objective 10

11. Answer c; Men are more likely to make internal attributions of lonely feelings; page 290; Learning Objective 11

12. Answer b; Intimate relationships foster personality growth and development; page 291; Learning Objective 12

13. Answer b; Pseudointimate style of relationships lacks a true commitment and is characterized by ambiguity and mixed emotions; page 292; Learning Objective 13

14. Answer a; Self-focused relationships are those in which persons' attention is directed toward their own feelings and how the other person feels about them; page 292; Learning Objective 14
15. Answer d; Maintaining a personal sense of self and personal identity is critical in adulthood; page 292; Learning Objective 15

Chapter **12**   Marriage, Family, and Adult Life Styles

Chapter Outline

I.   The Functions of Marriage and Selecting a Mate
   A.   The Functions of Marriage
     1.   Marriage is a legally and socially sanctioned relationship within the family system.
     2.   Its functions include replacement of members, reproduction, economic enhancement, social status, emotional support, and health benefits.
     3.   Married women and men are generally happier and less stressed than others, mainly due to interpersonal closeness.
     4.   Married men report the highest happiness level, possibly because they receive more emotional gratification from their spouse.
     5.   Married individuals have lower alcoholism rates, lower suicide rates, and greater longevity.
   B.   Deciding to Get Married and Selecting a Mate
     1.   Factors pushing one away from being single and pulling toward being married include: economic security, parental pressure, fear of independence, loneliness, cultural expectations, regular sex, desire for a family, and emotional attachment.
     2.   Factors pushing one away from being married and pulling toward being single include: restriction of a one-to-one relationship, obstacles to self-development, boredom, unhappiness, anger, potential communication problems, possible sexual frustration, blocked career opportunities, less variety of experience, and lack of freedom to change and experiment.
     3.   Homogamy is a person's tendency to marry someone who has personal characteristics similar to his or her own.
     4.   Endogamy is a person's tendency to marry someone in his or her own social group.
     5.   Desirable characteristics in a marital partner often vary according to one's culture (e.g., as shown with chastity and religion preferences).
II. Marital and Family Trends and Characteristics
   A.   Postponement of Marriage, Cohabitation, and Single Adults
     1.   The increase in never-marrieds has been pervasive across age groups.
     2.   The median age of marriage has been rising for the past thirty years.
     3.   There has been an increase in cohabitation, which is living together in a sexually intimate union without the legal sanction of marriage.
     4.   Most cohabitators are young adults and never-marrieds, although a sizeable portion have been divorced.
   B.   Divorce and Remarriage
     1.   In this century, the probability of a marriage ending in divorce increased from 10 percent to more than 50 percent.
     2.   Increasing numbers of children are growing up in single-parent families and in stepfamilies.

3. The United States has the highest remarriage rate in the world, with more than 40 percent of marriages including at least one person who is getting remarried.
4. About two-thirds of remarriages are preceded by cohabitation.

C. Women's and Men's Roles in Marriage and Family
1. More married women remain or return to the labor force.
2. The majority of mothers with children under the age of five is in the workforce.
3. Traditional divisions of labor and allocation of resources in marriage have been challenged.

D. Marriage and the Family in Ethnic Minority Groups
1. Large and extended families are more common among ethnic minority groups than White Americans.
2. Single-parent families are more common among Black Americans and Hispanic Americans than among White Americans.
3. When there are limited resources, early autonomy among children may be encouraged.
4. Impoverished parents may have a diminished capacity for supportive and involved parenting.
5. The community and family can filter out destructive racist messages, provide an ethnic frame of reference, provide role models and encouragement, and provide a buffer to stress.

E. Adolescent Parents
1. Each year more than one million American teenagers (1 in 10) become pregnant with four out of five of them unmarried.
2. The adolescent pregnancy rate in the United States is the highest of any in the Western world.
3. Recommendations to reduce the pregnancy rate are improved sex-education and family-planning information, greater access to contraception, and broad community involvement.

F. Family Violence
1. Family members can provide love, acceptance, and support, but are sometimes also a source of hostility, abuse, and neglect.
2. Amidst growing community concern, most family violence still remains a secret.
3. Child abuse is affected by parental personality characteristics, parental victimization as a child, and cultural attitudes.
4. Psychological maltreatment of children is more common than physical abuse of children, and it takes five forms: rejecting, isolating, terrorizing, ignoring, and corrupting.
5. A family scapegoat is a child who bears the burden for all the family's problems, and as adults they are loyal, personally rigid, full of anger, cold, emotionally needy, and self-condemning.
6. Probably one in four married couples involve spousal abuse.
7. Walker suggests a three-phase cycle of domestic violence: (1) Tension builds up with the battered person using coping skills to avoid abuse; (2) Tension escalates into an explosion of violence; and (3) Period in which the batterer is remorseful, loving, and generous.
8. Obstacles to change include the batterer's minimization of the violence, his dependency on spouse for intimacy, his development of jealousy and forcing his spouse to give up other outlets, and his low self-esteem and poor social skills.

G. Economic Distress in the Marriage and Family
   1. Employment instability, economic deprivation, and economic strain are negatively related to marital and family satisfaction.
   2. Economic hard times are associated with higher rates of marital dissolution, family disorganization, spousal and child abuse, and child neglect.
H. Fewer Children, No Children in Marriages
   1. Until the late 1940s, the majority of Americans thought at least three children was the ideal; now the majority view two or fewer as the ideal.
   2. The reduction is attributed to financial strains, increased contraceptive usage, more women in the labor force, and a change in attitude about attributes of only children.
   3. Adler viewed birth order as one influence on who we are and how we develop.
   4. The first-born child is likely to be adult-oriented, very responsible, and achievement-oriented with values similar to the parents.
   5. The middle child often chooses to achieve in areas in which the oldest child is not strongly developed and is often more sociable and concerned with justice and fairness.
   6. The youngest child may have many things done for the child or not taken seriously, and this child is likely to have more relaxed parents with more lenient discipline than did older siblings.
   7. Until recently, childless couples were pitied or believed to be selfish, but the choice is more accepted now, especially among highly educated and career-oriented couples.

III. The Family Life Cycle and Parenting
   A. Leaving Home and Becoming a Single Adult
      1. This is the first stage in the family life cycle.
      2. Launching is the process in which the youth moves into adulthood and exits his or her family of origin.
      3. It is a time to sort out what to keep. leave, and modify from the family of origin.
      4. The shift to adult-to-adult status between parents and children requires mutually respectful and personal form of relating.
   B. The Joining of Families through Marriage: The New Couple
      1. This is the second stage of the family life cycle.
      2. Two individuals from separate families of origin unite to form a new family system.
      3. Changing women's roles, increases in partners being from divergent cultural backgrounds, and increased physical distances from families place a stronger burden on couples to define themselves.
   C. Becoming Parents and Families with Children
      1. This is the third stage in the family life cycle.
      2. Entering this stage requires that adults now move up a generation and become caregivers to the younger generation.
      3. Babies place new restrictions on their mothers and fathers—limited freedom of movement and adding financial and emotional strain.
      4. Parenting requires a juggling of parent roles and self-actualizing adult roles.
      5. Fewer children and reduced demands of child care has resulted in more working women, more investment by men in fathering, and more institutional child care.

6. Early parenthood has the advantage of good physical energy and fewer medical problems with pregnancy and childbirth; late parenthood offers more planning, maturity, and better income.
7. Four parenting styles are authoritarian, authoritative, permissive-indifferent, and permissive-indulgent.

  D. The Family with Adolescents
    1. This is the fourth stage of the family life cycle.
    2. As adolescents pursue autonomy, parents may view them as changing from compliant children to noncompliant adolescents.
    3. Some parents clamp down and others become very permissive, but the best approach is a flexible relinquishing of control in areas where adolescents make mature decisions.

  E. Midlife Families
    1. This is the fifth stage in family cycle.
    2. It is a time of launching children.
    3. The empty nest syndrome proposed that launching children led to a decrease in marital and personal satisfaction, but actually marital satisfaction usually increases in the post-childbearing years.
    4. Parent-child similarity is most noticeable in religious and political areas, least in gender roles, life-style, and work orientation.
    5. Mothers and daughters had closer adult relationships than mother-son, father-daughter, and father-son combinations.
    6. Married men were more involved with their wives' kin than their own.

  F. The Family in Later Life
    1. This is the sixth and final stage in the family life cycle.
    2. Retirement alters a couple's life style, requiring adaptation, especially in traditional families.

IV. The Dynamics of Marital Adjustment
  A. Marital Expectations and Myths
    1. Unhappily married couples express unrealistic expectations about marriage.
    2. Males have more misconceptions about marriage than do females, and romantic individuals believe more misconceptions than others.

  B. Marital Satisfaction and Conflict
    1. Happiness is the strongest aspect of marital well-being with other significant components being equity, competence, and control.
    2. Bernard suggested that the main dimensions of marital adjustment are: (1) extent and degree of differences between marital partners; (2) the nature of the couple's communication; and (3) the quality of the partner's relationship.
    3. An important factor in marital success is the ability to handle conflict constructively.

  C. Gender, Marital Communication, and Marital Adjustment
    1. More men than women view their spouses as best friends, and fewer wives than husbands turn first to their spouse for support with a serious problem.
    2. Wives disclose more to their partners than husbands do, including more expression of tenderness, fear, and sadness while husbands often experience controlled anger.
    3. Many husbands have difficulty expressing their own feelings and thoughts.
    4. Women do more family work than do men, and they tend to enjoy meeting the needs of their loved ones more than they enjoy the activities themselves.

D. Dual-Career Marriages
   1. One of the main advantages is financial.
   2. Dual-career couples are more likely to have equal husband-wife relationships and the wives usually have higher self-esteem.
   3. Jugglers have little free time and identify the unrelenting pace of life as a persistent problem.

V. Divorce and Remarriage
   A. Divorce
      1. Divorce has increased for all socioeconomic groups, but more so among those with limited resources.
      2. Divorce rates are higher for youthful marriages, low educational level, low income, and premarital pregnancy.
      3. Former spouses often alternate between feelings of seductiveness and hostility with some thoughts of reconciliation.
      4. The stress of separation and divorce place both women and men at risk for psychological and physical difficulties.
      5. Many separation and divorces are highly emotional affairs that immerse the child in conflict.
      6. During the first year after the divorce, the child often experiences poor parenting.
      7. Children living with the same-sex parent were more socially competent and had higher self-esteem.
   B. Remarriage
      1. Younger women remarry more quickly than older women.
      2. The more money a divorced male has, the more likely he is to remarry, but for women the opposite is true.
      3. Boundary ambiguity is the uncertainty in stepfamilies of who is in or out of the family and who is performing or responsible for certain tasks in the family system.

VI. The Diversity of Adult Life Styles
   A. Cohabitating Adults
      1. Living apart prior to marriage predicts greater marital success than cohabitating.
      2. Perhaps cohabitators may be more committed to personal independence than individuals who do not cohabitate.
   B. Single Adults
      1. The number who live alone began to grow in the 1950s, rapidly increasing in the 1970s.
      2. Advantages include autonomous decisions, pursuing one's own interests, opportunity to try new things, and privacy.
      3. Common problems include intimate adult relationships, loneliness, and finding a niche in a marriage-oriented world.
   C. Gay and Lesbian Couples
      1. Homosexuals are sexually oriented toward persons of the same sex.
      2. Male homosexuals are often called gay and female homosexuals are called lesbians.
      3. The Judeo-Christian tradition approves only of sexual acts that can lead to conception within marriage, making homosexual relations unacceptable in some church doctrines.
      4. Homosexual couples are similar to heterosexual couples in most aspects.
      5. Although some homosexuals remain with the same partner for many years, homosexual relationships have a higher rate of instability than marital relationships.

Learning Objectives

After reading and studying the chapter, students should be able to:

1. Identify the functions of marriage and the process of getting married.
2. Know the alternative life styles that postpone marriage.
3. Understand the trend toward divorce and remarriage.
4. Understand the roles of men and women in marriages.
5. Identify the key characteristics of marriage and family among ethnic minorities.
6. Describe adolescents as parents and the challenges that exist for them.
7. Describe family violence and economic distress in families.
8. Describe families with few or no children.
9. Describe the processes of leaving home and living as a single adult.
10. Understand how new families are joined through marriage.
11. Describe and understand families at later time points in the family cycle.
12. Know what marital myths exist and how marital satisfaction is related to conflict.
13. Know how men and women communicate in marriages and how this is related to marital adjustment.
14. Define and describe dual-career marriages.
15. Understand the processes involved in divorce and remarriage.
16. Identify and understand the diverse range of adult life styles.

Guided Review

After you have read the chapter one time, search through the chapter to find the appropriate words to complete these statements. Material is covered in the same order as the chapter.

1. _____ is a legally and socially sanctioned _____ within the family system.
2. _____ women and men are generally happier and less stressed than their _____ counterparts, and marriage is especially rewarding for _____.
3. The primary factor responsible for married persons being happier than others is _____ _____.
4. Married _____ are happier than the other gender probably because they are more likely to receive _____ _____ from their spouses.
5. Married individuals have lower rates of _____ and _____ but greater _____.
6. Single men are more than _____ times as likely to die of _____ of the liver than are married men.
7. The highest incidence of suicide is among _____ men and _____ women.
8. Married persons live longer than unmarried persons probably because they have more _____ and _____.
9. Women in unhappy, unsupportive marriages have higher _____ levels, more _____ symptoms, increased levels of _____, and decreased _____ systems than happily married women.

10. Mental hospital admissions consistently show _____ rates for married than unmarried persons.

11. The decision to marry or not is influenced by many _____, _____, and _____ factors.

12. "Pushes" away from being single and "pulls" toward being married include: _____ security, pressure from _____, fear of _____, _____, _____ expectations to be married, regular _____, desire for _____, and _____ attachment.

13. Pushes away from being married and pulls toward being single include: restrictions such as a sense of feeling _____, obstacles to _____-_____, _____, _____, and _____, potentially poor _____ with a spouse, possible _____ frustration, blocked _____ opportunities, less exciting _____-_____ of marriage, and lack of _____ to change and experiment.

14. _____ is a person's tendency to marry someone with similar personal characteristics, and _____ is a person's tendency to marry someone from one's own social group.

15. The most important factor in marital selection in China, India, Indonesia, Iran, Taiwan, and the Palestinian Arab culture is _____.

16. South African Zulus, Estonians, and Colombians place a high value on _____ skills in their marital preference.

17. Individuals in Scandinavian countries marry _____ than those in Eastern European countries.

18. Today, fewer than one in _____ American families fits the description of a breadwinner father, a mother, and children.

19. Dramatic shifts toward the _____ of marriage and increases in _____ and _____ adulthood have recently occurred.

20. Between 1970 and 1990, the proportion of women never married _____, and nearly _____ for men.

21. Living together in a sexually intimate union without the legal sanction of marriage is called _____.

22. The probability that a marriage will end in a divorce has increased from approximately _____ percent at the beginning of the century to more than _____ percent currently.

23. Today, the average duration of a marriage is just over _____ years.

24. Between 1910 and 1960, about _____ percent of children lived in a single-parent family at some time; for children born in the 1980s, the figure is over _____ percent.

25. The United States has the _____ remarriage rate in the world, and more than _____ percent of marriages are remarriages for at least one of the couple.

26. In this country, the median interval between divorce and remarriage is just under _____ years.

27. Day care is a national issue as one in _____ mothers with a child under the age of 5 is in the labor force.

28. Large and extended families are _____ common among ethnic minority groups than among White Americans, allowing _____ interaction with grandparents, aunts, uncles, and cousins.

29. _____-parent families are more common among Black and Hispanic Americans, which means higher numbers of households with _____ resources and earlier _____ among their children.

30. Compared to White children, Black children are _____ times as likely to be poor, _____ times as likely to die of child abuse, _____ times as likely to be dependent on welfare, and _____ times as likely to live with a parent who never married.

31. The Black cultural tradition of an _____ _____ household, which traces to the _____ heritage, has helped many Black parents cope with adverse social conditions such as economic impoverishment.

32. Mexican children are more likely to play with _____ than with schoolmates or neighborhood children, and most of them grow up in families in which the _____ is the undisputed authority on all family matters.

33. Each year more than one million American teenagers—about one in _____—become pregnant with _____ of five of them unmarried.

34. The country with the highest adolescent pregnancy rate is _____ _____, and to reduce this rate, improved _____ _____ and _____-_____ information, greater access to _____, and broad community involvement and support is needed.

35. Most family violence remains a _____.

36. About half a million children are _____ _____ each year, and although professionals are mandatory reporters, at least _____ percent of suspected cases are not reported.

37. Child abuse is influenced by parents' _____ _____, whether parents were _____ _____ when they were young, and _____ attitudes.

38. In _____ and _____, where _____ punishment is rarely used to discipline children, the incidence of child abuse seems to be very _____.

39. More common than physical abuse of children is the _____ _____ of children, which occurs in a variety of ways.

40. All psychological maltreatment involves a concerted attack by an adult on a child's development of _____-_____ and _____ _____.

41. The five forms of psychological maltreatment are _____, _____, _____, _____, and _____.

42. The _____ _____ is the one child who bears the burden for all the problems in the family.

43. The family scapegoat feels _____ for all the family pain and as an adult remains _____ and _____ close to the family and tries to make amends for all that "they have done wrong"; they are described as _____, personally _____, full of _____, _____, emotionally _____, and _____-_____.

44. The first book to examine family violence, Pizzey's _____ _____ or the _____ _____ _____ wasn't published until _____.

45. Family violence probably affects at least one in _____ couples.

46. Lenore Walker's three-phase cycle of domestic violence is that (1) _____ builds up with the battered person using _____ skills to avoid abusive situations, (2) _____ of tension until the batterer _____ into a violent episode, (3) followed by a period in which the _____ is _____, loving, and generous and the _____ "chooses" to believe the change is _____.

47. Obstacles to the batterer's real change is that the batterer _____ and _____ the violence, the batterer's only source of _____ is the spouse, and in an isolated, closed system, _____ develops.

48. Another obstacle to change is the batterer's low _____-_____ , lack of skills and confidence to ask for what they want in a nonthreatening manner, and having family scripts full of _____ as a way to solve problems.

49. _____ instability and _____ hard times are negatively related to marital and family satisfaction.

50. Three reasons for the trend toward smaller families: (1) increased recognition of the _____ _____ a large family can cause; (2) increased use of _____ methods; and (3) increased number of women in the _____ _____ .

51. Alfred Adler believed that _____ _____ was a "pinch of salt" that flavors who we are and how we perceive the world.

52. The first-born child has a period of _____ attention from parents which ends with _____ when another sibling is born.

53. The _____ child has values most similar to the parents, and is conservative, dislikes _____ , prefers _____ , is ambitious, and prefers adults to children.

54. The middle child is born with an older sibling who is a _____ , therefore this child tries to _____ the first child or to develop achievements in different areas; typical characteristics are to be more _____ and to be more in tune with _____ .

55. The youngest child has one or more _____ but does not experience _____ ; this child might be powerful or might have trouble being taken _____ and is also at a risk of being _____ .

56. Until recently, childless couples were either _____ or considered to be _____ ; now, with a concern for _____ , some large families have been accused of being selfish.

57. About one in _____ married women will likely remain childless.

58. _____ _____ and becoming a _____ adult is the first stage in the family life cycle and involves the concept of _____ , or the process of moving into adulthood and exiting one's family of origin.

59. During the launching period, one formulates _____ _____ _____ , develops an _____ , and becomes more _____ before joining with another person to form a new family.

60. The _____ _____ is the second stage in the family life cycle in which two individuals from separate families of origin unite to form a new family system.

61. _____ _____ and _____ with _____ is the third stage in the family life cycle, and involves adults moving up a _____ and becoming _____ to the younger generation.

62. Problems that emerge when a couple first assumes the parental role are struggles with each other about taking _____ , as well as _____ or _____ to function as _____ parents to children.

63. Some new mothers experience the "_____ _____ ," a depressed state that lasts as long as _____ months.

64. Couples enjoyed more positive marital relations _____ the baby was born.

65. At some point during the early years of the child's life, parents do face the difficult task of juggling roles as _____ and as _____ -_____ adults.

66. Parenting involves several _____ skills and dealing with _____ demands, yet is done with very little formal education—most parents learn parenting practices from their own _____.

67. Fewer children and reduced demands of child care has resulted in these changes: (1) less _____ investment in the child's development; (2) increased time in _____; and (3) parental care supplemented by _____ _____.

68. In the 1930s, behaviorist John Watson suggested parents were too _____ with their children, and in the 1950s experts distinguished between _____ and _____ discipline, and emphasized the latter.

69. Baumrind wrote about three parenting styles: _____, _____, and _____-_____.

70. _____ parenting is a restrictive, _____ style that exhorts a child to follow a parent's directions and to respect _____ and _____; the children often have problems in the area of _____ _____.

71. _____ parenting encourages children to be _____ but still places limits and control on their actions; it is characterized by allowing extensive _____ give-and-take and by _____, _____ parents.

72. In _____-_____ parenting, the parent is very uninvolved in the child's life, while in _____-_____ parenting, the parent is highly involved but places few _____ or _____ on the child.

73. The family with adolescents represents the _____ stage of the family life cycle.

74. The old model of parent-adolescent relationships emphasizes parent-adolescent _____; the new model emphasizes that _____ serve as important attachment figures and support systems.

75. The _____ _____ _____ states that marital satisfaction will _____ when children leave the home, but actually, marital satisfaction _____ in the post-childrearing years.

76. When adult children live with their parents, both sides complain about loss of _____.

77. In middle adulthood, marital partners who engage in _____ _____ usually view their marriage as more positive than in earlier years.

78. Parent-adult child similarity is most noticeable in _____ and _____ areas, least in _____ roles, _____-_____, and _____ orientation.

79. The _____ in _____ _____ is the sixth and final stage in the family life cycle.

80. Retirement poses the most adaptation for _____ families.

81. Marital quality research by Crohan and Veroff determined that _____ was more clearly linked to all aspects of marital well-being than other aspects, but feelings of _____ in the marital role and feelings of _____ over marital outcomes were also important dimensions.

82. Bernard suggested three main dimensions of marital adjustment: (1) the extent and degree of _____ between marital partners; (2) the nature of _____ between the couple; and (3) the quality of the _____ between the partners.

83. Another important factor in marital success is the ability to handle _____ _____.

84. _____ are more likely to view their spouses as best friends; _____ disclose more to their spouses.

85. Typically, _____ do much more family work. About one in _____ husbands do as much family work as their wives.

86. Other than _____ benefits, dual-career marriages often have the advantage of having more _____ relationships and enhanced feelings of _____-_____ for the wives.

87. Overall, women who engage in _____ roles are better adjusted than those who engage in _____ roles; one disadvantage of "_____" is that there is too little _____ time.

88. While divorce has increased for all socioeconomic groups, those in _____ circumstances have a higher incidence of divorce; _____ marriage, low _____ level, low _____, and premarital _____ are all associated with increases in divorce.

89. Former spouses often alternate between feelings of _____ and _____, and may have thoughts of _____.

90. Separated and divorced individuals have higher rates of _____ disturbances, clinical _____, alcoholism, and _____ problems.

91. Special problems surface for the divorced woman who is a _____ homemaker.

92. Children in divorced families that are low in _____ function better than children in never-divorced, intact families that are high in _____.

93. On a short-term basis, _____ adjust better than their opposite-sex siblings; as teenagers, _____ engage in frequent conflict with their _____ and often behave in noncompliant ways.

94. The United States has the _____ remarriage rate in the world, with _____ women and _____ women remarrying sooner.

95. _____ _____ refers to the uncertainty in stepfamilies about roles and responsibilities.

96. Compared to living apart, cohabitation prior to marriage is related to _____ marital stability and _____ rates of marital dissolution.

97. Male homosexuals are often identified as _____ and female homosexuals as _____.

Guided Review Answers

1. Marriage, relationship; 2. Married, unmarried, men; 3. interpersonal closeness; 4. men, emotional gratification; 5. alcoholism, suicide, longevity; 6. three, cirrhosis; 7. divorced, married; 8. protection, support; 9. cholesterol, illness, depression, immune; 10. lower; 11. personal, interpersonal, sociocultural; 12. economic, parents, independence, loneliness, cultural, sex, family, emotional; 13. trapped, self-development, boredom, unhappiness, anger, communication, sexual, career, life-style, freedom; 14. Homogamy, endogamy; 15. chastity; 16. housekeeping; 17. later; 18. five; 19. postponement, cohabitation, single; 20. tripled, doubled; 21. cohabitation; 22. 10, 50; 23. nine; 24. 25, 50; 25. highest, 40; 26. three; 27. two; 28. more, more; 29. Single, limited, autonomy; 30. three, three, five, twelve; 31. extended family, African; 32. siblings, father; 33. ten, four; 34. United States, sex education, family-planning, contraception; 35. secret; 36. physically abused, 30; 37. personality characteristics, abuse victims, cultural; 38. China, Sweden, physical, low; 39. psychological maltreatment; 40. self-identity, social competence; 41. rejecting, isolating, terrorizing, ignoring, corrupting; 42. family scapegoat; 43. responsible, emotionally, physically, loyal, rigid, anger, cold, needy, self-condemning; 44. *Scream Quietly, Neighbors Will Hear,* 1974; 45. four; 46. tension, coping, escalation, explodes, batterer, remorseful, victim, permanent; 47. minimizes, denies, intimacy, jealousy; 48. self-esteem, violence; 49. Employment, economic; 50. financial strain, contraceptive, work force; 51. birth order; 52. undivided, dethronement; 53. oldest, change, authority;

54. pacesetter, overtake, sociable, injustice; 55. pacesetters, dethronement, seriously, spoiled; 56. pitied, selfish, overpopulation; 57. five; 58. Leaving home, single, launching; 59. personal life goals, identity, independent; 60. new couple; 61. Becoming parents, families, children, generation, caregivers; 62. responsibility, refusal, inability, competent; 63. postpartum blues, nine; 64. before; 65. parents, self-actualizing; 66. interpersonal, emotional, parents; 67. maternal, fathering, institutional care; 68. affectionate, physical, psychological; 69. authoritarian, authoritative, laissez-faire; 70. Authoritarian, punitive, work, effort, social competence; 71. Authoritative, independent, verbal, nurturant, warm; 72. permissive-indifferent, permissive-indulgent, demands, controls; 73. fourth; 74. conflict, parents; 75. empty nest syndrome, decrease, increases; 76. privacy; 77. mutual activities; 78. religious, political, gender, life-style, work; 79. family, later life; 80. traditional; 81. happiness, competence, control; 82. differences, communication, relationship; 83. conflict constructively; 84. Men, women; 85. women, ten; 86. financial, equal, self-esteem; 87. multiple, few, "juggling," free; 88. disadvantaged, youthful, educational, income, pregnancy; 89. seductiveness, hostility, reconciliation; 90. psychiatric, depression, psychosomatic; 91. displaced; 92. conflict, conflict; 93. girls, girls, mothers; 94. highest, younger, childless; 95. Boundary ambiguity; 96. less, higher; 97. gay, lesbian

Key Terms

For each term, briefly define the term in your own words and provide an example or situation (especially one you can visualize) that will help you retain the meaning of the concept. Key terms are presented in the order they are presented in the chapter.

1. marriage (p. 300)

2. homogamy (p. 301)

3. endogamy (p. 301)

4. cohabitation (p. 302)

5. leaving home and becoming a single adult (p. 308)

6. launching (p. 308)

7. the new couple (p. 308)

8. becoming parents and families with children (p. 310)

9. authoritarian parenting (p. 312)

10. authoritative parenting (p. 312)

11. permissive-indifferent parenting (p. 312)

12. permissive-indulgent parenting (p. 312)

13. family with adolescents (p. 313)

14. family at midlife (p. 313)

15. empty nest syndrome (p. 313)

16. family in later life (p. 314)

17. boundary ambiguity (p. 320)

18. homosexuals (p. 323)

19. heterosexuals (p. 323)

Study Aids

Students who do well on tests develop mnemonic aids to help them remember important terms and concepts. A few are suggested here, and you are encouraged to develop your own additional aids.

Homogamy and Endogamy. *Homo* is a prefix that means "the same," so *homogamy* is the tendency to marry someone with "the same" personal characteristics. *Endogamy* has to do with the tendency to marry someone from one's own social groups—you might remember that ethnic groups and economic groups, like endogamy, both start with the letter *e.*

The Family Life Cycle. It's easy to bring material about the six stages of this cycle into your active memory if you just key into the order of the stages using brief, telegraphic labels, such as the following:
 Launching
 New Couples
 With Children
 With Adolescents
 Midlife
 Later Life

Authoritarian, Authoritative, Permissive-Indulgent, and Permissive-Indifference Parenting. To help picture the different effects of parenting styles, picture a colt within a fence. In the *authoritarian* situation, the colt has a very small fenced-in area that doesn't allow much exploration; in the *authoritative* situation, the fence is farther out, allowing both exploration and the security of having boundaries. In the *permissive-indulgent* situation, the fence is so far away that the colt rarely runs up against it. This situation has lots of freedom and exploration, but the distance to the fence adds to the colt's insecurity. Finally, in the *permissive-indifference* situation, there is no fence at all—the colt has so much freedom to explore that the colt is lost.

Understanding Concepts

Answer these questions to develop your understanding of the important ideas in this chapter.

1. What are the most important functions of marriage in today's society?

2. What roles do homogamy and endogamy play in the selection of marital partners?

3. Summarize the trends in age of marriage, cohabitation, and single adulthood.

4. Compare and contrast the advantages and disadvantages of marriage versus cohabitation.

5. Summarize current divorce and remarriage trends.

6. How do African American and Hispanic American family structures differ from those of White Americans?

7. Differentiate between physical abuse of children and psychological maltreatment. What is a family scapegoat?

8. Describe the three-phase cycle of domestic violence proposed by Lenore Walker.

9. Describe the typical effects of birth order.

10. Briefly describe each of the six stages of the family life cycle.

11. Compare and contrast the following parenting styles: authoritarian, authoritative, permissive-indifferent, and permissive-indulgent.

12. What is the empty nest syndrome? Is it a reality or a misconception?

13. What factors influence marital satisfaction? What dimensions were emphasized by Jesse Bernard?

14. Discuss typical family work patterns of men and women. How does dual-career marriage affect family work patterns?

15. Summarize the primary effects of divorce on adults and on children.

16. Summarize the remarriage trend in the United States and how stepfamilies work.

Applying Concepts

Answer these questions to develop your ability to apply this chapter's material to your life and the world. Your own responses may differ from other students' in the class, and it is helpful to share your ideas with the other students.

1. Imagine that it is the 1950s. How might the views about marriage and family differ from our current views? Why do you think these differences would exist?

2. What are (or were) your pushes toward marriage and pulls away from being single?

3. Watch at least five television families and summarize how this media portrays marriage and parenthood. Do the shows reflect actual trends in society? What characteristics do they say are important in good relationships? What kinds of parenting styles are illustrated?

4. What are (were) the major factors involved in your own mate selection? What role do homogamy and endogamy play?

5. What are your own views on the advantages and disadvantages of cohabitation? Do you approve of its growing popularity?

6. List the roles that you believe men and women should have within marriage. How similar are your lists for wives and for husbands?

7. Describe the main features of the family structure in your family of origin (e.g., dual-career parents, single parent, extended family). What are the most important ways this family structure has influenced you?

8. What specific challenges are posed for inter-ethnic relationships, and what factors help support and foster them? How can people of two different religious backgrounds raise their children in a religious sense?

9. Why is the adolescent pregnancy rate in the United States so high? What could be done to reduce this rate?

10. If you were a counselor, how would you work with an adult who was psychologically maltreated in childhood and now is the family scapegoat?

11. What is your birth order position? How has this position affected your personality, your personal life goals, and how you interact with other persons? Check with your friends and find out their birth order position—do you get along better with persons of any particular position? Is it better for you to date/marry someone of the same, or different, birth order position?

12. Turn to Self-Assessment 12.1 and write about your family constellation. Summarize the most positive and negative influences from your family constellation.

13. Assess whether your life "fits into" or is quite different from the family life cycle described in the chapter.

14. Which parenting style did your parents use? Which style do you or would you use in rearing your own children? Do you think these parenting styles are also reflected in teaching styles and in administration styles?

15. Quiz yourself on your knowledge of marital myths and realities using Self-Assessment 12.2. Assess your overall accurate knowledge.

16. If you are currently married or in a committed relationship, use Self-Assessment 12.3 to assess your current happiness with your relationship. Summarize the results here. If the instrument does not apply to you currently, assess its value in helping marital partners improve their marriages.

17. Discuss how you currently split family work responsibilities, and how you would like to split these responsibilities.

18. Is marriage as a social institution changing, dissolving, or just adapting to other rapid social changes?

19. Would you legalize homosexual marriages? Why or why not?

20. Does American culture discriminate against people who choose to live a single life-style? Are there social expectations that single people simply cannot meet?

Chapter Practice Tests

Answer these multiple-choice test questions to help you assess your understanding of the chapter's material. Evaluate your answers to determine which sections you need to further review.

Practice Test A

1. All things taken together, men appear to
   a. benefit more from marriage.
   b. benefit less from marriage.
   c. benefit the same as women from marriage.
   d. neither benefit nor suffer from marriage.
   p. 301

2. Which of the following is true about cohabitation before marriage?
   a. The trend is decreasing.
   b. The trend is increasing.
   c. The trend has not changed in recent years.
   d. The trend is for cohabitation to replace marriage.
   p. 303

3. Which factor has most influenced changes in women's roles in marriage?
   a. women having more children
   b. women having less children
   c. children growing faster
   d. women entering the work force
   p. 303

4. Ethnic minority families possess a great deal of
   a. deficits.
   b. resilience.
   c. majority values.
   d. social disintegration.
   p. 304

5. High rates of teen pregnancy among American youth are most likely because adolescents in the U.S.
   a. have more sex.
   b. are less likely to use contraception.
   c. are more irresponsible.
   d. are more likely to drink.
   p. 305

6. Violent outbursts in relationships can often be triggered by
   a. jealousy.
   b. flashbacks.
   c. mingling friends.
   d. a family crisis.
   p. 306

7. Couples with lower levels of education are more likely to experience financial problems and are also more likely to
   a. remain childless.
   b. discipline their children.
   c. have more children.
   d. seek out help when they need it.
   p. 307

8. Launching involves a young adult
   a. running from their problems.
   b. reactively fleeing from a family.
   c. moving into adulthood.
   d. all of the above.
   p. 308

9. Parents who are very involved in their child's life and place few demands on them exhibit which style of parenting?
   a. permissive-indulgent
   b. permissive-indifferent
   c. permissive-providing
   d. authoritative-permissive
   p. 313

10. Adjustment to family life in traditional families in the later years is often
    a. more difficult for men.
    b. more difficult for women.
    c. equally difficult for men and women.
    d. less difficult for men unless the couple did not have children.
    p. 314

11. Conflict in relationships can be approached by discussion. In discussing conflicting issues, couples should
    a. consult a mediator.
    b. review their past conflicts and how they were resolved.
    c. establish ground rules.
    d. communicate about each other's expectations.
    p. 315

12. Many wives believe their husbands
    a. get angry too quickly.
    b. only express negative feelings.
    c. only love them when they have physical contact.
    d. do not express their feelings enough.
    p. 316

13. Women who engage in multiple roles involving marriage, family, and career, are more likely to be
    a. less well adjusted.
    b. too stressed to function.
    c. better adjusted.
    d. challenged more than men.
    p. 317

14. The stress of a divorce is likely to result in the experience of
    a. relief and adjustment.
    b. prolonged physical sicknesses.
    c. extreme depression.
    d. new insights into the self.
    p. 318

15. Homosexual couples may experience less stability than heterosexual couples because
    a. they receive fewer social supports to stay together.
    b. they do not have the financial resources heterosexuals have.
    c. they lack intimate communications.
    d. none of the above.
    p. 323

Practice Test B

1. Married people are more likely to be healthy if
   a. they are in a satisfying marriage.
   b. their spouse does not drink.
   c. they have a dual income.
   d. none of the above.
   p. 301

2. Research has shown that most people living together outside marriage have
   a. previously been married.
   b. never been married.
   c. different ethnic backgrounds.
   d. a fear of long-term commitments.
   p. 303

3. The majority of people who get divorced
   a. remarry.
   b. cohabitate.
   c. stay single.
   d. none of the above.
   p. 303

4. Women entering the work force have required that they
   a. rely on domestic help.
   b. demand more of their husbands.
   c. change their roles in marriage.
   d. adjust their self-expectations.
   p. 303

5. Ethnic minority families in the United States are more likely to
   a. be more like White families than previously thought.
   b. experience many deficits that are debilitating to children.
   c. all be alike.
   d. none of the above.
   p. 303

6. Teen pregnancy in the United States is
   a. higher than in any other country in the world.
   b. higher than in any other country in the Western world.
   c. a result of moral breakdown.
   d. less prevalent than ten years ago.
   p. 305

7. Psychological maltreatment of children involves
   a. all aspects of home life.
   b. the development of self-esteem.
   c. the development of self-identity.
   d. intellectual development.
   p. 306

8. Reductions in the number of children per family is the likely result of
   a. increased use of contraception.
   b. men assuming more control over child care.
   c. reduced social pressures to have children.
   d. reduced amount of available resources.
   p. 307

9. Leaving home to establish single adulthood involves
   a. a complete cut-off from the family of origin.
   b. developing independence.
   c. becoming financially stable.
   d. all of the above.
   p. 308

10. Women and men are likely to experience marriage
    a. with more or less the same perceptions.
    b. very differently.
    c. at different points in the family cycle.
    d. in much the same way.
    p. 316

11. Men increase their roles in the home usually when
    a. women enter the work force.
    b. couples enter their later years.
    c. they are threatened with divorce.
    d. none of the above.
    p. 317

12. Couples with higher levels of marital satisfaction and lower levels of marital conflict are more likely to
    a. be well off financially.
    b. have been together longer.
    c. alternate marital roles.
    d. communicate.
    p. 317

13. Most men and women agree with which of the following statements?
   a. Men and women should be equally responsible for family work.
   b. Women should be less involved in family work than they have been.
   c. Men and women should both be less involved in family work.
   d. Women should be primarily responsible for family work and men should help out.
   p. 318

14. Women are most likely to experience which of the following in relation to dual careers?
   a. reduced stress from getting out of the house
   b. poorer adjustment
   c. decreased investment in family
   d. none of the above.
   p. 318

15. Which of the following is true of children with a stepparent?
   a. They are more likely to be closer to the stepmother than the biological mother.
   b. They are more likely to be closer to a biological parent regardless of sex of the stepparent.
   c. They are more likely to be closer to a stepfather than to the biological father.
   d. They are rarely adjusted to stepparents at all.
   p. 320

Key for Practice Test A

1. Answer a; Research shows that men benefit more in terms of health and satisfaction from marriage than do women; page 301; Learning Objective 1
2. Answer b; Over the years, there is a trend toward people living together before getting married; page 303; Learning Objective 2
3. Answer d; Women entering the work force places necessary demands for change on traditional roles women have played in marriages; page 303; Learning Objective 4
4. Answer b; Research has shown that ethnic minority families tend to have a great deal of resilience resources for coping with change; page 305; Learning Objective 5
5. Answer b; Social barriers to contraceptive availability for adolescents has contributed to the high rates of teen pregnancy; page 305; Learning Objective 6
6. Answer a; Jealousy can turn to rage which then may lead to violence; page 306; Learning Objective 7
7. Answer c; Lower education and lower income families tend to have more children which further strains their financial resources; page 307; Learning Objective 8
8. Answer c; Launching is when young adults move out on their own to establish independence but not severing family ties; page 308; Learning Objective 9
9. Answer a; Permissive-indulgent parents are involved with the life of their child but also provide minimal guidance and rules on a child's behavior; page 313; Learning Objective 10
10. Answer a; Men report difficulty adjusting to family changes in later years of the family cycle; page 314; Learning Objective 11
11. Answer c; Ground rules establish a means for fairness and allow each member of the couple time and openness for discussing their perspectives and concerns; page 315; Learning Objective 12
12. Answer d; Wives often indicate that their husbands are reluctant to express feelings and that this can cause conflict in the marriage; page 316; Learning Objective 13

13. Answer c; Multiple roles that are balanced across areas of life can contribute to better adjustment; page 317; Learning Objective 14

14. Answer b; Prolonged stress, as occurs in divorce, can have very negative affects on health and wellness; page 318; Learning Objective 15

15. Answer a; Because of social prejudices, homosexual couples receive fewer supports that help couples stay together for long periods of time; page 323; Learning Objective 16

Key for Practice Test B

1. Answer a; Increased marital satisfaction has been found to be related to positive health benefits among married people; page 301; Learning Objective 1

2. Answer b; Most people who cohabitate have no previous history of being married; page 303; Learning Objective 2

3. Answer a; Remarriage is the most common path taken by persons who have been divorced; page 303; Learning Objective 3

4. Answer c; Adapting marital roles has been necessary for women who enter the work force; page 303; Learning Objective 4

5. Answer d; Ethnic minority families are highly diverse in their structure and roles for family members; page 303; Learning Objective 5

6. Answer b; Teen pregnancy is higher in the U.S. than any other country in the Western world, but not yet the highest in the entire world; page 305; Learning Objective 6

7. Answer c; Emotional and psychological abuse impairs the development of a sense of personal identity; page 306; Learning Objective 7

8. Answer a; Increased availability of contraception has resulted in couples having more fertility options and a reduction in the number of children per family; page 307; Learning Objective 8

9. Answer b; Independence is a key element of adult development and is initiated by moving out on one's own; page 308; Learning Objective 9

10. Answer b; Men and women have been found to have different expectations about marriage and to receive different benefits from being married; page 316; Learning Objective 10

11. Answer b; As couples enter their later years men become more involved in the daily workings of the home. This shift involves changing roles in careers as well as family structures that accompany older age; page 317; Learning Objective 11

12. Answer d; Open communication between marriage partners has been found to be related to the satisfaction experienced in the marriage; page 317; Learning Objective 12

13. Answer d; Contemporary views on men's and women's roles in the home emphasize the importance of sharing responsibilities; page 318; Learning Objective 13

14. Answer d; Dual careers pose increased stress for women due to multiple roles; page 318; Learning Objective 14

15. Answer b; Children with a stepparent are highly likely to favor their biological parent regardless of the sex of the child and the sex of the parent; page 320; Learning Objective 15

Chapter Outline

I. The Nature of Development
    A. Development is the pattern of movement or change that begins at conception and continues through the life span.
    B. Development includes biological, cognitive, and social processes.
    C. Adolescence begins from 10–12 years old and ends about 18–22 years old and is the developmental period of transition from childhood to early adulthood.
    D. Early adulthood is the developmental period that begins in late teens or early twenties and ends sometimes in the late thirties to early forties.
    E. Developmental research suggests that happiness and life satisfaction occurs about equally across the life span.

II. The Transition from Adolescence to Adulthood
    A. According to Kenniston, youth is the transitional period between adolescence and adulthood.
    B. In adolescence, one struggles for self-definition; in youth, one struggles for an autonomous self.

III. Physical Development
    A. Early and Middle Adulthood
       1. Most athletes reach their peak performance before the age of 30, often between 19 and 26.
       2. Early adulthood is the period of greatest health—few have chronic health problems and there are fewer colds and respiratory problems than in childhood.
       3. Many young adults use cigarettes, alcohol, drugs, and eat poorly.
       4. Concern about health status increases in middle adulthood, especially the issues of heart disease, cancer, and weight.
       5. Obesity increases the risk of dying in middle adulthood, as well as having hypertension and digestive disorders; about 20 million Americans are dieting at any time.
       6. The American culture emphasizes youthful appearance, and middle adulthood involves dealing with the signs of aging.
    B. Late Adulthood and Aging
       1. Active older adults tend to be healthier and happier.
       2. Sedentary older adults have a higher mortality rate than those who exercise moderately.
       3. In 1900, 1 in 25 was over 65; now it is 1 in 9; and, by 2050, it will be 1 in 4.
       4. Human life span has not changed, but life expectancy has increased.

IV. Cognitive Development
    A. Early and Middle Adulthood
       1. In adulthood individuals consolidate their logical thinking and become more systematic in approaching problems.
       2. Idealism decreases after adolescence and adults think logically and adapt to life as circumstances demand.

3. Most mental skills decline little with age, although some aspects of memory are affected, especially recent information and recall over recognition.
B. Late Adulthood
1. Wechsler suggested that intellectual decline was simply a part of the general aging process, that most of the decline is in the speed of processing information.
2. General knowledge and wisdom often increases well into late adulthood.
V. Social Development and Theories of Adult Development
A. Stage Theories of Adult Social and Personality Development
1. Most theories of adult development address themes of work, love, career, and intimacy.
2. Erikson's stages are intimacy versus isolation during early adulthood and generativity versus stagnation during middle adulthood.
3. Gould defines the twenties as a period of assuming new roles, and the thirties as a time of being stuck in our responsibilities; the forties includes a sense of urgency and a mid-life crisis.
4. Levinson says the two major tasks of adulthood are exploring the possibilities for adult living and developing a stable life structure; stages include the novice phases, developing family life and career, BOOM, and middle-age.
5. According to Levinson, the change to middle adulthood includes four major conflicts: (1) being young versus being old; (2) being destructive versus being constructive; (3) being masculine versus being feminine; and (4) being attached to others versus being separated from them.
6. Vaillant adds two stages—career consolidation stage, during early adulthood, and keeping the meaning versus rigidity, during middle adulthood.
7. All stage theories generally agree that adult development begins with change from identity to intimacy, then from career consolidation to generativity, and finally from searching for meaning to some final integration.
B. Crisis and Cohort
1. For Levinson, mid-life is a crisis between the past and the future.
2. Vaillant saw the forties as a decade of reassessing, but he also thought that most do not have a mid-life crisis.
3. According to Neugarten, attitudes, expectations, and behaviors are influenced by the period in which we live—or one's social clock.
4. Neugarten suggests that we are becoming less concerned about doing things at certain times.
C. The Life Events Approach
1. Life events (e.g., divorce, death of a spouse, job promotion) rather than stages may be responsible for changes in our adult lives.
2. Many factors (e.g., physical health, personality, family support) and self-perceptions influence how life events affect people.
D. Individual Variation
1. Personality development can be studies by focusing on either the similarities or the differences among people.
2. Pervasive personal preoccupation is maladaptive in both work and marriage.
E. Gender, Culture, and Adult Development
1. Stage theories do not adequately address women's concerns about relationships, interdependence, caring, and childbearing and childrearing.
2. Women's order of events varies more than men's order.

3. Middle-aged women in nonindustrialized societies tend to have fewer restrictions and more power.
4. Different stages may be appropriate for different cultures.

F. Stability and Change
1. James views the basic course of personality as set by the age of thirty.
2. Costa believes that extraversion, adjustment, and openness to new experiences do not change much during adulthood.
3. The California Longitudinal Study suggests that some stability exists, but also change occurs.

G. Late Adulthood
1. Activity theory suggests that active and involved older people are more satisfied and healthier.
2. Ageism is prejudice against older people.
3. Ethnic minority elderly face the double jeopardy of racism and ageism—and if female, add sexism.
4. Integrity versus despair is Erikson's eighth stage of development.

VI. Death and Dying
A. Facing One's Own Death
1. Knowledge of death's inevitability pushes one to establish priorities and structure to one's life.
2. Kübler-Ross proposes five stages of dying: denial, anger, bargaining, depression, and acceptance, although these stages are not an invariant sequence.

B. Perceived Control and Denial
1. Perceived control and denial may work together as an adaptive strategy for some older adults who face death.
2. In a nursing home setting, the "responsible" or "self-control" group had more improvement than the "dependent" group.
3. When Rodin taught nursing home patients to assertively say "no" to things they do not want, they had a lower cortisol level, which is related to lessened stress.

C. Coping with the Death of Someone Else
1. Most psychologists believe that it is best for dying individuals to know that they are dying.
2. Open communication is important, as is helping individuals focus on their strengths and on the remainder of their life.
3. Survivors suffer profound grief, financial loss, loneliness, and increased physical and psychological disorders.
4. Female survivors are more likely to have a network of relationships to help them cope.
5. Older widows do better than younger widows, perhaps because death of a partner is more expected; widowers usually have more money and are more likely to remarry.

Learning Objectives

After reading and studying the chapter, students should be able to:

1. Describe and understand the adolescent to adulthood transition.
2. Describe the processes of physical development in adulthood.

3. Describe the processes of cognitive development in adulthood.
4. Know the various stage theories of adult social and personality development.
5. Understand the life events approach to adult development.
6. Know how individual variation plays a role in adult development.
7. Understand the relationship between gender, culture, and patterns of adult development.
8. Understand both stability and change in adult development.
9. Identify the process of development in late adulthood.
10. Identify the factors associated with facing one's own death.
11. Describe the processes of perceived control and coping with death.

Guided Review

After you have read the chapter one time, search through the chapter to find the appropriate words to complete these statements. Material is covered in the same order as the chapter.

1. People develop in both similar and unique ways, and psychologists have paid the most attention to
   _____.

2. _____ is the pattern of movement or _____ that begins at _____ and continues through the life cycle.

3. Development is complex because it involves _____, _____, and _____ processes.

4. The most widely used classification of developmental periods is: _____ period, _____, _____ childhood, _____ childhood, _____ childhood, _____, _____ adulthood, _____ adulthood, and _____ adulthood.

5. The developmental transition from childhood to early adulthood is called _____, and it begins with rapid _____ changes, involves the pursuits of _____ and _____, and more time spent outside of the _____.

6. _____ _____ is the developmental period of one's twenties and into one's forties during which individuals establish _____ and _____ independence, pursue a _____, and seek _____ with one or more individuals.

7. Older adults are _____ satisfied with their lives as younger adults.

8. Regardless of age, about _____ in four adults report overall satisfaction with life.

9. Sociologist _____ proposed a transitional period of _____ between adolescence and adulthood which is a time of extended economic and personal temporariness.

10. In adolescence, a person struggles for _____-_____; in youth the struggle is in developing an _____ self and becoming socially involved.

11. One out of _____ individuals does not complete high school.

12. Two criteria that signal the end of youth and the beginning of early adulthood are _____ _____ and _____ _____ _____.

13. Most athletes reach their peak performance before the age of _____.

14. Both physical performance and _____ are likely to be their best during early adulthood, as few have _____ health problems and there are also fewer colds than in childhood.

15. At the same time, many young adults eat _____ and increase their use of _____, _____, and _____.
16. The three greatest health concerns during middle adulthood are _____ _____, _____, and _____.
17. Cancer related to _____ often surfaces for the first time in middle adulthood.
18. Approximately 20 million Americans are seriously _____ at this time.
19. _____ increases the probability of dying in middle adulthood by 40 percent, and is also associated with _____ and _____ disorders.
20. The more _____ older adults are, the _____ and happier they are.
21. An 11-year study at the Aerobics Institute in Dallas found that _____ participants were more than _____ as likely to die during that period than those who were moderately fit.
22. In 1900, one in _____ Americans were over 65; now the figure is one in _____, and by 2050 it will be one in _____.
23. The life _____, or _____ number of years a member of the _____ can live, has remained virtually unchanged, but life _____ has increased.
24. Improvements in _____, _____, _____, and _____-_____ have given us an average _____-_____ additional years of life since 1900.
25. Compared to adolescents, adults become more _____ in approaching problems, more proficient at developing _____ and deducing _____, less _____, and more able to _____ to circumstances of life.
26. Memory appears to decline with age more often with _____-term memory than _____-term memory.
27. Memory is more likely to decline when _____ and _____ are not used.
28. Information is harder to recall when it is _____ acquired or when the information is not used often.
29. Memory in middle adulthood also declines if the individual has poor _____.
30. Wechsler concluded that intellectual _____ was part of the general aging process, but most of the difference has to do with not being as _____.
31. In _____ _____ and _____, older adults often outperform younger adults.
32. Erikson's adolescence stage is _____ versus _____ _____, and in early adulthood, the stage is _____ versus _____.
33. Erikson's stage that occurs mainly in middle adulthood is _____ versus _____.
34. Through _____, the adult achieves a kind of immortality by leaving one's legacy to the next generation, while _____, or _____-_____, develops when individuals sense they have done nothing for the next generation.
35. In _____ generativity, adults conceive and give birth; through _____ generativity, children are nurtured and guided; through _____ generativity, skills are passed down to others; and through _____ generativity, some aspect of culture is created, renovated, or conserved.
36. Gould suggests that _____-_____ is as turbulent as adolescence because adults deal with being stuck with _____ and feeling a sense of _____ as life speeds by.
37. In his book _____ of a _____ _____, Levinson wrote about men's lives as a series of stages.

38. In early adulthood, the two major tasks are _____ the _____ and developing a stable _____ _____, and this stage is called the _____ phase.

39. During the thirties, men usually work to develop _____ _____ and _____, and toward the end of this decade, men are in the phase of _____ _____ _____ _____, or BOOM.

40. The transition to middle adulthood, which lasts about _____ years, involves dealing with four major conflicts: (1) being _____ versus being _____; (2) being _____ versus being _____; (3) being _____ versus being _____; and, (4) being _____ to others versus being _____ from them.

41. The _____ of Levinson's subjects found the mid-life transition (ages _____ to _____-_____) tumultuous and psychologically painful.

42. Vaillant adds the early adulthood stage of _____ _____ and the middle adulthood stage of _____ _____ _____ versus _____.

43. Stage theories tend to see adult development beginning with a change from _____ to _____, then from _____ _____ to _____, and finally from _____ for _____ to some final _____.

44. In contrast to Levinson, Vaillant believes that a _____ of adults experience a mid-life crisis.

45. _____ are groups of individuals born in the same year or time period, and Neugarten suggests that the social environment of a particular age group can alter its _____ _____, or the timetable for accomplishing life's tasks.

46. _____ _____ rather than stages may be responsible for changes in our adult lives.

47. How life events affect people is mediated by physical _____, _____, _____, _____ support, and _____, as well as by one's _____-_____.

48. Stage theories attempt to describe the _____, rather than the _____ _____, in adult development.

49. An important factor in functioning under stress is the ability to set aside _____ _____ and _____.

50. One criticism of stage theories is that they do not adequately address _____'s concerns about _____, _____, and _____, and do not attend to the importance of _____ and _____.

51. In nonindustrialized societies, middle-aged women typically have _____ restrictions than when they were younger.

52. James and Costa are two psychologists who emphasize the _____ of personality over time.

53. _____ theory says that being active and involved is related to satisfaction and health in late adulthood.

54. Prejudice against older people is called _____.

55. About one in _____ of all women working today can expect to be poor in old age.

56. Female ethnic-minority individuals are in the triple _____ of _____, _____, and _____.

57. Erikson's eighth stage of development during late adulthood is called _____ versus _____.

58. Knowledge of _____'s inevitability permits us to establish _____ and structure our _____ accordingly.

59. If faced with just six months to live, younger adults want to spend their time in _____, such as traveling, while older adults describe _____-_____ activities.

60. According to Kübler-Ross, the five stages of dying are _____ and _____, _____, _____, _____, and _____.

61. Nursing home residents who are given responsibility and control are more _____ and _____, _____, and _____, but if the control is taken back, they are _____ off than if they were never given control.

62. Rodin states that individuals who believe they have a high degree of _____ are more likely to feel their _____ can make a difference in their lives.

63. Being in control reduces _____ and its _____-_____ _____, including cortisol.

64. Of life events that require adjustment, _____ of a _____ is the most difficult adjustment.

65. Survivors often suffer profound _____, endure _____ _____, experience _____, and are more likely to have a _____ or _____ disorder.

66. Widows outnumber widowers by _____ to one.

67. Widows do _____ emotionally adjusting than do widowers because of their _____ of friends and relatives.

68. Widowers are more likely than widows to have more _____ and to _____.

Guided Review Answers

1. uniqueness; 2. Development, change, conception; 3. biological, cognitive, social; 4. prenatal, infancy, early, middle, late, adolescence, early, middle, late; 5. adolescence, physical, independence, identity, family; 6. Early adulthood, personal, economic, career, intimacy; 7. as; 8. three; 9. Kenniston, youth; 10. self-definition, autonomous; 11. four; 12. economic independence, independent decision making; 13. thirty; 14. health, chronic; 15. poorly, alcohol, cigarettes, drugs; 16. heart disease, cancer, weight; 17. smoking; 18. dieting; 19. Obesity, hypertension, digestive; 20. active, healthier; 21. sedentary, twice; 22. twenty-five, nine, four; 23. span, maximum, species, expectancy; 24. medicine, nutrition, exercise, life-style, twenty-two; 25. systematic, hypotheses, solutions, idealistic, adapt; 26. long, short; 27. organization, imagery; 28. recently; 29. health; 30. decline, fast; 31. general knowledge, wisdom; 32. identity, identity confusion, intimacy, isolation; 33. generativity, stagnation; 34. generativity, stagnation, self-absorption; 35. biological, parental, work, cultural; 36. mid-life, responsibilities, urgency; 37. *Seasons, Man's Life;* 38. exploring, possibilities, life structure, novice; 39. family life, career, becoming one's own man; 40. five, young, old, destructive, constructive, masculine, feminine, attached, separated; 41. majority, forty, forty-five; 42. career consolidation, keeping the meaning, rigidity; 43. identity, intimacy, career consolidation, generativity, search, meaning, integrity; 44. minority; 45. Cohorts, social clock; 46. Life events; 47. health, intelligence, personality, family, income, self-perception; 48. universals, individual variations; 49. unproductive worries, preoccupations; 50. women's, relationships, interdependence, caring, childbearing, childrearing; 51. fewer; 52. stability; 53. Activity; 54. ageism; 55. four; 56. jeopardy, ageism, sexism, racism; 57. integrity, despair; 58. death, priorities, time; 59. activities, inner-focused; 60. denial, isolation, anger, bargaining, depression, acceptance; 61. alert, active, happier, satisfied, worse; 62. control, actions; 63. stress, stress-related hormones; 64. death, spouse; 65. grief, financial loss, loneliness, physical, psychological; 66. five; 67. better, networks; 68. money, remarry

Key Terms

For each term, briefly define the term in your own words and provide an example or situation (especially one you can visualize) that will help you retain the meaning of the concept. Key terms are presented in the order they are presented in the chapter.

1. development (p. 332)

2. adolescence (p. 332)

3. early adulthood (p. 333)

4. middle adulthood (p. 333)

5. late adulthood (p. 333)

6. youth (p. 333)

7. intimacy versus isolation (p. 339)

8. generativity versus stagnation (p. 339)

9. career consolidation (p. 341)

10. keeping the meaning versus rigidity (p. 341)

11. cohorts (p. 342)

12. social clock (p. 342)

13. activity theory (p. 346)

14. ageism (p. 346)

15. integrity versus despair (p. 347)

16. selective optimization with compensation model (p. 349)

17. denial and isolation (p. 350)

18. anger (p. 350)

19. bargaining (p. 350)

20. depression (p. 350)

21. acceptance (p. 350)

Study Aids

Students who do well on tests develop mnemonic aids to help them remember important terms and concepts. A few are suggested here, and you are encouraged to develop your own additional aids.

> **Erikson's Adult Stages.** Use the sentence Ida Issues Girl Scout I.D.s to remember the first three stages of Erikson's theory. The first two I's help you to recall Intimacy versus Isolation, the G and S help you to recall Generativity versus Stagnation, and the I and D help you to recall Integrity versus Despair.

> **Kübler-Ross's Stages of Dying.** Remember DABDA to help you remember the five stages in their prototypal order:
> > Denial and isolation
> > Anger
> > Bargaining
> > Depression
> > Acceptance

Understanding Concepts

Answer these questions to develop your understanding of the important ideas in this chapter.

1. Define development, and briefly discuss why it is complex.

2. What is youth? What aspects of modern society increased the need to have a stage between adolescence and early adulthood?

3. How does college and career affect achievement orientation?

4. Compare and contrast physical development in early, middle, and late adulthood.

5. How does concern about one's health change from early through late adulthood?

6. Differentiate between life span and life expectancy. How has life expectancy changed in this century?

7. What are typical cognitive and memory changes during adulthood?

8. List the three adult stages of Erikson's theory, and briefly describe the important aspects of each of these stages.

9. Compare the ideas of Gould, Levinson, and Vaillant.

10. Discuss Neugarten's ideas about the effects of cohorts and social clocks.

11. How do life events approaches differ from stage theories?

12. Is personality stable or changeable during adulthood?

13. What is the activity theory?

14. What is ageism?

15. List and describe the five stages of dying as proposed by Kübler-Ross.

16. Discuss Rodin's work on the effects of control and responsibility on stress levels and life satisfaction.

17. Discuss the typical differences in the experiences of widows and widowers.

Applying Concepts

Answer these questions to develop your ability to apply this chapter's material to your life and the world. Your own responses may differ from other students' in the class, and it is helpful to share your ideas with the other students.

1. The chapter opens with Jim Croce's song "Time in a Bottle." Reread the lyrics, and then write about how you would spend the time that you could save.

2. Have you experienced youth? Are you still experiencing youth?

3. How did you know when you had moved from adolescence (or your youth) to adulthood? Was there a definite moment, or was it a gradual transition?

4. How would you assess your changes in physical development/condition during your adolescent through adult years?

5. How does the cultural emphasis on a youthful appearance affect you?

6. Do people who place greater value on physical strength and stamina in their youth have more difficulty adjusting to the physical declines that occur with aging?

7. Take Self-Assessment 13.1, which provides information about your personal life expectancy. According to your answers, what are your greatest unchangeable "liabilities"? Which "liabilities" could you modify?

8. Compared to your adolescence, have your thinking patterns changed?

9. Read the summary of Gould's stages in table 13.1. Has your life paralleled these stages so far? Where do you differ?

10. Do you believe that Levinson's ideas apply to both men and women? Why, or why not?

11. For each of the activities and events listed in table 13.2, mark the age at which you think is the best age to experience this major activity. Compare your answers with those of the 1950s and the 1970s. Are you similar? Does your life seem to match your own answers?

12. Do you think it is more important for psychologists to understand the similarities or the differences among individuals? Why?

13. As social roles continue to change, will there be a decrease in differences between men's and women's patterns of adult development?

14. In the future, will cultural and racial differences in patterns of adult development decrease or increase? Why do you take this position?

15. What are some examples of ageism in our culture? Do young adults who have negative attitudes toward the elderly fear their own growing old more than those who respect and understand the elderly?

16. Do other losses besides death also bring about the five stages of dying proposed by Kübler-Ross. Use an example to show the similarities or differences.

17. What would you do if you had six months to live? Would you engage in many activities or become inner focused? Why?

18. Take Self-Assessment 13.2 on death anxiety. Interpret your responses here.

19. If you were a nursing home administrator, what information in this chapter would you adapt to your work setting, and why?

20. Use the Life Review Chart in the Critical Thinking about Adjustment section. What changes have you been through, and where do you seem to be heading?

Chapter Practice Tests

Answer these multiple-choice test questions to help you assess your understanding of the chapter's material. Evaluate your answers to determine which sections you need to further review.

Practice Test A

1. Which of the following is the predominant characteristic of adulthood?
   a. independent decision making
   b. breaking off from family bonds
   c. increasing leisure activities
   d. sexual reproductive capacity
   p. 333

2. A person's best health tends to be during
   a. childhood.
   b. adolescence.
   c. young adulthood.
   d. middle adulthood.
   p. 334

3. People today are living longer lives because of which of the following?
   a. better nutrition
   b. the proliferation of medical care and hospitals
   c. cleaner living environments
   d. none of the above
   p. 335

4. Piaget's theory of cognitive development described adult functioning as
   a. the same as adolescent functioning.
   b. more systematic than adolescence.
   c. slower than in adolescence.
   d. disrupted and discontinuous.
   p. 336

5. Declines in intellectual functioning that occur in older age primarily involve
   a. speed of processing.
   b. wisdom.
   c. knowledge.
   d. recognition.
   p. 338

6. Being attached to others versus being separate from others is a conflict that occurs
   a. in adolescence.
   b. during the entire life span.
   c. in a transition into middle adulthood.
   d. as a part of the life review.
   p. 339

7. Comparing stage theories of adult development to each other shows that they tend to
   a. disagree on important dimensions.
   b. look more alike than different.
   c. point out the inconsistencies in development.
   d. show how Piaget was wrong.
   p. 340

8. Life events during adulthood are influenced by
   a. physical health.
   b. personality.
   c. family support.
   d. all of the above.
   p. 342

9. Stage theories of adult development tend to emphasize the
   a. negative aspects of aging.
   b. the universal aspects of aging.
   c. the biological aspects of aging.
   d. the individual aspects of aging.
   p. 342

10. The Gusii culture marks periods of adult development on the basis of
    a. chronological age.
    b. social age.
    c. life events.
    d. physical maturation.
    p. 345

11. According to Costa, which of the following is most likely to be true?
    a. Personality does not change in adulthood.
    b. Changes in men's and women's personality are similar.
    c. Changes in men's and women's personality are different.
    d. Adult personality undergoes many transitions.
    p. 345

12. Theorists disagree that adult personality
    a. is capable of change, but does not change.
    b. changes over adulthood.
    c. is not capable of change.
    d. all of the above.
    p. 346

13. Double jeopardy refers to which of the following forms of prejudice?
    a. ageism and racism
    b. ageism and sexism
    c. sexism and racism
    d. ageism and living in poverty
    p. 346

14. Which of the following is not one of the stages of death and dying described by Kübler-Ross?
    a. anger
    b. anxiety
    c. depression
    d. bargaining
    p. 349

15. Communication about death with a person in the process of dying may
    a. improve coping for the dying but not survivors.
    b. improve coping for survivors but not the dying.
    c. increase death anxiety of survivors.
    d. improve coping for all involved.
    p. 352

Practice Test B

1. Two important aspects of adulthood are
   a. distancing from family and intimate relationships.
   b. termination of old friendships and relationships.
   c. economic and decision-making independence.
   d. economic independence and intimate relationships.
   p. 333

2. More than at any other period in their life, people are their healthiest when they are
   a. children.
   b. adolescents.
   c. young adults.
   d. in middle adulthood.
   p. 334

3. Health among older adults is greatest for those who have
   a. been successful.
   b. health insurance.
   c. maintained working.
   d. exercised regularly.
   p. 335

4. As we get older, our memory is most likely to
   a. remain the same.
   b. decline in most ways.
   c. improve in most ways.
   d. decline in some ways but not others.
   p. 336

5. According to Levinson, an exploration of possible life-styles occurs during
   a. adolescence.
   b. early adulthood.
   c. middle adulthood.
   d. late adulthood.
   p. 340

6. Which of the following is a part of Erikson's theory?
   a. career consolidation
   b. intimacy
   c. generational leap
   d. integration
   p. 341

7. Life events that occur during adulthood are primarily
   a. coped with easily.
   b. coped with the same by all adults.
   c. coped with differently during different historical periods.
   d. coped with better by men than by women.
   p. 342

8. Erikson's theory, like other stage theories, is most likely to emphasize
   a. the positives.
   b. the universals.
   c. individual variation.
   d. the negatives.
   p. 342

9. When the broad perspective of adult development in taken, it is apparent that
   a. we are all more alike than we are different.
   b. we all share commonalities, but differ greatly.
   c. we all share commonalities and only differ slightly.
   d. men and women are more different than they are alike.
   p. 343

10. One problem with adult stage theories is that they
    a. are specific to a culture.
    b. describe male and female development.
    c. are unable to link adulthood to earlier years.
    d. do not adequately describe female development.
    p. 344

11. Costa's theory of personality in adulthood is characterized by
    a. change.
    b. stability.
    c. a balance of change and stability.
    d. change in early adulthood and stability in later adulthood.
    p. 345

12. Older persons who are in good health and have suitable income are more likely to
    a. be active.
    b. be satisfied with life.
    c. exercise.
    d. all of the above.
    p. 346

13. The primary process that occurs during Erikson's final stage of adult development is called
    a. generativity.
    b. ego involvement.
    c. life review.
    d. despair avoidance.
    p. 347

14. The stages of death and dying outlined by Kübler-Ross rely most heavily on which of the following?
    a. coping strategies for impending loss
    b. positive emotions
    c. factors that may be true for men but not women
    d. none of the above
    p. 350

15. Men are less likely to cope well after a loss because
    a. men tend to be emotionally unconnected to others.
    b. men lack support for emotional expression.
    c. men experience more losses.
    d. men are more likely to employ denial mechanisms.
    p. 352

Key for Practice Test A

1. Answer a; Adults are characterized by independent decision making and assuming responsibility for decisions made; page 333; Learning Objective 1
2. Answer c; Young adulthood occurs between the childhood sicknesses and the physical problems of older age; page 334; Learning Objective 2
3. Answer a; Increased nutrition is the primary reason for the improved health and length of life seen in this century; page 335; Learning Objective 2
4. Answer b; In Piaget's theory, development of cognitive abilities is marked by increased organization and systematicity; page 336; Learning Objective 3
5. Answer a; Advancing age results in a general slowing down of physical systems—this includes cognitive processing time; page 338; Learning Objective 3
6. Answer c; Middle age involves maintaining close ties as well as a re-emergence of independence; page 339; Learning Objective 4
7. Answer b; Stage theories of adult development overlap substantially in their characterizations of adulthood, but place a different emphasis on different aspects of adult life; page 340; Learning Objective 4

8. Answer d; Life events in adulthood involve multiple areas of living, including internal characteristics, family, and physical health; page 342; Learning Objective 5

9. Answer b; Although each individual is different, stage theories try to focus on the processes that cut across individuals and form universal themes; page 342; Learning Objective 6

10. Answer c; This is an example of a culture that attends more to life events than to chronological age in defining life periods; page 345; Learning Objective 7

11. Answer a; Costa views personality as a constant that remains fixed throughout adulthood; page 345; Learning Objective 8

12. Answer d; The greatest degree of conflict among theories of adult personality involves the degree to which personality changes; page 346; Learning Objective 8

13. Answer b; A person who is discriminated against because of age and sex has been subjected to double jeopardy; page 346; Learning Objective 9

14. Answer b; Kübler-Ross did not include a stage of anxiety in her description of stages of death and dying: anger, denial, bargaining, depression, and acceptance; page 349; Learning Objective 10

15. Answer d; Open communication can help all persons involved cope with an imminent death; page 352; Learning Objective 11

Key for Practice Test B

1. Answer c; Adulthood is the time when persons become independent in terms of the economic and decision-making aspects of their lives; page 333; Learning Objective 1

2. Answer c; Young adulthood is the healthiest period of the life span; page 334; Learning Objective 2

3. Answer d; Exercise offers many benefits to the long-term health of persons as they age; page 335; Learning Objective 2

4. Answer d; Memory declines are seen in older age for recall but not for recognition, showing that some aspects of memory decline with aging while others do not; page 336; Learning Objective 3

5. Answer b; Exploring life-styles and options is one of Levinson's development tasks for young adults; page 340; Learning Objective 4

6. Answer b; Intimacy is the development task of young adulthood for Erikson in his stage theory; page 341; Learning Objective 4

7. Answer c; Specific life events require different levels of coping depending on the social context within which they occur; page 342; Learning Objective 5

8. Answer b; Stage theories attempt to cut across individuals and point to universal aspects of development; page 342; Learning Objective 6

9. Answer b; Common themes run across different individuals in terms of their development, but each person's experiences and life events are unique; page 343; Learning Objective 6

10. Answer d; Most of the stage theories of adult development have focused on men and the themes identified do not readily transfer to women; page 344; Learning Objective 7

11. Answer b; Costa's theory emphasizes the long-term stability of adult personality; page 345; Learning Objective 8

12. Answer d; Among older adults, health and security are the strongest predictors of life satisfaction; page 346; Learning Objective 9

13. Answer c; Erikson stated that older persons engage in a life review process in order to establish ego integrity; page 347; Learning Objective 9

14. Answer a; The stages of death and dying describe the coping strategies for dealing with the catastrophic news of impending loss; page 350; Learning Objective 10

15. Answer b; Social supports help buffer the stress of loss and men tend to have smaller social networks than women; page 352; Learning Objective 11

Chapter Outline

I.   Abnormal Behavior: What Is It? What Causes It? How Can It Be Classified?
 A. What Is Abnormal Behavior?
   1. One way to define abnormal behavior is by what is atypical or infrequent.
   2. Atypical varies from era to era and from culture to culture.
   3. More useful is to define abnormal behavior as behavior that is maladaptive and harmful.
 B. What Causes Abnormal Behavior?
   1. Causes include biological, psychological, and sociocultural.
   2. Some criticize the medical model because it encourages labeling and using "sickness" to avoid personal responsibility.
   3. Psychological disturbances are universal, but frequency and intensity of abnormal behavior varies across cultures.
   4. About 15 percent suffer a mental disturbance at any time, with women having a slightly higher overall rate.
   5. Women have more mood and anxiety disorders; men have more substance-use and antisocial personality disorders.
   6. Only about one-third of those with mental disorders receive treatment.
   7. Women might have more mental disorders due to being in more trauma-inducing circumstances or being in "double-bind" situations, or, they might just be more likely to be labeled.
   8. Other risk factors for mental disorders include living in urban areas, being an ethnic minority (or living in an area with few persons of your ethnic background), and poverty.
   9. Interactionists consider the biological, psychological, and social factors that interact to produce abnormal behavior.
 C. How Can Abnormal Behavior Be Classified?
   1. The most widely used system to classify mental disturbances is the *Diagnostic and Statistical Manual of Mental Disorders.*
   2. The client's ethnicity may adversely influence assessment since cultural differences in nonverbal behavior and vocal styles may be misread as symptoms.
   3. People from the lowest socioeconomic backgrounds are diagnosed as having mental disturbances at twice the expected rate and are labeled with the most severe diagnoses.
   4. The benefits of classifying mental disorders include professional communication, research and theorizing, and accurate information about the disorder and possible treatments.
   5. The DSM appeared in 1952 and was revised in 1968, 1980, and 1987.
   6. The latest version of the DSM dropped the terms *neurotic* and *psychotic* as diagnostic labels because they were too broad and ill-defined.
   7. The DSM-III-R contains 18 major classifications and more than 200 specific disorders, and uses a multiaxial system including five dimensions or axes.

8. The axes include primary classification, personality disorders, physical disorders, psychosocial stressors, and highest level of functioning.
9. Psychiatrists primarily develop the DSM-III-R, which is why there is so much medical terminology.
10. Homosexuality is no longer part of the classification system, but other controversial issues, such as "self-defeating personality" are ongoing debates.
11. Rosenhan conducted a study in which normal individuals were easily labeled schizophrenics.
12. The International Classification of Disease (ICD) is widely used in other countries; the ICD still uses neuroses and psychoses as major categories.

II. Anxiety Disorders
  A. Generalized Anxiety Disorders
    1. Anxiety is a diffuse, vague, unpleasant feeling of apprehension or fear.
    2. Anxiety disorders include the symptoms of motor tension, jumpiness, trembling, inability to relax, hyperactivity, dizziness, a racing heart, perspiration, and apprehensive expectations and thoughts.
    3. Generalized anxiety disorder consists of unrealistic or excessive anxiety and worry about two or more life circumstances for at least six months.
    4. It includes muscle tension and hyperactivity.
  B. Panic Disorder
    1. Panic disorder is a recurrent anxiety disorder marked by the sudden onset of intense apprehension or terror.
    2. Anxiety attacks are often misinterpreted as heart attacks and involve shortness of breath, severe palpitations, chest pains, trembling, sweating, dizziness, and a sense of helplessness.
    3. Often panic attacks begin when stressful life events have been occurring, and often treatment with specific antidepressants and cognitive therapy are useful.
  C. Phobic Disorders
    1. Phobias are irrational fears of specific objects or situations.
    2. Phobic disorder exists when one or more phobias is persistent and pervasive enough that it significantly alters a person's life.
    3. Social phobias involve fear of public scrutiny.
    4. Agoraphobia is the fear of entering unfamiliar situations, especially open or public spaces, and it is the most common type of phobic disorder.
    5. Phobias might be defense mechanisms, or they might be classically conditioned; biological factors might also influence the development of phobias.
    6. There is a typical developmental order of phobias, beginning with a fear of loud noises, then of strangers, heights, and looming objects.
    7. Common preschool fears are sirens, thunder, animals, dark rooms, large machines, strangers, and separation from parents.
    8. School children often fear staying alone, tests, bodily injury, physical appearance, and death.
    9. Adolescents often have social performance and sexuality fears.
  D. Obsessive-Compulsive Disorders
    1. Obsessive-compulsive disorder (OCD) occurs when an individual has anxiety-provoking thoughts that will not go away (obsession) and urges to perform repetitive, ritualistic behaviors (compulsions).
    2. The most common compulsions are excessive checking, cleansing, and counting.

3. There seems to be a neurological basis for OCD, with the neurotransmitters serotonin and dopamine being involved.
4. Obsessive-compulsive personality disorder is a pervasive pattern of perfectionism and inflexibility.
5. The "20% mess up factor" can be used to break a perfectionism problem.

E. Post-Traumatic Stress Disorder
1. This disorder develops through exposure to any of several traumatic events, such as war, rape, floods, tornados, and plane crashes.
2. Symptoms can include flashbacks, constricted emotions, startle response, inability to sleep, memory and concentration difficulties, feelings of apprehension, and impulsive aggression.
3. About 15 to 20 percent of Vietnam veterans experience post-traumatic stress disorder, especially those who had no control over their time in Vietnam.

III. Somatoform Disorders
A. Hypochondriasis
1. Somatoform disorders are mental disturbances in which psychological symptoms take a physical form even though no physical causes can be found.
2. Hypochondriasis involves pervasive fear of illness and disease.
3. By contrast, psychosomatic illnesses are real physical illnesses.

B. Conversion Disorder
1. In this disorder, individuals experience specific, genuine physical symptoms even though no physiological problems can be found.
2. The name comes from psychoanalytic explanation that anxiety was "converted" to specific physical symptom.
3. It is not very common now.

IV. Dissociative Disorders
A. Psychogenic Amnesia and Fugue
1. Dissociative disorders involve sudden loss of memory or change in identity.
2. Psychogenic amnesia involves memory loss due to extensive psychological stress.
3. Fugue, which means "flight," involves both amnesia and a traveling into a new identity.

B. Multiple Personality
1. It is the most dramatic but least common dissociative disorder.
2. Two or more personalities or selves develop to deal with repeated exposure to trauma in childhood, especially sexual or physical abuse.

VI. Mood Disorders
A. Major Depression
1. Depression involves a cognitive triad of bad self, bad world, and bad future.
2. Mood disorders are characterized by wide emotional swings.
3. Major depression involves deep sadness, demoralization, and loss of interest in everything.
4. About 10 percent of men and 25 percent of women experience a major depression sometime. Women's depression is related to avoidant, passive, dependent behavior patterns, their higher experience of sexual and physical abuse, poverty, and marriage and having young children.

B. Bipolar Disorder
1. Bipolar disorder is a mood disorder characterized by extreme mood swings, from depression to mania.
2. About one percent of both men and women experience this sometime.

C. Suicide
1. Suicide rate in the United States tripled since the 1950s.
2. Men complete suicide three times more than women do, although women make more attempts; this occurs because of the methods used to commit suicide.
3. Although biological factors play a role, long-standing family instability and unhappiness play bigger roles.
4. Suicide rates are much higher in achievement-oriented cultures.
5. Catholicism and other religions may help decrease suicide rates for some populations.
D. Causes of Mood Disorders
1. Psychoanalytic explanations compare grief and depression, both of which center on losses.
2. Freud also viewed depression as the turning inward of aggressive instincts.
3. Bowlby emphasized the role of insecure attachment to the mother, lack of love as a child, and loss of parent during childhood.
4. Individuals who are depressed rarely think positive thoughts, and often use self-defeating ones.
5. According to Seligman, learned helplessness occurs when individuals are exposed to aversive stimulation over which they have no control.
6. Biogenetic explanations include genetic inheritance and chemical changes in the brain, such as levels of norepinephrine and serotonin.
7. Americans may be prone to depression because of society's emphasis on self.
8. Cultures with overt expression of grief have low depression rates.
VII. Schizophrenic Disorders
A. Characteristics of Schizophrenic Disorders
1. Schizophrenic disorders are severe psychological disorders characterized by distorted thoughts and perceptions, odd communication, inappropriate emotion, abnormal motor behavior, and social withdrawal.
2. The term comes from Latin meaning "split mind" and the mind is split from reality and thought patterns are fragmented.
3. Delusions, or false implausible beliefs, are common.
4. Hallucinations are perceptual mistakes.
5. Incoherent, loose word associations are called "word salad."
B. Forms of Schizophrenic Disorders
1. Disorganized schizophrenia involves severe delusions and hallucinations, withdrawal from human contact, and silly, childlike behavior.
2. Catatonic schizophrenia is characterized by bizarre motor behavior, including immobile stupor.
3. Paranoid schizophrenia is characterized by delusions of reference, grandeur, and persecution.
4. Undifferentiated schizophrenia is characterized by disorganized behavior, hallucinations, delusions, and incoherence.
C. Causes of Schizophrenia
1. Genetic factors seem to be involved in schizophrenia.
2. Deficits in brain metabolism, malfunctioning dopamine system, and distorted cerebral blood flow may cause schizophrenia.

3. The diathesis-stress view argues that a combination of environmental stress and biogenetic disposition causes schizophrenia.
4. The type and incidence of schizophrenia varies from culture to culture.
 D. Personality Disorders
  1. Personality disorders are psychological disorders that develop when personality traits become inflexible and thus maladaptive.
  2. The most problematic personality disorder for society is antisocial personality disorder.
 E. Substance-Use Disorders
  1. Substance-use disorder is characterized by a pattern of pathological use of frequent intoxification and an inability to control use, a significant impairment of social or occupational functioning, and/or physical dependence that involves serious withdrawal problems.
  2. Alcoholism is especially widespread.

Learning Objectives

After reading and studying the chapter, students should be able to:

1. Define abnormal behavior and know its causes.
2. Know the ways that psychologists try to classify abnormal behavior.
3. Identify and describe general anxiety disorder and panic attacks.
4. Identify and describe phobic disorders.
5. Describe the characteristics of obsessive-compulsive disorder.
6. Know the signs and symptoms of post-traumatic stress disorder and how it develops.
7. Identify and describe somatoform disorders.
8. Know what the dissociative disorders are and describe them.
9. Understand the differences and similarities of major depression and bipolar disorder.
10. Understand the characteristics and processes of suicide.
11. Understand the causes of mood disorders.
12. Understand the characteristics of schizophrenic disorders and the theories of their causes.
13. Define personality disorders.
14. Understand the key feature of substance-use disorders.

Guided Review

After you have read the chapter one time, search through the chapter to find the appropriate words to complete these statements. Material is covered in the same order as the chapter.

1. One way to define abnormal behavior is by using _____ behaviors, but this ignores the changes from on historical period to another and from one _____ to another.
2. Early in this century, many Americans believed _____ was sinful and caused everything from warts to insanity.
3. Abnormal behavior is behavior that is _____ and _____.

4. The causes of abnormal behavior include _____, _____, and _____.

5. Some criticize the medical model because it encourages _____ of mental disturbances and because viewing oneself as being "sick" may result in the avoidance of _____ for coping.

6. Many psychological disturbances are _____, appearing in most cultures, although there are cultural variations in _____ and _____.

7. The disorder labeled _____ appears in Malaysia, Philippines, and Africa, and involves a sudden, uncontrolled outburst of anger usually in males who are _____ before the onset.

8. Appearing in Western cultures, _____ _____ is an _____ disorder involving a relentless pursuit of thinness through starvation.

9. The disorder _____, which appears among the _____ Indian hunters involves a fear of being _____ and there is much worrying that one will be turned into a _____, craving for human flesh.

10. A recent study of 18,571 people showed that more than _____ percent had suffered from mental disturbance during the previous month; this incidence rate was _____ than had been predicted.

11. Overall, _____ had a slightly higher rate of mental disturbances than the other gender, especially in disorders of _____ and _____.

12. Men had higher rates of _____-_____ disorders and _____ _____ disorders.

13. When it comes to _____'s higher rate of depression, it might be that they get _____ by others more, that women display their _____ more, that it is the result of greater _____, and that they are more often placed in a "_____-_____" situation.

14. People who live closest to the _____ of a city have the greatest risk of developing a mental disturbance.

15. The _____ the number of ethnic members in one area, the higher their rate of mental health hospitalization.

16. The Hispanic population is diverse; for example, _____ Americans and _____ _____ have high rates of physician visitations while _____ Americans made fewer visits than any group.

17. Mental health issues of Hispanic women are involved by experiences of _____ and _____, with only the majority of _____ Americans born on the United States mainland.

18. Except for _____ women, Hispanic women have _____ incomes, _____ education, and _____ fertility rates than Anglo American women.

19. About _____ percent of Hispanic women work in professional or managerial roles.

20. The most widely used system to classify mental disturbances is the _____ _____ _____ _____ _____ _____ _____.

21. During diagnostic interviews, characteristics typical of Native Americans that might inadvertently signal mental distress include _____, _____, _____-_____, limited _____ contact, and _____ to talk about their personal lives.

22. Because it can be hard to trust a White professional, some Black clients defend themselves by saying essentially _____ phrases or by telling clinicians what they _____ to hear.

23. Since _____ Americans view mental disturbances as _____ behavior or _____, they may be unwilling to acknowledge serious mental problems except by recasting them as a _____ ailment.

24. People from the _____ socioeconomic backgrounds are diagnosed as having twice the expected rate of mental disturbances and the _____ severe diagnoses.

25. Classification systems allow professions a _____ system for _____ with each other.

26. _____ and _____ oppression are risk factors for mental disturbance.

27. A classification system can help psychologists _____ disturbances, providing information about the likelihood of a disturbance.

28. The classification of mental disorders based on the United States 1840 census had _____ category(ies), with _____ _____ and _____ making up one category.

29. The DSM-I was published in _____ and developed by the _____ _____ _____.

30. The term _____ refers to relatively mild mental disorders in which the individual has not lost _____ with _____.

31. _____ refers to severe mental disturbances involving lost contact with reality.

32. The DSM-III-R, the current major classification system contains _____ major classifications and more than _____ specific disorders.

33. The _____ system of the DSM-III-R uses _____ dimensions, and clients are measured on their _____ classification, their developmental or _____ disorders, relevant _____ disorders, recent _____ stressors, and one's _____ level of functioning in the last year.

34. Most health insurance companies reimburse their clients only for disorders in the _____ system.

35. Included in the DSM-II as a mental disorder, _____ was deleted from the DSM-III and III-R.

36. A controversial aspect of the DSM-III classification is the category called _____-_____ personality, commonly known as "_____," which some critics believe _____ the victim.

37. A classic study of _____ showed how easy it was to have eight "normal" individuals admit themselves into a psychiatric hospital with the diagnosis of _____.

38. In other countries, the major classification system is the _____ _____ of _____, established by the _____ _____ _____.

39. Unlike the DSM-II-R, the ICD classification system still includes _____ and _____ as major categories.

40. _____ is a diffuse, vague, unpleasant feeling of apprehension or fear, with its physical symptoms being the _____-or-_____ response of the _____ nervous system.

41. In _____ _____ disorder, a person experiences unrealistic or excessive _____ and worry about two or more life circumstances for at least _____ months.

42. _____ disorder is a recurrent anxiety disorder marked by sudden, spontaneous attacks of intense apprehension.

43. _____-_____ medications, _____ therapy, and _____ exercises are often employed in treating panic disorders.

44. An irrational fear of a specific object or situation is a _____, and if it is pervasive enough to significantly alter one's life it is called a _____ _____.

45. The most common type of phobic disorder is _____, which is the fear of entering _____ situations, especially _____ or _____ spaces.

46. Phobic disorder differs from generalized anxiety disorder by its association with _____ fears rather than vague ones, and panic disorders differ from generalized anxiety disorder by experiencing anxiety in _____ rather than almost all the time.

47. Explanations for phobias include _____ _____ from an actual experience and biological explanations, such as greater blood flow and metabolism to the _____ hemisphere of the brain.

48. There is a typical _____ order to fears or phobias, with one of the first being fear of _____ _____.

49. Common fears of babies between seven and twelve months are _____, _____, and _____ objects.

50. Early fears are based on _____ real things, but around the age of six years children become fearful of _____ _____.

51. Staying alone, school tests, bodily injury, physical appearance, and death are common fears during _____ _____ years.

52. Common fears in adolescence include fears about _____ _____ and _____.

53. _____-_____ disorder is an anxiety disorder in which the individual has anxiety-provoking, preoccupying thoughts called _____ and ritualistic, repetitive behaviors called _____.

54. The most common compulsions are excessive _____, _____, and _____.

55. Irregularities in the neurotransmitters _____ and _____ may be involved in obsessive-compulsive disorder.

56. The obsessive-compulsive personality disorder is a pervasive pattern of _____ and _____ in a variety of contexts.

57. The "20% mess up factor" is a suggested technique for individuals who demand _____ from themselves and others.

58. Individuals who experience traumatic events such as war, rape, accidents, and natural disasters are at risk for developing _____-_____ _____ _____.

59. "_____" are reliving events in nightmares or in awake, dissociative-like states.

60. The largest group of _____-_____ _____ disorder sufferers are female sexual abuse and assault victims.

61. Two types of _____ disorders are hypochondriasis and conversion disorder.

62. In hypochondriasis, an individual has a pervasive fear of _____.

63. Psychosomatic illnesses involve _____ physical illnesses.

64. _____ disorder involves specific, genuine physical symptoms without finding _____ causes.

65. In _____ _____, individuals report that their entire hand is numb from the tip of their fingers to a cutoff point at the wrist, which is a _____ pattern than with true physiological numbness.

66. _____ disorders involve a sudden loss of memory or change in _____ and three kinds are _____, _____, and _____ _____.

67. _____ amnesia is a dissociative disorder involving _____ loss caused by extensive psychological stress.

68. Amnesia involving amnesia and wandering away and assuming a new _____ is called _____.

69. _____ _____ disorder is the most dramatic and _____ common dissociative disorder.

70. The most common complaint of individuals who choose to go into counseling is _____.

71. The core thought associated with depression is that of "_____."

72. Profound depressions make up the _____ disorders, and depression occurs alone in _____ depression and alternates with mania in _____ disorder.

73. _____ is so widespread that it has been called the "common cold" of mental disorders.

74. About one in _____ men will have a major depression at some point, and about one in _____ women will.

75. Women's depression is related to _____, _____, _____ behavior patterns and by focusing more on _____ than on action and mastery strategies.

76. Extreme mood swings is characteristic of _____ disorder.

77. Since the 1950s, the rate of suicide in the United States has _____.

78. More _____ die from suicides, perhaps because of the _____ they use, and more _____ attempt suicide.

79. _____-related suicide attempts are more common now than in the past.

80. High pressure, _____-oriented cultures such as Japan and the United States have higher suicide rates.

81. The _____ religion of _____ Americans lowers their suicide risk but not for Puerto Ricans.

82. Freud compared the experience of depression with that of _____ and also suggested that depression was a turning inward of _____ instincts.

83. John Bowlby believed that an _____ attachment to the mother was an important determinant of depression in adulthood.

84. A longitudinal study of depression found that parents' lack of _____, high _____, and aggressive _____ orientation in early childhood was associated with depression among adolescent _____.

85. Individuals who are depressed rarely think _____ thoughts.

86. Beck believes that depressed people blame _____ more than is warranted.

87. According to _____ _____, the inability to avoid prolonged aversive stimulation produces an _____ state.

88. _____ which accompanies learned helplessness is often the result of a person's extremely negative, _____-_____ attributions.

89. Biological explanations of depression involve _____ _____ and _____ _____ in the brain.

90. Two neurotransmitters involved in depression are _____ and _____, which are at _____ levels during depression and _____ levels during mania.

91. Patients with unusually low _____ levels are _____ times as likely to commit suicide than individuals with normal levels.

92. Excessive secretion of _____ from the _____ gland occurs in depressed individuals.

93. Seligman has suggested that many young American adults experience depression because of our society's emphasis on _____, _____, and _____, coupled with erosion of _____ to others.

94. Some cross-cultural psychologists believe that _____ rituals in non-Western cultures reduce the risks of depression.

95. Women who are _____ _____ of _____ and young married women in unsatisfying, _____-_____ _____ have high rates of depression.

96. In cultures where _____ _____ and _____ are rare, such as in the Amish culture, the rate of depression for women is _____ _____ men's rate.

97. _____ disorders are severe psychological disorders characterized by distorted _____ and _____. odd _____, inappropriate _____, abnormal motor behavior, and _____ _____.

98. About one in _____ Americans will be diagnosed with schizophrenia in their lifetime.

99. About _____ of all mental hospital patients in the United States have schizophrenia.

100. _____ are utterly implausible false beliefs, while _____ are perceptions that are not present.

101. Incoherent, loose word associations are called _____ _____.

102. _____ schizophrenia is characterized by delusions, hallucinations, and silly, childlike gestures and behavior.

103. Catatonic schizophrenia is characterized by bizarre _____ behavior.

104. A catatonic who can be moved from one rigid position into another is exhibiting _____ _____.

105. Paranoid schizophrenia is characterized by delusions of _____, _____, and _____.

106. _____ schizophrenia is characterized by disorganized behavior, hallucinations, delusions, and incoherence.

107. Family and twin studies suggest that _____ _____ are involved in schizophrenia.

108. Deficits in _____ _____, a malfunctioning _____ system and distorted _____ _____ _____ may be involved in schizophrenia.

109. Persons with schizophrenia produce too much of the neurotransmitter _____.

110. The _____-_____ view argues that a combination of _____ stress and _____ disposition causes schizophrenia.

111. Blacks have _____ rates of schizophrenia than Whites in both the United States and Great Britain.

112. _____ is much more likely to be associated with schizophrenia than ethnicity.

1. atypical, culture; 2. masturbation; 3. maladaptive, harmful; 4. biological, psychological, sociocultural; 5. labeling, responsibility; 6. universal, frequency, intensity; 7. amok, withdrawn; 8. anorexia nervosa, eating; 9. windigo, Algonquin, bewitched, cannibal; 10. fifteen, higher; 11. women, anxiety, depression; 12. substance-use, antisocial personality; 13. women, labeled, emotion, discrimination, "double-bind"; 14. center; 15. fewer; 16. Cuban, Puerto Ricans, Mexican; 17. migration, immigration, Mexican; 18. Cuban, lower, less, higher; 19. 13; 20. *Diagnostic and Statistical Manual of Mental Disorders;* 21. nonassertive, hesitant, soft-spoken, eye, reluctance; 22. meaningless, want; 23. Japanese, inappropriate, malingering, physical; 24. lowest, most; 25. shorthand, communicating; 26. Poverty, racial; 27. predict; 28. one, mentally retarded, insane; 29. 1952, American Psychiatric Association; 30. neurotic, contact, reality; 31. Psychotic; 32. 18, 200; 33. multiaxial, five, primary, personality, physical, psychosocial, highest; 34. DSM-III-R; 35. homosexuality; 36. self-defeating, masochism, blames; 37. Rosenhan, schizophrenia; 38. International Classification, Disease, World Health Organization; 39. neuroses, psychoses; 40. Anxiety, flight, fight, autonomous; 41. generalized anxiety, anxiety, six; 42. Panic; 43. Anti-depressant, cognitive, relaxation; 44. phobia, phobic disorder; 45. agoraphobia, unfamiliar, open, public; 46. specific, waves; 47. classical conditioning, right; 48. developmental, loud noises; 49. strangers, heights, looming; 50. unfamiliar, supernatural beings; 51. elementary school; 52. social performance, sexuality; 53. Obsessive-compulsive, obsessions, compulsions; 54. checking, cleansing, counting; 55. serotonin, dopamine; 56. perfectionism, inflexibility; 57. perfectionism; 58. post-traumatic stress disorder; 59. "Flashbacks"; 60. post-traumatic stress; 61. somatoform; 62. illness; 63. real; 64. Conversion, physiological; 65. glove anesthesia, different; 66. Dissociative, identity, amnesia, fugue, multiple personality; 67. Psychogenic, memory; 68. identity, fugue; 69. Multiple personality, least; 70. depression; 71. loss; 72. mood, major, bipolar; 73. Depression; 74. ten, four; 75. avoidant, passive, dependent, feelings; 76. bipolar; 77. tripled; 78. men, methods, women; 79. Drug; 80. achievement; 81. Catholicism, Mexican; 82. grief, aggressive; 83. insecure; 84. affection, control, achievement, girls; 85. positive; 86. themselves; 87. learned helplessness, apathetic; 88. Hopelessness, self-blaming; 89. genetic inheritance, chemical changes; 90. norepinephrine, serotonin, low, high; 91. serotonin, ten; 92. cortisol, adrenal; 93. self, independence, individualism, connectedness; 94. mourning; 95. single heads, households, dead-end jobs; 96. alcohol abuse, aggression, equal to; 97. Schizophrenic, thoughts, perceptions, communication, emotion, social withdrawal; 98. 100; 99. half; 100. Delusions, hallucinations; 101. word salad; 102. Disorganized; 103. motor; 104. waxy flexibility; 105. reference, grandeur, persecution; 106. Undifferentiated; 107. genetic factors; 108. brain metabolism, dopamine, cerebral blood flow; 109. dopamine; 110. diathesis-stress, environmental, biogenetic; 111. higher; 112. Poverty

Key Terms

For each term, briefly define the term in your own words and provide an example or situation (especially one you can visualize) that will help you retain the meaning of the concept. Key terms are presented in the order they are presented in the chapter.

1. abnormal behavior (p. 362)

2. medical model (p. 363)

3. DSM (p. 366)

4. neurotic (p. 366)

5. psychotic (p. 366)

6. DSM-III-R (p. 367)

7. multiaxial system (p. 367)

8. anxiety disorders (p. 368)

9. generalized anxiety disorder (p. 369)

10. panic disorder (p. 369)

11. phobia (p. 369)

12. phobic disorder (p. 370)

13. agoraphobia (p. 370)

14. obsessive-compulsive disorder (p. 371)

15. obsessive-compulsive personality disorder (p. 372)

16. post-traumatic stress disorder (p. 372)

17. somatoform disorders (p. 372)

18. hypochondriasis (p. 372)

19. conversion disorder (p. 373)

20. dissociative disorders (p. 373)

21. psychogenic amnesia (p. 373)

22. fugue (p. 373)

23. multiple personality disorder (p. 373)

35. antisocial personality disorder (p. 383)

36. substance-use disorder (p. 383)

Study Aids

Students who do well on tests develop mnemonic aids to help them remember important terms and concepts. A few are suggested here, and you are encouraged to develop your own additional aids.

The Anxiety Disorders. Help yourself remember the five disorders that fit into this category by remembering GO3P to pull out the first letters of the disorders: Generalized anxiety, Obsessive-compulsive, Panic, Phobic, and Post-traumatic stress.

Somatoform Disorders. Remember that the word root *soma* means bodily (as in the word *psychosomatic*, somatic refers to physical). Therefore, somatoform disorders are going to center around physical concerns. The chapter discusses hypochondriasis and conversion disorder. **Hypochondriacs** have a great fear of illness but cannot really believe the doctor that they are healthy—envision *hypo*chondriacs as always believing they need **"hypos,"** needles, to make them better. **Conversion disorder** can be remembered in simplified Freud's terms of viewing it as *converting* psychological stress into a physical malfunctioning.

Schizophrenic Disorders. You can remember the four kinds of schizophrenia by thinking: CUPiD—using all the letters but the *i* to help you remember Catatonic, Undifferentiated, Paranoid, and Disorganized.

Understanding Concepts

Answer these questions to develop your understanding of the important ideas in this chapter.

1. Define abnormal behavior and discuss the causes of abnormal behavior.

2. What gender differences exist for mental disorders? Provide an explanation for these differences.

3. Describe the main features of the current revision of the *Diagnostic and Statistical Manual of Mental Disorders,* and discuss the advantages and disadvantages of having a classification system. Provide an example of one of the controversial aspects of the DSM-III-R.

4. Compare and contrast neurotic and psychotic.

5. Compare and contrast generalized anxiety disorder, panic disorder, and phobic disorder. In other words, how is anxiety experienced differently in each of these three disorders?

6. Explain the typical developmental order of fears.

7. Differentiate between obsessions and compulsions.

8. Discuss various biological explanations for anxiety disorders.

9. List the symptoms you might see in a person experiencing a post-traumatic stress disorder.

10. Compare and contrast hypochondriasis with psychosomatic illness.

11. Describe the main features of the dissociative disorders: amnesia, fugue, and multiple personality disorder.

12. Describe major depression and bipolar disorder.

13. What cultural factors are associated with a high suicide rate?

14. Provide three different explanations of depression.

15. Provide an example of learned helplessness.

16. List and describe each of the four types of schizophrenia: disorganized, paranoid, catatonic, and undifferentiated.

17. Compare and contrast delusions and hallucinations. Provide an example of each.

18. Provide two different explanations of schizophrenia.

Applying Concepts

Answer these questions to develop your ability to apply this chapter's material to your life and the world. Your own responses may differ from other students' in the class, and it is helpful to share your ideas with the other students.

1. Make a list of the maladaptive and harmful behaviors in your life. Make a list of the atypical behaviors in your life. Are the lists identical? Similar?

2. Create a culture-bound disorder that exists in the United States (e.g., "Mall-itis," or the tendency to "shop 'til you drop"). Provide a description of the disorder.

3. Diagnosing someone with a mental disorder is usually necessary for proper treatment. Diagnosing can also lead to expectations for abnormal behavior that can worsen a person's emotional state. Do the benefits of diagnosing/labeling outweigh the potential costs?

4. Evaluate your current rate of anxiety. What factors are contributing to your current anxiety? How are you handling your anxiety? Are you typically low, average, or high in anxiety?

5. Take Self-Assessment 14.1 to identify your fears and phobias. Do you have more simple phobias (objects and situations) or social phobias (involving people or social evaluation)? Can you identify the causes (e.g., classical conditioning, modeling, symbolism) of any of your fears? How much do these fears interfere with your life? Are there any that you would like to reduce?

6. Identify whether you have any problems related to perfectionism and its "buddy," procrastination. If yes, how do you deal with this issue? Try the "20% mess up factor" for a week and report on how it works.

7. Assess your own thought patterns for cognitions that are associated with depression ("loss" and the cognitive triad).

8. Measure yourself on Self-Assessment 14.2 about depression. Summarize the results.

9. What aspects of being a college student increase your anxiety and depression? What aspects help to alleviate your anxiety and depression?

10. Are there any conditions under which you think suicide is a viable option?

11. How would the treatment of depression differ if it is caused by biogenetic factors as opposed to psychosocial influences?

12. If genetic scientists are able to identify the exact gene, or genes, that contribute to the development of schizophrenia, people could have a blood test to detect if they and their children are at risk. What are the advantages as well as the moral and ethical implications of such a test?

13. What cultural factors affect the incidence of schizophrenia? Why?

Chapter Practice Tests

Answer these multiple-choice test questions to help you assess your understanding of the chapter's material. Evaluate your answers to determine which sections you need to further review.

Practice Test A

1. Behavior that is both maladaptive and harmful is usually considered
   a. abnormal.
   b. atypical.
   c. dangerous.
   d. deviant.
   p. 362

2. Which of the following is true of mental disorders?
   a. They occur at the same rates across various cultures.
   b. They occur at different rates across different cultures.
   c. They are biased against minorities.
   d. They are caused by poverty.
   p. 363

3. Chinese Americans are likely to be
   a. misdiagnosed as having a mental disorder.
   b. misdiagnosed as not having a mental disorder.
   c. inappropriately treated for their problems.
   d. all of the above.
   p. 366

4. Anxiety disorders share a relationship in common with the
   a. automatic nervous system.
   b. autonomic nervous system.
   c. parasympathetic but not the sympathetic system.
   d. none of the above.
   p. 368

5. Which of the following is not a symptom of phobic disorders?
   a. sweating
   b. changes in breathing
   c. fear
   d. compulsions
   p. 370

6. Moira has all of her towels arranged by color and reorganizes them on a daily basis. She has also created a list of the sizes and colors of towels she has as well as the same for her clothes. Moira probably suffers from
   a. panic disorder.
   b. schizophrenia.
   c. obsessive-compulsive disorder.
   d. phobia disorder.
   p. 371

7. Flashbacks, nightmares, constricted emotional expression, memory problems, and nervous tremors are all symptoms of someone who has
   a. been raped.
   b. been in combat.
   c. suffered post-traumatic stress disorder.
   d. all of the above.
   p. 372

8. Gary has developed the symptoms of paralysis, but his doctor and several specialists conclude he does not have a physiological problem. Gary probably suffers from
   a. schizophrenia.
   b. conversion disorder.
   c. personality disorder.
   d. psychosomatic illness.
   p. 373

9. People who suffer from multiple personality disorder are very likely to
   a. have experienced sexual trauma.
   b. suffer anxiety.
   c. hallucinate.
   d. imagine they are someone else.
   p. 373

10. Bipolar disorder includes which of the following?
    a. It involves less depression than major depression.
    b. It occurs in about 25% of adult women.
    c. It is the most common psychiatric diagnosis for men and women.
    d. It is characterized by recurrent cycles of mood change.
    p. 376

11. Suicides are most likely to occur in
    a. Western cultures.
    b. high-achievement countries.
    c. more depressed countries.
    d. all industrialized countries.
    p. 377

12. Depression varies across cultures and in Western cultures depression is more likely to be characterized by
    a. loss of interest in pleasures.
    b. self-defeating thoughts. center are likely to
    c. pervasive mood disturbance.
    d. sadness.
    p. 379

13. The diathesis-stress model of schizophrenia is an example of what type of theory of abnormal behavior?
    a. biological
    b. sociocultural
    c. psychoanalytic
    d. interactionist
    p. 382

14. Personality disorders are characterized by
    a. hysterical reactions.
    b. phobic anxiety.
    c. maladaptive and inflexible traits.
    d. aggressive behavior.
    p. 383

15. Which of the following is true about the gender differences in substance-use disorders?
    a. Biogenic causes are more common in men.
    b. The sex ratio is constant across cultures.
    c. Women are commonly substance abusive.
    d. Women abuse alcohol more often than men.
    p. 383

Practice Test B

1. Medical models of abnormal behavior emphasize
   a. biological influences.
   b. child-rearing practices.
   c. unconscious mental processes.
   d. life crises.
   p. 363

2. Classification systems for mental disorders may be flawed by
   a. their inappropriate application across cultures.
   b. their assignment of labels to people.
   c. their use against minorities.
   d. all of the above.
   p. 367

3. Research has shown that people who go to a

   a. be carefully evaluated.
   b. be assumed to be normal until otherwise diagnosed.
   c. be diagnosed with a mental disorder even if they do not have one.
   d. receive unfair treatment because of race.
   p. 368

4. Charles feels his heart beating and breaks out in perspiration a few times each day for no apparent reason. Charles may suffer from
   a. delusions.
   b. generalized anxiety disorder.
   c. schizophrenia.
   d. a phobic disorder.
   p. 369

5. In order for a person to have a phobic disorder, it is necessary that
    a. they be generally anxious.
    b. their fear is persistent and pervasive.
    c. the object they fear is not real.
    d. the fear existed in childhood.
    p. 369

6. Obsessions involve which aspect of the person?
    a. feelings
    b. thoughts
    c. behaviors
    d. autonomic reactions
    p. 370

7. The largest number of cases of post-traumatic stress disorder is probably among
    a. Vietnam veterans.
    b. rape victims.
    c. victims of natural disasters.
    d. victims of traffic accidents.
    p. 372

8. Jose has a pervasive and persistent fear that he has developed heart disease, despite the repeated findings of multiple medical tests. Jose probably suffers from
    a. phobic disorder.
    b. conversion disorder.
    c. hypochondriasis.
    d. psychosomatic illness.
    p. 372

9. Which of the following seems related to the onset of all dissociative disorders?
    a. extreme stress
    b. amnesia
    c. sexual abuse
    d. none of the above.
    p. 373

10. Major depression differs from bipolar disorder by the
    a. depth of depression.
    b. experience of manic elation.
    c. biological factors involved.
    d. extent of mental impairment.
    p. 374

11. Tom recently divorced his wife. Which of the following is likely to influence his becoming suicidal?
    a. blaming himself
    b. how much money his wife earned
    c. whether or not he has a job
    d. the level of achievement he had reached
    p. 377

12. Which theory states that depression is aggression turned inward?
    a. sociocultural
    b. learning
    c. cognitive theory
    d. psychoanalytic
    p. 378

13. The view that schizophrenia is caused by a combination of biological predispositions and environmental stress is expressed by
    a. the medical model.
    b. diathesis-stress model.
    c. biogenic-stress model.
    d. psychoanalysis.
    p. 382

14. People with personality disorders are most likely to respond to therapy by
    a. total cure.
    b. effort to change, but with little success.
    c. getting worse.
    d. none of the above.
    p. 383

15. Drug use becomes a disorder when a person
    a. has to steal to pay for it.
    b. is a part of a drug-using network.
    c. has a strong desire to try new drugs.
    d. experiences withdrawal after not using it.
    p. 383

Key for Practice Test A

1. Answer a; Abnormal behavior is defined by being harmful to oneself or others as well as maladaptive; page 362; Learning Objective 1
2. Answer b; Studies have shown that many of the well-described mental disorders occur frequently in some cultures while being almost absent in others; page 363; Learning Objective 1
3. Answer d; Complaints and problems related to mental health vary across cultures and often result in problems with diagnoses; page 366; Learning Objective 2
4. Answer b; Activation of the autonomic nervous system causes changes in the body that are characteristic of anxiety disorders; page 368; Learning Objective 3
5. Answer d; Phobias are intense irrational fears, but do not necessarily involve compulsions; page 370; Learning Objective 4
6. Answer c; Obsessive-compulsive disorder involves an excessive amount of attention to order and perfection that includes repetition and attention to detail; page 371; Learning Objective 5
7. Answer c; These are all symptoms of post-traumatic stress disorder that can be brought on by any one of several traumatic life experiences; page 372; Learning Objective 6
8. Answer b; Conversion disorder is when the symptoms of an illness are real to the patient but there is no evidence of actual disease to multiple doctors; page 373; Learning Objective 7
9. Answer a; Sexual trauma has been found to be a commonality among persons who suffer from multiple personality disorder; page 373; Learning Objective 8
10. Answer d; Bipolar disorder involves cycles of very deep depression and very elated euphoria; page 376; Learning Objective 9
11. Answer d; As societies become more industrialized and there is greater emphasis on achievement, the rates of suicide increase; page 377; Learning Objective 10
12. Answer b; The self-defeating thoughts that are common in depressions seen in Western cultures are not as prevalent in non-Western cultures; page 379; Learning Objective 11
13. Answer d; Diathesis-stress model states that there is a biological predisposition for schizophrenia but that environmental stressors are necessary for schizophrenia to develop, therefore emphasizing the interaction between biology and environment; page 382; Learning Objective 12
14. Answer c; Personality disorders involve rigid traits that are pervasively maladaptive; page 383; Learning Objective 13
15. Answer c; Women are common substance abusers in Western cultures, although the sex ratio does vary from society to society; page 383; Learning Objective 14

Key for Practice Test B

1. Answer a; Medial models emphasize the role of biological influences in the development of mental disorders; page 363; Learning Objective 1
2. Answer d; Classification systems for mental disorders have several potential limitations, some of which may be harmful if misused; page 367; Learning Objective 2
3. Answer c; Studies of people known not to have a mental disorder who go to psychiatric centers and receive diagnoses have demonstrated the biases in classification systems; page 368; Learning Objective 2
4. Answer b; Generalized anxiety disorder involves symptoms of autonomic nervous system arousal without any known event or thought related to the symptoms; page 369; Learning Objective 3

5. Answer b; A transient fear is not the same as a phobia. Phobias are persistent, lasting long periods of time, and pervasive, interfering with multiple aspects of life; page 369; Learning Objective 4

6. Answer b; Obsessions are repetitious and continuous thoughts that seem out of control by the person having them; page 370; Learning Objective 5

7. Answer b; Victims of sexual violence suffer extreme trauma that can result in post-traumatic stress disorder; page 372; Learning Objective 6

8. Answer c; Hypochondriasis is a persistent concern that one is severely ill, despite medial testing to the contrary; page 372; Learning Objective 7

9. Answer a; Stressful life events that are beyond coping capacities have been linked to most dissociative disorders; page 373; Learning Objective 8

10. Answer b; Major depression involves a deep depressed state, while bipolar disorder involves a cycling between deep depression and manic states; page 374; Learning Objective 9

11. Answer a; Self-blame for negative life events is the key element in considering suicide; page 377; Learning Objective 10

12. Answer d; Psychoanalytic theory states that aggressive impulses turned inward to the self cause depression. Thus, depression is viewed as self-destructive; page 378; Learning Objective 11

13. Answer b; The diathesis-stress model states that biological factors predispose a person to develop schizophrenia, but there are necessary environmental events that interact with the biological factors to cause schizophrenia; page 382; Learning Objective 12

14. Answer c; Personality disorders are usually not apparent to the person who has one but are readily apparent to others. Therefore, persons with personality disorders are less likely to respond to therapy; page 383; Learning Objective 13

15. Answer d; Withdrawal after not taking a drug indicates addiction, which is then considered a substance-use disorder; page 383; Learning Objective 14

Chapter Outline

I.   The Nature of Psychotherapy
   A. Defining Psychotherapy
       1. Psychotherapy is the process of working with individuals to reduce their problems and improve their adjustment.
       2. It does not include biomedical treatment (i.e., drugs and surgery).
       3. Psychodynamic and humanistic therapies are insight therapies.
       4. Eclectic therapists use a variety of therapeutic approaches.
   B. Therapists and Therapeutic Settings
       1. Mental health professionals include clinical psychologists, psychiatrists, and counselors.
       2. Therapeutic settings include community health centers, inpatient and outpatient hospital facilities, and private counseling offices.
       3. Many therapists prefer to work with young, attractive, verbal, intelligent, successful clients (YAVIS) over quiet, ugly, old, institutionalized, different clients (QUOID).
II. Psychodynamic Therapies
   A. Freud's Psychoanalysis
       1. Psychodynamic therapies emphasize the unconscious, therapist's interpretation, and early childhood experiences.
       2. Freud believed that current problems could be traced to childhood experiences, especially those involving sexual conflict.
       3. Free association involves saying whatever comes to mind, even if it seems trivial or embarrassing.
       4. Catharsis is the release of emotional tension by reliving an emotionally charged and conflicted experience.
       5. The therapist interprets the client's free association and dreams.
       6. Dream analysis involves looking at the latent rather than manifest content of dreams to obtain information about an individual's unconscious thoughts and conflicts.
       7. Transference occurs when the client relates to the analyst in ways that reproduce important earlier relationships.
       8. Resistance is the client's unconscious defense strategies that prevent the analyst from understanding the client's problems.
   B. Contemporary Psychodynamic Therapies
       1. Many psychodynamic approaches still emphasize unconscious thoughts about early childhood experiences to gain insight into emotionally-laden repressed conflicts.
       2. However, they often place more emphasis on the conscious than Freud did.
       3. The current emphasis is on the development of the self in social contexts.
       4. Kohut emphasizes early relationships/attachments with parents and getting the patient to identify and seek out appropriate relationships.

313

III.   Humanistic Therapies
    A.   Person-Centered Therapy
        1.   Humanistic therapies encourage clients to understand themselves and to grow personally with the emphases on conscious thoughts, the present, and growth and fulfillment.
        2.   Developed by Rogers, person-centered therapy emphasizes a warm, supportive atmosphere to aid client's improving self-concept and gaining of insight.
        3.   In this therapy, conditions of worth is replaced by unconditional positive regard.
        4.   In addition to unconditional positive regard, qualities of the therapist include genuineness and accurate empathy.
        5.   Active listening is the ability to listen to another person with total attention to what the person says and means, and restating and supporting what the client has said is helpful.
    B.   Gestalt Therapy
        1.   Perls believed that therapists should question and challenge clients to help them become more aware of their feelings and face their problems.
        2.   Perls dealt with unresolved past conflicts and used interpretation of dreams.
        3.   Unlike Freud, Perls emphasized living right now and being open about feelings.
        4.   Gestalt therapy emphasizes congruence between verbal and nonverbal behavior and role playing.
        5.   Compared to person-centered therapy, Gestalt therapy is more directive.
IV.   Behavior Therapies
    A.   Classical Conditioning Approaches
        1.   Behavior therapies use principles of learning to reduce or eliminate maladaptive behavior; they do not emphasize unconscious conflicts and self-awareness.
        2.   Systematic desensitization is treating anxiety by associating deep relaxation with successive visualizations of increasingly intense anxiety-producing situations.
        3.   Systematic desensitization is often an effective treatment for phobias.
        4.   Aversive conditioning involves repeated pairings of the undesirable behavior with aversive stimuli to decrease the behavior's rewards so the individual will stop doing it.
        5.   Aversive conditioning is used to help individuals avoid smoking, eating, and drinking.
    B.   Operant Conditioning Approaches
        1.   Behavior modification is the application of operant conditioning principles to change human behavior with the goal of replacing unacceptable responses with acceptable, adaptive ones.
        2.   A token economy involves reinforcing behaviors with tokens that can later be exchanged for desired rewards.
        3.   Because of their focus on changing behaviors rather than on modifying thoughts or gaining insight, behavioral therapy is especially useful with young children.
    C.   Cognitive Behavior Therapy
        1.   This approach helps individuals modify their thoughts as well as their behaviors.
        2.   According to Bandura, self-efficacy is especially important in successful therapy.
        3.   Self-instructional methods are aimed at teaching individuals to modify their own behavior.
V.   Cognitive Therapies
    A.   Rational Emotive Therapy
        1.   Believing one's thoughts are the main source of abnormal behavior; cognitive therapies attempt to change feelings and behaviors by changing cognitions.

2. Unlike psychoanalytic therapies, the focus in on overt symptoms instead of deep-seated unconscious thoughts.
3. Ellis asserts that individuals become psychologically disturbed because of their irrational, self-defeating beliefs.
4. All irrational beliefs are derived from three basic "masturbatory ideologies": (1) I must perform well and/or have approval of others; (2) Others must treat me fairly and considerately and they must not frustrate me; and, (3) My life circumstances should provide me with things easily and without frustration.
5. Irrational beliefs lead to three types of irrational thinking: demanding, catastrophizing, and rating of self and others.
6. The most important consequences of successful rational emotive therapy is self-acceptance.

B. Beck's Cognitive Therapy
1. Many of our thoughts are powerful, emotion-producing automatic thoughts.
2. The key core thought associated with the emotions are "gain" for joy, "loss" for sadness, "unfairly attacked" for anger, and "it'll get worse" for anxiety.
3. Cognitive distortions are corrected during cognitive therapy.

V. Group Therapies and Community Psychology
A. Group Therapies
1. Since many psychological problems develop in the context of interpersonal relationships, therapy with others can help correct these problems.
2. Group therapy is diverse.
3. The attractive features of group therapy are: information, universality, altruism, corrective recapitulation of the family group, development of social skills, and interpersonal learning.

B. Family and Couple Therapy
1. Family therapy is group therapy with family members.
2. Couple therapy is group therapy with married or unmarried couples whose major problem is their relationship.
3. Family systems therapy is based on the assumption that psychological adjustment is related to patterns of interaction within the family unit.
4. Validation is the therapist's understanding and acceptance of each family member's feelings and beliefs.
5. Reframing involves changing an individual's problem into a family problem.
6. The family systems therapist tries to restructure the coalitions in a family.
7. In a triangle, one family member is the scapegoat for two other members who are in conflict; in therapy, detriangulation is shifting the attention away from the scapegoat and dealing with the actual conflict.
8. Couples therapy addresses a variety of problems such as jealousy, sexual messages, delayed childbearing, infidelity, gender roles, two-career families, divorce, and remarriage.

C. Personal Growth and Self-Help Groups
1. Personal growth groups have their roots in humanistic therapies and emphasize personal growth, openness, and honest interpersonal relations.
2. Encounter groups promote self-understanding through candid group interaction.
3. Research shows that most encounter group participants had a positive, self-improving experience but that a small minority felt the experience was harmful.

4. Self-help groups are voluntary groups who meet regularly to discuss topics of common interest, and well-known groups include Alcoholics Anonymous, Weight Watchers, and Parents without Partners.

5. Self-help groups help individuals to feel less isolated and build hope, they provide an ideology to use as a guide, and they provide a setting for sympathy, confession, and emotional support.

VI. Is Psychotherapy Effective?

A. Research on the Effectiveness of Psychotherapy

1. In the 1950s, Eysenck did research that was critical of therapy because it suggested that two-thirds of individuals with neurotic symptoms improved regardless of whether they were in therapy.

2. In meta-analysis, the researcher statistically combines the results of many different studies.

3. A meta-analysis of 475 psychotherapy research studies indicated that individuals in therapy do improve more than those who do not.

4. Behavior therapies are most successful in treating specific behavioral problems (e.g., phobias, sexual dysfunctions) and cognitive therapies are most successful in treating depression.

5. Persons with a low tolerance of anxiety, low motivation, and psychological deterioration may worsen as therapy progresses.

6. Therapists may worsen client problems if they are aggressive, hasten client's self-disclosure, are impatient, or have bias toward or lack of understanding of ethnic, religious, gender, or other cultural differences.

B. Common Themes and Specificity in Psychotherapy

1. According to Frank, effective psychotherapists have the common elements of expectations, mastery, and emotional arousal.

2. The therapeutic relationship is important in successful psychotherapy, with client's confidence and trust in the therapist being essential.

3. One of the major questions in research is, "What treatment is most effective for this individual with that specific problem, and under which set of circumstances?"

C. Culture and Ethnicity

1. Only recently have psychologists become sensitive to the concerns of culture and ethnicity in psychotherapy.

2. Rather than using psychotherapists, ethnic minority individuals are more likely than others to discuss problems with friends or family.

3. Most ethnic minority persons prefer a counselor from their own cultural background, although effective therapy is accomplished when the therapist is culturally sensitive and can deal with persons who feel different, alienated, and misunderstood.

4. Language differences, class-bound values, and culture-bound values can impede psychotherapy with individuals from ethnic minority groups.

5. Some clinicians are devising culturally responsive treatments, such as using directive, structured approaches with Asian Americans, reframing of problems as medical for Hispanic Americans, and being externally focused, action oriented when counseling with Black Americans.

6. According to Sue, two processes should be present in initial sessions with ethnic minority clients: credibility and giving.

D. Gender
   1. Autonomy has traditionally been the goal of therapy, but exploration of gender issues has added relatedness as a major goal.
   2. Consciousness-raising groups focus on members' feelings and self-perceptions and emphasize defining one's own experience according to one's own criteria.
   3. Feminist therapies emphasize the societal contribution to personal problems, in that women have less political and economic power than men; to achieve mental health goals, female clients must be aware of the effects of social oppression on their own lives.
   4. Nonsexist therapy occurs when the therapist has become aware of and overcome personal sexist attitudes and behavior.
   5. Feminist therapists propose a three-phase route to women' mental health: (1) harmful adaptation, or acceptance of and dependence on the rules of a patriarchal society; (2) corrective action involving developing one's own identity and articulating personal goals; and (3) health maintenance, which includes alliances with other women to work toward better conditions for all women.
   6. Men and women bring many similar issues into counseling, but some are more common to one gender (e.g., controlling anger for men, eating disorders and depression for women).
   7. Little research has been conducted on the mental health factors that are unique for women.
   8. Therapists need to know accurate information about violence against women.
VII. Biomedical Therapies
   A. Drug Therapy
      1. Drug therapy is the most common form of biomedical therapy.
      2. Antianxiety drugs, or tranquilizers (e.g., Xanax, Valium), make individuals less excitable and more relaxed, but are also associated with drowsiness, impaired motor abilities, and dependency.
      3. Antipsychotic drugs, including neuroleptics, block the dopamine system in the brain and thereby diminish agitated behavior, reduce tension, decrease hallucination and delusions, improve social behavior, and produce better sleep patterns.
      4. With schizophrenics, neuroleptics effectively treat positive symptoms but have little effect on negative symptoms.
      5. Tardive dyskinesia, a major side effect of neuroleptic drugs, is characterized by grotesque, involuntary movements of the facial muscles and extensive twitching of the neck, arms, and legs, and is developed by about one-fifth of schizophrenics taking neuroleptics.
      6. Antidepressant drugs regulate mood, and tricyclics (including newer classes) and MAO inhibitors affect the neurotransmitters of norepinephrine and serotonin.
      7. Lithium is a drug that is widely used to treat bipolar disorder.
   B. Electroconvulsive Therapy
      1. ECT ("shock treatment") is sometimes used to treat severely depressed individuals (about 60,000 a year).
      2. Around for decades, it was once used indiscriminately, even as a punishment.
      3. Although ECT works with severe depression, scientists are not certain why it works, but it probably affects the neurotransmitters involved in depression.

C. Psychosurgery
1. Psychosurgery is a biomedical therapy that involves removal or destruction of brain tissue to improve the individual's psychological adjustment.
2. From the 1930s through the 1950s, many prefrontal lobotomies were performed.
3. Now, psychosurgery is more precise and is rarely used.

Learning Objectives

After reading and studying the chapter, students should be able to:

1. Understand the nature of psychotherapy.
2. Describe and understand the principles of psychodynamic psychotherapies.
3. Describe and understand the principles of humanistic psychotherapies.
4. Identify and understand the various behavior therapies.
5. Describe and understand the principles of cognitive therapies.
6. Know the functions of group therapies and community psychology.
7. Know what the research on psychotherapy effectiveness has shown.
8. Know the common themes and specificity in psychotherapy.
9. Know how culture and ethnicity interact with psychotherapy effectiveness.
10. Know how gender interacts with psychotherapy effectiveness.
11. Identify and understand the biomedical therapies.

Guided Review

After you have read the chapter one time, search through the chapter to find the appropriate words to complete these statements. Material is covered in the same order as the chapter.

1. _____ is the process of working with individuals to reduce their problems and improve their _____.
2. _____ therapy characterizes both _____ and _____ therapies because their goal is to encourage insight and awareness of one's self.
3. A therapist who uses a variety of therapeutic approaches is called _____.
4. _____ have a _____ degree and can prescribe drugs for mental disturbances while _____ _____ get their training in doctoral programs in psychology and use psychotherapy rather than drugs.
5. Since the first half of the century, psychotherapists have moved away from practicing primarily in _____ _____ and into other settings.
6. Psychotherapists have been criticized for preferring to work with _____, _____, _____, _____, and _____ clients.
7. Psychodynamic therapies emphasize the _____ mind, extensive _____ by the therapist, and the role of _____ _____ experiences.
8. Freud's therapeutic technique for analyzing an individual's unconscious thought is called _____.

9. _____ _____ is the technique of having individuals say aloud whatever comes to mind no matter how trivial or embarrassing.

10. Releasing _____ tension by reliving an emotionally charged and conflicted experience is called _____.

11. In _____ of free association and dreams, therapists look for symbolic, hidden meanings, or the _____ content.

12. The remembered aspects of a dream are its _____ content, and its symbolic, unconscious aspects are its _____ content.

13. In _____, the client relates to the analyst in ways that reproduce an important earlier relationship.

14. _____ is the client's _____ defense strategies that prevent the analyst from understanding the client's problems.

15. Contemporary psychodynamic approaches emphasize the development of the _____ in _____ contexts.

16. According to Kohut, early relationships with _____ figures are critical, and a therapeutic goal is to identify and seek out _____ relationship with others.

17. _____ therapies encourage self-understanding and personal growth, and they emphasize _____ thoughts rather than unconscious thoughts, the _____ rather than the past, and growth and fulfillment rather than curing an illness.

18. _____-_____ therapy developed by Rogers has the therapist providing a warm, supportive atmosphere to improve the client's _____-_____ and encouraging the client to gain _____ about problems.

19. The "strings" that can be attached to the positive regard we receive from others are called _____ of _____.

20. A warm and caring therapeutic environment in which the client is not the recipient of disapproval is an environment of _____ _____ _____.

21. The therapist's role is to be "_____," or not leading the client to any particular revelation.

22. A _____ therapist is one who does not hide behind a facade, and _____ _____ refers to the therapist's ability to identify with the client's emotions.

23. Fully attending to what a person says and means is called _____ _____.

24. Perls developed a humanistic therapy called _____ therapy in which the therapist questions and challenges clients to help them become more aware of their _____ and to fully face their problems.

25. The Gestalt therapist encourages _____ between verbal and nonverbal behavior and uses _____ _____ as a major technique.

26. _____ therapies use principles of learning to reduce or eliminate _____ behavior.

27. In _____ _____, one of the _____ _____ techniques, anxiety is treated by associating deep _____ with successive _____ of increasingly intense anxiety-producing situations.

28. In a desensitization _____, fearful situations are arranged in order from most to least frightening.

29. Systematic desensitization is often an effective treatment for _____, such as fear of giving a speech.

30. Also based on _____ conditioning, _____ conditioning involves repeated pairings of _____ behavior with aversive stimuli to _____ the behavior's rewards.

31. Behavior modification is the application of _____ _____ techniques to changing human behavior.
32. In a _____ _____, behaviors are reinforced with _____ that later can be exchanged for desired rewards.
33. _____ therapies are especially useful with young children.
34. _____ _____ therapy helps individuals adapt by modifying their thoughts as well as their behaviors.
35. The belief that one can master a situation and produce positive outcomes is called _____-_____.
36. _____-_____ methods are cognitive behavior techniques aimed at teaching individuals to modify their own behavior.
37. The cognitive therapies emphasize that one's _____ are the main source of abnormal behavior.
38. Cognitive therapies are _____ likely than the cognitive behavior therapies to use structured training sessions that require the individual to practice prescribed exercises.
39. Cognitive therapies differ from psychoanalytic therapies by focusing more on _____ symptoms and less on deep-seated _____ thoughts.
40. Ellis' _____ _____ _____ is based on the idea that _____ and _____-_____ beliefs cause psychological disturbance.
41. In rational emotive therapy, the ABCDE therapy process is that C is the _____ _____, which clients wrongly view as caused by A, the _____ _____, but is actually caused by B the individual's irrational _____ system. The therapist goes on to D, which stands for _____, and leads to more rational E, or _____.
42. Irrational beliefs lead to three types of irrational thinking, namely _____, _____, and rating of self and others.
43. Logically modifying irrational beliefs decreases self-_____ and increases self-_____.
44. Beck's cognitive therapy is especially effective in treating _____.
45. In cognitive therapy, depressed clients are first taught to identify _____-_____ and to notice when they are thinking _____ or _____ thoughts; then they learn how to substitute _____ thoughts and also receive _____ and motivating comments from the therapist.
46. Many of our thoughts are _____ thoughts which are brief but able to produce powerful _____ results.
47. In _____ _____, an individual focuses on one detail of a situation while ignoring other _____ aspects of a situation.
48. _____ involves relating external events to oneself without reasonable evidence.
49. _____ and _____ involves underrating one's _____ traits while exaggerating one's _____ traits.
50. Assuming that one knows the motives, intentions, and beliefs of others is called _____ _____.
51. In the NIMH study of cognitive therapy treatment of depression, more than 50 percent of those receiving _____ _____ improved in _____ weeks while in the _____ _____ only 29 percent improved.

52. The six attractive features of group therapy are: the individual receives _____ from others; they come to see that their concerns have _____; they provide _____ support; there can be _____ _____ of the family group; they help in the development of _____ _____; and they allow for _____ _____.

53. Although _____, _____, and _____ therapies may be used in family or couple therapy, the main form of therapy is _____ _____, which assumes that psychological adjustment is related to _____ of interaction within the _____ unit.

54. In _____, the therapist expresses an understanding and acceptance of each family member's feelings and beliefs.

55. _____ involves making an individual's problem a _____ problem.

56. The family systems therapist tries to _____ the coalitions in a family.

57. In some families, one member is the _____ for two other members who are in conflict but pretend not to be, and the therapist tries to disentangle, or _____, this situation by shifting attention away from the child to the conflict between the parents.

58. _____ _____ groups have their roots in the _____ therapies, and they emphasize increased openness and honesty in _____ relations.

59. An _____ _____ is a personal growth group designed to promote self-understanding through candid group interaction.

60. About _____ percent of the participants in an encounter group felt that the experience was harmful.

61. Family therapists who see Black clients believe it is important to provide _____ advice or assistance, emphasize their ethnic _____, and take into consideration their _____, such as the impact of racism, discrimination, and victimization.

62. _____-_____ groups are voluntary organizations of individuals who get together regularly to discuss topics of _____ _____.

63. Unlike later studies, a 1952 study by _____ suggested that psychotherapy was _____.

64. Using _____-_____, a researcher _____ combines the results of many different studies.

65. The _____ therapies are most successful in treating problems such as phobias and _____ dysfunctions, and _____ therapies are most successful in treating depression.

66. People with a low tolerance of _____, low _____, and strong signs of _____ _____ may worsen as therapy progresses.

67. Therapist qualities associated with poor therapy outcomes include being _____, pushing clients to _____-_____ too quickly, and being _____.

68. Jerome Frank concluded that effective psychotherapists have the common elements of _____, _____, and _____ _____.

69. The therapeutic _____ is an important ingredient in successful psychotherapy.

70. Specificity in psychotherapy means understanding what _____ is most effective for *this* _____ with *that* _____ problem, and under *which* set of circumstances.

71. Among the barriers that can impede psychotherapy's effectiveness with individuals from ethnic minority groups are _____ differences, _____-_____ values, and _____-_____ values.

72. Black clients maintain _____ eye contact than Anglo-American clients.

73. Asian-American clients are likely to feel uncomfortable with _____ expression and disclosing _____ information, but more likely to prefer a _____ and _____ approach.

74. Hispanic-American clients may prefer that their problem be reframed as a _____ problem.

75. _____ refers to the fact that somehow the therapist is believable, and _____ refers to the fact that clients receive some kind of benefit from treatment early in the therapy process.

76. Traditionally, _____ has been the idealized goal of therapy, but now a second goal of _____ has been added.

77. _____-_____ _____ are used to help women define their own experiences with their own criteria.

78. _____ therapies are based on a critique of society wherein women are perceived to have less _____ and _____ power than men have.

79. _____ therapy occurs when the therapist has awareness of and has overcome personal sexist attitudes and behavior.

80. According to one feminist approach to therapy, the three phases to mental health are: (1) _____ _____, in which women accept _____ and _____ rules; (2) _____ _____, in which women begin to develop their own _____ and to articulate _____ goals; and (3) _____ _____, which includes _____ in the new identity and _____ with other women.

81. Men are more likely to have issues revolving around controlling _____ or being unable to openly express their _____.

82. Women are more likely to experience _____, _____ disorders, and family _____.

83. The most common form of biomedical therapy is _____ therapy.

84. _____ drugs such as Xanax and Valium are commonly referred to as _____.

85. _____, the most widely used antipsychotic drugs, treat _____ symptoms but have little effect on _____ symptoms by blocking the _____ system's action in the brain.

86. A major side effect of neuroleptic drugs is _____ _____, characterized by involuntary facial muscle movement and twitching in the neck, arms, and legs.

87. Antidepressants, such as _____ and _____ _____, regulate _____.

88. Lithium is a drug that is widely used to treat _____ disorder.

89. _____ _____ is commonly called "shock treatment," and its most common use is in treating _____ _____ individuals.

90. Adverse side effects of ECT include _____ _____ or other cognitive impairment.

91. _____ is a _____ therapy involving removal or destruction of _____ tissue to improve the individual's psychological adjustment.

92. In the 1930s, Portuguese physician _____ developed a procedure known as a _____ _____, a surgical treatment in which fibers connecting the _____ lobe and the _____ were severed to supposedly alleviate symptoms of severe mental disorders.

93. Psychosurgery is now more precise, such as making a small lesion in the _____ or another part of the _____ system.

Guided Review Answers

1. Psychotherapy, adjustment; 2. Insight, psychodynamic, humanistic; 3. eclectic; 4. Psychiatrists, medical, clinical psychologists; 5. mental hospitals; 6. young, attractive, verbal, intelligent, successful; 7. unconscious, interpretation, early childhood; 8. psychoanalysis; 9. Free association; 10. emotional, catharsis; 11. interpretation, latent; 12. manifest, latent; 13. transference; 14. Resistance, unconscious; 15. self, social; 16. attachment, appropriate; 17. Humanistic, conscious, present; 18. Person-centered, self-concept, insight; 19. conditions, worth; 20. unconditional positive regard; 21. nondirective; 22. genuine, accurate empathy; 23. active listening; 24. Gestalt, feelings; 25. congruence, role playing; 26. Behavior, maladaptive; 27. systematic desensitization, classical conditioning, relaxation, visualizations; 28. hierarchy; 29. phobias; 30. classical, aversive, undesirable, decrease; 31. operant conditioning; 32. token economy, tokens; 33. Behavior; 34. Cognitive behavior; 35. self-efficacy; 36. Self-instructional; 37. thoughts; 38. less; 39. overt, unconscious; 40. rational emotive therapy, irrational, self-defeating; 41. emotional Consequence, Activating event, Belief, Disputation, Effects; 42. demanding, catastrophizing; 43. criticism, acceptance; 44. depression; 45. self-labels, distorted, irrational, appropriate, feedback; 46. automatic, emotional; 47. selective abstraction, relevant; 48. Personalization; 49. Minimization, magnification, positive, negative; 50. mind reading; 51. cognitive therapy, sixteen, comparison, group; 52. information, universality, altruistic, corrective recapitulation, social skills, interpersonal learning; 53. psychodynamic, humanistic, behavioral, family systems, patterns, family; 54. validation; 55. Reframing, family; 56. restructure; 57. scapegoat, detriangulate; 58. Personal growth, humanistic, interpersonal; 59. encounter group; 60. eight; 61. concrete, strengths, vulnerability; 62. Self-change, common interest; 63. Eysenck, ineffective; 64. meta-analysis, statistically; 65. behavior, sexual, cognitive; 66. anxiety, motivation, psychological deterioration; 67. aggressive, self-disclose, impatient; 68. expectations, mastery, emotional arousal; 69. relationship; 70. treatment, individual, specific; 71. language, class-bound, culture-bound; 72. less; 73. emotional, personal, directive, structured; 74. medical; 75. Credibility, giving; 76. autonomy, relatedness; 77. Consciousness-raising groups; 78. Feminist, political, economic; 79. Nonsexist; 80. harmful adaptation, dependency, patriarchal, corrective action, identity, personal, health maintenance, pride, alliances; 81. anger, emotions; 82. depression, eating, violence; 83. drug; 84. Antianxiety, tranquilizers; 85. Neuroleptics, positive, negative, dopamine; 86. tardive dyskinesia; 87. tricyclics, MAO inhibitors, mood; 88. bipolar; 89. Electroconvulsive therapy, severely depressed; 90. memory loss; 91. Psychosurgery, biomedical, brain; 92. Moniz, prefrontal lobotomy, frontal, thalamus; 93. amygdala, limbic

Key Terms

For each term, briefly define the term in your own words and provide an example or situation (especially one you can visualize) that will help you retain the meaning of the concept. Key terms are presented in the order they are presented in the chapter.

1. psychotherapy (p. 390)

2. insight therapy (p. 390)

3. psychodynamic therapies (p. 392)

4. psychoanalysis (p. 392)

5. free association (p. 392)

6. catharsis (p. 393)

7. dream analysis (p. 393)

8. manifest content (p. 393)

9. latent content (p. 393)

10. transference (p. 393)

11. resistance (p. 393)

12. humanistic psychotherapies (p. 394)

13. person-centered therapy (p. 394)

36. giving (p. 408)

37. conscious-raising groups (p. 408)

38. feminist therapies (p. 408)

39. nonsexist therapy (p. 408)

40. biomedical therapies (p. 410)

41. antianxiety drugs (p. 410)

42. antipsychotic drugs (p. 410)

43. tardive dyskinesia (p. 410)

44. antidepressant drugs (p. 410)

45. lithium (p. 410)

46. electroconvulsive therapy (ECT) (p. 411)

47. psychosurgery (p. 411)

Study Aids

Students who do well on tests develop mnemonic aids to help them remember important terms and concepts. A few are suggested here, and you are encouraged to develop your own additional aids.

> **Rogerian Therapist Characteristics.** Use A G E to help you remember the three desirable characteristics of therapists, the three letters stand for:
>> A = Acceptance, or unconditional positive regard
>> G = Genuineness, or not hiding behind a facade
>> E = Empathy (i.e., accurate empathy), or a sense of knowing what it would be like to be the client.

> **Ellis' Rational Emotive Therapy.** Ellis provides his own mnemonic aid since he abbreviates his therapy process into ABCDE. Learn the steps using his easy guide:
>> A is the Activating event, which individuals mistakenly think caused C.
>> B is the individual's Belief system (about A), which actually causes C.
>> C is the emotional consequence.
>> D is for Disputation, and in therapy the counselor disputes irrational aspects of B.
>> E is the effects or outcome of therapy—hopefully, having rational beliefs replace irrational beliefs.

> **Desirable Client Characteristics.** The chapter provides the mnemonic YAVIS to help you recall the characteristics of clients with whom counselors like to work—Young, Attractive, Verbal, Intelligent, and Social clients.

Understanding Concepts

Answer these questions to develop your understanding of the important ideas in this chapter.

1. Which therapies are insight therapies? What are the important features of insight therapies?

2. In psychoanalysis, discuss how an analyst uses free association, dream analysis, transference, and resistance in the task of interpretation.

3. Compare and contrast conditions of worth and unconditional positive regard. How does each affect our self-esteem and happiness?

4. List what behaviors and views you think each of the following therapists would exhibit: (1) a psychoanalyst; (2) a person-centered counselor; (3) a Gestalt therapist; (4) a behavior therapist; (5) a cognitive therapist.

5. Describe the two counseling techniques that are based on classical conditioning, namely, systematic desensitization and aversive conditioning.

6. Discuss the main features of a token economy program, and give an original example how it could be used in the classroom, in an institute, in a mental hospital, or by parents at home.

7. Describe the major features and basic process of Ellis' rational emotive therapy.

8. What is the core cognition for each of these emotions: joy, sadness, anger, anxiety? Give an example of a thought that can produce each of these emotions.

9. Compare and contrast individual therapy with group therapy.

10. What are some of the techniques used in family systems therapy? Define and give an example for each of the four techniques described in the text.

11. Distinguish among personal growth groups, encounter groups, and self-help groups.

12. Summarize research findings about the effectiveness of psychotherapy.

13. What therapist characteristics are important in effective counseling?

14. Distinguish between feminist therapy and nonsexist therapy.

15. What are the advantages and disadvantages of antipsychotic drugs, or neuroleptics?

16. Summarize the use of tricyclics, MAO inhibitors, and lithium in treating depression and bipolar disorders.

17. What has been the role of electroconvulsive therapy and psychosurgery in the treatment of mental disorders?

Applying Concepts

Answer these questions to develop your ability to apply this chapter's material to your life and the world. Your own responses may differ from other students' in the class, and it is helpful to share your ideas with the other students.

1. If you were to enter psychotherapy, would you choose an insight therapy or behavior or cognitive therapy? Why?

2. Read over Self-Assessment 15.1 and evaluate your reactions to it as a measure of counseling satisfaction. Are there any lines in which both ends of the measure are desirable, or both undesirable? Could this measure also be used to measure other situations, such as satisfaction with a class session?

3. How can the psychoanalyst know more about a person than the person himself can tell her? Is it possible for a psychoanalyst to confirm that their interpretations are indeed correct?

4. Choose a specific situation (e.g., taking a test, giving a speech) that increases your anxiety level. Develop a 10- to 15-item hierarchy of things that are associated with your anxiety that could be used as a basis for systematic desensitization.

5. What type of ethical concerns might be expressed over the use of aversive conditioning techniques?

6. Design a behavior modification program (i.e., the application of operant conditioning principles) to change one of your behaviors (e.g., improve your study skills, keep your dormitory room neater). Write an appropriate behavioral contract.

7. Do behavior therapists really address persons' psychological problems or do they just scratch the surface, never really getting to the root of the problem?

8. Take Self-Assessment 15.2 and evaluate your irrational values. What are some of your basic irrational beliefs? Then, think about and list your irrational beliefs pertaining to being a college student.

9. In designing a national health program, would you include counseling? Would you provide coverage for individual and group therapy? For family and couple therapy? Why, or why not?

10. Design an outline for a workshop—dealing with ethnic minority and low-income individuals in therapy—that would be provided for the mental health professionals' audience.

11. Do you think that both autonomy and relatedness are major goals of therapy? Why?

12. Several years ago, consciousness-raising groups were popular with women, and, to a lesser degree, with men. Do you think that these groups are passé, or is there a great need for them now? Why?

13. What is your opinion about the use of drug therapy to treat mental disorders such as depression, anxiety, and schizophrenia? Under what conditions would you use antidepressants if you were depressed?

Chapter Practice Tests

Answer these multiple-choice test questions to help you assess your understanding of the chapter's material. Evaluate your answers to determine which sections you need to further review.

Practice Test A

1. Psychotherapies are typically based on
   a. medicine.
   b. theories of personality.
   c. religions.
   d. educational models.
   p. 390
2. The major thrust of Freud's theory of personality was
   a. the unconscious.
   b. resistance.
   c. regressed learning.
   d. evil versus good.
   p. 392

3. Contemporary psychoanalytic therapy differs from Freud's psychoanalysis in which of the following ways?
   a. the amount of emphasis placed on social contexts
   b. the reliance on psychoanalytic theory
   c. the amount of emphasis placed on family experiences
   d. the amount of emphasis placed on the unconscious
   p. 394
4. A nondirective role with clients would be emphasized by
   a. Freud.
   b. Perls.
   c. Rogers.
   d. Kohut.
   p. 394

5. Humanistic psychotherapies all consider which of the following to be important?
   a. use of dreams in therapy
   b. encouraging individuals to take responsibility
   c. confronting clients about their feelings
   d. directing the path therapy will take
   p. 394

6. Behavior therapists use which technique to increase self-efficacy?
   a. behavior modification
   b. token economy
   c. aversive conditioning
   d. self-instruction
   p. 395

7. Beliefs about one's own abilities are not addressed in which type of therapy?
   a. behavior modification
   b. self-instruction
   c. cognitive behavior therapy
   d. all of the above
   p. 398

8. The focus of rational emotive therapy is
   a. learning to relax under successive levels of anxiety.
   b. learning to instruct oneself in behavior change.
   c. challenging irrational beliefs.
   d. eliminating self-defeating thoughts.
   p. 398

9. Beck's cognitive therapy and rational emotive therapy differ most in which way?
   a. Beck focuses more on negative thoughts than feelings.
   b. Rational emotive therapy is much briefer.
   c. Rational emotive therapy does not require special training to conduct.
   d. Beck's therapy is more specific to depression.
   p. 400

10. A personal growth group designed to promote self-understanding through confrontation is
    a. family therapy.
    b. EST.
    c. encounter groups.
    d. psychodrama.
    p. 403

11. Most of the benefit of psychotherapy appears to occur
    a. early in treatment.
    b. as a person remains in treatment.
    c. after years of therapy.
    d. none of the above.
    p. 405

12. Specificity in psychotherapy indicates that
    a. different circumstances warrant different treatments.
    b. specific therapies only work for some people.
    c. specialized training is necessary to be a therapist.
    d. psychotherapeutic techniques are the essential part of therapies.
    p. 406

13. Clients receive some benefit early in the therapy process when the therapist is
    a. credible.
    b. not culturally deprived.
    c. giving.
    d. of the same ethnic background.
    p. 406

14. Men and women who enter psychotherapy are likely to
    a. be very different in what services are needed.
    b. have some issues that are gender specific.
    c. respond better to different therapies.
    d. differ in their commitment to completing therapy.
    p. 408

15. Medications that diminish agitated behavior, reduce psychotic thinking, and improve social functioning are
    a. neuroleptics.
    b. MAO inhibitors.
    c. tricyclics.
    d. lithium.
    p. 410

Practice Test B

1. A psychotherapist is most likely to treat
   a. a wide range of persons from diverse backgrounds.
   b. people who tend to be of a middle-class and upper-class background.
   c. people who require medications.
   d. all of the above.
   p. 391
2. Contemporary psychoanalytic therapy
   a. is completely different from Freud's traditional approaches.
   b. continues to avoid face-to-face contact between the client and therapist.
   c. places less emphasis on social contexts and relationships than Freud's therapy.
   d. differs more on the surface from Freud's therapy than in actual basic principles.
   p. 394
3. Carl Rogers likely emphasized which of the following in his therapy?
   a. challenging a person to think
   b. questioning motives
   c. warmth and acceptance
   d. none of the above.
   p. 394
4. Which of the following psychotherapy theorists would have confronted individuals in therapy?
   a. Freud
   b. Perls
   c. Rogers
   d. Kohut
   p. 394

5. Hannah's mother gives her a straw for doing her homework and bonus straws for her behavior. The straws can then be traded in for candy or toys. This is an example of
   a. systematic desensitization.
   b. token economy.
   c. aversive condition.
   d. self-instruction.
   p. 397
6. Clients are most active in their own changing process through which of the following techniques?
   a. systematic desensitization
   b. self-instruction
   c. aversive condition
   d. token economy
   p. 398
7. Irrational thinking as the cause of emotional problems is the basic principle of
   a. behavior modification.
   b. Beck's cognitive therapy.
   c. rational emotive therapy.
   d. all cognitive therapies.
   p. 398
8. Beck's cognitive therapy and rational emotive therapy are most alike in that they both
   a. specifically target depression.
   b. focus on "must" beliefs.
   c. use self-instruction.
   d. use changing thoughts to change behavior.
   p. 400
9. Personal growth groups have their roots in which theory?
   a. humanistic
   b. cognitive
   c. behavioral
   d. psychoanalytic
   p. 403

335

10. Which of the following is a potential benefit of group therapy?
    a. helping others
    b. getting feedback on how you come off to others
    c. learning from the experiences of others
    d. all of the above
    p. 404

11. According to the ethics of therapy, which of the following is true?
    a. A therapist can have sex with a client after therapy is over.
    b. A therapist can have sex with a client if the client initiates it.
    c. A therapist and client can have sex together before therapy starts but not after.
    d. none of the above.
    p. 405

12. A confident and trusting relationship between the therapist and client is fundamental to
    a. only interpersonal therapies.
    b. individual but not group therapies.
    c. psychoanalytic and humanistic therapies only.
    d. all psychotherapy.
    p. 406

13. Psychotherapists of majority background who treat clients of ethnic minority background face problems when
    a. the client misses appointments.
    b. the therapist imposes cultural values on the client.
    c. the client is culturally deprived.
    d. the therapist is culturally deprived.
    p. 406

14. Which therapy is characterized by the therapist becoming aware of their own sexist bias and overcoming it?
    a. nonsexist therapy
    b. feminist therapy
    c. equity therapy
    d. consciousness-raising groups
    p. 408

15. Which of the medications causes tardive dyskinesia?
    a. tricyclics
    b. lithium
    c. neuroleptics
    d. MAO inhibitors
    p. 410

Key for Practice Test A

1. Answer b; Theories of personality describe normal personality development and functioning and can therefore be used to explain maladjustment; page 390; Learning Objective 1

2. Answer a; For Freud, the unconscious mind contained conflicts between the id, ego, and superego that form the basis for personality functioning; page 392; Learning Objective 2

3. Answer a; Today's approaches based on psychoanalysis continue to emphasize many of the traditional aspects that Freud emphasized but place an added importance on social forces; page 394; Learning Objective 2

4. Answer c; Carl Rogers founded client-centered therapy which is the most nondirective of psychotherapies; page 394; Learning Objective 3

5. Answer b; Humanistic psychotherapies emphasize the individual choices people make and the responsibility each person holds for their decisions; page 394; Learning Objective 3

6. Answer d; Self-instruction is a technique that allows persons to control their own behavior and therefore increase self-efficacy; page 395; Learning Objective 4

7. Answer a; Behavior modification techniques focus attention only on behavior and the surrounding environment. There is no attention paid to beliefs, attitudes, or other cognitive dimensions; page 398; Learning Objective 4

8. Answer c; Rational emotive therapy is based on the premise that negative emotions are caused by irrational belief systems. Therefore, therapy directly challenges such beliefs; page 398; Learning Objective 5

9. Answer d; Beck's cognitive therapy was developed from Beck's theory of depression to specifically treat depression; page 400; Learning Objective 5

10. Answer c; Encounter groups focus on challenging group members to be honest with themselves and their feelings and to confront each other about the honesty they present; page 403; Learning Objective 6

11. Answer b; Psychotherapy takes time and effects are seen as therapy progresses rather than early on; page 403; Learning Objective 7

12. Answer a; Specific treatments appear to be called for to address specific problem areas, suggesting that therapies may need to be prescribed to particular problems; page 406; Learning Objective 8

13. Answer c; Developing a psychotherapeutic relationship appears to offer some benefits early in the course of therapy when a therapist is giving; page 406; Learning Objective 9

14. Answer b; Men and women face many different life challenges and are therefore likely to have different issues to address in therapy; page 408; Learning Objective 10

15. Answer a; Neuroleptics are used to treat severe thought disorders; page 410; Learning Objective 11

Key for Practice Test B

1. Answer b; Psychotherapy tends to be utilized only by verbal, educated, and primarily middle-class persons; page 391; Learning Objective 1

2. Answer d; Modern applications of psychoanalytic therapy have altered some of the techniques of therapy, but they are based on the original theory; page 394; Learning Objective 2

3. Answer c; Rogers placed an emphasis on the quality of the therapeutic relationship; page 394; Learning Objective 3

4. Answer b; Gestalt therapy, founded by Perls, confronts persons to look at their motives, feelings and beliefs; page 394; Learning Objective 3

5. Answer b; Token economies give rewards for behaviors that can be accumulated and used to get desired objects; page 397; Learning Objective 4

6. Answer b; Self-instruction allows a person to control their behavior change through individually employed behavior change; page 398; Learning Objective 4

7. Answer c; Rational emotive therapy challenges a person's thinking and beliefs on the premise that thoughts cause feelings; page 398; Learning Objective 5

8. Answer d; Both rational emotive therapy and Beck's cognitive therapy hold that changes in thought will result in changes in emotional states; page 400; Learning Objective 5

9. Answer a; Humanistic theories formed the basis for encounter groups and other group psychotherapies; page 403; Learning Objective 6

10. Answer d; Group therapy has the benefit of learning from others and their experiences, as well as receiving their feedback; page 404; Learning Objective 6

11. Answer d; Sex between a therapist and client is always considered unethical on the part of the therapist; page 405; Learning Objective 7

12. Answer d; All psychotherapies are grounded on the assumption that there is a trusting and confidential relationship between the therapist and the client; page 406; Learning Objective 8
13. Answer b; Therapist imposition of cultural values on clients can cause serious disruption to therapy and even harm to clients; page 406; Learning Objective 9
14. Answer a; Nonsexist therapy is the product of a therapist's efforts to do away with biases and sexist beliefs; page 401; Learning Objective 10
15. Answer c; Neuroleptics are used to treat severe thought disorders and can cause serious motor disturbances, such as tardive dyskinesia, after prolonged use; page 410; Learning Objective 11

Chapter Outline

I.   The Scope of Health Psychology
     A. Leading Causes of Death in the United States
         1. The leading cause of death are heart diseases, cancers, accidents, cerebrovascular diseases, pulmonary diseases, pneumonia and influenza, diabetes mellitus, suicide, chronic liver disease, homicide, and HIV/AIDS.
         2. Heart disease, cerebrovascular diseases, accidents, and lung and liver disease have declined over the past decade, the others have increased, especially HIV/AIDS.
     B. Individual Decisions and Health
         1. Daily decisions can affect health and life quantity/quality immediately and for years in the future.
         2. People often deal poorly with the reality of the dangers from some lifestyle choices.
         3. Young adults, for example, believe HIV/AIDS is for others although one college student in 500 tests positive for HIV, and only half are using condoms during first intercourse.
     C. Health Psychology Definitions
         1. Health psychology is a multidimensional approach to health that emphasizes psychological factors, lifestyle, and the nature of the health care delivery system.
         2. Behavioral medicine attempts to combine medical and behavioral knowledge to reduce illness and to promote health.
II. Health Habits and Lifestyles
     A. Smoking
         1. In 1985, one-fifth of all deaths in the United States was cigarette smoking related, including 30 percent of cancer deaths, 21 percent of coronary heart disease deaths, and 82 percent of chronic pulmonary disease deaths.
         2. More women die from lung cancer than from breast cancer.
         3. Passive smoke carries health risks, including more respiratory and middle ear diseases in the children of smokers.
         4. Fewer people smoke today and almost half who have ever smoked have quit.
         5. Over 50 million Americans continue to smoke.
         6. Nicotine is an addictive stimulant that easily crosses the blood barrier into the brain where it releases acetylcholine and endorphins.
         7. Smoking also works as a negative reinforcer.
         8. Smoking usually begins in childhood or adolescence, with female adolescents more likely than their male peers to smoke.
         9. Schools have succeeded in teaching teens about the long-term health consequences of smoking but with little effect on smoking behavior.
         10. The *Keep It Clean* program emphasizes the negative effects of smoking, and seems to affect young people's smoking choices.

339

B. Body Image and Lifestyle Choices
  1. Body image is the way that people perceive themselves and the way they think others see them.
  2. Self-perceived body image often has a stronger effect on lifestyle habits and self-esteem than factual presentations.
  3. "The beautiful is good" bias affects evaluations of chubby and thin children by their peers.
  4. Every culture does aesthetic self-management, but tasks and goals vary; at times these tasks demand interference with normal functioning.
  5. Many Americans are dissatisfied with some aspects of their body image, especially their weight; this dissatisfaction can influence both poor and good lifestyle changes.
  6. Body dysmorphic disorder (BDD) is a preoccupation with some imagined deficit (especially a facial feature) in a normal-appearing person.
  7. Self-mutilation is more common among adolescents than among other age groups, and it involves self-condemnation and body alienation.
  8. Body image distortions play a major role in eating disorders and activity disorders.
C. Nutrition and Eating Behavior
  1. By following the best recommendations, Americans could lower their risks for coronary disease by at least 20 percent.
  2. Limit fats to 30 percent of daily calories (especially cut back on saturated fats), increase carbohydrates, including vegetables, pasta, and cereals, and moderately consume proteins.
  3. Heavy use of dietary supplements is not recommended.
  4. The basal metabolism rate (BMR) is the minimum amount of energy an individual uses in a resting state.
  5. The BMR is slightly higher for males than for females, and the BMR declines during adulthood.
D. Obesity, Dieting, and Eating Disorders
  1. Genetics plays a significant role in body weight, and only 10 percent of children who do not have an obese parent becomes obese. It rises to 40 percent with one obese parent, and to 70 percent with two obese parents.
  2. Fat is stored in adipose cells. When filled, you do not get hungry, but if you gain weight, the number of fat cells may permanently increase.
  3. About one-half of adults and one-fourth of adolescents are overweight; 80 percent of obese adolescents become obese adults.
  4. At any one time, a third of American women and a quarter of the men are trying to lose weight; about 90% of dieters regain all or most of their lost weight within one to five years after the dieting.
  5. Amphetamines has only a short-term effect on weight loss and creates problems with blood pressure and addiction.
  6. Exercise is useful in burning calories and also in raising the metabolic rate for hours.
  7. Successful weight control has three main components: change habits to lose less than a pound a week; eat fewer calories especially fat calories; add moderate exercise.
  8. Anorexia nervosa is an eating disorder that involves the relentless pursuit of thinness through starvation and often with hyperactive behavior.

9. Anorexia nervosa is caused by several factors, including societal emphasis on thinness, high achievement motivation, needing an area of life that seems controllable, and hypothalamic activity.

10. Bulimia is an eating disorder in which the individual consistently follows a binge-and-purge eating pattern, and it is often associated with depression.

    E. Exercise

       1. Aerobic exercise refers to sustained exercise that stimulates heart and lung activity.

       2. Regardless of other risk factors, exercising to burn at least 2,000 calories a week cuts heart attack risk by two-thirds.

       3. Exercise should be pleasurable, not painful.

       4. Exercise also improves self-concept and reduces anxiety and depression.

       5. Activity disorder is an intense, driven, compulsive exercise pattern often combined with restrictions that can damage the person's body.

       6. Individuals with activity disorder tend to be high achievers, independent, and high in self-control and perfectionism.

       7. Activity disorder is resistant to change because of strong cultural support, pleasure including pleasure from endorphins, weight concerns, and cyclic patterns.

III. Coping with Illness

    A. Recognizing, Interpreting, and Seeking Treatment for Symptoms

       1. Many individuals are inaccurate at recognizing the symptoms of illness.

       2. We are better at recognizing the symptoms of illnesses with which we are familiar than for ones that are unfamiliar.

       3. Seeking treatment depends on perception of severity and the likelihood that medical treatment will relieve or eliminate them.

       4. Busy, active people are less likely to notice symptoms than others.

    B. The Patient's Role

       1. The "good patient" role is one of passivity, unquestioning and proper behavior, but the patient may actually feel helpless, powerless, anxious, and depressed.

       2. The "bad patient" role is when the patient complains to the staff, demands attention, disobeys staff orders, and generally misbehaves. The positive aspects are the refusal to become helpless and taking an active role; the negative aspects are aggravation of some conditions and negative reactions from medical staff.

       3. Compliance depends on patients' belief in the danger and in an effective, concrete coping strategy.

       4. Gender and ethnicity of the physician can affect interaction with the patient.

       5. Most medical research studies are conducted only with men with their results generalized to women; women's health issues (e.g., wanted and unwanted pregnancies, eating disorders, breast diseases) are under-researched.

IV. Psychoactive Drugs

    A. The Uses of Psychoactive Drugs

       1. Psychoactive drugs act on the nervous system to alter our state of consciousness, modify our perceptions, and change our moods.

       2. Psychoactive substances are attractive because they help people adapt to an ever-changing environment, reducing tension and frustration, relieving boredom and fatigue, and aiding escape from harsh realities.

3. Use of psychoactive drugs for personal gratification and temporary adaptation can lead to drug dependence, personal and social disorganization, and a predisposition to serious and sometimes fatal diseases.
4. Tolerance means that a greater amount of the drug is needed to produce the same effect.
5. Addiction is a physical dependence on a drug.
6. Withdrawal is the undesirable intense pain and craving for an addictive drug.
7. Psychological dependence is the need to take a drug to cope with problems and stresses.

B. Depressants
1. Depressants are psychoactive drugs that slow down the central nervous system, body functions, and behaviors.
2. Alcohol acts primarily as a depressant and slows down the brain's activities.
3. Alcohol is the most widely used drug in our society, and 13 million define themselves as alcoholics.
4. Alcohol is the substance most abused by adolescents and by college students.
5. Cultural attitudes about drinking are related to alcohol abuse, with Muslims, Mormons, and Orthodox Jews having lower rates of alcoholism.
6. Many, but not all, view alcoholism as a disease with biological causes.
7. Two views of treating alcoholism involve abstinence, such as with Alcoholics Anonymous, and reeducation into social or controlled drinking, using behavior modification techniques and cognitive therapy.
8. Other depressants are barbiturates and tranquilizers, and both are habit-forming and produce symptoms of withdrawal when a person stops taking them.

C. Opiates
1. Opiates depress the central nervous system's activity.
2. Opiates include morphine and heroine, and they are physically addictive drugs leading to craving and painful withdrawal.
3. The neurotransmitters most dramatically affected are the endorphins.

D. Stimulants
1. Stimulants increase central nervous system activity and are physically addictive.
2. Stimulants include caffeine, nicotine, amphetamines (often prescribed as diet pills), and cocaine.
3. Stimulants increase heart rate, breathing, and temperature, but decrease appetite.
4. The total number of cocaine users has declined in the last few years, however, the number of regular and daily users has increased.
5. Cocaine's addictive powers are so strong that six months after treatment, more than 50 percent of cocaine abusers return to the drug.

E. Hallucinogens
1. Hallucinogens are drugs that modify a person's perceptual experiences.
2. Both LSD (lysergic acid diethylamide) and marijuana (active ingredient THC) are hallucinogens.
3. The physical effects of marijuana include faster pulse rate, higher blood pressure, red eyes, coughing, and dry mouth and psychological effects include a variety of excitatory, depressive, and hallucinatory characteristics.

V. Toward Healthier Lives
   A. Gender and Life Expectancy and Health
      1. Boys and men are at greater risk for death at every age in the life span.
      2. Males are more likely than females to die from homicide, respiratory cancer, suicide, pulmonary disease, accidents, cirrhosis of the liver, and heart disease.
   B. Behavioral Medicine and the Future
      1. There is a need to develop preventive services targeting diseases.
      2. Health promotion and behavior modification in areas of healthier lifestyle are necessary.
      3. Improve environment and workplace safety.
      4. We need to understand the needs of special populations.
   C. Ethnicity and Life Expectancy and Health
      1. Blacks have a higher mortality rate than whites for 13 of the 15 leading causes of death.
      2. Black women are the most vulnerable of all ethnic minority women to health problems.
   D. Health Policy
      1. America's health costs are near one trillion dollars annually.
      2. Health costs can come down if people live healthier lives.
      3. Businesses that promote health among their employees save money; promotions include smoke-free work environments, on-site exercise programs, and bonuses to quit smoking and lose weight.
      4. Governments can promote health by restricting tobacco and liquor ads, requiring seat belts and mandatory helmets for motorcycle riders, and providing free blood pressure and other health checks.

Learning Objectives

After reading and studying the chapter, students should be able to:

1. Understand the scope of health psychology and what health psychology is not.
2. Know the effects of smoking on health.
3. Identify the various body image and lifestyle choices.
4. Know how nutrition and eating behaviors affect health.
5. Identify and describe the various eating disorders.
6. Understand how exercise interacts with health.
7. Know how people come to recognize and seek treatment for illness symptoms.
8. Identify and describe the patient's role in coping with illness.
9. Understand the compliance process when it comes to medical treatments.
10. Understand the use and effects of psychoactive drugs.
11. Identify and describe the various psychoactive substances and their effects.
12. Know how lifestyle changes can impact the development of healthier lives.

Guided Review

After you have read the chapter one time, search through the chapter to find the appropriate words to complete these statements. Material is covered in the same order as the chapter.

1. The top five causes of death in this country are (1) _____ _____,
    (2) _____, (3) _____, (4) _____ _____, and
    (5) _____ _____.
2. The next six causes of death in the United States are (6) _____ and _____,
    (7) _____ _____, (8) _____, (9) chronic _____ disease,
    (10) _____, and (11) _____/_____.
3. Three of the top causes of death that have increased over the last decade are _____,
    _____, and especially _____/_____.
4. About one college student in _____ tests positive for HIV.
5. About one in _____ adolescents uses a condom during the first intercourse.
6. _____ psychology is a _____ approach that emphasizes psychological factors,
    _____-_____, and the nature of the health care delivery system.
7. _____ medicine attempts to combine medical and behavioral knowledge to reduce
    _____ and to promote _____.
8. In 1985, cigarette smoking accounted for more than one in every _____ deaths.
9. The most common form of cancer in women is _____ cancer.
10. Because of _____ smoke, children of smokers are at special risk for _____ and
    _____ _____ diseases.
11. Smoking among men fell from over 50 percent in 1965 to about _____ percent in 1989.
12. Smokers are addicted to _____, a _____ that increases energy and alertness, while
    releasing _____ and _____ neurotransmitters, which have a calming and pain-
    reducing effect.
13. _____ adolescents are more likely to be smokers than the other gender.
14. There are _____ restrictions on children's access to cigarettes today than in 1964, and the
    existing restrictions are _____ reinforced.
15. Cheryl Perry's programs featuring *Keep It Clean,* and *Health Olympics,* and *Shifting Gears* are designed
    to reduce teenagers' _____.
16. _____ _____ is the way that people perceive themselves and the way they think
    others see them.
17. The "_____ _____ _____" bias is that attractiveness is associated with
    positive characteristics and behavior.
18. Dieting, exercising, tanning, clothing, facial cosmetics, and liposuction are American tools of
    _____ self-management.
19. The _____ women of Burma use _____ _____ _____ to
    elongate their necks into their cultural ideal, and in earlier centuries, _____ women were
    subjected to _____-_____ procedures that reduced the foot to _____-
    _____ its normal size.
20. _____ _____ _____ (BDD) is a preoccupation with some
    _____ deficit in a normal-appearing person.

21. _____-_____ is more common among _____ than among other age groups and involves an attitude of "I hate my body," a subset of generalized self-condemnation.

22. Body image distortions play a major role in _____ disorders and _____ disorders.

23. Good nutritional guidelines include limiting _____ to 30 percent of daily calories, especially _____ fats; increasing _____, with more _____, _____, and _____ carbohydrates such as pasta, whole-wheat breads, and cereals; and, eat only moderate amounts of _____.

24. Megadoses of vitamins and minerals have no known _____ and can be _____.

25. _____ _____ _____ is the minimum amount of energy an individual uses in a resting state and it varies by _____ and _____.

26. Some individuals _____ a tendency to be overweight, with only _____ percent of children without an obese parent becoming obese, _____ percent of children with one obese parent becoming obese, and about _____ percent of children with two obese parents becoming obese.

27. Fat is stored in _____ cells, and the amount of fat in one's body is an important factor in determining your body weight's _____ _____.

28. Obese persons who were obese as children have _____ fat cells, and obese persons who were not obese as children have _____ fat cells.

29. About one in _____ adolescents is overweight and about one in _____ middle-aged adults is overweight.

30. _____ percent of obese adolescents become obese adults.

31. At any time, one in _____ American women and nearly one in _____ American men are trying to lose weight.

32. Some have used _____ to help them lose weight, but the weight loss effects of this drug is short-lived and has potential adverse side effects of increased _____ _____ and possible _____.

33. More effective is _____, which burns up calories and raises the _____ _____ for several hours afterward.

34. The characteristics of successful weight control are (1) don't _____ but change to habits that lead to slow, steady weight loss of less than a _____ weekly; (2) eat fewer _____ and less _____; and (3) add moderate _____.

35. _____ _____ is an eating disorder that involves the relentless pursuit of _____ through starvation, and it mostly affects _____ during adolescent and early adulthood years.

36. Anorexics have a distorted _____ _____, perceiving themselves as beautiful even when they become skeletal.

37. As the anorexic continues self-starvation and the _____ content of the body drops, _____ usually stops.

38. Psychological factors of anorexia include motivation for _____ and _____, denial of _____, coping with _____ parents, and anorexics are usually products of a family with high demands for _____.

39. Physiologically, the _____ becomes abnormal in anorexic adolescents.

40. _____ is an eating disorder in which the individual consistently follows a _____-and-_____ eating pattern.

41. The female athlete who is most likely to have an eating disorder is a _____; among males, it is the _____.

42. _____ _____ refers to sustained aerobic exercise that stimulates _____ and _____ activity.

43. Regardless of other risk factors, if you exercise enough to burn at least 2,000 calories a week, you cut your risk of heart attack by about _____-_____.

44. The level of aerobic training that showed psychological benefits was _____.

45. Often combined with symptoms of an _____ disorder, the _____ disorder is an intense, driven compulsive exercise pattern, which is maintained even at the cost of physical and social damage.

46. Most of us are not _____ at recognizing the symptoms of an illness.

47. We are better at recognizing the symptoms of illnesses with which we are _____.

48. Whether treatment is sought depends on our perception of the _____ of the symptoms and the _____ that medical treatment will help.

49. When people direct their attention _____, they are less likely to notice symptoms than when they direct their attention _____.

50. Therefore, people with interesting jobs and active social lives are _____ likely to report symptoms.

51. In the "_____ _____" role, the patient is passive, unquestioning, and "proper."

52. The positive aspect of the "bad patient role" is that patients take an _____ role in their own health care.

53. Some women believe that their doctors devalue their complaints as "_____" rather than physical in origin.

54. _____ research is conducted on women's health issues than on men's issues, and many important research studies are done only with men.

55. Besides gender, research needs include looking at the effects of _____ and _____ on disease incidence and on treatment outcomes.

56. The quality of _____ is associated with a lower rate of _____ depression and a _____ rate of recovery from coronary bypass surgery and from surgery for breast cancer.

57. _____ drugs act on the nervous system to alter our state of _____, modify our perceptions, and change our moods.

58. _____ means that a greater amount of the drug is needed to produce the same effect.

59. Addiction is a _____ dependence on a drug, and _____ is the undesirable intense pain and craving for an addictive drug.

60. _____ dependence is the need to take a drug to cope with problems and stresses.

61. Depressants are psychoactive drugs that _____ the central nervous system, body functions, and behaviors, and the most widely used depressant is _____.

62. Alcoholism is the _____ leading killer in the United States.

63. The substance most abused by adolescents is _____.

64. Three religious views associated with low incidence of alcoholism are _____, _____, and _____.

65. The most common belief in America is that alcoholism is a _____ with _____ causes.

66. For _____ only, there seems to be a _____ factor if alcohol abuse begins before the age of twenty.

67. In Goodwin's study of the rate of alcoholism among male _____, a subject with an alcoholic _____ parent had _____ times greater risk of alcoholism, or _____ percent chance instead of _____ percent.

68. The _____-step program of Alcoholics Anonymous emphasizes _____, _____ support, and faith in a _____ _____.

69. Cognitive therapies can be helpful in treating alcoholism by dealing with _____ beliefs that lead to low _____ _____.

70. According to Ellis, addictions may be maintained because drinking works more _____ and _____ than _____ irrational comments, but drinking leads to the self-label of "_____" and increased _____ and _____.

71. Some addicts are _____ _____ and engage in addictive behaviors because they want excitement.

72. _____ are depressant drugs that induce sleep or reduced anxiety, and _____ are depressant drugs that reduce anxiety and induce relaxation, and both are _____- _____ and there can be symptoms of _____ when a person stops taking them.

73. Opiates _____ the central nervous system's activity, and opiates include _____ and _____.

74. The neurotransmitters most dramatically affected by the opiates are the _____, and use of opiates produces a strong _____ addiction that leads to _____ and painful _____ when the drug becomes unavailable.

75. Since most heroin addicts inject the drug _____, when they share _____ with other addicts, they increase the risk of getting _____.

76. _____ are psychoactive drugs that increase the _____ nervous system's activity, and the most commonly used ones are _____, _____, _____, and _____.

77. Stimulants increase _____ _____, _____, and _____, but decreases _____, and they can be _____ addictive.

78. Cocaine comes from the _____ plant and is mostly _____ or _____ to produce a rush of _____, which is followed by depression, lethargy, insomnia, and irritability.

79. Cocaine has damaging physical effects, and can even trigger a _____ _____, _____, or brain _____.

80. Treating cocaine addiction has been relatively _____, with more than _____ returning to the drug by six months later.

81. _____, also called _____ drugs, are _____ drugs that modify a person's perceptual experiences and produce visual images that are not real with the most well-known dramatic drug in this category being _____ _____ _____, or LSD.

82. _____, a hallucinogen, comes from the hemp plant and has _____ as its active ingredient.

83. Seven of the 10 leading causes of death in the United States are associated with the _____ of health behaviors.

84. At every age in the life span, _____ are at greater risk for death, with the biggest gender difference in cause of death being _____.

85. The health objectives for the year 2000 established by the Society for Public Health Education include developing _____ services, conducting health _____, improving the environment and workplace _____, and meeting the needs of _____ populations.

86. Of all ethnic minority women, _____ women are the most vulnerable to health problems.
87. In the United States, both _____ and _____ lobbying groups have made it difficult for health-related legislation to be _____.

Guided Review Answers

1. heart diseases, cancers, accidents, cerebrovascular diseases, pulmonary diseases; 2. pneumonia, influenza, diabetes mellitus, suicide, liver, homicide, HIV/AIDS; 3. pneumonia, diabetes, HIV/AIDS; 4. 500; 5. two; 6. Health, multidimensional, life-style; 7. Behavioral, illness, health; 8. five; 9. lung; 10. passive, respiratory, middle ear; 11. 30; 12. nicotine, stimulant, acetylcholine, endorphin; 13. Female; 14. fewer, rarely; 15. smoking; 16. Body image; 17. "beautiful is good"; 18. aesthetic; 19. Karen, brass neck rings, Chinese, foot-binding, one-third; 20. Body dysmorphic disorder, imagined; 21. Self-mutilation, adolescents; 22. eating, activity; 23. fats, saturated, carbohydrates, vegetables, fruits, complex, protein; 24. benefits, toxic; 25. Basal metabolism rate, age, sex; 26. inherit, 10, 40, 70; 27. adipose, set point; 28. more, larger; 29. 4, 2; 30. 80; 31. 3, 4; 32. amphetamines, blood pressure, addiction; 33. exercise, metabolic rate; 34. diet, pound, calories, fat, exercise; 35. Anorexia nervosa, thinness, females; 36. body image; 37. fat, menstruation; 38. attention, individuality, sexuality, overcontrolling, achievement; 39. hypothalamus; 40. Bulimia, binge, purge; 41. gymnast, wrestler; 42. Aerobic exercise, heart, lung; 43. two-thirds; 44. moderate; 45. eating, activity; 46. accurate; 47. familiar; 48. severity, likelihood; 49. outward, inward; 50. less; 51. "good patient"; 52. active; 53. "emotional"; 54. Less; 55. age, ethnicity; 56. optimism, postpartum, higher; 57. Psychoactive, consciousness; 58. Tolerance; 59. physical, withdrawal; 60. Psychological; 61. slow, alcohol; 62. third; 63. alcohol; 64. Muslims, Mormons, Jews; 65. disease, biological; 66. males, genetic; 67. adoptees, biological, 3.6, 18, 5; 68. 12, abstinence, peer, higher power; 69. irrational, frustration tolerance; 70. quickly, easily, refuting, "worthlessness," guilt, depression; 71. sensation seekers; 72. Barbiturates, tranquilizers, habit-forming, withdrawal; 73. depress, morphine, heroin; 74. endorphins, physical, craving, withdrawal; 75. intravenously, needles, AIDS; 76. Stimulants, central, caffeine, nicotine, amphetamines, cocaine; 77. heart rate, breathing, temperature, appetite, physically; 78. cocoa, snorted, injected, euphoria; 79. heart attack, stroke, seizure; 80. unsuccessful, half; 81. Hallucinogens, psychedelic, psychoactive, lysergic acid diethylamide; 82. Marijuana, THC; 83. absence; 84. males, homicide; 85. preventive, promotion, safety, special; 86. Black; 87. citizen, industry, approved

Key Terms

For each term, briefly define the term in your own words and provide an example or situation (especially one you can visualize) that will help you retain the meaning of the concept. Key terms are presented in the order they are presented in the chapter.

1. health psychology (p. 418)

2. behavioral medicine (p. 419)

3. body image (p. 421)

4. body dysmorphic disorder (BDD) (p. 421)

5. basal metabolism rate (BMR) (p. 422)

6. anorexia nervosa (p. 425)

7. bulimia (p. 426)

8. aerobic exercise (p. 426)

9. activity disorder (p. 427)

10. "good patient" role (p. 429)

11. "bad patient" role (p. 429)

12. psychoactive drugs (p. 430)

13. tolerance (p. 430)

14. addiction (p. 431)

15. withdrawal (p. 431)

16. psychological dependence (p. 431)

17. depressants (p. 431)

18. barbiturates (p. 433)

19. tranquilizers (p. 433)

20. opiates (p. 433)

21. stimulants (p. 433)

22. amphetamines (p. 433)

23. hallucinogens (p. 433)

24. LSD (p. 433)

25. marijuana (p. 433)

Study Aids

Students who do well on tests develop mnemonic aids to help them remember important terms and concepts. A few are suggested here, and you are encouraged to develop your own additional aids.

Nutritional Guidelines. Use Prat*Fall* to remember that Proteins and Fats should be reduced, and use Climb to remember to "increase" Carbohydrates.

Eating Disorders. To remember the key aspect of the eating disorders, use the first and last letter of **AnorexiA** to remind you of *Abstain* from eating and *Activity* disorder and use the first letter of **Bulimia** to remind you of *Binge* eating.

Types of Psychoactive Drugs. Remember a sentence such as "Does She Hop?" to use the first letter of each word to remember **Depressants, Stimulants,** and **Hallucinogens.**

Understanding Concepts

Answer these questions to develop your understanding of the important ideas in this chapter.

1. Compare and contrast the terms *health psychology* and *behavioral medicine.*

2. Explain the aspects of cigarette smoking that make it difficult to give up.

3. Compare and contrast body dysmorphic disorder and self-mutilation. How is one's body image involved in both of these disorders?

4. Summarize the major recommendations for good nutrition.

5. We are a nation obsessed with food, spending an extraordinary amount of time thinking about, gobbling, and avoiding food. What causes people to be overweight? What is the best way to lose weight?

6. What is the nature of anorexia nervosa and bulimia? What do they have in common, and how are they different?

7. What are the primary benefits of exercise?

8. Describe activity disorders and discuss the factors that make these disorders difficult to overcome.

9. List factors that influence one's ability to recognize symptoms of an illness.

10. Compare and contrast the characteristics and behaviors of "good patients" and "bad patients."

11. Distinguish the physiological effects of depressants, stimulants, and hallucinogens.

12. What's the difference between a physical addiction and a psychological addiction?

13. Discuss the problem of alcoholism in the United States, including ethnic differences.

14. Summarize the Society for Public Health Education's health objectives for the year 2000.

Applying Concepts

Answer these questions to develop your ability to apply this chapter's material to your life and the world. Your own responses may differ from other students' in the class, and it is helpful to share your ideas with the other students.

1. Summarize the effects of medical advances and lifestyle choices in the current list of leading causes of death.

2. What is your personal position on how actively the government should regulate healthy lifestyle choices? For example, would you mandate seatbelt usage? Helmets for motorcyclists and bicyclists? Regulate cigarette and liquor advertising and personal use? Should government enforce annual physical exams?

3. Although Perry's (1988) study was highly successful in increasing adolescents' health behaviors, it has not been widely used in schools. Why not? What may get in the way of using the results of a scientific study in public programs?

4. How has your body image affected your life? Give examples of both positive and negative effects? Have you been influenced by the "beautiful is good" bias? What are the important aspects of aesthetic self-management?

5. Assess your own nutritional behavior? Do you eat the right foods? The right amounts? What changes should you make in your eating, and do you plan to actually make any of these changes?

6. How has our nation's obsession with food and weight affected you? Do you often diet? Do you have any of the characteristics of eating disorders?

7. How might athletic trainers deal with the number of female athletes (especially gymnasts, skaters, and runners) who develop eating disorders?

8. Assess your own exercise program. Does it need to be modified? Have you ever had symptoms of an activity disorder?

9. How good are you at recognizing and interpreting medical symptoms and seeking appropriate treatment?

10. Conduct a breast or testes self-examination on yourself and summarize your reactions to doing this task.

11. Some people actively seek information concerning their health while other people will do everything to avoid finding out about their health status. What kinds of things may lead a person to avoid seeing a doctor and seeking health care?

12. What would you like to see done about the drug problem in the United States? How would you split resources among prevention and education, treatment, and prosecution? Why?

13. Some people seem to be attracted to taking certain drugs, while other people like to use other types of drugs. What personality characteristics may be different for people who use cocaine (a stimulant) as opposed to those who use alcohol (a depressant)?

14. Design your own personal health objectives for the year 2000.

15. Can a government be successful in promoting behavior that ensures the health of its citizens?

16. Take Self-Assessment 16.3 and evaluate your personal knowledge of AIDS risk behavior.

Chapter Practice Tests

Answer these multiple-choice test questions to help you assess your understanding of the chapter's material. Evaluate your answers to determine which sections you need to further review.

Practice Test A

1. Health psychology is best described as
   a. a combination of medical and biological knowledge.
   b. a basis for psychologists to prescribe drugs.
   c. a multidimensional approach to health.
   d. being closely related to psychiatry.
   p. 418

2. Current trends in smoking show that
   a. more people smoke now than ever.
   b. about half of smokers have quit.
   c. smokers increase each year.
   d. less women are smoking than ever before.
   p. 420

3. Body dysmorphic disorder involves which of the following?
   a. an obese person
   b. self-mutilation
   c. eating disorders
   d. none of the above
   p. 421

4. Health experts recommend that a person
   a. eat a large amount of protein.
   b. eat relatively few carbohydrates.
   c. does not use dietary supplements.
   d. reduce amounts of fiber.
   p. 422

5. Which of the following is true of fat cells?
   a. Obese people have more of them.
   b. Obese people have the same number but they are bigger.
   c. When they are filled is when people get hungry.
   d. They are unrelated to actual weight.
   p. 424

6. Exercise will
   a. raise the body's set point.
   b. lower metabolic rate.
   c. eliminate fat cells.
   d. none of the above.
   p. 424

7. Aerobic exercise at moderate levels has which effect?
   a. minimal effects
   b. as many effects as intense exercise
   c. the potential to substantially improve fitness
   d. only psychological benefits
   p. 424

8. A person who leads a stimulating and active life may be more likely to
   a. require hospitalization when they become ill.
   b. see a doctor when they need to.
   c. recognize physical symptoms.
   d. overlook physical symptoms.
   p. 426

9. "Bad patients" tend to
   a. get out of the hospital sooner.
   b. take an active role in their treatment.
   c. comply with doctor orders.
   d. get the medications they want.
   p. 429

10. Patient compliance with recommended treatments can be improved by
    a. threats from medical doctors.
    b. more informed patients.
    c. improved medications.
    d. better doctor-patient communication.
    p. 429

11. People are attracted to psychoactive substances because
    a. drugs help them escape realities.
    b. drugs adapt to the challenges of a changing world.
    c. drugs make people feel good.
    d. all of the above.
    p. 430

12. The drug most frequently abused by adolescents is
    a. alcohol.
    b. marijuana.
    c. heroin.
    d. cocaine.
    p. 431

13. Which treatment has been effective in treating alcoholism?
    a. behavioral therapy
    b. psychoanalytic
    c. group therapy
    d. rational emotive therapy
    p. 432

14. The active ingredient in marijuana is
    a. LSD.
    b. narcotic.
    c. delta-9-tetrahydrocannabinol.
    d. delta-9-THC.
    p. 433

15. The U.S. government's health objectives for the year 2000 includes which of the following?
    a. decreasing insurance costs
    b. increased development of medications
    c. prevention
    d. increasing hospital availability
    p. 436

Practice Test B

1. Medical and behavioral knowledge are combined to reduce illness with
    a. psychology.
    b. health psychology.
    c. behavioral medicine.
    d. medical psychology.
    p. 418
2. Cigarette craving occurs because
    a. nicotine affects the chemistry of the brain.
    b. the flavor is overwhelming to the senses.
    c. the brain requires stimulation.
    d. all of the above.
    p. 420
3. Smoking prevention programs that have been successful with adolescents emphasize
    a. the "just say no" message.
    b. education about the ill effects of smoking.
    c. anti-smoking ad campaigns.
    d. peer influences.
    p. 420
4. Preoccupied with a body disfigurement that does not exist is referred to as
    a. self-mutilation.
    b. anorexia nervosa.
    c. body dysmorphic disorder.
    d. none of the above.
    p. 421
5. Dietary supplements
    a. should be used only when necessary.
    b. can replace most foods.
    c. are required to meet recommendations.
    d. are necessary for a balanced diet.
    p. 422

6. Exercise does which of the following?
    a. lowers the body's set point for weight
    b. raises metabolic rate hours after exercise
    c. burns calories
    d. all of the above.
    p. 426
7. Sylvia is constantly active and refuses to eat much more than a salad a day. She probably suffers from
    a. bulimia.
    b. hyperactivity.
    c. body dysmorphic disorder.
    d. none of the above.
    p. 427
8. The chances that a person will seek medical treatment increases when
    a. there is a potential cure for the problem.
    b. the person has had the problem before.
    c. the person recognizes the symptoms as serious.
    d. all of the above.
    p. 428
9. Having had a heart attack in the past makes you more likely to
    a. ignore symptoms in the future.
    b. go to the doctor with new symptoms.
    c. recognize and attend to symptoms to other diseases.
    d. read and learn more about heart disease.
    p. 429
10. Good patients are also more likely to
    a. fake being sick.
    b. experience a sense of helplessness.
    c. fight back.
    d. be noncompliant.
    p. 430
11. Attention to women's health issues in research has
    a. only recently increased.
    b. still not become similar to men's.
    c. always been acceptable.
    d. declined in recent years.
    p. 430

12. Psychoactive substance use can best be described as a
    a. great time for all.
    b. better place with a friendly face.
    c. way out with a high price.
    d. means to a better end.
    p. 430

13. Alcohol interferes with which two brain functions?
    a. thought and emotion
    b. thought and perception
    c. control and judgement
    d. control and emotion
    p. 431

14. LSD
    a. is no longer popular.
    b. is a central nervous system depressant.
    c. converts to morphine in the brain.
    d. is made of THC.
    p. 433

15. Most of the major causes of death are
    a. inherited.
    b. preventable.
    c. not preventable.
    d. none of the above.
    p. 436

Key for Practice Test A

1. Answer c; Health psychology takes several tacks in addressing health problems both in prevention and once they have occurred; page 418; Learning Objective 1
2. Answer b; Vast numbers of people have quit smoking, but unfortunately many have started and restart; page 420; Learning Objective 2
3. Answer d; Body dysmorphic disorder involves persons without and distinguishable problem who feel their body is disfigured; page 421; Learning Objective 3
4. Answer c; Dietary supplements are not recommended by most health experts; page 422; Learning Objective 4
5. Answer a; Obesity is related to the number of fat cells that a person has in his or her body; page 424; Learning Objective 5
6. Answer d; Exercise burns calories, raises the body's metabolic rate even hours after, and lowers the body's set point; page 424; Learning Objective 5
7. Answer c; Even moderate aerobic exercise can increase fitness substantially; page 424; Learning Objective 6
8. Answer d; Attention to external stimulation can cause a decrease in attention to internal processes; page 426; Learning Objective 7
9. Answer b; Taking on an active role in treatment can be viewed as a hassle by medical professionals but tends to benefit the patient; page 429; Learning Objective 8
10. Answer d; Communication of the benefits of treatment and the costs of not complying with treatment can lead to better compliance; page 429; Learning Objective 9
11. Answer d; There are a multitude of reasons why people use drugs, most of which make it difficult to stop once they start; page 430; Learning Objective 10
12. Answer a; Alcohol is the most frequently abused drug among teens and is the most readily accessible; page 431; Learning Objective 11
13. Answer d; Because belief systems facilitate the use of alcohol, such as "I can stop whenever I want," rational emotive therapy has been effective at challenging these beliefs; page 432; Learning Objective 11

14. Answer c; Delta-9-tetrahydrocannabinol is the agent that gives marijuana its psychoactive effects; page 433; Learning Objective 11
15. Answer c; Prevention is cost effective in terms of dollars to prevent unnecessary pain and suffering; page 436; Learning Objective 12

Key for Practice Test B

1. Answer b; Health psychology combines medical and behavioral technologies; page 418; Learning Objective 1
2. Answer a; Nicotine alters the structure of brain cells making it so that when the nicotine is gone the person craves it; page 420; Learning Objective 2
3. Answer d; Adolescents respond well to peer pressure and therefore peer influence has been successful in smoking prevention; page 420; Learning Objective 2
4. Answer c; Body dysmorphic disorder is when persons believe they have a specific body disfigurement but they actually do not; page 421; Learning Objective 3
5. Answer a; Dietary supplements do not replace nutrition gained from food and should only by used when necessary; page 422; Learning Objective 4
6. Answer d; Exercise has numerous health benefits including changes in metabolism and lowering the body's set point for weight; page 426; Learning Objective 5
7. Answer d; These characteristics resemble anorexia more than any of the answers provided; page 427; Learning Objective 6
8. Answer d; Seeking medical attention is highest when a symptom is recognized as a potential problem and there is a known cure for the problem; page 428; Learning Objective 7
9. Answer b; Past experience with a health problem increases the chances that new symptoms will be recognized and treated; page 428; Learning Objective 7
10. Answer b; Overcompliance can be seen as being a "good patient," but can also result in learned helplessness; page 429; Learning Objective 8
11. Answer b; Although there have been changes to include more women in studies of health, women are still under-represented in this research; page 430; Learning Objective 9
12. Answer c; Drug use has immediate benefits but at a high cost in the long run; page 430; Learning Objective 10
13. Answer c; Alcohol has many effects on the brain, but most predominantly impairs control and judgement; page 431; Learning Objective 11
14. Answer a; Although still around and used, LSD is not as popular as it was in the 1960s and 1970s; page 414; Learning Objective 11
15. Answer b; Most of the major causes of death, such as cancer, heart disease, and AIDS, are preventable by changes in behavior and lifestyle; page 415; Learning Objective 12